When Terrorism Strikes Home

Defending the United States

James A. Fagin

East Stroudsburg University of Pennsylvania

PEARSON

Boston • New York • San Francisco
Mexico City • Montreal • Toronto • London • Madrid • Munich • Paris
Hong Kong • Singapore • Tokyo • Cape Town • Sydney

Series Editor: *Jennifer Jacobson*
Series Editorial Assistant: *Elizabeth DiMenno*
Senior Marketing Manager: *Kelly May*
Production Editor: *Patrick Cash-Peterson*
Editorial-Production Service: *Lynda Griffiths*
Composition Buyer: *Linda Cox*
Manufacturing Buyer: *JoAnne Sweeney*
Electronic Composition: *Peggy Cabot*
Cover Administrator: *Kristina Mose-Libon*

For related titles and support materials, visit our online catalog at www.ablongman.com.

Between the time website information is gathered and then published, it is not unusual for some sites to have closed. Also, the transcription of URLs can result in typographical errors. The publisher would appreciate notification where these errors occur so that they may be corrected in subsequent editions.

Library of Congress Cataloging-in-Publication Data

Fagin, James A. (James Arlie)
    When terrorism strikes home : defending the United States / James A. Fagin.
        p. cm.
    Includes bibliographical references and index.
    ISBN 0-205-40581-9
        1. Terrorism—United States.   2. War on Terrorism, 2001–   I. Title.

    HV6432.F334 2005
    363.32'0973—dc22

                                                            2005049155

Photo credits: p. 1: SIPA Press; p. 19: CORBIS; p. 47: AP/Wide World Photos; p. 85: Pearson Education/PH College; p. 115: Getty Images; p. 151: AP/Wide World Photos; p. 185: CORBIS; p. 215: Federal Emergency Management Agency (FEMA); p. 251: AP/Wide World Photos; p. 287: CORBIS.

Contents

5   *Defending Main Street, USA   115*

6   *Defending Aviation against Terrorism   151*

7 *Defending the Homeland: Weapons of Mass Destruction   185*

Preface to Instructors

"What is the terror alert color of the day?" If this question were asked prior to September 11, 2001, there would be no reference for responding to it. There was no such thing as a terror alert color code. Much has changed in a very short period of time. Although those who are older can remember conflicts with a foreign enemy such as the Vietnam War, the Korean War, or World War II, few of today's young students have such a remembrance. The war on terrorism is the first war they have ever experienced. With U.S. troops deployed in Afghanistan and Iraq and the media and government officials often warning of the threat of domestic attacks by terrorists, it feels like a real war to America's youth. A generation that has lived in relative peace finds that not only are Americans at war, but for the first time since the American Civil War, the battlegrounds are familiar U.S. landmarks such as New York City, Washington, D.C., and Pennsylvania.

When Terrorism Strikes Home: Defending the United States provides a frame of reference to help explain the war on terrorism. It provides students with a brief but adequate history of terrorism and then goes on to examine the major "domestic" issues raised by the war on terrorism. By "domestic" issues, I mean those issues that directly affect everyone living in the United States. Whether it is something as simple as not being able to have a lighter in a sterile area of an airport or a more serious concern like the U.S. government's ability to provide for the safety of its citizens within the rule of law, the war on terrorism affects everyone.

This book is not a political thesis, a psychological analysis, a sociological study, or a history lesson. However, it does contain elements of each. It is an examination of great events that affect the very structure of democracy, our quality of life and our faith and belief in local, state, and federal government as they unfold before us on a day-to-day basis. Each day history is being written as new terror threats and counterterrorism laws and strategies present themselves.

When Terrorism Strikes Home can be used in a wide variety of courses and with a wide variety of students. It can serve as a supplementary text or as a primary text. It can be used in introductory classes or in graduate classes. The book does not focus on theory and history, although enough of each is included to provide the student with a good academic foundation. It focuses on the impact the war on terrorism has on individuals, society, and government. It examines how the war on terrorism has affected first responders like police and fire departments, how it has transformed local and state government planning, and how it has defined a new relationship between state and federal government. The war on terrorism has also increased the importance of federalism, as the federal government has assumed the lead in counterterrorism and protection of the homeland.

When Terrorism Strikes Home: Defending the United States may be divided into four sections:

1. Introduction and history (Chapters 1 and 2)
2. How the United States has responded to the threat of terrorism on U.S. soil (Chapters 3, 4, and 5)
3. An examination of the major efforts the United States has chosen to identify as its primary priorities, such as aviation, weapons of mass destruction, and recovery in the event of a terrorist attack (Chapters 6, 7, and 8)

4. A discussion of more complex topics in the war on terrorism, such as future threats and the impact the war on terrorism is having on society and government (Chapters 9 and 10)

The complexity of thought increases as the text progresses from Chapter 1, "Introduction: The Awakening of the United States to Terrorism," to Chapter 10, "The Cost of Freedom." The early chapters are descriptive; the later chapters provoke reflective thought and analysis. The last two chapters address critical issues with no right answer. If *When Terrorism Strikes Home* is used in an undergraduate course, you should focus on the descriptive nature of the chapters. If the text is used in an upper-level or graduate course, you should focus on the complexity and reflective nature of the chapters.

Three types of boxes provide an opportunity to enhance the text with real-life details for the undergraduate student or to act as a springboard for upper-division and graduate students. The Case Study boxes point students to topics for further research. The Consider This boxes raise important questions that often have complex answers where sincere and honest persons can disagree about not only the conclusion but also the facts. The Up Close and Personal boxes provide the chance to examine the intersection of theory and practice. These boxes can be used to stimulate thought and discussion in upper-division credit classes and graduate classes. They may also be used for discussion topics or can be assigned as the thesis for a reaction paper or research assignment.

The book contains a number of aids to assist students in retention. Each chapter starts with an overview of the chapter and concludes with a chapter summary. These can be useful for both instructor and students. They provide instructors with quick overviews to help fine-tune lectures and provide students with a reference to determine whether they understand the major points in the chapter. Following each chapter are two sets of questions and a list of important terms and concepts to allow students to check comprehension and retention of the information in the chapter. These questions may also be used as study aids in preparation for examinations. The first set of questions can be used by students (and instructors) to check comprehension of the major concepts in the chapter. The second set of questions can be used in discussion groups or can be assigned as essay topics.

Lecture outlines can be created using the chapter headers at the beginning of each chapter. Consider adding contemporary topics, updates to the text material (especially for topics such as the Patriot Act and enemy combatants), and a discussion of local impact to these outlines. For example, guest lecturers could provide information on local first responder preparations and capacities or city planners could provide local information on emergency planning. The questions and lists of important terms and concepts at the end of the chapters can be used to develop test questions.

Preface to Students

"What is the terror alert color of the day?" This may be a common question today but if this question were asked prior to September 11, 2001, there would be no reference for responding to it. There was no such thing as a terror alert color code. Much has changed in a very short period of time.

The war on terrorism is the first war since the American Civil War in which the battlegrounds are familiar U.S. landmarks such as New York City, Washington, D.C., and Pennsylvania. *When Terrorism Strikes Home: Defending the United States* provides a brief history of terrorism to help you understand the background and history of terrorism and then goes on to examine the major "domestic" issues raised by the war on terrorism. By "domestic" issues, I mean those issues that directly affect everyone living in the United States. Whether it is something as simple as not being able to have a lighter in a sterile area of an airport or a more serious concern like the U.S. government's ability to provide for the safety of its citizens within the rule of law, the war on terrorism affects everyone.

This book is not a political thesis, a psychological analysis, a sociological study, or a history lesson. It is an examination of great events that affect the very structure of democracy, our quality of life and our faith and belief in local, state, and federal government as they unfold before us on a day-to-day basis. Each day history is being written as new terror threats and counterterrorism laws and strategies present themselves.

When Terrorism Strikes Home focuses on the impact the war on terrorism has on individuals, society, and government. It examines how the war on terrorism has affected first responders like police and fire departments, how it has transformed local and state government planning, and how it has defined a new relationship between state and federal government. It examines how the war on terrorism has increased the importance of federalism, as the federal government has assumed the lead in counterterrorism and protection of the homeland.

When Terrorism Strikes Home: Defending the United States has 10 chapters. The text may be divided into four sections:

1. Introduction and history (Chapters 1 and 2)
2. How the United States has responded to the threat of terrorism on U.S. soil (Chapters 3, 4, and 5)
3. An examination of the major efforts the United States has chosen to identify as its primary priorities, such as aviation, weapons of mass destruction, and recovery in the event of a terrorist attack (Chapters 6, 7, and 8)
4. A discussion of more complex topics in the War on Terrorism such as future threats and the impact the war on terrorism is having on society and government (Chapters 9 and 10)

The complexity of thought increases as the text progresses from Chapter 1, "Introduction: The Awakening of the United States to Terrorism," to Chapter 10, "The Cost of Freedom." The early chapters are descriptive and the later chapters provoke reflective thought and analysis. The last two chapters address critical issues with no right answer.

Three types of boxes enhance the text with real-life details and act as a springboard to stimulate thought and discussion. The Case Study boxes illustrate specific examples and topics. The Consider This boxes raise important questions that often have complex answers. The Up Close and Personal boxes provide the chance to examine the intersection of theory and practice.

The book contains a number of aids to assist you in retaining the content. Each chapter starts with an overview of the chapter and concludes with a chapter summary. Following each chapter are two sets of questions and a list of important terms and concepts to check your comprehension and retention of the information in the chapter. These questions may also be used as study aids in preparation for examinations. The first set of questions checks whether you understood the major concepts in the chapter. The second set of questions asks you to apply the information in the chapter.

Acknowledgments

No book is written in a vacuum. Behind every book is a team of people who assist the author. Writing takes time and much of that time was taken from my wife and family. I thank them for their support, encouragement, and sacrifice. I thank Jennifer Jacobson, my editor at Allyn and Bacon. She was a cheerleader, a counselor, a literary critic, and very generous with her patience. It was her initiative and support that started this project and helped me complete it. I would not have entered into the project without her encouragement and I would not have completed the book without her support and patience. Also, I thank Emma Christensen at Allyn and Bacon for her help in working with the manuscript.

Dr. Ross Prizzia and Dr. Gary Helfand are professors of public administration at the University of Hawaii–West Oahu. They teach courses and conduct research in disaster management and have published articles on Disaster Response in Hawaii. They have developed the only FEMA and State Board of Regents approved certificate program in Disaster Preparedness and Emergency Management in Hawaii. I am grateful for their assistance and contributions as authors of Chapter 8, "The Day After: Rebuilding Main Street, USA."

Often it is difficult to acknowledge the full slate of persons who help bring a book to fruition. Thus, I collectively thank all those at Allyn and Bacon who have made this book possible. I especially would like to mention the reviewers whose feedback helped shape the manuscript: James Jengeleski, Shippensburg University; Robert Ostergard, Binghamton University; Brian King Shott, Grand Valley State University; and Theodore Wallman, University of North Florida.

1

Introduction

The Awakening of the United States to Terrorism

The fear of attack by international terrorists has transformed the American landscape. The war on terrorism has resulted in the largest government reorganization since World War II. There are many daily reminders of the government's battle against international terrorists, such as this armed patrol of U.S. cities.

> *The struggle against international terrorism is different from any other war in our history. . . . The enemy is no one person. It is not a single political regime. Certainly it is not a religion. The enemy is terrorism—premeditated, politically motivated violence perpetrated against noncombatant targets by subnational groups or clandestine agents. Those who employ terrorism, regardless of their specific secular or religious objectives, strive to subvert the rule of law and effect change through violence and fear. These terrorists also share the misguided belief that killing, kidnapping, extorting, robbing, and wreaking havoc to terrorize people are legitimate forms of political actions.[1]*
>
> —President George W. Bush, November 6, 2001

Chapter Outline _____

Introduction: Defending the Homeland

In his 2002 State of the Union Address, President Bush said, "Our war against terror is only beginning. . . . Tens of thousands of potential terrorists have been trained by Al Qaeda in Afghanistan since 1996 and are now spread throughout the world like ticking time bombs—set to go off without warning. . . . Digging through Al Qaeda's hideouts, we have found diagrams of American nuclear power plants and public water facilities along with instructions for manufacturing chemical weapons and maps of major American cities and their landmarks." President Bush's remarks highlighted Americans' fears of international terrorism and the new focus on anti-terrorism, especially in the prevention of attacks by terrorists in the United States. In his 2005 State of the Union Address, President Bush cited whey he called "unprecedented actions to protect Americans" from terrorism as one of the accomplishments of his first term of office.

For more than 50 years, public opinion polls have indicated the U.S. public has been most concerned about three things: war, crime, and the economy. On September 11, 2001, a new fear was added to the list: fear of terrorism. Prior to September 11, 2001, there were few successful acts of terrorism committed by international terrorists in the United States. The public was aware of the fact that American tourists abroad could be attacked by terrorists; U.S. military personnel, ships, and bases could be the target of terrorists; and international aviation could be susceptible to attack by terrorists. But there was no widespread acceptance of the fact that thousands of ordinary U.S. citizens going about their daily business in the United States could ever be the targets of international terrorists.

Fear of and response to anticipated attacks of terrorists, especially international terrorists, is now a focal issue in government, business, society, and our private lives. In the fight against terrorism, wars are declared on once obscure Middle East countries. Americans have less freedom and privacy as new anti-terrorism legislation is introduced with promises that although we may have less freedom and privacy, we will be safer. Having a personal refuge in the event of a terrorist attack involving radioactive material or biological agents has become essential to many citizens. Citizens have stockpiled duct tape, plastic sheeting, and emergency food and water, fearing an attack by international terrorists may occur in their neighborhoods.

As a result of this new paradigm there have been many changes in government, in business, and in individual behavior and attitudes. These changes have occurred rapidly. In fact, they have occurred so rapidly that many Americans have not been able to adjust to or comprehend the extent of the changes. For example, for many people, the various terror alert colors create confusion rather than provide meaningful information. An informal poll by the Associated Press asked people whether they could name the various alert color codes and identify the color of the moment. Few could provide the correct colors or the current alert level.[2] New legislation, new governmental agencies, and new doubts about safety have raised more questions than answers. The Bush administration has declared a "war on terrorism" but few of us are sure of the objectives of this war or even who the enemy is. However, everyone is sure that it has affected our government, society, and personal freedoms.

The purpose of *When Terrorism Strikes Home: Defending the United States* is to examine the unique history and distinctiveness of terrorism in this country and the challenge of defending the United States against international terrorist attack while preserving the hallmarks of individual liberty and freedom. This book examines the impact of terrorism in the United States on government, society, and individual freedoms. It will concentrate primarily on the impact of terrorism by international terrorists since September 11, 2001.

Although the origins of the current threat of international terrorism may be rooted in the Middle East with allegations and counterclaims of international and/or historical injustices or ethnic conflict, this book chooses to leave such analysis of international terrorist groups, ideologies, and political/ethical debates to others to address. The focus of *When Terrorism Strikes Home* is on examining the challenge of responding to international terrorist attacks on U.S. soil. In discussing this challenge, this book presents a fair, reasoned, and descriptive analysis of the impact of terrorism and the anti-terrorism response on various aspects of the government, business, society, homeland defense, the criminal justice system, and individual behavior and attitudes.

For the purposes of this book, the definition of *terrorism* will be narrowed to focus on terrorism that occurs in the United States or its territories. But it also includes terrorist incidents committed by individuals or groups not acting on behalf of a foreign power (domestic terrorism) and U.S. persons or foreign nationals in the United States who are targeting national security interests on behalf of a foreign power (international terrorism). This definition includes terrorism committed by groups or individuals based and operating entirely within the United States and terrorism committed by groups or individuals trained, sponsored, funded, or under foreign direction. Thus, this book is concerned with domestic terrorism and a fairly narrow aspect of international terrorism—international terrorist attacks in the United States or its territories.

Although *When Terrorism Strikes Home* focuses on the impact of terrorism on persons in the United States, this does not mean that the author has blinders and does not recognize and appreciate the impact of international terrorism and the foreign policy and military response of the United States on other countries and world citizens. However, to attempt to cover the whole of terrorism and all its parts would far exceed the scope of this book.

Overview of When Terrorism Strikes Home

Chapter 2 presents a brief history of international terrorism and terrorism in the United States. Some of the unique aspects of terrorism in the United States includes its birth as a nation rebelling against the English monarchy, the fear of and response of the new Americans to the native people living in the United States, the fear of immigrants, and the terrorism rooted in pro-slavery, anti-slavery, and civil rights movements.

Chapter 3 discusses the various executive orders and laws that have been adopted in the strategy to defeat terrorism.

Chapters 4 and 5 look at the threat of international terrorism in the United States since the 9/11 attacks and the government's response.

Chapters 6 and 7 examine two key threats that have been identified as high priorities: aviation and weapons of mass destruction.

Chapter 8 discusses one of the most complicated problems in the war on terrorism—how to mitigate the potential harm of a terrorist attack on the United States.

Chapters 9 and 10 look at other significant issues and threats in the war on terrorism, such as cyber-attacks by terrorists, border security and the illegal immigration problem, the effort to stifle terrorism by reducing its financial resources, and the high costs of a constant state of vigilance and anti-terrorism programs.

Real Threats and Irrational Fears

Since the terrorist attacks on the World Trade Center and the Pentagon, billions of dollars have been spent on security and anti-terrorism preparations. More than money, people's attitudes and feelings of security have been permanently changed. A memorial article on the September 11 terrorist attacks summarized the new American consciousness: "On September 10, we were living in a country with 19 terrorists poised to kill as many of us as possible, but we thought we were safe. From the next day forward, we thought otherwise."[3] Now, people often worry about terrorist attacks or fear that suspicious-looking people may be terrorists. Even events highly unlikely to be the result of a terrorist attack are suspect. For example, when the *Columbia* space shuttle broke up on reentry over the Midwest, early news reports asked, "Could it be due to terrorism?" This question was raised despite the fact that it is inconceivable that terrorists would have the technology to destroy the *Columbia* in flight. When a failure of the electrical grid plunged the Midwest into darkness, immediately people wanted to know if it was the result of a terrorist attack. The public fears both being a victim of terrorism and perceived terrorists. To some degree these fears are justified and to another degree public fear is irrational.

The fear is real in that in 2003, the State Department reported there were 208 terror attacks worldwide resulting in 625 deaths and 2,646 people wounded. In a March 2003 news conference President Bush warned, "There [is] a 'real threat' of a new terror attack."[4] Former Attorney General Ashcroft repeated the warning that there is a very real potential that the al-Qaida[*] terrorism network could again strike the United States in August 2003. Attorney General Ashcroft said, "U.S. officials have worked hard to track suspected terrorists and foil their plans. I believe we've disrupted dozens and dozens and dozens, over 100 terrorist-related attacks around the world since 9/11."[5] President Bush promised the U.S. public that the various government agencies would respond appropriately to the threat of terrorism. Despite these reassurances, the public remains fearful of terrorism.

Despite the actions taken by the government to promote safety, many citizens have an irrational fear of attack by terrorists. Often these fears are translated into irrational actions against innocent people of Middle East descent living in the United States. Many of these people of Middle East descent fear that they will be targeted for violence based on irrational fears linking them to terrorism. For example, a Muslim woman who wears a hijab, or traditional headscarf, reported she is afraid to stand at a bus stop for fear of a car swerving to hit her. Also, some men named Mohammed have changed their name to Michael to avoid persecution and prejudice.[6] Airlines are leery of Middle Eastern–looking passengers. For example, an Arab American member of President Bush's security detail was denied passage on a commercial airline flight after being bumped from *Air Force One* because of a change in the president's schedule because the pilot suspected him of being a terrorist despite his Secret Service credentials.[7] A comedian scheduled to open for comic Jackie Mason was told hours before the show that he could not perform because of his Palestinian descent and the fear that the audience would react with hostility to his appearance on stage.[8]

In the extreme, people of Middle Eastern descent have been the subjects of random attacks, such as when Larme Price allegedly shot and killed four Middle East male victims. Mr. Price's mother said that after the September 11 attacks "he walked around scared all the time, he couldn't sit still. He said 'I'm going to join the war.'" In the statement released by the police, Mr. Price said, "he wanted to kill people of Middle Eastern descent."[9]

Fear of terrorism is not confined just to big cities. Even people in small towns react to unusual events, immediately fearing it could be a terrorist attack. For example, the residences of Geneseo, Illinois, a town of 6,400, were alarmed and feared terrorist activity that resulted in local law enforcement agencies receiving 100 phone calls when a military pilot who wanted to impress his grandmother flew his military jet low over his hometown.[10]

---

[*]There are several variations of the spelling of al-Qaida. The term and pronunciation is a transliteration from Arabic. The U.S. Department of State's *Patterns of Global Terrorism* uses the spelling "al-Qaida." The U.S. media more often uses the spelling "al-Qaeda," whereas overseas media tend to use the spelling "al-Qaida." Another common variation is "al-Qaidah." Both "al-Qaida" and "al-Qaeda" are commonly used as spellings by Internet websites. The author has elected to use the U.S. Department of State's spelling of the organization's name.

Awakening to Terrorism in the United States

Until September 11, 2001, there were very few acts of terrorism by international terrorists in the United States. The perpetrators of terrorist-type attacks for the most part were domestic extremist groups, such as animal rights groups, eco-terrorism groups, anti-abortionists, white supremacists, and anti-government/tax groups.[11] The Federal Bureau of Investigation defines this type of terrorism as *domestic terrorism:* "Domestic terrorism is the unlawful use, or threatened use, of force or violence by a group or individual based and operating entirely within the United States or its territories without foreign direction committed against persons or property to intimate or coerce a government, the civilian population, or any segment thereof, in furtherance of political or social objectives."[12]

After September 11 there has been an awakening to the vulnerability of the United States to international terrorist attacks. What was once considered unlikely or impossible is now acknowledged as a real threat. In assessing the threat of international terrorist attacks in the United States in mid-2003, the State Department Office of the Coordinator for Counterterrorism concluded, "Despite solid progress, the danger persists. Al-Qaida is still planning attacks. Every al-Qaida operations officer captured so far was involved in some state of preparation for a terrorist attack at the time of capture. Recent audiotapes by al-Qaida leaders contain exhortations to further violence. . . . These threats must be regarded with utmost seriousness. Additional attacks are likely."[13] Apparently, people are taking these threats with utmost seriousness. For example, when advised by the Department of Homeland Security to stock up on duct tape and plastic sheeting to prepare for possible biological or nuclear terrorism, the country's largest duct-tape manufacturer was running its factories 24 hours a day as sales tripled in a week.[14]

Many critics have accused the Bush administration of promoting public fear while failing to deal effectively with the threat of terrorism. Former New York City Mayor Michael R. Bloomberg called the advice from the government to stock up on duct tape and plastic sheeting "preposterous."[15] Critics such as Senator Joseph I. Lieberman (D-CT) accused the Bush administration of being "too slow, too protective of the status quo, and too unwilling to back up tough talk with real resources when it comes to improving our homeland defenses."[16] Critics may belittle the threat of terrorist attacks and some individuals may even continue as if there were no threat of danger, but in general the threat of terrorism occupies a central place in U.S. society. Law enforcement and intelligence agencies have heightened their response to possible terrorist attack. Members of Congress have been warned about the possibility of assassination attempts.[17] The news media continue to provide a constant stream of information, interviews, and warnings about the threat of terrorism.

Responding to Terrorism in the United States

Despite the serious concern about the war on terrorism, there is a surprising lack of understanding of the complexity of the concept of terrorism. The anti-terrorist response of the government has cast a broad net and as a result some unusual problems have been created in the fight against terrorism. Anti-terrorist measures appear to impact not only potential terrorists but also many ordinary citizens. One of the problems causing ineffective anti-terrorist

BOX 1.1 • *Consider This: Where to Go If You Want More Information*

The following websites contain useful information for persons interested in further information about terrorism in the United States.

Government Websites

U.S. Department of Homeland Security
www.dhs.gov

The Department of Homeland Security has primary responsibility for defense against terrorism in the Untied States.

Federal Bureau of Investigation
www.fbi.gov

The Federal Bureau of Investigation is a multitask law enforcement agency but its primary mission since 9/11 has been investigation of terrorism in the United States and domestic intelligence. The website provides information about the FBI's efforts in fighting terrorism. It includes a listing of wanted terrorists, a tip line, information about terrorism warnings, and advice on what to do with suspicious packages.

U.S. Department of State
www.state.gov

The U.S. Department of State website contains information about travel warnings, crisis awareness, and preparedness, as well as information about countries and regions. There are links to State Department publications on terrorism such as *Patterns of Global Terrorism*.

Ready.gov
www.ready.gov

Ready.gov is a website of the Department of Homeland Security. It informs citizens about what actions to take to promote safety in the event of a terrorist attack.

Office of Victims of Crime, U.S. Department of Justice, Office of Justice Programs
www.ojp/usdoj.gov

The Office of Victims of Crime (OVC) offers various services to victims of terrorism and criminal mass violence, including contacts for information and incident-specific hotlines and websites for victims only.

FirstGov.gov
firstgov.com

FirstGov.gov is a gateway website that will allow the user to access the webpage of government agencies. It provides links to all of the various departments of the federal executive branch.

Federal Emergency Management Agency (FEMA)
www.fema.gov

The Federal Emergency Management Agency—a former independent agency that became part of the new Department of Homeland Security in March 2003—is tasked with responding to, planning for, recovering from, and mitigating against disasters, including terrorist attacks using weapons of mass destruction.

Nongovernment Websites

Illinois Institute of Technology, Galvin Library Government Publications Access
www.gl.iit.edu

Archives of official documents of the United States and international governments concerning terrorism are available at www.gl.iit.edu/govdocs/terrorism.htm.

George Washington University, The National Security Archive
www.gwu.edu/~nsarchiv/

The National Security Archive is an independent nongovernmental research institute and library located at George Washington University. The archive collects and publishes declassified documents acquired through the Freedom of Information Act (FOIA).

American Civil Liberties Union
www.aclu.org

The ACLU website is the official website of the American Civil Liberties Union. Although not ded-

(continued)

BOX 1.1 • Continued

icated to the topic of terrorism, it frequently contains critiques of anti-terrorist legislation, policies, and government actions.

The Hate Directory
www.bcpl.net/~rfrankli/hatedir.htm

The Hate Directory is regularly updated and includes a directory of hate groups on the Internet, racist games available on the Internet, Web Rights, as well as racist-friendly web-hosting services. All links are clickable but the directory is a nonprint-

able PDF document. A copy of the Hate Directory is available for a fee.

Question

1. Government and private agencies have attempted to provide the public with extensive information about terrorism. Do you think the average person is aware of or accesses the scores of sources of information about terrorism?

actions and legislation is the net widening resulting from new legislation and anti-terrorist actions. Because of this widening net, citizens engaged in behaviors very remote from terrorist activities fall under federal scrutiny. For example, in an effort to control explosive materials, the Safe Explosive Act, passed in November 2002, prevented some miners in Pennsylvania from obtaining dynamite to work their mines because of the lack of notice to them regarding the new federal requirements for registration and background checks. The fact that they had been purchasing dynamite for years and were properly registered with state agencies was irrelevant.[18] Also, model-rocket hobbyists fell under federal scrutiny when it was determined that the propellant used in high-power rocketry (APCP and black powder) could be used by terrorists to construct an explosive device.[19] The banning of all persons but passengers from airport terminals has resulted in reduced revenue for airport shops and restaurants. The banning of lighters and matches from airplanes and in the secure area of airports has caused widespread inconvenience for many people. Thus, although citizens want to support the government's anti-terrorist actions, the appropriateness and effectiveness of some intrusions are questioned.

There is no single, globally accepted definition of terrorism. States and local governments have definitions of terroristic actions ranging from misdemeanor crimes, such as terroristic threatening (e.g., the verbal threat to harm someone) to felony crimes involving the use of violence or death (e.g., the bombing of abortion clinics). Nor do federal codes provide a conclusive definition of terrorism. Various executive orders, presidential decision directives, and congressional statutes address the issue of terrorism and although these have some commonality, the definition of terrorism is still elusive. Sometimes there are conflicts regarding the definition of terrorism, and the constitutionality of government laws and actions are challenged in court. Persons accused of terrorism can be apprehended and/or convicted under a multitude of existing criminal statutes, new federal laws (e.g., the USA Patriot Act) or executive orders such as the Enemy Combatant Executive Order.[20] International law and the United Nations do not provide a uniform standard that can be applied in defining terrorism because of the sharp divergence of opinion among nations as to what actions constitute terrorism, crime, internal/civil conflict, and freedom fighting.

In the United States, the legal definition of terrorism has been defined since 1983 by Title 22 Section 2656f(d) of the U.S. Code, defining terrorism as "premeditated, politically motivated violence perpetrated against noncombatant targets by subnational groups or clandestine agents, usually intended to influence an audience."[21]

To provide further specificity to the definition, the Federal Bureau of Investigation divides terrorism into "domestic terrorism investigations" and "international terrorism investigations." The guidelines for investigating *domestic terrorism* apply to investigations of persons who reside in the United States who are not acting on behalf of a foreign power, and who may be conducting criminal activities in support of terrorist objectives. The guidelines for investigating *international terrorism* apply to investigating persons or foreign nationals in the United States who are targeting national security interests on behalf of a foreign power.[22] These definitions are very broad and can include numerous actions that can be defined as terrorism. Also, there is the potential of a blurring of the distinction between domestic and international terrorism. For example, the Federal Emergency Management Agency (FEMA) makes little distinction between international terrorism and domestic terrorism in its efforts to mitigate the harm of a terrorist attack.

Finally, there are actions in the United States that historically have not been commonly considered as terrorism but, if examined and compared to the contemporary understanding of terrorism, are indeed examples of terrorism. Chapter 2 discusses some examples of this type of terrorism.

Prior to the September 11, 2001, attacks, most terrorist incidents in the United States were bombing attacks, arson, and vandalism. Furthermore, most of these attacks involved small extremist domestic groups. Most, if not all, of the members of these groups were U.S. citizens. The most common motivations for the use of violence was the group's radical stand on a single issue, such as anti-abortion, animal rights, tax protest, or racial/ethnic hatred. Some of the groups were extreme religious-cults or simply psychologically unbalanced individuals. Bombs were the most common form of attack, but a few of the groups attempted to use—and some successfully used—biological agents in their attacks. The number of terrorist attacks by these groups was fairly few. For example, the Federal Bureau of Investigation reported a total of only 101 terrorist incidents in the United States from 1983 to 1991. These terrorist incidents were handled by local, state, and federal law enforcement agencies. Few attacks caused widespread panic or concern. The Federal Bureau of Investigation considered the persons responsible for these acts of terrorism as a small criminal minority in a larger social context.[23] There was little fear that such domestic terrorist incidents would impact national security, significantly disrupt social order, or threaten the infrastructure of the U.S. government.

Federal Government Policy and Strategy

Prior to the terrorist attacks of September 11, 2001, there was little or no need to examine international terrorist attacks in the United States, as this phenomenon was extremely rare. Nearly all international terrorism occurred outside the United States. It is true that U.S. citizens or property were the target of these attacks, but the attacks themselves did not occur on U.S. soil. Because of this fact, (1) fear of international terrorists attacking U.S. citizens and property was relatively low among the general population and (2) the jurisdiction and response of the United States was often limited. Responses to terrorist attacks on U.S. citizens and property were primarily the responsibility of the executive branch of government. These responses were usually in the form of political and diplomatic responses or a military response involving the use of force against a specific target suspected of being responsible for the attack. Often, the response of the United States was limited to diplomatic efforts and cooperative assistance to other countries to help identify the terrorist(s) and bring the terrorist(s) to a court, usually an international court, with jurisdiction to try the person(s).

Following the 9/11 attacks, the federal government adopted a national security strategy emphasizing the need (1) to destroy terrorist organizations, (2) to win the "war of ideas," (3) to strengthen America's security at home and abroad, and (4) to focus on identifying and defusing threats before they reach the United States.[24] These national security goals are to be accomplished by use of the 4D strategy: Defeat, Deny, Diminish, and Defend.[25] Basically this strategy called for the *Defeat* of terrorist groups of global reach through the direct or indirect use of diplomatic, economic, information, law enforcement, military, financial, intelligence, and other instruments of power.[26] *Deny* refers to strategies to deny terrorist groups access to resources and weapons of mass destruction. *Diminish* refers to reducing the capacity of terrorist groups both in the scope of their tactical plans and their geographical reach. Finally, *Defend* refers to strategies to defend the United States against attacks and to minimize the damage in the event of an attack.

According to U.S. policy, international terrorist groups are classified according to their threat severity and their geographical capacity.[27] Figure 1.1 shows how terrorists groups are classified according to these two criteria. The terrorist group al-Qaida is classified as having a high threat severity and capacity to attack globally. Less of a threat severity to the United States are terrorist groups that operate regionally (i.e., their operations transcend at least one international boundary). The least threat to the United States are state-level groups that operate primarily within a single country.[28] The goal of the United States, as reflected in Figure 1.2 is to respond to terrorism so as to lessen the threat of global and regional groups by

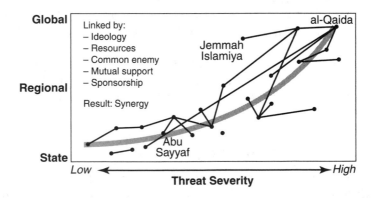

FIGURE 1.1   *Transnational Terrorist Networks*

Source: National Strategy for Combating Terrorism (Washington, DC: State Department, 2003), p. 9.

OPERATIONALIZING THE STRATEGY

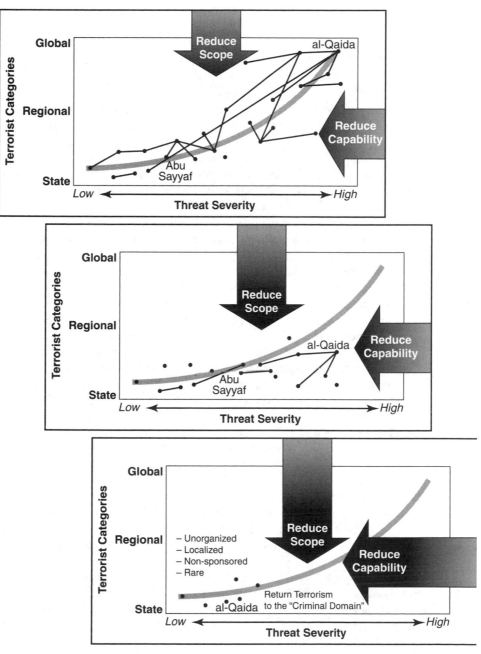

FIGURE 1.2   *From Terrorism to Criminal Activity*

Source: National Strategy for Combating Terrorism (Washington, DC: State Department, 2003), p. 13.

reducing them to state-level groups or to reduce their impact to "the criminal domain" to be handled by state-level law enforcement agencies and resources.

Criminals and Terrorism: Is There a Difference? Does It Matter?

As a result of the belief that international terrorist attacks in the United States could threaten national security and the infrastructure of government and society, new legislation and investigative procedures have emerged that give the executive office, law enforcement agencies, and criminal justice system new powers. New questions have emerged as government agencies exercise these recent powers. For example, if a madman places a bomb in a building and kills hundreds of people, is he a terrorist or a criminal? If a person kills a dozen persons in the act of armed robbery, is he a terrorist? If it is believed that money from illegal drug trafficking finances terrorism, is a drug dealer aiding terrorism? If a person provides fake identification documents that allow another person to enter the United States and blow up a building, is the person who provided the fake identification documents aiding terrorism? If a lawyer defends a client accused of terrorism, is he or she aiding terrorism? If a member of Greenpeace, PETA (People for the Ethical Treatment of Animals), or an anti-war protest group conducts public protests against government policy, could that person be investigated as a terrorist? Can suspected terrorists, including U.S. citizens, be held indefinitely without being charged with a crime and without access to the courts and a lawyer? Does a person have to commit an act of violence to be a terrorist or is he a terrorist because of his ideology? If a person gives to a charity that supports international terrorism but is unaware of such support, is the donor aiding and abetting terrorism? If there is legislation that allows the government to strip terrorists of certain constitutionally protected rights, including the right to revoke the citizenship of natural-born Americans, and allows indefinite detention without the right to contact an attorney, what criteria should determine who can be treated this way and who is protected by "normal" constitutional rights? What is the appropriate role of the military and the CIA in preventing international terrorists from terrorist actions in the United States?

Using new powers, the State Department has designated groups, "charities," and organizations as Foreign Terrorist Organizations (FTOs) (see Figure 1.3). Under section 219 of the Immigration and Nationality Act, as amended by the Antiterrorism and Effective Death Penalty Act of 1996, the designation FTO carries legal consequences. It is unlawful to provide funds or other material support to a designated FTO. Representatives and certain members of a designated FTO can be denied visas or excluded from the United States. Financial institutions must block funds of designated FTOs and their agents and must report the blockage to the United States Department of Treasury.[29] Once placed on such a list, it can be very difficult for the group to refute the classification as a FTO as there are no appeal procedures.

Because of these questions and many more, the distinction between *criminal* and *terrorist* has become an important topic of discussion. The United States Constitution and various federal and state laws provide accused criminals with a number of rights and protections. In the war on terrorism, the government has consistently demonstrated an agenda dedicated to reducing the rights of accused terrorists. In the name of fighting terrorism,

FIGURE 1.3 *Foreign Terrorist Organizations*

Abu Nidal Organization (ANO)
Abu Sayyaf Group (ASG)
Al-Aqsa Martyrs Brigade
Armed Islamic Group (GIA)
'Asbat al-Ansar
Aum Supreme Truth (Aum) Aum Shinrikyo, Aleph
Basque Fatherland and Liberty (ETA)
Communist Party of Philippines/New People's Army (CPP/NPA)
Al-Gama'a al-Islamiyya (Islamic Group, IG)
HAMAS (Islamic Resistance Movement)
Harakat ul-Mujahidin (HUM)
Hizballah (Party of God)
Islamic Movement of Uzbekistan (IMU)
Jaish-e-Mohammed (JEM)
Jemaah Islamiya (JI)
Al-Jihad (Egyptian Islamic Jihad)
Kahane Chai (Kach)
Kurdistan Workers' Party (PKK, KADEK)
Lashkar-e-Tayyiba (LT)
Lashkar I Jhangvi (LJ)
Liberation Tigers of Tamil Eelam (LTTE)
Mujahedin-e Khalq Organization (MEK or MKO)
National Liberation Army (ELN)—Colombia
Palestine Islamic Jihad (PIJ)
Palestine Liberation Front (PLF)
Population Front for the Liberation of Palestine (PFLP)
Population Front for the Liberation of Palestine-General Command (PFLP-GC)
Al-Qaida
Real IRA (RIRA)
Revolutionary Armed Forces of Colombia (FARC)
Revolutionary Nuclei
Revolutionary Organization 17 November (17 November)
Revolutionary People's Liberation Party/Front (DHKP/C)
Salafist Group for Call and Combat (GSPC)
Sendero Luminoso (Shining Path or SL)
United Self-Defense Forces/Group of Colombia (AUC)

Source: National Strategy for Combating Terrorism (Washington, DC: State Department, 2003), p. 99.

the government has often been granted new investigative powers that some critics condemn as violation of constitutionally protected rights of privacy and civil rights.

The 1999 *Report on Terrorism in the United States* included the statement, "All suspected terrorists placed under arrest are provided access to legal counsel and normal judicial procedures, including Fifth Amendment guarantees."[30] Some new anti-terrorism strategies do not provide for such constitutionally protected rights, arguing that terrorists are "enemy combatants," not criminals. Even the trial of persons *accused* of terrorism has raised difficult questions of justice. The government prosecution has in some cases refused to provide the defendant the right to court-ordered documents or witnesses, citing the potential harm to national security that would occur if such documents or witnesses were make public.[31] The denial of such rights to terrorists raises serious questions regarding the ability of the criminal justice system to handle the trial of international terrorists.

In the past, the criminal justice system stated that all who are accused of crimes have equal rights before the court. It has been a cornerstone of the U.S. judiciary that citizens and noncitizens enjoyed the same constitutional rights and were subject to the same laws. Some critics of the government's use of military tribunals, new intelligence-gathering powers, and intrusion into individual privacy voice concern over the loss of civil rights and the impact such loss has on a democratic government. For example, Senate Judiciary Committee Chairman Patrick Leahy (D-VT) believes that rather than respecting the "checks and balances that make up our constitutional framework, the executive branch has chosen to cut out judicial review in monitoring attorney-client communications and to cut out Congress in determining the appropriate tribunal and procedures to try terrorists."[32] New York University law professor Burt Neuborne criticized government actions against accused terrorists, saying, "The Constitution is not a device to empower the government to engage in wholesale arrests, secret military trials, [and] eavesdropping on attorney-client [conversations]. It's not a sword that allows the government to simply alter the rules of justice."[33]

It is argued that stripping terrorists of any rights has the potential to degenerate the rights of all citizens. This dilemma as to whether terrorists are criminals entitled to all the rights and privileges afforded to any criminal in the criminal justice system or whether by virtue of their grave threat to national security they should be arrested, prosecuted, and punished by different judicial standards will be further discussed throughout this book.

Conclusion: How Did We Get to This Point?

In 1998, the Business Exposure Reduction Group issued a report that echoed the confidence in the war against terrorism when it concluded: "Terrorism is not widespread, terrorist groups are not proliferating at an uncontrollable rate and terrorism has and can be contained."[34] In 2000, the Federal Bureau of Investigation repeated this message of confidence when it reported, "For the sixth consecutive year, there were no successful acts of international terrorism perpetrated in the United States."[35] Since 9/11, however, no one is minimizing the potential harm posed by international terrorists in the United States.

The government's response to terrorism has created new roles and relationships for local, state, and federal law enforcement agencies. Anti-terrorism operations planning has mandated the cooperation of previously semi-autonomous agencies such as the Department of Justice, State Department, Central Intelligence Agency, Federal Bureau of Investigation, Federal Emergency Management Agency, Department of Defense, Department of Energy, Environmental Projection Agency, and Department of Health and Human Services. New government agencies have been created to counter terrorism (the Office of Homeland Security). Also, new legislation (USA Patriot Act) and new standards of conduct and response by local, state and federal law enforcement agencies have emerged. For example, numerous "tourists" have been arrested and deported for photographing bridges, tunnels, and other infrastructures under the assumption that such photographs could be a threat to national security. Since the 9/11 attacks new terms such as *enemy combatants* and *military tribunals* are used to define new anti-terrorism strategies. Anti-terrorist efforts have turned toward prevention and cutting off the funding of terrorism as well as responding to terrorist attacks. New concerns are raised about cyber-terrorism, weapons of mass destruction (WMD), aviation security, border security, and funding of terrorists.

The result of this new appreciation of the dangers of international terrorists in the United States has changed the response of the government and law enforcement agencies to terrorist and terrorist incidents. Prior to September 11, 2001, an uncoordinated response by local, state, and federal law enforcement agencies to terrorist-type incidents was the norm. Perpetrators of such incidents were considered criminals and were dealt with by use of the criminal justice system. Since 9/11, however, many people consider the criminal justice system ineffective in dealing with international terrorists in the United States and criticize the uncoordinated efforts by law enforcement as endangering national security. The federal government, particularly the Federal Bureau of Investigation and the Department of Homeland Security, has assumed lead roles in anti-terrorist activities. The Immigration and Naturalization Service (INS) has been dismantled and new aggressive laws and agents are responsible for border security. These new expectations are often overwhelming local and state law enforcement agencies. Often, local and state law enforcement agencies find that they are inadequately equipped as first responders to terrorist incidents. Many airports cannot afford new mandated security measures. New immigration and border controls impact legitimate businesses and foreign students. A higher standard of performance is being asked of law enforcement agencies, but many of these agencies do not have the resources or expertise to fulfill these expectations.

Americans have entered a new era in which there is a realization that defending the homeland against terrorism is an immediate and important priority. However, this awakening to the threat of terrorism in the United States has also been accompanied by many questions. How did we go from domestic peace and tranquility to watching the daily alert color? How did we go from no terrorist attacks by international terrorists for six years in a row to daily fear of attack? Were there warning signs that were missed about the impending threat of terrorism to the United States? The remaining chapters of this book will provide insight and information regarding these questions. It will show how, in many ways, Americans and government agencies failed to heed clear warning signs of domestic terror by international terrorists and how terrorism in the United States has been much more common than previously acknowledged.

In fact, it could be argued that the United States was born from a terrorist movement as it went to war with England for its freedom. Even Yasser Arafat has often made reference that his actions and motives resemble those of George Washington—often to the displeasure of U.S. audiences who fail to see or refuse to see the resemblance. The examination of the challenge of terrorism in the United States touches nearly all aspects of government and society, but the primary focus of this book will be the effect on homeland security. In a time when fear influences the judgment of many, a reasoned and balanced inquiry to a very serious problem is essential.

Chapter Summary

- Attacks by international terrorists in the United States have caused fear and a plethora of reactions, legislation, and questions.
- The purpose of *Terrorism in the United States: Defending the Homeland* is to examine the unique history and distinctiveness of terrorism in America and the challenge of defending the United States against international terrorist attack while preserving the hallmarks of individual liberty and freedom.
- The terrorist attacks of September 11, 2001, on the World Trade Center and the Pentagon are a watershed which marks the awakening of Americans to the real threat of attack by international terrorists in the United States. Since 9/11, government, society, businesses, and individuals respond differently to the challenge of defending the homeland against terrorism.
- Prior to 9/11, domestic terror attack by international terrorists were rare, but following 9/11, preventing such attacks has become one of the primary concerns of government.
- While nearly everyone recognizes the harm that can be done by a terrorism attack in the United States, many criticize the response of the government and argue that while Americans are giving up privacy and constitutionally protected rights, little headway is being made in defending the homeland.
- Terrorism is a complex concept and is not adequately defined in the United States or in international law.
- It is important to define terrorism because if terrorism is differentiated from ordinary criminal activity and if those accused of terrorism are subject to different standards of investigation, prosecution, and punishment, it is important to know what actions and behaviors justify this different treatment by the criminal justice system.
- Domestic terrorism by international terrorists is such a new phenomenon in the United States that many are confused and lack information about defending the homeland against terrorism.
- In a short time there has been a significant reorganization of numerous government and law enforcement agencies in the effort to provide an effective anti-terrorism response.
- In responding to domestic terrorism by international terrorists, many new concepts and ideas are being proposed.

Terrorism and You _____

Understanding This Chapter

1. Examine the content of the terrorism-related websites cited in this chapter. Do you find the information from the government personally helpful and/or reassuring? Why or why not?

2. Irrational fear of persons of Middle Eastern descent or sometimes even people who appear to *look* like persons of Middle Eastern descent has resulted in alleged acts of racial discrimination and violence. What is the harm of such irrational acts of violence? How can these irrational fears be minimized?

3. The FBI makes a distinction between *domestic terrorism* and *international terrorism*. Do you believe this is a valid distinction that serves a legitimate purpose? Explain your answer.

4. Some critics of the government's anti-terrorism response do not dispute the existence of the threat but the methods used by the government to fight terrorism. These critics argue that as a result of broad laws, vague criteria for defining terrorism, and an attempt to cover very remote threats, ordinary citizens who in no way are involved in terrorism will come under government scrutiny, regulation, and control. How can the rights and privacy of individuals be balanced against the security of the nation and society?

Thinking about How Terrorism Touches You

1. Has the threat of terrorist attack made any changes in your lifestyle, attitude, or behavior? Do you feel less safe in public places? Explain your answers.

2. To what extent would you give up personal freedoms and privacy to the government to help promote anti-terrorist efforts?

3. Terrorism is currently one of the most important topics in the United States. Do you think that in 5 or 10 years the U.S. public and government will be more concerned about terrorism, less concerned about terrorism, or no change in the concern about terrorism? Why?

4. Did you feel "surprised" by the sudden realization of the vulnerability of the United States to domestic terror attacks by international terrorists? Why or why not?

5. Do you believe that there should be a differentiation in law, investigation, prosecution, and punishment of terrorists and criminals? If no, why not? If yes, why and what should be the differentiation?

Important Terms and Concepts

Al-Qaida Terrorism Network
Checks and Balances
Civil Rights
Constitutionally Protected Rights
Department of Homeland Security
Domestic Terrorism
Enemy Combatants
Equal Rights before the Court

Federal Bureau of Investigation
International Terrorism
Net Widening
9/11
Safe Explosive Act
Terror Alert Colors
Title 22 Section 2656f(d) of the U.S. Code

Endnotes

1. *National Strategy for Combating Terrorism* (Washington, DC: Department of State. Publication 11038. April 2003), p. 1.

2. Siobhan McDonough, "Red, Yellow, Orange, Whatever," *Pocono Record,* June 7, 2003, p. A2.

3. Nancy Gibbs, "What a Difference a Year Makes," *Time,* September 11, 2002, p. 28.

4. Brian Knowlton, "Bush Acknowledges 'Real Threat' of Terrorism," New York Times Online, www.nytimes.com, July 31, 2003.

5. Associated Press, "Attorney General Ashcroft Says There Is a 'Very Real Potential,'" New York Times Online, www.nytimes.com, August 3, 2003.

6. Nancy Gibbs, "What a Difference a Year Makes," *Time,* September 11, 2002, p. 28.

7. "Guard for Bush Isn't Allowed Aboard Flight,"

New York Times Online, www.nytimes.com, December 27, 2001.

8. "Opening Act for Jackie Mason Canceled Because He Is of Palestinian Descent," *Pocono Record,* August 29, 2002, p. A5.

9. Robert F. Worth, "Police Arrest Man in Slaying of 4 Shopkeepers," New York Times Online, www.nytimes.com, March 31, 2003.

10. Associated Press, "Military Jet's Fly-By Scares Ill. Town," New York Times Online, www.nytimes.com, February 14, 2003.

11. Counterterrorism Threat Assessment and Warning Unit, Counterterrorism Division, *Terrorism in the United States 1999* (Washington, DC: U.S. Department of Justice, 2000), pp. 1–2.

12. Counterterrorist Threat Assessment and Warning Unit, National Security Division, *Terrorism in the United States 1999* (Washington, DC: U.S. Department of Justice, 2000), p. ii.

13. United States Department of State, *Patterns of Global Terrorism 2003* (Washington, DC: Department of State Publication, April 2003), p. ix.

14. Nancy Gibbs, "A Nation on Edge," *Time,* February 24, 2003, p. 23.

15. Richard W. Stevenson, "Trying to Walk the Line between Fear and Ridicule," New York Times Online, www.nytimes.com, February 15, 2003.

16. Ibid.

17. Nancy Gibbs, "A Nation on Edge," *Time,* February 24, 2003, p. 22.

18. "Law Keeps Dynamite from Miners," *Pocono Record,* June 3, 2003, p. C3.

19. Eric Lichtblau, "Model-Rocket Bill Stirs Debate," New York Times Online, www.nytimes.com, July 30, 2003.

20. Counterterrorist Threat Assessment and Warning Unit, National Security Division, *Terrorism in the United States 1997* (Washington, DC: U.S. Department of Justice, 1999), p. i.

21. Counterterrorist Threat Assessment and Warning Unit, National Security Division, *Terrorism in the United States 1997* (Washington, DC: U.S. Department of Justice, 1998), p. i, 28 C.F.R. Section 0.85; United States Department of State, *Patterns of Global Terrorism 2002* (Washington, DC: Department of State Publication, April 2003), p. xiii.

22. Counterterrorist Threat Assessment and Warning Unit National Security Division, *Terrorism in the United States 1999* (Washington, DC: U.S. Department of Justice, 2000), p. i.

23. Counterterrorist Threat Assessment and Warning Unit, National Security Division, *Terrorism in the United States 1998* (Washington, DC: U.S. Department of Justice, 1999), p. ii.

24. *National Strategy for Combating Terrorism* (Washington, DC: Department of State. Publication 11038. April 2003), p. 2.

25. Ibid., p. 25.

26. Ibid., p. 15.

27. Ibid., p. 9.

28. Ibid., p. 8.

29. Ibid., p. 100.

30. Counterterrorism Threat Assessment and Warning Unit Counterterrorism Division, *Terrorism in the United States 1999* (Washington, DC: U.S. Department of Justice, 2000), p. i.

31. Philip Shenon, "U.S. Will Defy Court's Order in Terror Case," New York Times Online, www.nytimes.com, July 15, 2003.

32. NPR Special Report: Liberty vs. Security, www.npr.org/programs/specials/liberties/011205.index.html, April 27, 2003.

33. Ibid.

34. Larry C. Johnson, "Is Terrorism Getting Worse?" Berg Associates, LLC: www.BERG-Associates.com.

35. Counterterrorism Threat Assessment and Warning Unit, Counterterrorism Division, *Terrorism in the United States 1999* (Washington, DC: U.S. Department of Justice, 2000), p. 1.

Terrorism in the United States

A Historical Overview

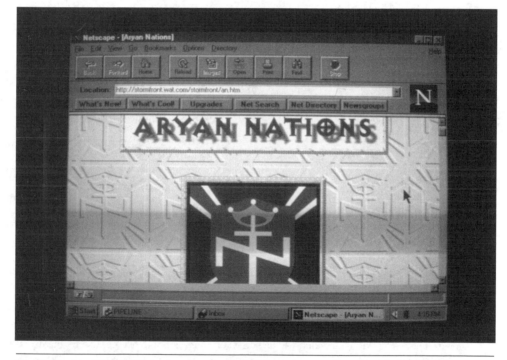

The September 11, 2001, attacks were not the first terrorist acts committed in the United States. Our country's history includes many examples of the use of terrorism by extremist groups. However, none of these previous terrorist attacks had the impact of the September 11, 2001, attacks.

The new kamikazes of the 21st century bore no flags or markings. They hid behind ordinary citizens, and their targets included ordinary Americans. By hijacking civilian airliners and riding them into the World Trade Center and the Pentagon, they used the very accessibility of an open society to wound that society. Nobody doubts America's clear military superiority. But the lesson of yesterday seemed to be that even such power is vulnerable and may offer no redress against terror. . . . In the short run, the terrorists accomplished their objectives. . . . The terrorists are in the fight for the long haul.[1]

—Michael R. Gordon, September 12, 2001

Chapter Outline

Learning Objectives

- The reader will understand that it is difficult to define terrorism because of the values and moral judgments necessary to define it.
- The reader will understand what a person or group hopes to accomplish by the use of terrorism.
- The reader will understand how groups that use terror see themselves.
- The reader will understand some key characteristics of violence that is classified as terrorism.
- The reader will appreciate the extensive worldwide history of the use of terrorism and how modern vocabulary has been shaped by early examples of terrorism.
- The reader will understand that terrorism is rooted in American history.
- The reader will understand why, in the twentieth century, Americans feared the terror posed by Communist revolutionaries and other Communist-Marxist–inspired governments and groups.

Introduction: Why Terrorism?

The September 11, 2001, terrorist attacks resulted in the largest number of civilian deaths in the United States by a foreign enemy. The magnitude and unexpectedness of the mass destruction of those terrorist attacks, and the subsequent revelation that hundreds or thousands of other terrorists are planning and willing to carry out future attacks has caused a fundamental change in the attitude of Americans toward terrorism and terrorists. This shift of paradigm has been swift and radical. The 9/11 attacks have been compared to the surprise attack of the Japanese on Pearl Harbor that resulted in the entry of the United States into World War II. However, unlike the Pearl Harbor attack, there is no clearly identified enemy against which to retaliate. The terrorist group(s) responsible for the September 11 attack is not clearly defined, does not reside in a single nation, and cannot easily be defeated by a military assault.

Furthermore, the threat of future attacks is perceived as much closer and personal than the attack on Pearl Harbor because it is believed that terrorists are plotting to attack targets such as bridges, nuclear power plants, shopping malls, schools, government buildings, hotels, and other nonmilitary targets. Terrorism is not unique to modern times; however, the technology of modern civilization, the metropolitan population centers, and the global communication and transportation capacity have created unprecedented opportunities for terrorists, both in terms of the destruction they can create and the level of public anxiety their acts can generate.[2]

This chapter will review the historical roots of terrorism in the United States; later chapters will focus on contemporary terrorism threats to the nation. The chapter will discuss how terrorism has deep roots in American history, especially the American Revolutionary War, terror against Native Americans, the American Civil War, and racism following the Civil War. In addition, this chapter will examine the reaction of the U.S. government and people to the Red Scare and the Cold War and how this reaction was similar to the reaction to the September 11, 2001, attacks by terrorists.

Historical Roots of the Definition of Terrorism

Terrorism and terrorist activities predate even the origins of the word *terror*. Thus, before there was the word *terrorism*, there was terrorism. Terrorism has always been associated with violence, politics, toppling governments, and religion. Defining terrorism is difficult because the definition reflects a value statement concerning the legitimacy in the use of violence as a means to achieve an end. Hence, in nearly any heated debate concerning the definition of terrorism, the argument fails to be resolved because either side can throw out the cliché "One man's terrorist is another man's freedom fighter." The argument comes to a dead end as neither side will admit to the moral legitimacy of the other side. For example, in the trial to prosecute Mohammed Ali Hassan al-Moayad, the sheik charged with providing material support to al-Qaida and the Palestinian militant group Hamas, one of the conflicts between the prosecution and the defense is the definition of the word *Jihad*. The prosecution has secretly recorded tapes in which the sheik referred to Jihad countless times. The prosecution asserts that these references refer to terroristic activity against the United States. The defense claims the definition of Jihad is being mistranslated and misunderstood.[3] The defense asserts that the definition of Jihad is "the struggle for self-perfection and charitable work. Anything that basically furthers the cause of Islam and is understood to be doing good."[4]

Defining terrorism is similar to the problem of defining pornography. Not even the United States Supreme Court has been able to craft an unqualified definition of pornography but nearly everyone seems to be of the opinion that although they are unable to define pornography, "they know it when they see it." Like pornography, the problem with this approach is that given the diverse value systems of people, societies, and government, it is impossible to arrive at an universal definition as to who is a terrorist and who is a freedom-fighter hero engaged in a heroic battle for national independence.

The matter is complicated by the fact that terrorism is a strategy, a philosophy, rather than a group or a set of defining beliefs. As a strategy, any one person or any group can inflict terrorism. Terrorism does not define who the person or group is; rather it is only a strategy adopted by the individual or group. Groups with opposing viewpoints and beliefs can both use terrorism—even against each other. Terrorism is not a philosophy or belief system that unites groups or defines who belongs or does not belong to a group. Persons and groups with common beliefs can be divided on their belief in the morality of terrorism as a strategy to advance their cause. Environmentalists, for example, may share common beliefs about the need to take action to protect the environment but hold opposing views about the legitimacy of violence as a means to achieve political action.

Individuals, small groups, and nations can make use of terrorism. A small group of persons who are unable to achieve military or political victory over a larger group through use of conventional military power or political strategies may embrace terrorism as a strategy. Terrorism can be used by nations to maintain power and the status quo. When used by the state, the purpose of terrorism is to discourage anyone from challenging the power and authority of the state.

When terrorism is used by individuals or small groups who are challenging the state, there may be several objectives but the root objective is to demonstrate to the general population of the nation that the government is unable to provide for the safety and general welfare of its citizens. The irony of this strategy is that it is the terrorists who carry out the attacks against the government, infrastructure, and citizenry to demonstrate that the government cannot protect its citizens. Thus, the terrorists are in reality attempting to demonstrate the government cannot provide protection and preventive action against the terrorist group who are the perpetrators of the attacks. The message of the terrorists seems to be: "If government cannot stop a small group like us, how can they protect you against really serious threats?"

David versus Goliath

Terrorism is often portrayed as a "David versus Goliath" scenario. In this scenario a small but vociferous group opposed to the dominance of the more powerful group engages in strategies employing violence, such as attacks on military or governmental personnel, governmental and social infrastructure, or the general citizenry. These attacks are often characterized as "hit and run." That is to say, the terrorists do not engage in a military campaign to capture and hold geo-political territory, but inflict injury against the government and then blend back into the citizenry to avoid counterattack by the government. To some degree there is a distinction between the adoption of such tactics by rural-based groups and urban-based groups. The use of such tactics by rural-based groups is called *guerrilla warfare* and the actors are called *guerrillas*. The use of such tactics by urban-based groups is called *terrorism* and the actors are called *terrorists*. The importance of the distinction between the two, if there is a distinction, does not seem to be as important as it was in the 1970s when the use of political violence started to emerge.

Terrorism does not count on military prowess to topple the governing structure and power. The strategy of terrorism is to use time in its favor. As the opening quote of this chapter concludes, "The terrorist is in the fight for the long haul."

Those who use terrorism hope to promote one or more of the following conclusions by the government and citizens:

- Government agencies, such as the police and military, are unable to protect the citizenry from random attack.
- The cost of counterterrorist activity and preparation in terms of dollars spent and dollars diverted from other government services, such as health, education, and general welfare, is not worth it. Therefore, the government should concede to some or all of the terrorists' demands.
- The government presents a false front to citizens as to the government's respect for civil rights and privacy. The terrorists hope to demonstrate by the "overreaction" of the government against the terrorists that the government poses a more serious danger and harm than the terrorists.
- The activities of terrorists are morally justified given the ends advocated by the terrorists. Anti-abortionists, for example, believe that the bombing of abortion clinics and the murder of medical personnel who perform abortions is a form of self-defense of the unborn.
- The morality of terrorists is right and proper to extend to the entire population even if their values represent a minority of the population. For example, eco-terrorists hope that the general population will view the "humane treatment" of animals in the same light as they do; anti-abortionists hope that legislation will be adopted to stop the practice of abortion; and religious extremists desire that everyone will adopt the same religious beliefs and practices of their faith.
- Citizens will perceive the lies and deceit of the government and will rebel against the government. Citizens will rebel to different degrees, ranging from giving aid and comfort to the terrorists to active support and carrying out of terrorist attacks.
- History will judge terrorists to be justified in their means. Terrorists believe that their beliefs are morally, politically, and spiritually correct. Rejection of these beliefs will turn to acceptance. This belief is illustrated by the parting words of Charles Taylor, dictator of Liberia, as he was forced from office in 2003, "History will treat me kindly."

The Ends Justify the Means

Terrorists are often called *fanatics, radicals, extremists, fundamentalists,* and other terms that imply that they are outside the norm of civilized behavior and sensibility. One of the reasons for these labels is that the philosophy of the terrorist often sees the world in terms of "black and white," "win or lose," or "us against them."

The philosophical position of terrorists is that they have the higher moral ground, and compromise, bargaining, or negotiating is inappropriate. This philosophy is boosted by the belief by the members of the group that they possess knowledge of a truth that is not perceived or known by those outside the group. Racial terrorism, for example, is often predicated on the belief by the group members that they have been ordained by their god as a superior race of people over those they terrorize. Given this bipolar view of the world, members of terror groups see the world as divided into those who support their cause and those who do not. Anyone who does not support their cause is against their cause.

No Innocent Parties

One of the most distinctive characteristics of terrorism is that terrorists do not given credence to the concept of "innocent bystanders," "neutral parties," "civilians," or "noncombatants." Unlike organized national military groups that have rules of engagement that identify citizens and targets that are inappropriate to attack or harm, terrorists believe any person is a legitimate target of violence. This belief that there are no innocent parties is one of the ideologies of terrorism that is most often and most stridently protested by governments and the general citizenry. The general public has great difficulty accepting the moral argument that violence resulting in the death of children, women, and "innocent people" is justified by the ends of the group. In fact, the definition of terrorism in the United States is based on the premise that terrorism harms "innocent parties."

The reaction of the general public to denial of innocent parties is often very strong. For example, Professor Ward Churchill of the University of Colorado at Boulder penned an essay in which he wrote that those killed in the 9/11 World Trade Center attacks were not innocent parties, because they neglected the impact of foreign policy on citizens of the Middle East. (He was referring to the U.S. embargo on Iraq.) Of those killed in the World Trade Center, he said,

> They were too busy braying, incessantly and self-importantly, into their cell phones, arranging power lunches and stock transactions, each of which translated, conveniently out of sight, mind and smelling distance, into the starved and rotting flesh of infants. . . . If there was a better, more effective, or in fact any other way of visiting some penalty befitting their participation upon the little Eichmanns inhabiting the sterile sanctuary of the twin towers, I'd really be interested in hearing about it.

Professor Churchill's denial of innocence of those killed caused a firestorm of protest across the nation. (In response to the criticism, Professor Churchill acknowledged that he conceded that some of the victims—such as children, janitors, and those who just happened to be in the area at the time of destruction—were "innocent.")

Very few people or groups call themselves terrorists.[5] *Terrorists* or *terrorism* is the label applied not by the perpetrators of the violence but by the governments opposed to the perpetrators. This label condemns the actions of the perpetrators as unjust, immoral, and criminal. It is not uncommon for the perpetrators to be stereotyped by the government or government-sponsored media as "crazed, madmen beyond reason and civilization." Racial epitaphs are often used to describe the terrorists as a further way to denigrate their actions and motives. On the other hand, the perpetrators of violence often see themselves as engaged in a struggle of epic proportions—fighting the battle of good against evil, right against wrong, or on a quest for a righteous end to a historical egregious and immoral event.

The use of violence to achieve the goals of the group is one of the thorniest questions in examining terrorism and in crafting a universal definition of terrorism. Can terrorism be a legitimate response to a real grievance? Can there be an act, event, religion, leader, or government so immoral, so contrary to the inherent rights of humans, so repressive of the rights of liberty, justice, and the pursuit of happiness that it is justified to use indiscriminate violence and terror in the quest to right this wrong? The birth of the United States was predicated on the assertion by the founding fathers that indeed there are wrongs so grievous that the use of force is justified.

Early Worldwide Examples of Terrorism

Terrorism as a tactic to achieve and to maintain political dominance, social change, and/or religious values has been used throughout history. In each age the tactics used have reflected the technologies available to the parties, but the basic principle has been similar throughout history. It is impossible to definitively determine the origins of terrorism, but its use as a tactic by dominant parties to maintain the status quo and by those who would challenge the status quo has been chronicled from the earliest of historical writings. For example, the ancient Greek historian Xenophon (c. 431 BC–c. 350 BC) wrote of the effectiveness of psychological warfare against enemy populations.[6] Roman emperors routinely resorted to the use of widespread violence against perceived opposition parties as a method to squash rebellion.

Contemporary focus has concentrated on terrorism originating in the Middle East, but historically the use of terrorism has been pervasive throughout the world and in all records of political and religious conflict. Historically, terrorism has been most closely associated with political control and religious conflicts. The worldwide nature of terrorism is seen in the fact that key vocabulary words—such as *zealot, assassin,* and *thugs*—associated with defining terrorism have come from such diverse countries as the Middle East, India, and Russia. Even the word *terror* is derived from the strategies used during the French Revolution.

Zealot

The origins of *zealot,* one of the earliest terms associated with terrorism, dates back to the first-century Roman occupation of the Middle East. In contemporary language, *zealot* is a term that is frequently used to describe the members of a terrorism group. The term implies that the members have a fanatical commitment to the group and that they would do anything, including homicide and suicide, for the group. The original Zealots of the first century were members of a Jewish group opposed to Roman domination and values. The Zealots would target Romans, Greeks, and Jews for murder. The purpose of these murders was to send a message to the Roman authorities and those Jews who collaborated with them that their very lives were threatened so long as the Roman government continued it domination.[7] Given the relative military strength of the powerful Roman army and the number of Zealots, there was virtually no chance that the Zealots could have intimidated Roman authorities through the use of threat or military attack. Therefore, the Zealots resorted to killing Roman authorities (and Jews who collaborated with them) in daylight and in front of witnesses.[8] Although this tactic was very effective in creating fear, it was "classical terrorism" in that the attacker usually forfeited his life in the brazen attack.

Assassin/Fedayeen

The words *assassin* and *Fedayeen* emerged from the Middle East when Hassan Ben Sabbah (c. 1060) attempted to convince the Shia, centered in Cairo, and the Sunni, with its core in Baghdad, to forsake their own interpretations of the Koran and accept the Ishmaili version.[9] Unable to achieve conquest over the opposing parties, Hassan Ben Sabbah organized a band of followers to commit political murder as a means of persuasion. This group of men called themselves *Fedayeen* or *fedai*, which translates to "Men of Sacrifice."[10] The victims of the Fedayeen were politicians or clerics who refused to adopt the purified version of Islam. Their victims were often attacked in daylight in public places at religious sites on holy days. This tactic publicized their cause, but it nearly always resulted in the sacrifice of the attacker.

It was believed that the suicidal attacks were committed with such fanaticism because the attackers underwent ritualistic drug taking (hashish) prior to undertaking their missions.[11] Based on this common belief, the members of the group were called *Assassins*, which meant "hashish-eaters."[12] The term *assassin* has come to mean any murder that is motivated by political ideology or religious values.

As is the characteristic of modern-day terrorists, members of the Fedayeen were willing to sacrifice their lives to advance the cause of their group. What would cause a person to make such a commitment? Fedayeen members were willing to commit suicide missions primarily because Hassan Ben Sabbah selected individuals who were fearless, lower than average intellects, and completely committed to spreading the religious values of their group. Also, they did not fear the consequences of their suicidal attack, as they believed that their sacrifice would guarantee them entry into paradise.[13] (Modern Middle Eastern revolutionaries, who also call themselves Fedayeen, profess this belief.) It is believed that this band of political murderers carried out hundreds of murders and their existence continued after the death of their leader, Hassan Ben Sabbah.[14]

Thugs

Another term associated with terrorism is *thugs*. The word is derived from the Indian religious cult *Thuggee*. Members of the Thuggee cult ritually strangled their victims as an offering to the Hindu goddess of terror and destruction, Kali.[15] The cult was allegedly a hereditary cult with both Muslim and Hindu members who practiced large-scale robbery and murder of travelers by strangulation.[16] Their victims were usually travelers chosen at random. Unlike the Zealots and Assassins, Thugees did not commit violence to exercise political or social influence, but were inspired primarily by their religious beliefs that demand

BOX 2.1 • *Consider This: Is There Prejudice against Muslims?*

Is there prejudice against Muslims in the United States? Some point to incidents such as the following in support of their conclusion that there is:

- In 2003, the FBI order field supervisors to count the number of mosques and Muslims in their areas as part of the anti-terrorism effort. Civil rights advocates and Arab American leaders denounced the survey as a form of racial profiling.[17] Prior to counting mosques, the Justice Department identified foreign males in the United States from certain predominately Muslim countries and FBI agents were sent to conduct "voluntary interviews" with them. These interviews asked questions about the men's religious beliefs and with whom they associated.

- In November 2003, residents of Voohrees, New Jersey, protested against the building of a mosque on the grounds that it could attract people connected to terrorists.[18]

- In February 2005, the Muslim population of Falls Church, Virginia, protested that federal law enforcement officials were scrutinizing mosques, private Muslim schools, fund raisers, and Muslims in the area for terrorists based on racial profiling.[19]

- Surveys indicate that in some U.S. cities Muslims are cited by the police for violations more often than other races.

- Surveys of Arab Americans report that a significant number of those polled said they felt they were discriminated against because of their race.

Questions

1. Do you think that the 9/11 attacks have led to Americans discriminating against Muslims? Explain your answer.

2. Do you think there is widespread understanding by Americans about the principles of the Muslim religion, beliefs, and culture? If not, what are some of the consequences of this lack of knowledge? What could be done to improve relations between the U.S. population and Muslims?

human sacrifice. Despite the absence of political motives, the Thugs created a significant problem for the Indian government: They reportedly murdered 1 million people from the seventh to the mid-nineteenth century.[20]

The defeat of this widespread random violence became one of the main goals of the British government ruling India. The British rulers of India suppressed Thugs in the 1830s due largely to the extensive efforts of William Sleeman. Between 1831 and 1837, British courts in India hanged nearly 4,000 Thugs. The problem of the Thuggee cult was so great that a police organization known as the Thuggee and Dacoity Department was established within the government of India and remained in existence until 1904, when it was replaced by the Central Criminal Intelligence Department.[21] The defeat of the cult was one of the reasons the Indians were loyal to the British Crown for several decades following their suppression.[22]

The term *thug* entered the English language in 1839 with the publication of Philip Meadows Taylor's novel, *Confessions of a Thug. Thuggee* is a relatively obscure term to most people in the United States, but it was popularized in the media by the 1939 film *Gunga Din* and the 1984 Indiana Jones film, *Indiana Jones and the Temple of Doom.*[23] In these films Thuggee cult members attempt to resume their reign of terror but are thwarted by the film's hero.

Terror, Terrorism, Terrorist

The origins of the terms *terror, terrorism,* and *terrorists* are rooted in the French Revolution's Reign of Terror (1793–1794). Their use in the French Revolution pretty much mirrors contemporary use. The French Revolution was directed toward eliminating government by a privileged group, abolishing feudalism, economic reform, and the implementation of a government dedicated to liberty, equality, and fraternity.[24] However, the leaders of the revolution believed that violence was an essential tactic in this quest.

French society of the eighteenth century was stratified by birth. Its three traditional divisions, or "orders," were the clergy, the nobility, and the common people, or third estate. Class privileges were passed on primarily through inheritance. The clergy and nobility placed the burden of taxes to support the government primarily on the common people. The French participation in the American Revolution had increased the huge debt of the French government. On May 5, 1789, representatives of each of the three orders met to consider the challenge of general fiscal reform. The focus of the meeting quickly moved toward sweeping political and social reforms and a claim of authority by the common people, or third estate. King Louis XVI disbanded the meeting but the assembly challenged the king. The group, calling itself the National Assembly, demanded a constitutional government on June 20, 1789. Initially, Louis XVI refused to recognize the demands of the National Assembly but he quickly yielded to their demands within a week. The demand for reform was not satisfied, however, and on July 14, 1789, Parisians stormed the Bastille fortress in revolt against the monarchy and feudalistic government. Following this revolt, members of the third estate pillaged and burned chateaus, destroying records of feudal dues. The violent actions of the third estate, known as the *grande peu,* or "great fear," was instrumental in the nobles and clergy renouncing their privileges on August 4, 1789.[25]

The National Assembly abolished most feudal privileges, including tax exemptions, tithes, obligatory labor on roads, and the payment of seigneurial dues. On August 11, 1789, the National Assembly formally abolished the Feudal System. On August 26, 1789, the National Assembly adopted the *Declaration of the Rights of Man and the Citizen.* In October, women joined the revolution and marched on Versailles, demanding equality for women. In November, all church property was expropriated. In June 1790, all aristocratic, hereditary titles were abolished. On July 14, 1790, the first anniversary of the revolution was celebrated on the fields of the *Champ de Mars,* the Festival of the Federation. Thus, the belief in the use of violence as a tool in transforming a repressive, class-orientated monarchy into a society based on reason and equality seemed to be proven correct.

The Reign of Terror.   The French Revolution was far from over, however. Demands for equality from women and black inhabitants of French colonies extended the definition of equality far beyond that originally envisioned by the revolutionaries. Both the fear of foreign invasion and the push for war to spread the revolution created factionalism, chaos, and instability in the revolutionary government. Fear of food shortages among commoners, especially those in Paris, and the desire to find relief from the unsatisfactory living conditions they felt had resulted from a government both mismanaged and insensitive generated a fear of "spontaneous anarchy."[26] These forces led to the Reign of Terror from 1793 to 1794, from whence comes the modern ideologies that define terrorism.

As the revolution achieved more popular support, its leaders became more intolerant of diversity of ideologies and suggestions as to how the new society should be structured. In April 1793, the government was ruled by a war dictatorship operating through the Committee of Public Safety, the Committee of General Security, and numerous agencies such as the Revolutionary Tribunal. The leaders of this war dictatorship controlled virtually all aspects of the government.[27]

Headed by Georges Danton and Maximilien Robespierre, this small group of revolutionary leaders sought to eliminate all competing political parties and ideologies. One of the tactics of the Committee of Public Safety was execution by use of the guillotine. The committee sought to eliminate any opposition by having the adversaries arrested and executed. During the Reign of Terror from 1793 to 1794, approximately 11,000 individuals were sentenced to death as enemies of the state.[28] By the summer of 1794, public reaction against the terror reached a peak and several of the so-called ultra-revolutionaries were arrested and executed in March 1794. Robespierre's power over the Committee of Public Safety waned despite his call for new purges. The members of the committee turned against him and Robespierre was arrested on July 27, 1794, and beheaded the next day.[29]

It is recorded of Robespierre that he was a "ruthless individual, incorruptible, dictatorial, impersonal, and determined to sweep away all who opposed the Revolution. . . . He was feared and unloved. He was the image of the modern revolutionary whose profession and passion are political."[30] Following the removal of the Committee of Public Safety, a new constitution and a bicameral legislature was adopted in 1795. This constitutional government reigned until its overthrow by Napoleon Bonaparte in 1799.

Despite the many positive changes to emerge from the French Revolution (i.e., establishing the precedents of such democratic institutions as elections, representative government, and constitutions), the Reign of Terror is described as the "modern precursor of modern totalitarianism."[31] British political philosopher Edmund Burke, who popularized the term *terrorism* in his writings, demonized the secular terrorism of the Reign of Terror.[32]

Class Warfare

One of the pillars justifying modern terrorism is the ideology of class warfare. Although class warfare was an important element in the French Revolution, the concept of class warfare as it applies to modern terrorism is rooted in communism. Numerous contemporary revolutionary groups have justified their revolutionary movement based on the original ideologies posited by Karl Marx and Frederick Engels in their founding document, *The Manifesto of the Communist Party,* first published in London in 1848. Some of the major revolutionary ideologies that are grounded in the original ideologies of communism include Leninism, Stalinism, and Maoism. Countries that have been instrumental in promoting terrorism—such as Cuba, North Korea, and China—ascribe to Marx's principles. Countless revolutionary groups have justified their violent attacks against government by citing the underlying principles of communism.

Communism identified class conflict as the source of evil and conflict in society. *The Manifesto of the Communist Party* says,

The history of all hitherto existing society is the history of class struggles. Freeman and slave, patrician and plebian, lord and serf, guild-master and journeyman, in a word, oppressor and oppressed, stood in constant opposition to one another, carried on by uninterrupted, now hidden, now open fight, a fight that each time ended, either in a revolutionary reconstitution of society at large, or in the common ruin of the contending classes.[33]

To end this class struggle, Marx and Engels advocated, "The immediate aim of the Communists is the same as that of all other proletarian parties. Formation of the proletariat into a class, overthrow of the bourgeois supremacy, conquest of political power by the proletariat."[34]

Communism advocates the overthrow of existing governments all of which are considered oppressive of the proletarian, or worker class of people.[35] Communism, as defined by Marx and Engels, considers the violent overthrow necessary because they did not believe that the bourgeoisie, or ruling class, would give up power by electoral means or nonviolent reforms. Furthermore, communism does not provide for the peaceful coexistence of the various classes in society. Communism argues that there can be no reform of the class structure that would make it acceptable; therefore, it was to be destroyed, not reformed. Thus, class hatred is a good thing and class collaboration is a bad thing, and there is no "middle ground" or compromise in the values of the bourgeoisie and proletarian.

The overthrowing of all existing governments throughout the world by violent means was the central theme presented by Communists. The closing statement of *The Manifesto of the Communist Party* declares, "The Communists disdain to conceal their views and aims. They openly declare that their ends can be attained only by the forcible overthrow of all existing social conditions. Let the ruling classes tremble at a communist revolution. The proletarians have nothing to lose but their chains. They have a world to win. Proletarians of all countries, unite!"[36]

The Russian Revolution

In October 1917, led by Vladimir Lenin and Leon Trotsky, Communists succeeded in violently overthrowing the Russian Tsarist government and implementing a state founded on Communist principles. Because of the uncompromising rhetoric of communism advocating the overthrowing of all capitalist states, the establishment of a state based on the principles of revolutionary violence caused great alarm throughout Europe and the United States. The United States was particularly fearful of the intentions of the new revolutionary government of Russia because the United States was seen as the primary example of the capitalist state condemned by Communist ideology.

The concept of class warfare is one of the major pillars of modern terrorism ideology and, until the attacks of September 11, 2001, on the World Trade Center and the Pentagon, the United States government, for the most part, focused on terrorism originating from Marxist-inspired groups and states. Much of the political debate, legislative response, and public concern regarding the threat of terrorism in the United States centered on responding the to Marxist-Communist–inspired terrorism in what was known as the Red Scare and the Cold War.

Early Terrorism in the United States

Terrorism has deep roots in American history. For example, the United States obtained its status as a free state only after a prolonged revolutionary war with Britain. Terrorism played a role in the settling of the American West as well as in the American Civil War and after the war. Terrorism has also been a common tactic in racial conflict in the United States. Often, the term *terrorism* has not been applied to these situations. Today, terrorism seems to be reserved for violence originating from groups in the Middle East. However, if one examines the scope and nature of the actions, it is evident that the strategy of terrorism played an important role in these events.

The American Revolutionary War

In the eighteenth century, Great Britain considered the American colonies as part of the British Empire. Many of the early colonists thought of themselves as British citizens and did not want to separate from Great Britain. However, a group of individuals in the colonies considered British rule onerous and oppressive of individual liberties and when they were unable to effect change through traditional political means, they called for a violent overthrow of British rule of the American colonies. The document calling for this violent revolution, the *Declaration of Independence,* opened with the words,

> When in the course of human events, it becomes necessary for one people to dissolve the political bands which have connected them to another, and to assume among the powers of the earth, the separate and equal station to which the Laws of Nature and of Nature's God entitle them, a decent respect to the opinions of mankind requires that they should declare the causes which impel them to the separation. . . . That whenever any form of government becomes destructive of these ends, it is the right of the people to alter or to abolish it, and to institute new government.

Many modern revolutionary movements often compare their struggle to that of the American colonies against Great Britain. These revolutionaries cite the very same arguments put forth by the American colonists in the Declaration of Independence, claiming justification in the violent overthrowing of the ruling government based on the right of self-government and equality. The dilemma posed by the U.S. condemnation of the struggle of these countries for independence is that it is often impossible to distinguish the difference between their efforts to achieve independence and the struggle for independence in the American Revolutionary War. In effect, the United States was born of a violent revolutionary movement against an alleged oppressive government, and that makes it difficult for the United States to condemn contemporary "freedom fighters" who take up the cause of self-government and overthrow a repressive government.

Terror against Native Americans

After the United States obtained its liberation from British rule, the belief in manifest destiny gave rise to the idea that all land from the Atlantic to the Pacific belonged to the newly formed country called the United States of America. In pursuit of this goal, American expansionism resulted in westward migration. One of the problems with this westward migration was that there were Native people living in nearly all of the land to which the Americans desired to migrate, or the land was claimed by a foreign government. To enable westward expansion large sections of land were purchased from Russia and France. Other sections of land in California, Arizona, New Mexico, and Texas, which could not be purchased from Mexico, were taken by military force. However, in those lands where Native American Indians were living, the treatment of these people as they were forcibly and violently removed from their native lands appears to be justifiably called terrorism.

The history of the expatriation of the Native American Indian is a sordid chapter in American history. English colonists displaced many tribes of Native Americans living along the East Coast but the apex of violence against these people occurred during the western movement. In the 1800s, Native Americans occupying the western United States were to a large degree seen as dangerous and savage. Despite the fact that the United States was founded on the principles of freedom and equality, these rights were not extended to the Native Americans. The wars waged by the United States military against Native Americans were often characterized by indiscriminate slaughter of men, women, and children. It was not uncommon for the military to completely destroy Native American settlements and kill everyone in the settlement. Defeated tribes were subjected to brutal conditions, confined to hostile lands with little ability to sustain the tribe, and ruled by incompetent and corrupt governmental agents.

Treatment of Native Americans by the general public was not much better than by the military. Few Americans during the nineteenth century advocated equal rights for Native Americans and Native Americans enjoyed few protections of law. Miners, farmers, settlers, and citizens of emerging cities felt little moral concern as they routinely used violence to force Native Americans from the land they desired. Most treated Native Americans with brutality and racism. Murder, beatings, exile, and denial of justice were routine responses to Native Americans' claim of sovereignty, land ownership, and humanity. Most likely such treatment of Native Americans was motivated out of fear and greed: fear of the Native Americans and greed to possess the land they claimed. When examined from the point of view of the Native Americans, the violent actions of the military and citizenry against them appears little different from what is today called terrorism.

Unfortunately, abuse of Native American Indians continues to be a concern. In 1992, on the 500th anniversary of the arrival of Europeans in the Americas, Amnesty International called for an end to the abuse of indigenous people. In its call for human rights Amnesty International said, "For centuries, governments have often treated the rights of indigenous people with contempt—torturing, 'disappearing,' and killing them in the tens of thousands and doing virtually nothing when others murder them."[37] Amnesty International noted that even today most abuses against Native Americans continue to be committed with impunity.

The American Civil War

The American Civil War is an often overlooked period of terrorism in the United States. Professor Daniel Sutherland says that significant terrorist activities occurred during the Civil War, especially in the South. Rebel and Unionist civilians engaged in guerilla warfare in order to control their community.[38] According to Sutherland, "In the early years of the war, bands of rebels from Maryland burned homes and destroyed homes of Unionists, or those who lived in the Confederate states who remained loyal to the Union."[39] Terrorist attacks by civilians were a common tactic by citizens of both the Confederacy and the Union. Another example of civilian terrorism was civilian violence against other civilians prior to the arrival of military troops and civilian terrorism against areas where the military troops did not go. Also, outlaws would disguise themselves as military soldiers and swoop down on civilians to steal horses and valuables. As a means of inflicting injuries on the opposing force, civilians would often attempt to derail railroad trains carrying supplies and troops.[40] Although not often reported in the history of the Civil War Professor Sutherland argues, "The sheer violence of guerilla warfare crippled the Confederacy. The terrorism and violence forced people to lose confidence in the Confederate government and its ability to protect its citizens."[41]

Sherman's March to the Sea. Perhaps one of the most dramatic examples of terrorism during the Civil War was General Sherman's "March to the Sea." On November 12, 1864, General Sherman and his 62,000 Union troops marched from Atlanta to Savannah, Georgia. The troops formed a 60-mile-wide line and marched toward the Atlantic Ocean. Civilian homes, farms, and businesses in the path of the advancing Union army were destroyed. As the troops marched toward the sea they looted food, tore up and destroyed railroads, and burned nearly everything in their path. When the Union troops reached Atlanta Sherman looted what he wanted from the city and then proceeded to burn anything in Atlanta that he did not need or that could be used by the Confederacy. The burning of Atlanta became a media icon when it was portrayed in the 1939 movie *Gone with the Wind.* Sherman's march struck terror in the hearts and minds of southerners as the brutal destruction convinced them that the strength of the Confederate army was vastly inferior to the Union's might. Even today, many residents of Atlanta harbor ill feelings toward what they consider a brutal and terrorist act.

Sherman's "scorched earth" policy was one of the first examples of "modern war," taking the war to the supporting civilian population and destroying the will of the population to resist.[42] This tactic of destroying the will of the population to resist was to be used again as a means to obtain Germany's and Japan's surrender in World War II by large-scale attacks on civilian populations.

Racism in the United States and Terrorism

The loss of the American Civil War and the impact of Amendments Thirteen through Fifteen on the political and social life of the southern states were far-reaching and turned the political and social order upside-down. Families that had been powerful figures in southern government and business for generations were suddenly prohibited from voting or holding office. With a new system of apportionment, the political power of freed slaves, combined with the elimination of virtually every potential white candidate, created a new political power that favored freed slaves. Taken at face value, if these Amendments were enforced, freed slaves would hold most, if not all, of the political positions in southern states and would be the majority of businessmen.

Congress attempted to provide the opportunity for freed slaves to gain political power, even dominance, in the South following the American Civil War. This attempt was not without its critics. Andrew Johnson addressed the Congress on December 25, 1868:

> The attempt to place the white population under the domination of persons of color in the South has impaired, if not destroyed, the friendly relations that had previously existed between them; and mutual distrust has engendered a feeling of animosity which, leading in some instances to collision and bloodshed, has prevented the cooperation between the two races so essential to the success of industrial enterprise in the Southern States."[43]

Johnson's remarks were prophetic. Despite the attempt of Congress to prevent segregation and retaliation, the white population of the southern states rebelled.

Unable to exercise legitimate political power, vote, or influence, the white population turned to the use of terrorism and violence. Whites formed white supremacy organizations such as the Ku Klux Klan, the White Brotherhood, the Men of Justice, the Constitutional Union Guards, and the Knights of the White Camelia to keep freed slaves from voting, running for office, and engaging in free enterprises. The most notorious of these white supremacy groups was the Ku Klux Klan (KKK), which is discussed, in greater detail in the Case Study.

Why the Ku Klux Klan Emerged

The American Civil War ended with Lee's surrender at Appomattox on April 9, 1865. Shortly following the defeat of the South, Congress passed the Thirteenth Amendment (December 6, 1865) that prohibited slavery. When it became evident that the southern states were not providing freed slaves the rights of citizenship, Congress passed the Fourteenth Amendment (July 9, 1868) that granted citizenship to anyone born or naturalized in the United States. It also provided that "no State shall deprive any person of life, liberty, or property, without due process of law; nor deny to any person within its jurisdiction the equal protection of the laws."

Furthermore, the Fourteenth Amendment attempted to provide freed slaves with the opportunity to hold political office by the adoption of two provisions. The first provision changed the way that U.S. Representatives should be apportioned. Prior to the American Civil War, Representatives were apportioned by counting only three-fifths of the slave population.[44] The Fourteenth Amendment provided that only Native Americans not taxed should be excluded from the count in determining the number of federal representatives that a state was entitled to have. This significantly increased the number of representatives from southern states as freed slaves were now fully counted in determining the number of state representatives.

The second provision in the Fourteenth Amendment to increase the political power of freed slaves was the prohibition against anyone who "engaged in insurrection or rebellion against the [United States] or given aid and comfort to the enemies thereof from holding any political office." This prohibited nearly all white males from holding political office or appointment. This prohibition, combined with the newly won right to vote, provided freed slaves an unprecedented opportunity for political power. However, this opportunity was

BOX 2.2 • *Case Study: The Ku Klux Klan*

One of the most notorious domestic terrorist groups emerging out of the reconstruction effort following the American Civil War was the Ku Klux Klan (also known as the KKK, the Klan, or the Invisible Empire). It had its origins in the defeat of the South, but even today the KKK is synonymous with acts of terrorism, such as lynching, bombings, burning of homes, violence, brutality, racism, and cross burning.

Between 1868 and 1870, the Ku Klux Klan played an important role in restoring white rule in North Carolina, Tennessee, and Georgia.[45] In addition to preventing freed slaves from voting, the Klan attacked successful black businessmen and quickly moved against any attempt to form black protection groups. The primary weapon of the Klan was terror. The Klan operated at night and was known as the Invisible Empire. Members would inflict vengeance on black citizens by breaking into their houses at night, dragging them from their beds, torturing them, burning their homes, and stealing their possessions. The arrival of Klan members on horseback in the middle of the night struck terror in the hearts of freed slaves and was indeed an effective method to get them to abandon their right to vote, demands for equality, and equal opportunity in owning and conducting businesses.[46]

The first branch of the Ku Klux Klan was established in Pulaski, Tennessee, in May 1866. Most of the leaders were former members of the Confederate Army, and its first national leader or Grand Wizard was Nathan Forrest, a Confederate general during the American Civil War.[47] The name Ku Klux Klan comes from *kuklos,* the Greek word for "circle."[48] The Ku Klux Klan arose due to the stripping of power from white politicians, leaders, and influential persons who ruled the southern states during and before the American Civil War. White supremacists were unable to retain political power and control through traditional means and so they resorted to the use of terror to win back their power. The Klan was successful in restoring white supremacy and as a result, membership waned during the late 1800s. The success of the white supremacy

movement was evident in the 1896 Supreme Court case *Plessy v. Ferguson,*[49] which upheld the doctrine of segregation of the races.

William J. Simmons, a preacher, revived the Ku Klux Klan in 1915. The works of Thomas Dixon, *The Clansmen* and *The Leopard's Spots,* and D. W. Griffith's film, *The Birth of a Nation,* influenced him. Griffith's film portrayed blacks as "tribal, lazy and violent criminals who crave white women."[50] In the twentieth century, membership in the Klan was bolstered by the belief that the economic woes of whites were caused by blacks, Jewish bankers, and immigrants. The revived clan was centered in the midwestern states and was largely Democratic, whereas the first wave of Klan membership was Republican and in the southern states. Klan membership increased during the Great Depression and again after World War II.

In the 1950s and 1960s, the Ku Klux Klan actively opposed the civil rights movement, especially voter registration drives in the South. For example, in 1960, 42 percent of the population of Mississippi was black but only 2 percent were registered to vote. Those who attempted to encourage blacks to register to vote were murdered or threatened with violence. Blacks who registered to vote faced the same fate. Today, the Ku Klux Klan claims membership throughout the United States and even abroad.

Questions

1. If you were to compare the violence of the Ku Klux Klan and other white supremacist groups to the violence of international terrorists, how would you describe the relative danger to the United States from each? Is one more dangerous than the other? Explain your answers.

2. Do you believe that interracial violence is a serious threat to homeland security? Why or why not?

3. What is the best way to stop the violence of the Ku Klux Klan and other white supremacist groups? Should laws restrict their freedom of speech? Why or why not?

never realized due to a reign of terror by southern white supremacists against freed slaves who attempted to exercise the right to vote and sympathizers who supported this movement. This reign of terror gave "dramatic warning to all black inhabitants that the iron clad system of white supremacy was not to be challenged by deed, word, or even thought."[51]

The Ku Klux Klan's strong opposition to African Americans voting extended well into the twentieth century. For example, Dr. E. P. Pruitt, Grand Dragon of the Federated Klans of Alabama, said in a speech in Georgia in 1954: "Southern whites, occupying that super-position assigned to them by the Creator, are justifiably hostile to any race that attempts to drag them down to its own level! Therefore let the nigger be wise in leaving the ballot in the hands of a dominant sympathetic race, since he is far better off as a political eunuch in the house of his friends, than a voter rampant in the halls of his enemies!" Even after the passage of the Civil Rights Act of 1964, the Klan opposed racial equality and integration of the races.

The white population of the southern states refused to cooperate with the government's plan for a new political power in the South. To disenfranchise freed slaves of the rights provided by the Thirteenth, Fourteenth, and Fifteenth Amendments, southern states used violence to intimidate freed slaves and enacted "Jim Crow" law, effectively depriving freed slaves of the right to vote, to hold office, to engage in business, and to have equal protection under the law. Jim Crow laws provided that a person could not vote unless his grandfather was eligible to vote in the last election. Of course, no freed slaves qualified to vote under this restriction, as their ancestors were slaves.

Congress passed the Reconstruction Act of 1867 that placed military troops in the southern states to provide temporary military rule and protection of the rights of freed slaves. The temporary military government ruling the southern states was to remain in place until the state ratified the Fourteenth Amendment, which, in theory, provided for the free exercise of the rights for freed slaves. By 1870, all of the rebellious states had returned to the Union, but suffrage for freed slaves was effectively nullified despite ratification of the Fourteenth Amendment.

Members of these white supremacists groups saw themselves as "right-minded men" protesting against "conditions not to be endured; not a movement of weaklings or theorists, but of desperate men, challenging fate, and swearing that life, liberty and the pursuit of happiness should be theirs and their children's at any cost."[52] In their minds, they engaged in a campaign of murder, lynching, and brutality in the name of justice and God.

Terror Tactics of the KKK

Amendments Thirteen, Fourteen, and Fifteen provided a brief window of opportunity for African American political power in the South. However, any hope of equality and assimilation into the political and economic structures by African Americans was quickly dashed by the opposition of white supremacy groups that rose to restore white supremacy. These white supremacy groups used terrorism as their primary tactic to preserve their position of political and social power. These terror tactics were, in fact, effective, and despite Congress's attempt to provide the freed slaves with political equality and voice, the white supremacy of the South was maintained through the use of an effective campaign of terror against freed slaves.

Lynching.   One of the most effective tactics in interracial terrorism was the practice of lynching. The term *lynching* was named for Colonel Charles Lynch, who used the practice during the American Revolutionary War to deal with Tories and criminals.[53] Although lynching was common as early as the colonial period, its early use was mostly a form of extra-legal execution generally used against accused criminals. After the American Civil War, the victims of lynchings were primarily, but not exclusively, blacks. Victims were lynched for various reasons, including "registering to vote, arguing with a white man, disrespect to a white woman, shoplifting, drunkenness, elopement, insults and refusing to give evidence, . . . being obnoxious, disorderly conduct, indolence, suing white man [sic], vagrancy and unpopularity."[54] Accusations that a black man sexually assaulted a white woman would frequently provoke the crowd to lynching the accused even before a trial or lynching the defendant after conviction rather than wait for his official execution. It is difficult to estimate the number of lynchings but one estimate is that there were 10,000 lynchings between 1878 and 1898.[55]

Lynchings were acts of terror, not just extra-legal justice. Lynching involved far more than simply hanging the victim. Victims were often humiliated, tortured, burned, dismembered, castrated, beaten, whipped, and shot. It was not uncommon for the victim to be shot hundreds of times prior to being lynched.[56] Lynchings were most often public events. Photographs were taken of the event. Often, the victim's fingers and toes were cut off, his teeth pulled out by pliers, and castration was performed before the audience. At times, these "souvenirs" would be sold.[57] Victims would be lynched in public places and left hanging for people to see. Postcards were made from the photographs of the lynchings.

Lynchings were carried out without fear of prosecution. The first recorded prosecution of a white man for punishment for a lynching was not until 1909 (*U.S. v. Shipp,* 214 U.S. 386, 1909).[58] Lynchings were often performed in front of a crowd of thousands of people, yet no one was ever prosecuted. Often the mob was led by local police or local police aided and abetted in the lynching. This ability to treat blacks with such savagery and brutality and to do so with impunity was indeed an effective terror strategy. Some newspapers such as the *New York Times* and the *Atlanta Constitution*[59] condemned lynchings, but most press coverage of lynchings was typically unsympathetic to the victim. The tone of most articles implied support or at least tolerance of the vigilante justice.[60]

Blacks suffered grievously as local, state, and federal law enforcement turned a blind eye toward lynchings. Legislation proposed in the 1930s that would have made it a federal crime for any law enforcement officer who failed to exercise his responsibilities during a lynching incident failed to gain enough votes to pass.[61] Jim Crow laws and the ability of whites to inflict brutality and death on blacks without fear of punishment seemed to condone the racial terrorism of the time. Lynchings have been described as "the most powerful machine of racism, violence and murder our nation has ever seen before or since."[62]

This interracial terrorism was not to be without repercussions. Race riots resulted when blacks fought back. Race riots started to emerge shortly before 1900. One of the first race riots was in November 1898, in Wilmington, North Carolina, resulting in about 30 blacks killed.[63] During the summer of 1919, there were 26 race riots. Race riots have been described as the response of "disillusioned Black people to the southern reign of terror."[64] During the civil rights movement of the 1960s, blacks expressed their frustration with racial inequality and injustice through race riots that resulted in the deaths of hundreds and in millions of dollars of property damage.

Cross Burning.   Another key terror tactic of the KKK was cross burning. To warn a person that he was in disfavor with the Klan, the Klan would place a burning cross on the person's property at night. This could be accompanied with threats and sometimes brutality against the offender. It was understood that if this warning was not heeded and the person did not leave town or cease the offending practice or rhetoric, the person would most likely be lynched, killed, or beaten. Cross burning became closely identified with the Ku Klux Klan because of this practice of terrorism and the use of large burning crosses in their meetings. In their meetings conducted at night Klan members would surround a large burning cross and pledge their allegiance to the Klan.

The Klan continues the practice of cross burning both in its ceremonial ritual and as a terrorisitc warning even today. However, a 2003 Supreme Court case ruled that cross burning can be an "instrument of terror" and states have the authority to ban or limit such activities. Lawyers for the Klan argued that cross burning is a form of free speech and is protected under the First Amendment.[65] The Supreme Court ruled in a 5–4 decision that cross burning was different from other forms of symbolic speech. The history of racial intimidation attached to cross burning outweighed the free speech protection of Ku Klux Klansmen.[66] The Supreme Court ruled that unlike other forms of symbolic protest such as flag burning, cross burning conveys a message of racial hatred and an implicit threat to African Americans. Cross burning inspires fear and is meant to do so; whereas other forms of symbolic speech do not necessary imply the intimidation or imminent threat that is associated with cross burning.[67] This ruling permits states and communities to pass laws that prohibit or limit cross burning as an illegal act of intimidation.

To what extent cross burning can be completely prohibited will be settled by future cases. The Supreme Court's opinion called for the consideration of "contextual factors" when trying to prove whether a defendant's symbolic acts were intended to intimidate. Cross burnings at Ku Klux Klan rallies that are not directed at specific persons may be permissible.[68]

The Red Scare and the Cold War

The September 11, 2001, attacks were not the first attacks by foreign terrorists on United States soil. Prior to the 9/11 attacks there were terrorist attacks by Communist revolutionaries at the beginning of the twentieth century. Communist revolutionaries, known first as Bolsheviks and anarchists and later simply as Communists, carried out a number of terror attacks in the United States. From the early twentieth century until the end of the Cold War fear of Communist revolutionaries in the United States and abroad greatly influenced U.S. politics, civil liberties, the labor movement, and public opinion. The fear of communism is known as the Red Scare and the Cold War.

Origins of the Red Scare

The origins of the Red Scare were in the 1917 violent overthrow of the Russian Tsarist government and the formation of the Communist-based Bolshevik government. As previously mentioned, the newly formed Russian revolutionary government advocated the violent overthrow of capitalistic governments throughout the world, and the United States was at the top of the list as the premier example of capitalism. The reaction of the U.S. government and to some degree public reaction to the perceived threat from Communist revolutionaries in many ways was similar to the reaction to the September 11, 2001, attacks.

This fear of the "Bolshevik menace" gained national prominence when Bolshevik anarchists in the United States undertook a reign of terror aimed at prominent American capitalists and politicians. In April and June of 1919, Bolshevik terrorists attempted 38 bombings against influential figures such as J. P. Morgan, John D. Rockefeller, and Supreme Court Justice Oliver Wendell Holmes.[69] When they exploded a bomb on the front lawn of A. Mitchell Palmer's Washington, DC, home, the newly appointed Attorney General declared war on the anarchists. As in the 9/11 attacks, there was a swift and decisive reaction to the bombers in general and to the larger Communist revolutionary movement. Attorney General Palmer believed that Communist agents from Russia were planning to overthrow the U.S. government and he believed this was a credible threat.[70] He invoked the wartime Espionage Act of 1917 and the 1918 Sedition Act to arrest, without warrants, thousands of Russian immigrants.[71] Many were arrested on the slimmest of suspicions and evidence. Membership in the Communist Party, public statements favorable to the Communists overthrow, or support of the labor union movement often was sufficient evidence for arrest.

When criticized for his arrest and deportation of aliens Palmer replied,

> I have been asked to what extent deportation will check radicalism in this country. Why not ask what will become of the United States Government if these alien radicals carry out the principles of the Communist party? In place of the United States Government we would have the horror and terrorism of Bolshevik tyranny such as the destroying of Russia now. The whole purpose of communism appears to be the mass formation of the criminals of the world to overthrow the decencies of private life, to usurp property, to disrupt the present order of life regardless of health, sex or religious rights. These are the revolutionary tenets of the Communist Internationale. These include the IWW's, the most radical socialists, the misguided anarchists, the agitators who oppose the limitations of unionism, the moral perverts and the hysterical neurasthenic women who abound in communism.[72]

Motivated by this belief, Palmer arrested, without warrants, approximately 16,000 Soviet resident aliens. Many of these were detained without charges and without trial for long periods of time. Many of the arrested persons were members of the Industrial Workers of the World movement. Some 245 suspected Communist agents were deported to Russia. These arrests and deportations were known as the "Palmer raids." Attorney General Palmer viewed these Communists as responsible not only for the bombings but also for a wide rage of social ills in the United States.[73] Most prominent among the problems allegedly caused by the Communists was the emerging labor union movement.

Fear and hatred of Communists rose to such a point that the response of the government and citizens appeared to be completely out of proportion to the reality of the threat. Attorney General Palmer claimed that Communist agents from Russia were planning to overthrow the U.S. government on the second anniversary of the Russian Revolution, November 7, 1919. As a preventive measure to defeat the anticipated overthrow attempt, 10,000 suspected Communists and anarchists were arrested. Despite the lack of evidence against these suspects, they were held without trial for a long time; 245 were deported to Russia with much publicity announcing the defeat of the overthrow attempt.[74]

BOX 2.3 • *Up Close and Personal: Lynne Steward Convicted*

Lynne F. Steward, age 65, is an outspoken lawyer who has defended many defendants who have been critical of the United States. She was the defense attorney for Sheik Omar Abdel Rahman, who was convicted for a 1993 plot to bomb the United Nations, the Lincoln and Holland Tunnels, and other New York landmarks. He is serving a life sentence and Steward was working with him to obtain an appeal of his conviction. During her conferences with Sheik Rahman it was alleged by government officials that contrary to restrictions by the Justice Department that prohibited Sheik Rahman from communicating with possible terrorists, Steward conveyed communications to and from Sheik Rahman to facilitate such communications. The Justice Department charged her with five felony counts of providing material aid to terrorism and lying to the government. In February 2005, after a trial lasting more than seven months, Lynne Steward was convicted on all five charges.

Attorney General Alberto R. Gonzales said of the convictions, "[They] send a clear, unmistakable message that this department will pursue both those who carry out acts of terrorism and those who assist them with their murderous goals."[75]

Steward said the rules imposed by the special administrative measures adopted by the Justice Department that barred the sheik, who was in solitary confinement, from communicating with anyone outside prison except for his wife and lawyers was an eroding of constitutional rights. Steward signed an agreement to uphold the conditions of the special administrative measures. The Justice Department was able to obtain a conviction based on her violation of these rules.

According to Steward, the charges against her were the government's attempt to subvert civil liberties and to punish lawyers who represented those accused of terrorism. Steward issued a statement, saying, "I will fight on, I'm not giving up. I know I committed no crime. I know what I did was right."[76]

Question

1. Labeling lawyers who defended those accused of un-American activities as Communists was a common practice of the FBI during the Red Scare. Do you think the prosecution of Lynne Steward is a message by the Justice Department to cause other lawyers to be concerned about representing clients accused of terrorism? Explain your answer.

The November 7, 1919, attack by Communist revolutionaries did not occur. However, Palmer announced that the Communist revolution in America was likely to take place on May 1, 1920. When he made this prediction, mass panic took place.[77] Often, innocent Russian immigrants became the target of anti-revolutionary violence. For example, Joseph Yenowsky, a Russian immigrant, was convicted and sentenced to six months in prison for allegedly making a public statement that Lenin was "the greatest, the most brainiest man on earth today."[78] Sometimes the prejudice was extreme. For example, in 1920, George Goddad was shot by a member of the color guard at an amphitheater in Chicago when he failed to remove his hat and stand during the playing of the national anthem.[79]

In January 1920, another 6,000 were arrested and held without trial, justified by the claim that these subversives were planning the overthrow of the United States. When the May revolution failed to appear, Palmer lost public confidence. However, his assistant, John Edgar Hoover, quickly rose to the position of Director of the Federal Bureau of Investigation, which he retained until 1972. As Director of the FBI, Hoover continued the fight against the red menace.

The FBI and the Red Scare

The first Red Scare focused on immigrants, but starting in the 1950s Hoover and others turned the focus on U.S. citizens who supported Communism. Hoover, for example, created a card index of over 450,000 people with left-wing political views who he advised Palmer to have rounded up and deported. When lawyers would represent the accused radicals that were arrested in the anti-Communists sweeps, Hoover would add their names to the list of suspected Communists and anarchists.[80]

Hoover continued his aggressive prosecution of the Federal Communist Party throughout his career. In 1924, he was appointed director of the Bureau of Investigation. Under Hoover's leadership much of the activity of the FBI was directed toward fighting the threat of Communism in the United States. Hoover saw the threat as coming from within as well as abroad. For example, he was convinced that several senior officials in the U.S. government were secret members of the Communist Party and undertook to gather extensive intelligence files to investigate whether this was true. Hoover was a supporter of the investigations of the House of UnAmerican Activities Committee and supplied much information to the committee in the course of its investigation. In the 1950s, Hoover was instrumental in getting writers, directors, and performers blacklisted who were suspected by the FBI of having memberships in subversive organizations.

The Red Scare became the Cold War after World War II, as the United States and the Soviet Union were the dominant world superpowers. The opposition to communism was evidence by such acts as the Federal Employee Loyalty Program, which required every federal employee to sign a statement that he or she was not a member of the Communist Party and did not support the ideology of the Communist Party. Many states adopted similar acts for state employees.

The Cold War

The peak of the anti-communism movement occurred under the Eisenhower Administration. In 1950, Senator Joseph McCarthy (R-WI) claimed he had a list of 205 Communist Party members who were employed in the U.S. State Department. McCarthy's anti-communism campaign has been referred to as a "reign of terror." McCarthy's extreme fear of communism was shared by many Americans who feared that communism posed a serious threat to national security.[81]

Hoover said that communism "stands for the destruction of our American form of government: it stands for the destruction of American democracy; it stands for the destruction of free enterprise; and it stands for the creation of a 'Soviet of the United States' and ultimate world revolution." Hoover viewed communism as a threat to national security. As such, he focused the powers of the FBI on fighting the potential threat of subversive Communists in the United States, as illustrated by the fact that in 1959 Hoover had 489 agents spying on Communists but only 4 investigating the Mafia.[82] Throughout his career Hoover continued to conduct investigations, amass secret files, and gather incriminating material about anyone suspected of being a Communist, a Communist sympathizer, or a Communist supporter.

Today, some have tried to compare the war on terrorism with the Cold War against communism. They describe the war on terrorism as a conflict against a global enemy that would threaten freedom and democracy. Terrorists are the "bad guys" and are to be opposed at all costs.

Conclusion: Terrorism by Any Other Name

A famous play line by William Shakespeare says, "A rose by another other name would still smell as sweet." The fact that the term *terrorism* did not emerge until the late eighteenth century does not mean that there was no terrorism prior to the French Revolution's Reign of Terror. Nor does the fact that the term *terrorism* is not frequently used to describe the use of violence by one group on another that occurred throughout American history mean that it was not terrorism.

The pillars of terrorism are murder, violence, the advancement of political agendas and ideologies, and religious extremism. Many of these elements were common in the early history of the United States.

Terrorism is a strategy that can be simply defined as a violent means to an desired end. The important point to remember is that the ethical questions that arise from the use of violence, murder, and intimidation to achieve a goal are not diminished because the goal is a "good" goal rather than an "evil" goal.

As the United States engages in a war on terrorism it is important to remember the past. Counterterrorism policies formulated without incorporating the lessons learned in the past may prove to be ineffective and result in undesired consequences.

Chapter Summary

- Terrorism is associated with violence, politics, toppling governments, and religion.
- Terrorism is difficult to define because it is a value term. It implies that the violence used to achieve the goals of the group is not justified. However, the use of terrorism is common to many "good" causes in history, including the American Revolutionary War, the American Civil War, and the French Revolution.
- Terrorists do not try to achieve military victory but count on creating public opinion that will result in the changes they seek.
- Terrorists do not call themselves "terrorists." *Terrorism* is a label used by the dominant power to create an image of the terrorists as "evil."
- Terrorists see the world in black and white. There is no middle ground. They believe they have the higher moral ground and often believe they have divine knowledge.
- Terrorists do not recognize the concepts of innocent bystanders, neutral parties, civilians, or noncombatants.
- Early terms associated with terrorism, such as *zealot, assassin, thug, terror*, and *class-warfare,* come from many countries around the world.
- The use of terrorism can be found in early American history in the American Revolutionary War, the treatment of Native Americans, the American Civil War, and the interracial violence that occurred following the American Civil War.

- One of the most horrific terror campaigns in the United States was the lynching of African Americans. Lynchings were common from 1870 to 1915 and continue up to the present day. Lynchings were much more than extra-legal justice. The victims were brutalized, tortured, and put on public display as a warning to others.
- The Ku Klux Klan was one of the most notorious domestic American terrorism groups.
- In the twentieth century, Americans feared the terror posed by Communist revolutionaries and other Communist-Marxist–inspired governments and groups.
- Attorney General A. Mitchell Palmer led the initial assault against the Red Scare starting in 1919. J. Edgar Hoover continued the assault on communism throughout his reign as Director of the Federal Bureau of Investigation (1924–1972).
- The reaction of the U.S. public and government to the Red Scare in many ways resembles the reaction to the September 11, 2001, attacks and the subsequent war on terrorism.

Terrorism and You

Understanding This Chapter

1. What do terrorists hope to gain by the use of violence? How does the use of violence by terrorists differ from the violence of a military campaign?

2. What is the origin of some important terms associated with terrorism?

3. Many Americans may not be aware of domestic terrorism prior to September 11, 2001, but there are many incidents in American history of the use of domestic terrorism. Describe the use of terrorism during the American Revolutionary War, during the American Civil War, in the treatment of Native Americans, and in interracial violence.

4. Why was the Ku Klux Klan endorsed by most southern whites after the American Civil War? How did the Ku Klux Klan of the nineteenth century differ from the Ku Klux Klan of the twentieth century?

5. From the freeing of the slaves with the passage of the Thirteenth Amendment in 1865 to the passage of the Civil Rights Act of 1964, the struggle by blacks for freedom, equality, and justice has been opposed by some whites. What violence was used against blacks to intimidate them from seeking equality and justice? Do you think this violence amounted to "terrorism"? Why or why not?

6. What are the similarities between the reaction of the government and public to the Red Scare and Communism and the current war on terrorism?

Thinking about How Terrorism Touches You

1. Do you believe that terrorism can be a legitimate response to a real grievance? Explain what type of grievance, injustice, or suppression of freedom would justify the use of terrorism.

2. In his fight against communism, J. Edgar Hoover often advocated for greater law enforcement powers. Former Attorney General John Ashcroft made a similar argument as he led the Justice Department's fight against terrorism. Do you believe that any of your personal rights

and freedoms have changed as a result of greater law enforcement powers being granted to the FBI or other federal agencies? Why or why not?

3. To what degree, if any, do you think today's interracial conflict between blacks and whites is affected by the historical use of violence against blacks?

4. At what point does a historical act of violence against a person or group of persons cease to be a valid justification for violent retribution? What responsibility do contemporary members of a group have for the violence that their distance ancestors did to members of another group in the past?

5. Do you believe that conflict between the classes is the primary source of conflict in the world? Have you been injured or denied anything because of the social/political class to which you belong? Have you benefited at the expense of others because of the social/political class to which you belong? Marx and Engels believed that there were no nonviolent means of resolving the conflict between classes. Do you agree? Why?

Important Terms and Concepts

American Civil War
American Revolutionary War
Assassin/Fedayeen
Class Warfare
Cold War
Communist
Cross Burning
D. W. Griffith
David versus Goliath
Fifteenth Amendment
Fourteenth Amendment
Frederick Engels
French Revolution Reign of Terror
Hassan Ben Sabbah
J. Edgar Hoover
Joseph R. McCarthy
Karl Marx
Ku Klux Klan
Lynching

Manifesto of the Communist Party
March to the Sea
Maximilien Robespierre
Mitchell Palmer
Nathan Forrest
Plessy v. Ferguson
Reconstruction Act of 1867
Red Scare
Terrorism
The Birth of a Nation
Third Estate
Thirteenth Amendment
Thomas Dixon
Thuggee
Thugs
Vladimir Lenin
William J. Simmons
Zealot

Endnotes

1. Michael R. Gordon, "When an Open Society Is Wielded as a Weapon Against Itself," New York Times On-line, www.nytimes.com, September 12, 2001.

2. James Fagin, "The Impact of Technology and Communications upon International and Transnational Terrorism," *International Journal of Comparative and Applied Criminal Justice,* Vol. VI, No. 1, Spring 1982, p. 96;

Counterterrorism Threat Assessment and Warning Unit, Counterterrorism Division, *Terrorism in the United States 1999* (Washington, DC: U.S. Department of Justice, 2000), p. 15.

3. William Glaberson, "Defense in Terror Trail Paints a Rosier Picture of 'Jihad,'" New York Times Online, www.nytimes.com, February 25, 2005.

4. Ibid.

5. Adam Roberts, "The Changing Faces of Terrorism," BBCi History, www.bbc.co.uk/history/war/sept_11/changing_faces_01.shtml, August 27, 2002.

6. "History of Terrorism," Terrorism Files.Org, www.terrorismfiles.org, July 5, 2003.

7. Mark Burgess, "A Brief History of Terrorism," Center for Defense Information, www.cdi.org, August 30, 2003.

8. Ibid.

9. "Terrorism Began Centuries Ago as Middle Eastern Religious Conflict," *Sam Houston State University News,* www.shsu.edu/~pin_www/RothTerror.html, August 30, 2003.

10. Ibid.

11. Mark Burgess, "A Brief History of Terrorism," Center for Defense Information, www.cdi.org. August 30, 2003.

12. Ibid.

13. Ibid.

14. Terrorism Began Centuries Ago as Middle Eastern Religious Conflict," *Sam Houston State University News,* www.shsu.edu/~pin_www/RothTerror.html, August 30, 2003.

15. Mark Burgess, "A Brief History of Terrorism," Center for Defense Information, www.cdi.org, August 30, 2003.

16. "Thuggee," Wikipedia: The Free Encyclopedia, www.wikipedia.org/wiki/Thuggee. August 30, 2003.

17. Eric Lichtblau, "F.B.I. Tells Offices to Count Local Muslims and Mosques," New York Times Online, www.nytimes.com, January 28, 2003.

18. Associated Press, "Plans for Mosque Brings Protest in N.J." New York Times Online, www.nytimes.com, November 6, 2003.

19. James Dao and Eric Lichtblau, "Case Adds to Outrage for Muslims in Northern Virginia," New York Times Online, www.nytimes.com, February 27, 2005.

20. Mark Burgess, "A Brief History of Terrorism," Center for Defense Information, www.cdi.org, August 30, 2003.

21. "Thuggee," Wikipedia: The Free Encyclopedia, www.wikipedia.org/wiki/Thuggee. August 30, 2003.

22. Ibid.

23. Ibid.

24. "The French Revolution," *The Columbia Encyclopedia,* 6th edition, 2001. Great Books Online, www.bartleby.com/65/fr/FrenchRe.html, August 30, 2002.

25. Ibid.

26. Raymond Betts, "Europe in Retrospective: A Brief History of the Past Two Hundred Years," *Britannia,* www.britannia.com/history/euro/1/2_2.html.

27. Ibid.

28. Ibid.

29. Ibid.

30. Ibid.

31. "The French Revolution," *The Columbia Encyclopedia,* 6th edition, 2001. Great Books Online, www.bartleby.com/65/fr/FrenchRe.html, August 30, 2002.

32. Mark Burgess, "A Brief History of Terrorism," Center for Defense Information, www.cdi.org, August 30, 2003.

33. Karl Marx and Frederick Engels, *Manifesto of the Communist Party,* www.anu.edu.au/polsci/marx/classics/manifesto.html, September 1, 2003.

34. Ibid.

35. Related to underlying ideologies of communism but distinct from it are the philosophical beliefs exposed by anarchists. The Communist ideology advocated that the working class should take over the existing capitalist state, turning it into a workers' revolutionary state, which would put in place the democratic structures necessary, and then the state itself would eventually become unnecessary and would be discarded. On the other hand, the anarchists argue that it is the state that is the source of evil and oppression and the way to progress is the complete destruction of the state without any new governmental body replacing it.

36. Karl Marx and Frederick Engels, *Manifesto of the Communist Party.* www.anu.edu.au/polsci/marx/classics/manifesto.html, September 1, 2003.

37. "Amnesty Calls for End to Abuse of American Indians," http://nativenet.uthscsa.edu/archive/n1/9210/0052.htm, October 1, 2003.

38. Ty West, "History Pro Says Terrorism Has American Roots Going Back to the Civil War," Dateline Alabama, www.datelinealabama.com/article/2003/0/07/3709_war_art.php3, September 1, 2003.

39. Ibid.

40. Ibid.

41. Ibid.

42. Illinois Regiments in the March to the Sea, www.rootswweb.com/~ilcivilw/battles/sea.htm, September 1, 2003.

43. "Reconstruction Acts," Teaching History Online, www.spartacus.schoolnet.co.uk/USASreconstruction.htm, September 1, 2003.

44. The Constitution of the United States of America, Article I: Section 2.

45. "Ku Klux Klan," *Spartacus,* www.spartacus.schoolnet.co.uk/USAkkk.htm, September 13, 2003.

46. Ibid.

47. Ibid.

48. "Ku Klux Klan," Wikipedia: The Free Encyclopedia, www.wikipedia.org/wiki/Ku_Klux_Klan, September 1, 2003.

49. *Plessy v. Ferguson* (1896). 163 US 537.

50. "The Ku Klux Klan," Court TV's Crime Library, www.crimelibrary.com/notorious_murders/mass/lynching/klan_4.html?sect=8, September 13, 2003.

51. "The History of Lynching," Court TV Crime Library, www.crimelibrary.com/notorious_murders/mass/lynching/lunching_2.html?sect=8, September 11, 2003.

52. "History of the Original Ku Klux Klan," www.reactor-core.org/secret/history-of-the-original-ku-klux-klan.html, September 13, 2003.

53. "Lynching," Wikipedia: The Free Encyclopedia, www.wikipedia.org/wiki/lLynching, September 1, 2003.

54. Mark Gado, Lynching in America: Carnival of Death." Court TV's Crime Library, www.crimelibrary.com/classics2/carnival/, September 13, 2003.

55. "Jim Crow Law," Wikipedia: The Free Encyclopedia, www.wikipedia.org/wiki/Jim_Crow_laws, September 13, 2003.

56. Mark Gado, "Lynching in America: Carnival of Death." Court TV's Crime Library, www.crimelibrary.com/classics2/carnival/, September 13, 2003.

57. Ibid.

58. Ibid.

59. Ibid.

60. Ibid.

61. Ibid.

62. Ibid.

63. Robert A. Gibson, "The Negro Holocaust: Lynching and Race Riots in the United Sates, 1980–1950 [sic]," Yale-New Haven Teachers Institute, www.yale.edu/ynhti/curriculum/units/1979/2/79.02.04.x.html, September 13, 2003.

64. Ibid.

65. CBS News, "High Court Upholds Cross-Burning Ban," www.cbsnews.com/stories/2003/04/07supremecourt/main548121.shtml, September 13, 2003.

66. CNN.com, "Supreme Court Upholds Virginia Ban on Cross Burning," www.cnn.com/2003/LAW/04/07/scotus.cross.burning.

67. Julie Hilden, "The Supreme Court Confronts Cross-Burning and the First Amendment Once Again, Because It Failed to Make This Knotty Area of Law Clear the First Time, FindLaw's Legal Commentary, http://writ.findlaw.com/hilden/20021115.html.

68. "Limits on Cross Burning," *The Christian Science Monitor,* www.csmonitor.com/2003/0409/p10s03-comv.html, September 13, 2003.

69. "Crackdown!" *Smithsonian Magazine,* www.smithsonianmag.si.edu/smithsonian/issues02/feb02/red_scare.html, September 3, 2003.

70. "Red Scare," *Spartacus,* www.spartacus.schoolnet.co.uk/USAredscare.htm, September 5, 2003.

71. "Crackdown!" *Smithsonian Magazine,* www.smithsonianmag.si.edu/smithsonian/issues02/feb02/red_scare.html, September 3, 2003.

72. "Red Scare," *Spartacus,* www.spartacus.schoolnet.co.uk/USAredscare.htm, September 5, 2003

73. "The Palmer Raids," Between the Wars: The Red Scare, http://chnm.gmu.edu/courses/hist409/red.html.

74. "Red Scare," *Spartacus,* www.spartacus.schoolnet.co.uk/USAredscare.htm, September 5, 2003.

75. Julia Preston, "Lawyer Is Guilty of Aiding Terror," New York Times Online, www.nytimes.com, February 11, 2005.

76. Ibid.

77. Ibid.

78. "The Palmer Raids," Between the Wars: The Red Scare, http://chnm.gmu.edu/courses/hist409/red.html.

79. Ibid.

80. "John Edgar Hoover," *Spartacus,* www.spartacus.schoolnet.co.uk/USAhooverE.htm, September 7, 2003.

81. "The Events of the Red Scare," http://aselle.troop474.org/red/events.html, September 7, 2003.

82. "John Edgar Hoover," *Spartacus,* www.spartacus.schoolnet.co.uk/USAhooverE.htm, September 7, 2003.

3

Defending the Homeland

The Rule of Law

When national security is felt to be threatened, often new laws are passed aimed at providing the government with expanded powers to fight the perceived threat. These new laws are frequently criticized for curtailing liberties and infringing on constitutionally protected rights.

We shall vigorously apply U.S. laws and seek new legislation to prevent terrorist groups from operating in the United States or using it as a base for recruitment, training, fund raising or other related activities.[1]

—President William Clinton, Presidential Decision Directive 39

[W]hen a society feels itself at risk, it turns to whoever promises security and often sets aside its constitution, laws, and civil liberties.[2]

—Dennis Jett, former U.S. ambassador to Peru
and Dean of the International Center at the University of Florida

Those who would trade liberty for security deserve neither.

—Benjamin Franklin

Chapter Outline

Learning Objectives

- The reader will appreciate how law has been used as a primary strategy in reducing U.S. vulnerability to terrorism.

- The reader will know what advantages and disadvantages are associated with the use of law as a strategy to counter terrorism.
- The reader will know the major laws and presidential directives that have been used in the fight against terrorism.
- The reader will be knowledgeable of potential conflict between national security and civil liberties in using legislation to prosecute terrorists.
- The reader will understand the provisions of the USA Patriot Act and the advantages and challenges related to the Patriot Act.

Introduction: Responding to Terrorism through Law

One of the primary strategies for defending the United States against terrorism is the use of laws to prohibit behavior, to grant powers to fight terrorism to governmental agencies, to provide access to records, and to arrest those whom the government deems dangerous.

This chapter will examine the use of law as a primary strategy in defending the United States in the war on terrorism. It will discuss how the use of law has been a common response during times of threat to national security. When national security is felt to be threatened, often new laws are passed aimed at providing the government with expanded powers to fight the perceived threat. In general, aliens and immigrants have been the focus of these new laws. These new laws are often criticized for curtailing liberties and infringing on constitutionally protected rights.

Defending the Homeland with Law

Presidential Decision Directive Number 39 issued in 1995 declared that the vigorous prosecution of those who violated anti-terrorism laws was one of the keystone strategies to protect the United States against terrorism by foreign enemies. However, the strategy of vigorous prosecution and the seeking of new legislation are not without its critics. Dennis Jett, former U.S. ambassador to Peru and Dean of the International Center at the University of Florida, reported that more than 69,000 people in Peru were killed between 1980 and 2000 in political violence in the name of combating terrorism. He observed that the governments of Peru and other nations are often tempted to circumvent their constitutions in times of perceived threats to national security.[3] His implication was that the U.S. government might fall into the same offense against democracy as it seeks to use new laws to fight terrorism. Thus, although the use of law is one of the primary strategies in the war on terrorism, it is a double-edge sword that offers both effective anti-terror legislation and potential erosion of constitutional rights and abuse of the innocent.

Law as a Double-Edged Sword

In law, terrorism is defined as criminal behavior. As such, the law is effective in preventing terrorism in that it prohibits behaviors deemed to be criminal or enabling criminal behavior.

Those who violate such laws are subject to fines, imprisonment, or death. However, the law can be a double-edged sword in that while it punishes certain behaviors defined as criminal or enabling criminal activity, citizens of good intent may be caught up in these laws.

For example, in early 2003, as the United States prepared to act militarily against Iraq, one of the objectives of the Bush Administration was to remove all American citizens from the country of Iraq. To achieve this objective, presidential directives and State Department policies were issued that prohibited travel to Iraq, and Treasury regulations prohibited the importation of anything to Iraq or the spending of U.S. currency in Iraq. In February 2003, approximately 20 U.S. citizens opposed to the bombing of Iraq chose to demonstrate against the imminent bombing by traveling to Iraq to act as human shields to protect the civilian infrastructure of Iraq from potential U.S. bombs. Americans have the right of free speech and may protest U.S. foreign policy, but this right is not an unrestricted right. Despite the moral objections of the citizens or their "good" intentions to protect "innocent civilians," their behavior was in violation of law and they were subject to civil penalties of fines up to $275,000 and/or imprisonment up to 12 years.

In August 2003, many of those U.S. citizens who went to Iraq to act as human shields began to receive notices from the U.S. Treasury Department of Foreign Assets Control, advising them of their violation of the restrictions on travel to Iraq. Some citizens questioned the charges as politically motivated, but the U.S. Department of Treasury denied these charges. A spokesperson for the Treasury Department said the enforcement of U.S. law was without regard to the person's motivation for breaking it.[4]

Many laws have been passed to fight terrorism. As these laws are examined, one discovers that laws aimed at fighting terrorism often have unintended consequences or impact citizens not directly linked to terrorism.

Early Legislation to Promote National Security

Early legislation to promote national security was not framed in the current terms of a war on terrorism, but the intent was indeed similar. From the earliest days of its founding, the United States has feared subversive attacks from foreign agents. Historically, as now, one of the purposes of national security legislation was to diminish the likelihood of attack by providing for the deportation of persons thought to be a threat to national security. Two of the earliest laws that attempted to promote national security through the deportation of enemy agents were the Alien Act of 1798 and the Sedition Act of 1798.

Another strategy of early legislation to promote national security was to give the government greater powers and to curtail constitutionally protected civil liberties. Early examples of this type of legislation include the Alien Act of 1798, the Sedition Act of 1798, the Force Act, the Ku Klux Act, the Espionage Act of 1918, and the Sedition Act of 1919.

The Alien Act and the Sedition Act

On July 6, 1798, only 10 years after George Washington was inaugurated as President of the United States, the Alien Act was passed and on July 14, 1798, the Sedition Act was approved.[5] The purpose of these public laws was to enhance national security by providing the government the power to deport people who were suspected of being a danger to national security. The Alien Act declared,

> That whenever there shall be a declared war between the United States and any foreign nation or government, or invasion or predatory incursion shall be perpetrated, attempted, or threatened against the territory of the United States, by any foreign nation or government, and the President of the United States shall make public proclamation of the event, all natives, citizens, denizens, or subjects of the hostile nation or government, being males of the age of fourteen years and upward, who shall be within the United States, and not actually naturalized, shall be liable to be apprehended, restrained, secured and removed, as alien enemies."[6]

This sweeping authority provided the government the power to quickly apprehend and deport those suspected of dangerous activity. The law did not provide that foreign nationals had to do anything illegal nor did the government have to prove they were a threat to national security to merit deportation. All male foreigners residing in the United States who were age 14 and older and who were citizens of the hostile country were subject to deportation.

The Sedition Act was passed shortly after the Alien Act. Its stated purpose was to prohibit anyone (but it was aimed particularly at foreign nationals) from advocating for any cause of a hostile nation and it made it a crime to oppose "any measure or measures of the government of the United States." The purpose of the Sedition Act purportedly was to prevent riots, uprisings, or unlawful assemblies. However, the language of the law was so vague that the Sedition Act prohibited virtually any public speech or written document critical of any action of the government or a public official. The scope of the legislation is rather difficult to appreciate given today's emphasis on personal liberties. The legislation prohibited the publication or assisting in the publication of material that was critical of anything the government did or any attempt to oppose any law of the United States. This legislation even prohibited anyone from speaking against the Sedition Act or calling for its repeal.[7]

The Sedition Act clearly had the potential to curtail the First Amendment's freedom of speech rights as virtually any criticisms of the government or elected representatives and president could be deemed unlawful. The Sedition Act prohibited criticism regardless of the intention of the speech or writings. Even efforts at constructive debate to expose the faults of certain actions so that more effective action may be followed could be considered unlawful under the Sedition Act.

Despite the prohibition against criticism of the Sedition Act, the flaws of this legislation were sharply criticized and there was a public outcry concerning the constitutionality of the law. Regardless of the risk of arrest and prosecution, several prominent politicians protested these two laws. For example, the Alien Act and the Sedition Act were protested as unconstitutional by the Kentucky Resolutions of 1798 authored by Thomas Jefferson and the Virginia Resolution of 1799 authored by James Madison. The Kentucky Resolutions and the Virginia Resolution condemned the Alien Act and the Sedition Act as "palpable violations of the said constitution" and declared that failure to protest the unconstitutionality of the acts would be "a reproachable inconsistency, and criminal degeneracy."[8]

The Force Act and the Ku Klux Act

The Force Act and the Ku Klux Act are examples of fighting terrorism through legislation by expanding the powers of the government. The Force Act and the Ku Klux Act following the

American Civil War were some of the earliest examples of legislation in the United States to deal specifically with domestic terrorist groups. These acts expanded government authority by authorizing the president to use federal troops to enforce federal laws, specifically the Fourteenth and Fifteenth Amendments, in the southern states. This was not the first time such legislation authorized the use of federal troops to enforce federal law. In January 1833, a bill passed by Congress in response to South Carolina's passage of an ordinance of nullification protesting the Tariff of Abominations in 1828 gave President Andrew Jackson the power to use the armed forces to enforce federal law.[9] The Force Act and the Ku Klux Act, however, were aimed specifically at defeating the terrorism of a domestic group of citizens, the Ku Klux Klan, and not at the government in general, as was the case in South Carolina's protest against federal tariffs.

There were two Force Acts: one passed by Congress on May 31, 1870, and the other on February 28, 1871. This legislation authorized the use of federal troops to enforce the Fifteenth Amendment as it related to black suffrage. The Ku Klux Act was passed on April 20, 1871. It authorized the use of federal troops to enforce the guarantee of civil rights granted by the Fourteenth Amendment. These laws provided President Grant with the authority to suspend habeas corpus, or the right to appeal the constitutionality of detention or imprisonment. President Grant used the authority of the act on several occasions. The most extensive use of the Force Act was when the president suspended habeas corpus in nine South Carolina counties and appointed commissioners who arrested hundreds of southerners for conspiracy.[10] The Ku Klux Act was short-lived; in *United States v. Harris* (1882) the Supreme Court declared the act unconstitutional.[11]

The Espionage Act of 1918 and the Sedition Act of 1919

The Espionage Act of 1918 and the Sedition Act of 1919 were powerful legislative acts that provided broad powers to the government to ensure national security related to the war effort in World War I. During the years preceding the entry of the United States into World War I and after its entry into the war, legislation was passed to promote national security by prohibiting certain actions by what were believed to be enemy agents residing within the United States. Fearing anti-war activities and attacks by foreign enemy agents, Congress passed legislation that was aimed at suppressing anti-war rhetoric, censoring criticism of the government's war effort, and prohibiting activities that would obstruct the war effort or aid the enemy.

The original Espionage Act of 1917 was reasonable and focused in its intent. The original intent of the Espionage Act was to make it a crime to interfere with the operation or success of the military or naval forces; to promote the success of its enemies; to cause or attempt to cause insubordination, disloyalty, mutiny, or refusal of duty in the military or naval forces; or to obstruct the recruiting or enlistment service of the United States. Violation of the law was a felony punishable by a maximum fine of $10,000 (quite a sum in 1917 dollars) or imprisonment for up to 20 years.

The Sedition Act of 1918, however, was much broader in its focus and intent. The legislation prohibited any anti-war effort or aid to the enemy but was vague in the description of what acts constituted such criminal conduct. The act prohibited many activities that were only remotely related to hindering the U.S. war effort. For example, the legislation was used extensively to hinder the organizational efforts of labor unions, arguing that labor union movements curtailed the production of essential products "necessary or essential to the prosecution of the war." The legislation was used to prosecute persons advocating for social and economic reform in the United States based on the argument that Section 3 of the Sedition Act prohibited virtually any criticism of any type of the United States. Technically, the prohibition applied to protests or criticisms that "promoted the cause of its enemies" but often any public protest, regardless of motivation or cause, was considered linked with aiding the enemy.

Following the entry of the United States into World War I, various amendments were added to these acts that increased the authority of the government to prohibit behavior or censor public speech. For example, it was against the law even to display the flag of an enemy nation. Also, the Sedition Act gave the Postmaster General and local postmasters the power to refuse to deliver any mail that the postmaster at any post office thought was in violation of any of the provisions of the Sedition Act. It was not necessary for postmasters to seek court approval or review in exercising this authority. Postmasters could, on their own authority, decide what was unlawful material to send through the U.S. mail. Even criticism of the Sedition Act was prohibited. The powers granted to the government by the Sedition Act resulted in a virtual ban on free speech concerning any social, labor, or justice issue.

Despite widespread arrests for activities with little relationship to the war effort, the Sedition Act enjoyed great public support. The United States Supreme Court offered little relief from the injunctions of free speech imposed by the Sedition Act or its broad application to ancillary subjects such as the labor movement, calls for social justice, or criticisms of corruption or injustice. Over 1,500 people were arrested for disloyalty under the Sedition Act. Foreigners were frequently targeted for arrest, interrogation, and deportation. Although many of those arrested were foreigners, a number of those arrested were prominent social reformers of the time, such as Eugene Debs, Kate Richards O'Hare, Phillip Randolph, and Emma Goldman. Due to her influential social position, urban reformer Jane Addams was not arrested for her critique of poverty in the Chicago area and the war but she was labeled unpatriotic, disloyal, and un-American.

The Beginning of the Age of Terrorism—1980s: Defending the Homeland by Presidential Directives and Legislation

The primary focus of legislation of the nineteenth and early twentieth centuries concentrated on deporting suspected enemy agents, prohibiting "propaganda," and expanding government powers. Contemporary anti-terrorism legislation continues to focus on these goals but it also has another purpose. Often, contemporary legislation defines which governmental agency is responsible for responding to and/or preventing various types of terrorist activities. The need to use law to define who is responsible for what illustrated the degree to which the United States lacked formal plans, policies, practices, and procedures for responding to international terrorism.

Much, if not all, of the contemporary anti-terrorism legislation and presidential directives have been reactive. In other words, the legislation and directives have attempted to provide oversight, to prohibit activities, and to expand governmental powers after a particularly horrific terrorist event revealed that the United States lacked laws to prohibit certain terrorist behaviors or punish those accused of the act. Legislation and directives were often the result of various acts of terrorism that emphasized the escalating nature of international terrorism. Some of the significant acts of terrorism of the 1970s include:

- The Red Brigades in Italy assassinated over 300 political and public figures and kidnapped or crippled hundreds of others.
- The Irish Republican Army Provisional Wing committed many bombings and assassinations of public figures who were opposed to the formation of Northern Ireland as an independent nation-state.
- In 1972, the first use of a commercial airlines by a terrorist group occurred when a group of Black Panthers hijacked a plane out of Florida and took it and the ransom money they obtained to Africa.
- The world watched in shock as the Palestinian Liberation Organization (PLO) kidnapped and murdered 11 Israeli athletes during the 1972 Winter Olympic games in Munich, Germany.

During the 1970s, U.S. troops, civilians, and property were targeted for attack by terrorists, causing the United States Congress to focus on crafting anti-terrorism legislation. At the close of the 1970s, the Iranian Hostage Crisis (1979) captured U.S. news headlines as a group of "radical students" stormed the U.S. embassy in Teheran, Iran, and held 65 U.S. citizens hostage for 15 months. The apparent inability of the Carter Administration to secure the return of the hostages for this prolonged period of time resulted in the public demand for a more effective capacity to respond to terrorism.

The Reagan Administration: Organizing the Government's Response to Terrorism

One of the interesting aspects of the Reagan Administration's efforts to enhance national security was extensive use of anti-terrorism strategies that often were initiated and directed by classified documents and policies. Thus, unlike the public criticism and protest that were associated with some of the anti-terrorism legislation of the Clinton and George W. Bush Administrations, there was often little public reaction due to the secrecy that cloaked the government's strategies. Such secrecy was possible because the Reagan Administration favored the use of classified National Security Decision Directives (NSDD) rather than public laws. It was only years later, when these National Security Decision Directives were declassified, that the general public became aware of the efforts that the government had taken to counter terrorism.

Four classified National Security Decision Directives were particularly important in shaping the response to terrorism: National Security Decision Directives 30, 179, 205, and 207. These directives established policies and procedures that defined the U.S. response to terrorism. Many of the strategies established by these directives have been continued and enhanced in legislation that followed.

National Security Decision Directive 30: Defining Who Is Responsible for What.
One of the first concerns of the Reagan Administration was to develop effective strategies
to prevent and respond to hijacking of commercial aircraft by terrorists. National Security
Decision Directive 30, issued April 10, 1982, was first classified "secret"; therefore, the general public did not know if its existence or content until it was declassified. The purpose of
National Security Decision Directive 30 was to counter aviation hijacking. In an effort to
better respond to the increasing number of incidents involving the use of commercial aircraft by international terrorists, NSDD 30 sought to provide an effective and coordinated response to hijacking by establishing which government agency would be the lead agency
responsible for various types of terrorist attacks. NSDD 30 assigned the following agencies
as the "lead agency" for specific types of terrorist attacks:

- The State Department was responsible for responding to international terrorists outside the United States.
- The Department of Justice was responsible for responding to terrorist incidents within the United States or within any of its territories. Furthermore, it charged the Federal Bureau of Investigation with the responsibility as lead agency within the Department of Justice for operational response.
- The Federal Aviation Agency was the lead agency for responding to hijackings.
- The Federal Emergency Management Agency was responsible for planning for and managing the public health aspects of a terrorist incident and recovery from the consequences of such incidents.

National Security Decision Directive 30 was important for two reasons. First, NSDD
30 outlined a strategy of coordinated and cooperative effort by the various federal law enforcement agencies. Federal law enforcement agencies are semi-autonomous agencies often
with conflicting and overlapping authority and responsibility. In a sense, NSDD 30 provided an official chain of command for responding to terrorism. By delineating which agency
would be the lead agency for which event, the Reagan Administration sought to eliminate
ineffective and inefficient response caused by interagency conflict, lack of cooperation
among federal agencies, and lack of accountability. Second, NSDD 30 was important because for the most part it assigned local and state law enforcement agencies a secondary role
to the federal law enforcement agencies in responding to acts of terrorism. In every case
NSDD 30 named a federal agency as the lead agency for responding to acts of terrorism.
Prior to NSDD 30, acts of terrorism often were considered criminal incidents and as such
the primary responsibility for responding to a criminal incident often was vested in local and
state law enforcement agencies. With NSDD 30, local and state law enforcement agencies
were primarily relegated as support agencies to the lead federal law enforcement agency.

National Security Decision Directives 179 and 180: Task Force on Combating Terrorism and Aviation. The 1985 classified documents National Security Decision Directives 179 and 180 were early documents to explicitly acknowledge the potential threat of
terrorism to national security and to world peace. With the creation of NSDD 179, a governmentwide task force headed by the vice president was charged with investigating the
threat of terrorism to the national security of the United States. This task force was called

the Task Force on Combating Terrorism. One of the conclusions of the Task Force on Combating Terrorism was that international terrorism was becoming an increasing threat to U.S. citizens and national security. The task force concluded, "Terrorists are waging a war against, not only the United States, but all civilized society in which innocent civilians are intentional victims and our servicemen are specific targets." The Task Force on Combating Terrorism further refined the responsibilities and accountability for various federal agencies in the event of a terrorist attack to ensure interagency cooperation and coordination before, during, and after a terrorist incident. The task force also reported that adequacy of public awareness and support of the threat of terrorism are essential to the war on terrorism.

Still concerned about the threat of terrorism to commercial aviation, National Security Decision Directives 179 and 180 expanded the Federal Air Marshal Program and called for more research and development on the detection of explosive and incendiary devices, hijack prevention, and security system enhancements.

National Security Decision Directives 205 and 207: State-Sponsored Terrorism and Non-Concessions Policy. In 1986, President Reagan issued National Security Decision Directive 205, which acknowledged the threat to national security posed by state-sponsored terrorism. It declared that certain states (in this case, Libya was the primary concern) sponsored, trained, and deployed terrorists to attack aviation targets, U.S. military targets, and U.S. citizens abroad. The threat posed by state-sponsored terrorism has continued to elevate and today it has become one of the most difficult problems in combating terrorism.

Issued in the same year, NSDD 207 established the National Program for Combating Terrorism. It outlined guidelines for preventing and responding to acts of terrorism. Many of these guidelines have continued to shape the nation's response to terrorism. Perhaps one of the most well known policies to emerge from these guidelines was the policy of negotiating with terrorists for the release of hostages and other demands. The directive established a "no-negotiations policy" in responding to terrorists' demands. According to NSDD 207, the "United States policy on terrorism is unequivocal: firm opposition to terrorism in all its forms whether it is domestic terrorism perpetrated within United States Territory, or international terrorism conducted inside or outside U.S. territory by foreign nations or groups. The policy is based on the conviction that to accede to terrorist demands places more U.S. citizens at risk. This non-concessions policy is the best way of protecting the greatest number of people and ensuring their safety." It continues to be the cornerstone of United States policy in negotiating with terrorism.

Public Laws to Combat Terrorism. In addition to presidential initiatives to combat terrorism, Congress passed several landmark laws starting in the 1980s aimed at fighting terrorism. Legislation passed by Congress attempted to provide international cooperation in the fight against terrorism, to cut off funds to terrorists, to promote aviation security, to bolster diplomatic security overseas, and to take action against the growing threat of biological attack by terrorists.

One of the early major legislative acts passed by Congress aimed at fighting terrorism was the 1984 Act to Combat International Terrorism (Public Law 98-533). This act recognized that the United States could not effectively respond to terrorism by itself and urged the president to enhance efforts to seek international cooperation in combating terrorism. It also adopted a tool to fight terrorism that continues to be used in the war on terrorism. The law authorized the offering and paying of rewards for reporting information about international terrorism. For example, the paying of rewards for information leading to the capture of wanted persons in the Iraq and Afghanistan conflict was a major strategy used by the U.S. government.

In 1985, Congress moved to cut off funding to terrorists by passing Public Law 99-83. This legislation prohibited the granting of foreign aid to countries that the Secretary of State determined to be contributing to terrorism (1985 USC Sec. 2371). Congress also attempted to help other countries fight terrorism by allowing certain arms on the U.S. munitions list to be made available for counterterrorism efforts by foreign countries.

Congress became concerned that commercial civilian aviation was particularly vulnerable to terrorist attack. Thus, in 1985, Congress amended the Federal Aviation Act of 1958 so that the Secretary of Transportation would be able to assess effectiveness of security measures at foreign airports.

Also, in 1986, the Omnibus Diplomatic Security and Antiterrorism Act of 1986 (Public Law 99-399) expanded the jurisdiction of the Federal Bureau of Investigation to include investigation of acts of terrorism directed against U.S. citizens overseas. It also established the Bureau of Diplomatic Security within the State Department to enhance the ability of the State Department to ensure the security of U.S. facilities and nationals abroad.

Congress's concern of the possible use of biological agents by terrorists is reflected by the Biological Weapons Anti-Terrorism Act of 1989 (Public Law 101-298). This legislation evolved from the international Convention on the Prohibition of the Development, Production and Stockpiling of Bacteriological (Biological) and Toxin Weapons and on Their Destruction. The agreement resulting from the international convention was signed by more than 100 nations. The key purpose of the domestic legislation was to protect the United States against the threat of biological terrorism. The legislation identified a list of select agents and toxins relevant to human disease that are prohibited or whose possession is controlled. The legislation provided for the prosecution of those persons found to be in possession of a biological agent and/or toxin with the intention of using it as a weapon. Also, the Biological Weapons Anti-Terrorism Act statute provided for the prosecution of individuals who utilize hoax devices.

The Clinton Administration: The Foundation of Post-September 11, 2001, Legislation

During the Clinton Administration the official anti-terrorism policy of the United States was

> to deter, defeat and respond vigorously to all terrorist attacks on our territory and against our citizens, or facilities, whether they occur domestically, in international waters or airspace or on foreign territory. The United States regards all such terrorism as a potential threat to national security as well as a criminal act and will apply all appropriate means to combat it. In doing so, the United States shall pursue vigorously efforts to deter and preempt, apprehend and prosecute, or assist other governments to prosecute, individuals who perpetrate or plan to perpetrate such attacks.

One of the goals of the Clinton Administration was to reduce the vulnerability of the United States to terrorism, at home and abroad. Again, presidential directives and

BOX 3.1 • *Up Close and Personal: The Integrity of the Rule of Law*

One of the founding principles of the United States is the rule of law. The rule of law declares that the standards of behavior and privilege are established not by kings, religious leaders, dictators, or political leaders, but by rules and procedures that define and prohibit certain behaviors as illegal or criminal and that prescribe punishments for those behaviors. All people, regardless of rank, title, position, status, or wealth, are accorded the same rights and privileges under the law.[12] The rule of law limits the actions of government against its citizens.

Many are questioning whether the rule of law is a casualty of the war on terrorism. Some argue that in its zeal to protect the homeland, the federal government has abandoned the rule of law. For example, Omar Khadr was 15 years old when he was captured in Afghanistan and transported to Guantanamo Bay. He was accused of throwing a grenade that killed a U.S. medic near Khost. He claims that while at Guantanamo he has been regularly shackled and left alone for long periods. Critics claim that Omar Khadr's detention and treatment violate the Convention on the Rights of the Child, a treaty of which the United States is a signatory.[13] (The United States eventually released all children from Guantanamo.)

Another complaint accuses the United States of torture. Mamdouh Habib, an Australia citizen who was captured and detained at Guantanamo Bay before he was released and returned to Australia, claims he was abused while in custody. He states that he was burned with cigarettes, was interrogated using electric shock, was beaten, was doused with ice water, and was hung by handcuffs from the ceiling. Eventually, Mr. Habid was released from Guantanamo Bay without being charged with anything.[14] In another case, Khaled el-Masri, a German citizen, claims he was kidnapped by U.S. agents and transported from Germany to Afghanistan. During his capture, he was interrogated by U.S. agents who tortured him to obtain confessions. He said he was told, "You are in a country where the laws don't apply to you."[15] Khaled el-Masri was eventually secretly returned to German without ever knowing who kidnapped him and why. German authorities are investigating his claims.

Another accusation of the abuse of the rule of law is the changing of the rules of evidence for those accused of terrorism. In some cases the federal government is refusing to reveal its evidence against those accused of and detained for terrorism on the grounds that to reveal the evidence against the person would compromise national security. Federal judges are being asked to keep persons detained in prison based on "secret evidence." Federal prosecutors are asking to be able use secret evidence to litigate cases against accused terrorists.[16]

Finally, the enacting of laws that may be difficult or impossible to enforce is challenging the rule of law. For example, in the desire to prevent passengers from bringing lighters and matches aboard commercial airplanes, Congress passed a law banning lighters and matches from the secure area of an airport. However, the Transportation Security Administration (TSA) has serious concerns about how this law will be enforced.[17] Will it also be necessary to ban smoking in the secure areas of airports because smokers without matches or lighters will be unable to light up? One suggestion has been that the airports install "wall-mounted" lighters in the smoking areas.[18] Also, how will those with legitimate needs for matches and lighters (e.g., restaurants needing matches to light candles on tables) be exempted? The challenge of screening passengers for matches and lighters is virtually impossible, as it is common for people to carry matches, which cannot be detected by any existing technology. Each passenger would have to be extensively searched, including examining the contents of their pockets, purses, and carry-on items.

Questions

1. Do you think the federal government has violated the rule of law in aggressively pursuing accused terrorists in the war on terrorism? Why or why not?
2. If it is true that the government agents have kidnapped and tortured suspected terrorists, what should be done to correct this illegal activity?

BOX 3.1 • Continued

3. Do you believe that in a time of crisis the rule of law "may have to be broken or bent a little" for the safety of the greater society? Explain your position.
4. In the desire to enhance security against terrorism, can laws be passed that literal-ly are impossible to enforce fairly and consistently? Do you think the law against matches and lighters at airports is an example of such a law? Explain your answers.

legislation were seen as effective strategies to reduce the vulnerability of the United States to terrorism.

One of the major concerns continued to be the hijacking of commercial civilian aviation. Responding to this concern, Congress passed the Aviation Security Improvement Act of 1990 (Public Law 101-604). This legislation established the Office of Director of Intelligence and Security within the Office of the Secretary of Transportation. This office was responsible for developing transportation security. The law required the Federal Aviation Administration to develop counterterrorism strategies for aviation.

In addition to concern over terrorist attacks on aviation there continued to be concern over the coordination of the response of the various federal agencies. Several presidential directives in the mid-1990s were directed toward improving U.S. anti-terrorism capacity by improving interagency cooperation. In April 1992, President Clinton issued a National Security Decision Directive entitled "Managing Terrorist Incidents." This NSDD expanded and clarified NSDD 30 from the Reagan Administration that established the responsibilities of the State Department, the FBI, and the FAA in responding to terrorist incidents. In addition to delineating the responsibilities of the various federal agencies, President Clinton's National Security Decision Directive called for the establishment of the Terrorist Incident Working Group. This group would be responsible for coordinating efforts among the various federal agencies to respond to terrorism. It also established the Interdepartmental Group on Terrorism that was responsible for formulating policies to counter terrorism.

Presidential Decision Directive 39.   In 1995, President Clinton further defined the responsibilities of the various federal agencies in Presidential Decision Directive (PDD) 39. In this directive President Clinton revisited the assigned responsibilities of the various federal agencies. The directive expanded the list of federal agencies and duties to include responding to weapons of mass destruction (WMD) incidents, as well as the roles of the Defense Department and the Central Intelligence Agency. This directive provided the following responsibilities for each of the federal agencies:

- *Attorney General:* Responsible for reducing vulnerability to terrorism of government facilities in the United States and critical national infrastructure.
- *Federal Bureau of Investigation:* Responsible for reducing vulnerabilities to terrorism by an expanded program of counterterrorism. The FBI is the lead federal agency for responding to domestic weapons of mass destruction incident. A WMD incident

includes the threat or use of a WMD and defines a WMD as any destructive device (explosive or incendiary), chemical or biological agent, or release of life-threatening levels of radioactive material.

- *State Department:* Responsible for reducing vulnerabilities of all personnel and facilities at nonmilitary U.S. government installations abroad.
- *Defense Department:* Responsible for the security of all U.S. military personnel (except those assigned to diplomatic missions) and facilities.
- *Department of Transportation:* Responsible for the security of all airports in the United States and all aircraft and passengers and all maritime shipping under the United States flag.
- *Secretary of State and Attorney General:* Responsible for using all legal means available to exclude from the United States persons who pose a terrorist threat and deport or otherwise remove from the United States any such aliens.
- *Central Intelligence Agency:* Responsible for reducing the vulnerability of the United States to international terrorism through an aggressive program of foreign intelligence collection, analysis, counterintelligence, and covert action in accordance with the National Security Act of 1947 and Executive Order 12333.

Despite these presidential directives and congressional legislation, concern about terrorism in the United States continued to rise. In the mid-1990s, two landmark laws were passed to enhance the U.S. anti-terrorism capacity: the Omnibus Counterterrorism Act of 1995 and the Anti-Terrorism and Effective Death Penalty Act of 1996.

The Omnibus Counterterrorism Act of 1995 and the Anti-Terrorism and Effective Death Penalty Act of 1996 (Public Law 104-132)

The purposes of the Omnibus Counterterrorism Act of 1995 were to provide for federal prosecution of acts deemed to be terrorism and to change the immigration law to allow for the deportation of aliens accused or suspected of terrorism. The legislation was spurred by the proliferation of international terrorist incidents beginning in the 1980s. In fact, the Senate bill recited a long list of worldwide terrorist incidents in which U.S. citizens were the targets of attack or were injured in the attack in justification of the bill.[19] The legislation was justified by the claim that "present Federal law does not adequately reach all terrorist activity likely to be engaged in by aliens within the United States and law enforcement officials have been hindered in using current immigration law to deport alien terrorists because the law fails to provide procedures to protect classified intelligence sources and information."[20]

The act significantly shifted the balance between local and state law enforcement and federal law enforcement. It allowed the federal government to claim criminal jurisdiction over people alleged to have committed acts of terrorism in the United States and who use the United States as the place from which to plan terrorist attacks overseas. Also, the act expanded federal jurisdiction over bomb threats. This increased jurisdiction provided the federal government with criminal jurisdiction over bombing incidents that previously would have been state offenses. The Omnibus Counterterrorism Act of 1995 criminalized fundraising for terrorism and provided the first regulation of nonweapons-grade nuclear material. Nonweapons-grade nuclear material is nuclear material that can be used to make a "dirty" bomb. The act also clarified and extended U.S. criminal jurisdiction over certain terrorism offenses overseas, such as the bombing of U.S. embassies.

Following the 1995 Oklahoma City bombing, the Omnibus Counterterrorism Act was amended to provide for more effective prosecution of domestic terrorism as well as international terrorism. Specifically, the amendment required the inclusion of taggants in standard explosive device raw materials, provided for a 10-year mandatory penalty for transferring firearms or explosives with knowledge that they will be used to commit a crime of violence, and criminalized the possession of stolen explosives. It permitted law enforcement agencies to gain access to financial and credit reports in anti-terrorism cases, and expanded law enforcement power to track telephone traffic with "pen registers" and "trap and trace" devices. The act provided law enforcement with the power to obtain records, such as hotel/motel records, common carrier records, storage facilities records, and vehicle rental records that were deemed critical to terrorism investigations utilizing a national security letter process that did not require a search warrant.

The Omnibus Counterterrorism Act of 1995 was opposed by the American Civil Liberties Union. The ACLU in an open letter to President Clinton and congressional leadership stated,

> We are strongly opposed to provisions of the Omnibus Counterterrorism Act of 1995, H.R. 896 or S. 390, which allow the government to engage in activities contrary to constitutional principles of due process, free speech, and freedom of association. We are also strongly opposed to proposals to increase the government's authority to monitor groups, domestic and international, in the absence of reasonable suspicion of criminal activity.[21]

The Omnibus Counterterrorism Act and its amendments were short-lived, as it was replaced by the Anti-Terrorism and Effective Death Penalty Act of 1996. This legislation was to be the backbone of terrorist legislation until the passage of the Patriot Act following the September 11, 2001, terrorist attacks. The legislation incorporated legislation of the Omnibus Counterterrorism Act of 1995 and the Antiterrorism Amendments Act of 1995. Provisions of the Anti-Terrorism and Effective Death Penalty Act include:

- The legislation provided broad new federal jurisdiction to prosecute anyone who commits a terrorist attack in the United States or who uses the United States as a planning ground for attacks overseas.
- The legislation banned fund-raising in the United States that supports terrorist organizations.
- The legislation provided for extensive revision of Immigration and Naturalization Services (INS) regulations regarding access to confidential INS files through court order, waiver of authority concerning notice of denial of application for visas, asset forfeiture for passport and visa offenses, forfeiture of passport and visa for criminal offenses, and criminal alien deportation procedures. The act allowed for the deportation of accused terrorists from U.S. soil without being compelled by law to divulge classified information on which the deportation was initiated. It allowed accused or suspected terrorists to be barred from entering the United States. It expanded the criteria for deportation to include crimes of moral turpitude. Also, the act permitted the deporta-

tion of nonviolent alien offenders prior to completion of their sentence of imprisonment.

- The law required plastic explosives to contain chemical markers. It enabled the government to issue regulations requiring the chemical taggants to be added to some other types of explosives so that police can better trace bombs to the criminals who make them.
- The law increased federal controls over biological and chemical weapons.
- The act increased the penalties for many terrorist crimes.
- The legislation banned the sale of defense goods and services to countries that the president determines are not cooperating fully with U.S. anti-terrorism efforts.
- The act allowed the Secretary of State in conjunction with the Attorney General and the Secretary of Treasury to designate an organization as a terrorist organization if it is determined that it is a foreign organization that engages in terrorist activity, and that activity poses a threat to the United States and/or its citizens.
- The law streamlined federal appeals for convicted criminals sentenced to the death penalty. It also included habeas corpus reform, including limits on successive applications and death penalty litigation procedures.[22]

The original bill contained several provisions that were struck from the legislation and did not become law. Sponsors of the bill had wanted *but did not get* the following investigative tools and powers:[23]

- Increase wiretap authority in terrorism cases, power to seek multipoint wiretaps
- The requirement that black power and smokeless powder contain taggants that would allow law enforcement to trace the material back to its manufacturer
- Increased access without court order or search warrant to hotel, phone, and other records in terrorism cases
- Mandatory penalties for transfer of firearms that are used in a violent felony
- Longer statute of limitations to allow law enforcement more time to prosecute terrorists who use weapons such as machine guns, sawed-off shotguns, and explosive devices
- A ban on cop-killer bullets

This list of provisions that were struck from the bill is interesting to examine, as they will reemerge in post–September 11, 2001, legislation, including some of them that will be included in the Patriot Act.

Post-September 11, 2001, Legislation

After the terrorist attacks of September 11, 2001, more executive orders and legislation followed in the attempt to protect the United States from terrorist attacks. The two most controversial legal strategies to emerge in post-September 11 legislation were the Enemy Combatant Act and the USA Patriot Act. Both have been criticized as unconstitutional, destructive of privacy rights, ineffective, and worst than the harm they seek to prevent. Despite these arguments they continue to be the centerpiece in fighting domestic and international terrorism in the United States.

Enemy Combatant Executive Order

President George W. Bush authorized a military assault against Afghanistan, citing state-sponsored terrorism by that nation, specifically the September 11, 2001, attacks, as the justification for his action. Following the U.S. invasion of Afghanistan, President Bush issued an executive order concerning how certain prisoners who were captured in Afghanistan would be detained and treated. The executive order, issued November 13, 2001, has been extremely controversial, as it resulted in 680 captured persons being detained in a military prison compound in Guantanamo Bay, Cuba, without charges, access to an attorney, or protection of constitutional rights.

The Geneva Convention.   The Geneva Convention of 1864 and its subsequent revisions proscribe the treatment and rights accorded to persons captured on the battlefield during military combat. Normally, prisoners captured in combat would be entitled to the rights and protections of the Third Geneva Convention of 1949, also known as the Prisoner-of-War Pact. The Geneva Convention Prisoner-of-War Pact proscribes that prisoners will not be questioned and do not have to reveal information other than their name, rank, and serial number. It provides for humane treatment with regard to housing and food. It guarantees fair treatment and protection against criminal charges for the soldiers' battlefield participation except in certain circumstances when the captured solider is charged with war crimes. It also provides that in the event of charges against a prisoner, the prisoner has the right to a civilian attorney of his or her choice and has the right to a trial in a civilian court. The provisions of the Geneva Convention provide for the right of prisoners to communicate and to receive communication. It also provides the right of inspection of the imprisonment of prisoners by international humanitarian organizations such as the Red Cross.

Unlawful Combatants Are Not Prisoners of War.   President Bush's executive order declared that captured members of al-Qaida are "unlawful" or "enemy combatants." According to President Bush's executive order, unlawful combatants are not entitled to prisoner of war status under the Geneva Convention nor are they accorded the rights and privileges they would have if they were prisoners of war.[24] Bush's executive order provides that as unlawful enemy combatants, the prisoners will be held without access to U.S. civilian courts, without the right of appeal, and are not entitled to the protections of the United States Constitution or the Prisoner of War provisions of the Geneva Convention.

The status of unlawful enemy combatant is usually applied to spies or enemy saboteurs who are behind enemy lines without uniform.[25] Normally, prisoners of war can be captured and detained but cannot be tried and punished for their participation in combat. However, unlike prisoners of war, unlawful combatants such as spies can be tried and punished by military tribunals for their action.

The United States has not evoked the use of unlawful combatant status since World War II. In 1942, President Franklin D. Roosevelt had six German saboteurs captured in the United States tried by a military court and executed. "The Supreme Court upheld the

BOX 3.2 • *Consider This: What Are Military Tribunals?*

Bush's executive order provides that Afghanistan enemy combatants will be tried by a military tribunal of three to seven judges, all of whom must be commissioned military officers.[26] The captured enemy combatants can be charged with international terrorism or with knowingly harboring a member of the organization known as al-Qaida or an international terrorist.[27] To be subject to trial by a military tribunal, the subject must be a member of the Taliban or al-Qaida and a non-U.S. citizen. Although the executive order primarily targets accused terrorists captured in Afghanistan, it is not restricted to such persons and can be used for international terrorists captured in the United States.[28] A military tribunal differs significantly from a military court martial.[29] Military courts are governed by the Uniform Code of Military Justice and the rules of evidence are similar to those in civilian courts (see Figure 3.1). The defendant is accorded rights similar to a defendant in a civilian trial, including the right to an attorney, the right to examine the evidence against him or her, the right to a public trial, and the right to appeal. The verdict of a military court can be appealed to the United States Supreme Court.

FIGURE 3.1 • *Uniform Code of Military Justice*

The Uniform Code of Military Justice (UCMJ) is a single law code that applies to all U.S. military personnel throughout the world. Generally, civilians are not tried under the authority of the Uniform Code of Military Justice, as they are entitled to a trial in a civilian court. The Uniform Code of Military Justice can be found at www.au.af.mil/au/awc/awcgate/ucmj.htm.

Ronald W. Meister, a New York lawyer who is a former Navy lawyer and judge, said military tribunals are "a totally different animal" compared to the military court martial system.[30] Military tribunals for the trial of accused Taliban and al-Qaida terrorists eliminate a number of due process rights of the defendant, significantly modify the rules of

evidence, and do not provide for an appeal to a civilian court. In a military court martial the defendant has many of the same rights as the defendant in a civilian court, including the right to confirm witnesses, to challenge evidence, and to be informed of the charges against him or her. In a military court martial a three-fourths vote is required for a guilty verdict; whereas in the military tribunals proposed by President Bush a two-thirds vote is required for a guilty verdict. The maximum penalty that can be imposed in both the military court martial and the military tribunal is death. In the case of the death penalty, a unanimous verdict is required. The proof required for guilty in both courts is guilt beyond a reasonable doubt, the same as in a civilian criminal court.

A major difference between the court martial and the military tribunal is the rules of evidence governing the trial. Military court martial trials use similar standards as civilian courts in regard to the admission of evidence. Military tribunals may consider "any evidence that a reasonable person would find useful."[31] This rule of evidence would allow hearsay and other kinds of evidence that would typically be excluded in civilian trials to be used in a tribunal trial. Because of the lack of appeals provided in the tribunals, writs of habeas corpus would not be available to the defendant in a military tribunal. Current rules provide that attorneys who represent accused terrorists in military tribunals must sign a list of promises and agree to certain conditions regarding disclosure of information. The American Bar Association strongly objects to many of these conditions. One point of contention is the government's ability to listen to conversations between suspects and their lawyers.[32] The American Bar Association is critical of the prohibition against providing defense lawyers with evidence that might help their cases, as in civilian criminal cases, and the prohibition against civilian lawyers from consulting with others to build their cases.[33] Both of these restrictions are supposedly to protect national security. Because of the limitations imposed by the government, the American Bar Association and other associations of criminal defense lawyers voice criticism that

BOX 3.2 • Continued

defendants will not receive a fair trial before a military tribunal.[34]

Questions

1. Do you believe enemy combatants will get a fair trial before a military tribunal? Why or why not?
2. Do you think trying persons captured on the battlefield in a foreign country before a mil-

itary tribunal is a violation of the Geneva Convention? Explain your answer.
3. Do you think that the fact that the United States is aggressively interrogating captured combatants and plans to bring them to trial before a military tribunal will impact how captured U.S. soldiers may be treated? Explain your answer.

proceeding, saying that people who entered the United States for the purpose of waging war were combatants who could be tried in a military court."[35] However, many have challenged the rationale that persons captured on the battlefield in Afghanistan are similar to spies or enemy saboteurs without uniform and are therefore unlawful combatants.[36]

The White House's justification for classifying Afghanistan prisoners as unlawful combatants is that the subjects were terrorists, not members of an organized state military, and as such were engaged in unconventional war against the United States. A White House spokesperson, defending the use of enemy combatant status, stated, "We have looked at this war very unconventionally, and the conventional way of bringing people to justice doesn't apply to these times."[37] Furthermore, it was argued by White House officials that tribunals were necessary "to protect potential American jurors from the danger of passing judgment on accused terrorists . . . and the disclosure of government intelligence methods, which normally would be public in civilian courts."[38] Thus, President Bush has declared that terrorists classified as unlawful combatants will be tried by military law.

Criticisms of the Enemy Combatant Executive Order.   One reason President Bush's executive order is controversial is because under the order, the president himself—not a Court—determines who is an accused terrorist and therefore who is subject to trial by a military tribunal. Furthermore, this decision cannot be appealed to a civilian court, even the United States Supreme Court.[39] Another reason is that critics of Bush's executive order argue that it is a breach of international law guaranteeing fair treatment of prisoners of war. The Geneva Convention provides that no prisoner is to be tried by a court that fails to offer the essential guarantees of independence and impartiality, that prisoners have the right to be represented by an attorney of their choice, and that they have the right of appeal.[40]

Also, the treatment of "enemy combatants" is criticized as it is argued that prisoners of war cannot be interrogated for information under the rights guaranteed by the Geneva Convention, and prisoners held in the civilian court system cannot be interrogated without the protections provided by legal counsel and the Constitution. However, prisoners held as enemy combatants have no protection against interrogation and have no access to legal counsel. It is this ability to interrogate prisoners without restraint, without access to legal counsel, and without the right to remain silent that causes critics to protest. (Some critics have alleged

BOX 3.3 • *Case Study: Why Gitmo?*

Prisoners captured on the battlefield in Afghanistan were transported to the United States Naval Base in Guantanamo Bay, Cuba, commonly referred to as "Gitmo." The Bush Administration deliberately selected this site. It is perhaps the only place in the world were the prisoners could be held as enemy combatants. If the prisoners were held in the United States, on any other military base, in any U.S. territory, or at any U.S. military base in a foreign county, the prisoners would most assuredly have access to the civil courts to challenge their detention as enemy combatants. If they were held on a military base in a foreign country, the prisoners could petition to the civil courts of the country in which the U.S. military base was located and the United States would not be able to block this appeal. If the prisoners were incarcerated in a facility under the control of the United States, they would have certain constitutional rights, such as the right to have an attorney, to know the charges against them, and to have access to the court to file motions and petitions.

Gitmo is a unique location. Despite the fact that Cuba is a Communist country with no diplomatic relations with the United States, the United States has a lease (signed in 1934) granting the United States indefinite use of a 45-square-mile corner of the island in return for an annual payment of $4,085.[41] The Bush Administration claims that since the naval base is leased from a Communist country, it is not officially on U.S. soil and therefore the prisoners held at Guantanamo Bay are not entitled to the constitutional rights guaranteed to noncitizens on American soil.[42] The United States has no diplomatic relationship with Cuba, and thus the prisoners cannot appeal to the Cuban courts. It is the perfect place to detain the prisoners as enemy combatants because they are cut off from access to the United States Supreme Court and from the civilian courts of Cuba or any other country.

Initially, 110 men were transported by the military to Gitmo in January 2002. They were held in wire cages rather than "regular prison cells" at a site called Camp X-Ray. To accommodate additional prisoners, a larger facility called Camp Delta was built. Camp Delta has better facilities than Camp X-Ray but it still is not equivalent to the accommodations provided to prisoners in the United States prison system. The combatants are from 42 countries. Some of the detainees were as young as 13 to 15 years old.[43] However, the youngest detainees have been released to their country of citizenship. Although most are from Middle Eastern countries, several of the detainees are from Canada, Sweden, Britain, and Australia. At its peak, Gitmo housed 680 prisoners. The number of prisoners has decreased as the United States has released a small number of the prisoners who are citizens of foreign countries outside the Middle East.

It is the claim of the Bush Administration that as enemy combatants held on non-American soil, these prisoners are beyond the jurisdiction of U.S. Courts. Solicitor General Theodore B. Olson argued before the Supreme Court, "Aliens detained by the military abroad have only those rights that are determined by the executive and the military, and not the courts."[44] However, lawyers representing detainees from Kuwait, Britain, and Australia challenged this claim. They argued that the lease provides that the United States exercises sole and absolute control of Guantanamo Bay and therefore the base should be treated for jurisdictional purposes as part of the United States.[45] The detainees they represent claim that they were not fighters either for the Taliban or for al-Qaida. They claim they were humanitarian volunteers who were captured by bounty hunters.[46] The lawyers claim that their clients are entitled access to civilian courts to challenge their open-ended detention.

To assert this right, the lawyers have filed a writ of habeas corpus and the United States Supreme Court has agreed to hear the arguments. Critical of the government's arguments, the Center for Constitutional Rights argued, "For over a year and a half, hundreds of people have been imprisoned in Guantanamo without charges, access to lawyers or to their families. . . . This lawless situation must not continue. . . . Never has America taken the public position that it is not bound at all by the rule of law."[47]

Lawyers for the detainees have filed an appeal with the United States Supreme Court and the

BOX 3.3 • Continued

Court has agreed to hear the appeal. The Court's ruling will determine whether the Bush Administration's claim that the detainees are outside the jurisdiction of the civilian courts will be upheld. If the Supreme Court decides that the detainees are under the jurisdiction of the federal courts, the cases will go back to district court for a decision on the merits of the detainees' claims of access to a civilian federal court.[48]

The prisoners at Gitmo can be held indefinitely unless the Court intervenes and contradicts the Bush Administration's claim that the prisoners have no access to the civilian courts. Justice Department officials deny that the prisoners will be held indefinitely. Justice Department officials said the detainees will be provided access to an attorney after their interrogation is completed and they have provided intelligence to the government.[49] Critics of the policy on enemy combatants argue that President Bush lacks the judicial authority to remove constitutionally protected rights and they continue to press for a review of the policy by the United States Supreme Court.

Questions

1. Should prisoners detained at Guantanamo Bay have access to civilian courts? Why or why not?
2. If terrorists can be held at Guantanamo Bay and denied access to the civilian courts, do you think it would be possible for other persons to be held by the U.S. government without access to the civilian courts? Explain your answer.
3. The Bush Administrations argues that the U.S. Supreme Court does not have jurisdiction to overrule President Bush's executive orders to hold enemy combatants in Guantanamo without access to the civilian courts. Lower federal courts have ruled against the government on this claim. What do you think will be the arguments for and against this claim when it appears before the U.S. Supreme Court?

that the military has used torture in interrogating persons held as unlawful combatants.) The justification cited by the Bush Administration for such interrogation is the desire to obtain information about possible plans for terrorist attacks on the United States and/or information that would lead to the capture of other terrorists. The Bush Administration claims that this ability to interrogate the prisoners has produced a wealth of information regarding terrorist plots against the United States and the operation of al-Qaida.

United States Senator John McCain, a naval aviator who spent more than five years as a prisoner of war in North Vietnam, disputes the intelligence value that can be obtained from the prisoners at Guantanamo Bay. Senator McCain argues that most useful operational intelligence information goes stale after about four months. The prisoners have been detained for years and have had no contact with the outside world during that time. McCain argues that the detainees can provide little information of value.[50] Critics argue that the elimination of due process for Afghanistan prisoners accused of terrorism and the open-ended indefinite detention of them without charges or access to the courts may provoke other countries to take a similar policy toward U.S. soldiers and/or civilians.[51]

Executive Order Extended to the United States and Citizens. When President Bush issued his executive order declaring that the Afghanistan prisoners captured on the Afghanistan battlefields were enemy combatants, there was the expectation that its use would be limited to non–U.S. citizens and combatants captured on foreign battlefields. In a unique move, the Bush Administration expanded the power of the enemy combatant executive order by declaring "Al-Qaida made the battlefield the United States."[52] Based on this argument, the president declared a Qatari student who entered the United States on a student visa an enemy combatant and he declared a U.S. citizen arrested at Chicago's O'Hare International Airport an enemy combatant. The ability of President Bush to extend the jurisdiction of the enemy combatant executive order to noncitizens residing within the United States and citizens in the United States has been described as a "sea change in the constitutional life of this country."[53]

Qatari student Ali Saleh Kahlah al-Marri entered the United States on September 10, 2001, on a student visa. In December 2001, based on intelligence information that he was a "sleeper" operative assigned to help other members of al-Qaida "settle" in the United States, he was picked up by the Federal Bureau of Investigation. He was first held as a material witness in the 9/11 investigation and later charged with lying to the Federal Bureau of Investigation and credit card fraud.[54] On June 23, 2003, less than one month before his civilian trial, President Bush issued a declaration that "Ali Saleh Kahlah al-Marri is, and at the time he entered the United States in September 2001 was, an enemy combatant."[55] The White House claims the classification of Mr. al-Marri was intended to allow officials to interrogate him about al-Qaida.[56] Civil liberties advocates and military law experts criticized the application of the executive order to Mr. al-Marri.

They argue that removing Mr. al-Marri from the civilian court system by declaring him an enemy combatant just weeks before his scheduled trial is a tactic to coerce a plea from Mr. al-Marri and from other terrorists being held on criminal charges. Justice Department officials denied the charge.[57] However, a senior FBI official commented that the "Marri decision held clear implications for other terrorism suspects. If I were in their shoes, I'd take a message from this."[58] Defense Secretary Donald H. Rumsfeld said of the tactic that it "demonstrated the White House's continued commitment to using a range of military and legal weapons to pursue terrorism suspects."[59]

Perhaps the greatest criticism of the Enemy Combatant Executive Order is reserved for the case of Jose Padilla, a U.S. citizen who was taken into custody at Chicago O'Hare Airport in May 2002. He was suspected of being part of a "dirty bomb" plot by al-Qaida.[60] Mr. Padilla was a former Chicago gang member with a long criminal record who converted to Islam. The government arrested him after he returned from a trip to Pakistan. Officials claimed he was "associated" with al-Qaida, met officials of the group in Afghanistan, and received training in explosives in Pakistan. In June 2003, President Bush declared him an enemy combatant and Mr. Padilla was moved from a federal jail in Manhattan to a Navy brig in Charleston, South Carolina.[61]

Jose Padilla is the only U.S. citizen arrested in the United States declared to be an enemy combatant and held indefinitely without charges or without access to an attorney or the civilian courts.[62] In November 2003, lawyers arguing on behalf of Mr. Padilla to a three-judge panel of the United States Court of Appeals for the Second Circuit in Manhattan argued that the government was "distorting principles of American liberty by expanding battlefield concepts to civilian life. . . . The President seeks an unchecked power to substitute military power for the rule of law." The court appeared to be sympathetic to the arguments of the defense. Rosemary S. Pooler, one of the judges hearing the arguments, declared, "As terrible as 9/11 was, it didn't repeal the Constitution."

New Legal Questions. The enemy combatant executive order has created new legal questions. As the situation evolves and changes, new challenges emerge. Critics express concern that trials by military tribunal may be used as a tactic to get less important al-Qaida detainees to provide information about senior operational al-Qaida personnel.[63] The prospect of trying foreign citizens, some belonging to countries that are considered allies of the United States, has created foreign policy tensions and concern. For example, a spokesperson for the British Foreign Office has called on the United States "to conduct the tribunals with fairness on issues like access to lawyers, standards of evidence and the right to appeal in the case of a guilty verdict. Clearly, we want the Americans to give us assurances that the international minimum standards of fair trials will be met."[64]

The Bush Administration is feeling the effect of these pressures. Five Pakistanis held at the Guantanamo Bay detention center in Cuba were released in November 2003. As a result of Pakistani government efforts, 21 of the 58 Pakistanis have been released from Guantanamo Bay since November 2002. In March 2004, five British citizens were released from Guantanamo Bay. In January 2005, the United States agreed to release the last four Britons and one Australian who had been held without charge or trial at Guantanamo Bay. Interestingly, the release of detainees often proves to be only the beginning of another problem. One of the Pakistani prisoners released from Guantanamo Bay has filed a lawsuit seeking $10.4 million in damages from the United States for his "illegal detention, torture and humiliation."[65] Often, those returned from Guantanamo Bay back to their native countries have been released without charges being filed against them.[66] This action causes the United States to fear that these combatants will rejoin al-Qaida in its attacks against the United States.

The USA Patriot Act

On October 11, 2001, the USA Patriot Act breezed through the Senate, 96 to 1. The next day it passed the House, 337 to 79, and President Bush signed it on October 26, 2001.[67] Despite its quick and overwhelming approval, the USA Patriot Act (commonly called the Patriot Act) has become one of the most controversial anti-terrorism legislative acts to date. The extent of the opposition to the Patriot Act is seen in the fact that an estimated 150 local governments and the states of Alaska, Hawaii, and Vermont have passed resolutions objecting to the legislation.[68]

Despite this criticism, former Attorney General John Ashcroft, one of the most passionate supporters of the Patriot Act, defended the act by pointing out that there had not been a successful attack on U.S. soil since the Patriot Act was passed. He attributed this accomplishment to the fact that the Patriot Act has closed "gaping holes in our ability to investigate terrorists."[69] Other supporters of the Patriot Act argue that even if there is no firm evidence that the Patriot Act has been responsible for the lack of terrorist attacks on U.S. soil, the legislation was necessary. The argument is that if there had been another terrorist attack and the legislation had not been passed, the U.S. government would have been criticized for its failure to pass effective anti-terrorism legislation.[70]

Supporters of the Patriot Act argue that it provides law enforcement personnel with the necessary tools to gather intelligence, to act proactively against terrorists' plots, and to protect against another terrorist attack in the United States. The key provisions of the USA

Patriot Act provide greater surveillance powers to law enforcement agents, expansion of the definition of crimes that fall under the authority granted by the Patriot Act, and removal of some civil liberties protections for those accused or detained under the Patriot Act.

The Patriot Act authorized federal law enforcement personnel to use investigation tactics previously denied to them or available only by court order. Figure 3.2 provides a summary of the new authority granted to law enforcement.

The authority of law enforcement agents to execute searches has been greatly expanded under the Patriot Act. One of the most controversial provisions is the "sneak-and-peek" warrant authorized by the Patriot Act. The "sneak-and-peek" warrant gives law enforcement agents the authority to conduct a search without informing the suspect of the search. Thus, law enforcement agents could enter a house or business, or execute a search warrant of records, in secret. The suspect would not know that the search had been conducted. It also gives law enforcement agents much great authority to demand that Internet providers give up information on their customers.

Another controversial section of the Patriot Act is Section 215. Under the authority of Section 215, the FBI is authorized to demand access to records without a warrant or probable cause. Under this provision, any third party—including doctors, libraries, bookstores,

---

FIGURE 3.2 • *Summary of the Key Provisions of the USA Patriot Act*

- Expands the range of crimes trackable by electronic surveillance.
- Allows police to use roving wiretaps to track any phone a terrorism suspect might use. Previously, the law provided that a wiretap of each individual phone was necessary. This provision allows law enforcement to obtain a single wiretap to listen in on any phone the suspect uses, including cell phones.
- Permits law enforcement to conduct searches with delayed notification—the so-called sneak-and-peak provision.
- Allows FBI agents, with secret court orders, to search personal records (business, medical, library, etc.) without probable cause in national-security terrorism cases.
- Lowers legal barriers in information sharing between criminal investigators and intelligence officials.
- Provides new tools for fighting international money laundering.
- Makes it a crime to harbor terrorists.
- Increases penalties for conspiracy, such as plotting arson, killing in federal facilities, attacking communications systems, supporting terrorists, or interfering with flight crews.
- Makes it easier for law enforcement agents to obtain search warrants any place where "terrorist-related" activities occur; allows nationwide search warrants (including the monitoring of Internet use, email, and computer bills) in terrorism investigations.
- Allows the Attorney General to detain foreign terrorism suspects—but charges, deportation proceedings, or release must come within a week.
- Sends more federal agents to patrol the United States–Canada border.
- Ends surveillance and wiretap measures in 2005.

Source: Adapted from Warren Richey and Linda Feldman, "Has Post–9/11 Dragnet Gone Too Far?" *The Christian Science Monitor,* www.csmonitor.com, September 12, 2005.

universities, and Internet service providers—must turn over records on their clients or customers and they are forbidden to inform the subject or the public of the action. There is no judicial oversight of this power.

In support of the USA Patriot Act, supporters point to the success of the government in discovering terrorist plots and arresting terrorists in the United States. They point to the fact that since September 11, 2001, six alleged terrorist cells have been broken up in Buffalo, Detroit, Seattle, Portland, Tampa, and North Carolina.[71] A plot to destroy the Brooklyn Bridge was discovered and prevented before the terrorists could act upon it. Alleged "sleeper agents" have been discovered and arrested in numerous cities throughout the United States. All in all, supporters contend that the USA Patriot Act has made the United States safer from terrorism.

Criticisms of the USA Patriot Act

Former Vice President Al Gore declared in a public address, "I believe the Patriot Act has turned out to be, on balance, a terrible mistake. . . . The Patriot Act must be repealed."[72] Many agree with Mr. Gore's analysis. Critics argue that even the name is offensive as "it implies that the purpose of the act is to promote patriotism and that those not cooperating with it are somehow less patriotic."[73] Since passing the Patriot Act, Congress has expressed its reservation with its implementation by various amendments to cut the use of federal funds for the Patriot Act, particularly the "sneak-and-peek" searches of people's homes and offices and the repeal of the library and personal records searches.[74]

Former Attorney General John Ashcroft argued that the Patriot Act has historical precedent in that the Kennedy Administration used the same strategy in its attack on organized crime. In its fight against organized crime, President Kennedy ordered law enforcement agents to arrest mobsters for "spitting on the sidewalk if that's how you can get them."[75] While Ashcroft argues that the Patriot Act tactics are similar to those used by the Kennedy Administration, critics argue that the Patriot Act violates civil liberties as it "expands the sidewalk" to allow for the arrest of persons performing constitutionally protected speech and actions.[76]

Alarmed that the Patriot Act may violate constitutional rights, some police departments have refused to cooperate with FBI agents in terrorism investigations. Most prominent was the refusal of the Portland, Oregon, Police Department to interview foreign students as requested by the FBI. The Portland Police Department refused to conduct the interviews, claiming that the FBI did not offer any specific information about any crimes with which the individuals might be involved. Furthermore, the Portland Police believed that the questions that the FBI wanted them to ask the students were inappropriate, as they asked about noncriminal matters such as religious beliefs and other questions not specifically related to criminal activity or knowledge.[77]

Criticism of the Patriot Act is closely associated with criticism of former Attorney General John Ashcroft, who is seen as the prime architect of the legislation. Critics of Ashcroft accused him of "a seemingly insatiable appetite for more federal law-enforcement power."[78] Other critics are more direct, as illustrated by Jim Hightower's strong criticism of the Patriot Act. Hightower said,

After two years of "protecting" our freedom by suspending our freedoms, here's what scares me: Not al Qaeda, but our own homegrown autocrats—Ashcroft and other political extremists and opportunists who fan the embers of fear, then drape a veil of patriotism over their push to impose a police-state mentality on our Land of the Free. . . . These people are NUTS! And dangerous. They can't find Osama bin Laden . . . , but they have amassed a shiny new arsenal of police powers so they can always find you and me.[79]

Senator Howard Dean said, "Ashcroft is not a patriot. John Ashcroft is a descendant of Joseph McCarthy."[80]

The Bush Administration defends the use of the Patriot Act by pointing to the over 5,000 foreign nationals who have been detained since the September 11, 2001, attacks, but critics quickly point out that very few of those detained were ever charged with any crime.[81] As a result of these thousands of dismissed charges, there were over 1,000 complaints of Patriot Act–related abuse of civil rights or civil liberties during the first six months of 2003.[82] For example, a report released in December 2003 by the Department of Justice's inspector general concluded that at one federal prison in Brooklyn, some staff members physically abused many illegal immigrants arrested after the September 11 attacks, taunted them, and illegally taped their meetings with lawyers.[83]

Critics argue that the Patriot Act permits people to be locked up not for what they have done but for suspicion of what they might do.[84] As a result of this orientation, many persons of Middle East descent have been picked up and detained, often in secret and without any charges being filed against them. Some critics charge that numerous civil rights violations have occurred under the Patriot Act but that only a few of the abuses have surfaced because the victims of this abuse are afraid to complain. David Cole, in his book *Enemy Aliens,* accuses the government of treating thousands of people as suspected terrorists who turned out to have nothing to do with terrorism.

For example, one of the many charges of abuse is the case of Mahner Arar. Mr. Arar, who holds dual Canadian and Syrian citizenships, was detained as a terrorist suspect at New York's John F. Kennedy Airport in September 2002. Although never charged, he was deported to Syria a month later without the knowledge of Canadian officials. He spent 10 months in solitary confinement in Syria and said he was tortured before being released to return to his family in Ottawa.[85] Former U.S. Attorney General John Ashcroft said that the Syrian embassy in Washington denied that Arar was tortured.[86] Critics are skeptical of the denial and call the deportation of Mr. Arar to Syria "torture-by-proxy."[87] Christopher Pyle, in the *San Francisco Chronicle,* cited an unnamed intelligence official who confirmed the practice of torture-by-proxy. He said the intelligence agencies use the practice of surreptitiously shipping a suspect to another country where it is known that police routinely practice torture "extraordinary rendition."[88]

Mr. Arar denied any connect to terrorism despite the fact that he signed confessions to the contrary. He said the confessions were obtained by torture and were not true: "I agreed to sign any document they put before me, even those I wasn't allowed to read. And eventually I would say anything at all to avoid more torture."[89] Mr. Arar was eventually returned to Canada and released without being charged with anything. One former Canadian official, commenting on the Arar case, was quoted as saying, "Accidents will happen" in the war on terror.[90] Protests by the Canadian government resulted in reassurances by Attorney General John Ashcroft that in the future the Canadian government would be notified before any

Canadian citizen was deported to another country. Mr. Arar has filed a lawsuit against the U.S. government. However, government attorneys claim that the case cannot be adjudicated because it "would involve the revelation of state secrets."[91]

Never Again: Defense of the Patriot Act and the Call for Expanded Powers

Despite the widespread and vocal criticism of the Patriot Act, the Bush Administration continues not only to defend the Patriot Act but also to champion it, arguing that "the stakes are too high to risk another attack. In an era of nuclear, chemical, and biological weapons of mass destruction, it is too costly to permit even a single al-Qaida operative to strike again."[92] In response to attacks on the Patriot Act, former Attorney General John Ashcroft rebutted, "If we knew then what we know now, we would have passed the Patriot Act six months before September 11 rather than six weeks after the attacks."[93] Ashcroft has defended the aggressive pursuit and prosecution of terrorists, claiming, "The cause we have chosen is just. The course we have chosen is constitutional."[94]

In his 2004 State of the Union Address, President Bush said of the threat of terrorism, "Our greatest responsibility is the active defense of the American people. Twenty-eight months have passed since September the 11th, 2001—over two years without an attack on American soil—and it is tempting to believe that the danger is behind us. The hope is understandable, comforting—and false. . . . The terrorists continue to plot against America and the civilized world."[95]

The Movement for Expanded Power: Patriot II

Indeed, it does appear that the possibility of another terrorist attack on U.S. soil is very real. In August 2003, a research company reported that the United States is the fourth most likely of 186 countries to be the target of a terrorist attack within the next 12 months.[96] President Bush endorsed this assessment with a message to Congress to "untie the hands of law enforcement and enact broader search-and-seizure powers and wider use of the death penalty to combat terrorism."[97] President Bush has argued that because of the imminent threat of a terrorist attack on U.S. soil, greater powers need to be given to law enforcement agencies rather than curtail the powers granted them by the Patriot Act. In his 2004 State of the Union Address, President Bush pointed out that "key provisions of the Patriot Act are set to expire next year [2005]. The terrorist threat will not expire on that schedule. . . . You need to renew the Patriot Act."[98] John Ashcroft has chided critics for becoming complacent and apathetic after the September 11 attacks, saying, "Just two years have passed but already it has become difficult for some Americans to recall the shock, anger, grief and anguish of that day."[99]

Former Attorney General Ashcroft has argued the Patriot Act does not give enough power to law enforcement and there is a need for expanded law enforcement powers. He argued for expanding the power of federal agents to use wiretaps, surveillance, and other investigative methods and to share intelligence information to give law enforcement the technological tools to anticipate, adapt, and out-think terrorists planning attacks.[100] The

Bush Administration argues that legislation is needed that would provide expanded search-and-seizure powers to federal law enforcement agents and alter the definition of terrorism to allow the government to pursue the "lone wolf" terrorist.

The Bush Administration has argued for a number of other provisions to be included in what is being commonly called the Patriot II bill. Figure 3.3 provides a list of major pro-

FIGURE 3.3 • *Major Provisions of the Legislative Draft of the Bill Entitled Patriot II: The Domestic Security Enhancement Act of 2003*

- Patriot II would enhance the Department of Justice's ability to deny releasing material on suspect terrorists in government custody through the Freedom of Information Act (FOIA) requests.
- The law would restrict public access through the FOIA to "worst-case scenario" reports required by the Environmental Protective Agency for companies that use potentially dangerous chemicals. Such "worst-case scenario" reports are considered potential "roadmaps for terrorists."
- The law would authorize creation of a DNA database on "suspected terrorists." The definition of *suspected terrorist* is broad and includes noncitizens suspected of certain crimes or of having supported any group designated as terrorist. Critics claim that if a person who makes a contribution to a "charitable" group that is later deemed to be a terrorist group, even if the person was unaware of the terrorist nature of the organization, he or she could fall under the jurisdiction of this law.
- Patriot II would allow local and state police greater surveillance powers of individuals and organizations. Due to alleged abuses in the 1960s and 1970s, much of the intelligence-gathering power of local and state police agencies was terminated.
- Patriot II would create a presumption of "flight risk/harm to the community" for pretrial detention in cases involving terrorism. This would reverse the burden of proof. Normally, the prosecution must demonstrate that the defendant is a flight risk or is a potential danger to the community. Patriot II would shift the burden to the defendant to provide that he or she was not a flight risk or potential harm to the community.
- One of the more controversial sections of Patriot II provides for "expatriation of terrorists." It would give the Justice Department the authority to infer from conduct that a citizen who is a member of, or engaged in material support to, a group that the United States has designated as a "terrorist organization" will relinquish his or her U.S. citizenship and would be presumptive grounds for expatriation. This section does not require that the person actually engage in any terrorist act—only that he or she becomes a member of or provide material support to a terrorist group.
- The FBI would be granted powers to conduct searches and surveillance based on intelligence gathered in foreign countries, without first obtaining a court order. This is a significant change from present law, which creates a firewall between "domestic" and "foreign" intelligence.
- Patriot II would criminalize the use of encryption to conceal incriminating communications.
- Patriot II would expand the list of crimes eligible for the death penalty.
- The law would allow an individual with no affiliation with a foreign government or a terrorist organization to be deemed a "foreign power" for purposes of FISA (Foreign Intelligence Surveillance Act) surveillance of that person and those associated with him or her. This is the "lone wolf" provision. The bombing of the federal building in Oklahoma by Timothy McVeigh is an example cited for the necessity of the lone wolf power.

visions to be included in Patriot II. As has been seen in previous anti-terrorism legislation, many of the provisions are those powers not granted in previous bills.

It is argued that legislation expanding law enforcement search and seizure and intelligence powers could be used against domestic political protestors.[101] Critics believe that such legislation would authorize the government to investigate persons associated with such movements as Operation Rescue, Greenpeace, People for the Ethical Treatment of Animals (PETA), animal rights groups, radical anti-abortion groups, and environmental activists as if they were international terrorist groups. Drug dealers, for example, could be deemed "narco-terrorists" or contributing to the support of terrorism or a terrorist group.[102] Opponents argue that legislation authorizing such expansion of law enforcement powers would infringe on constitutionally protected civil liberties and rights afforded to the accused in a court of law.

Prosecuting Terrorists to the Fullest Extent of the Law

Retail stores often post notices declaring, "Shoplifters will be prosecuted to the fullest extent of the law." These notices are intended to dissuade the potential shoplifter, but many career criminals know that the threat of prosecution lacks any "teeth" because proprietors find that prosecuting a shoplifter to the fullest extent of the law is time consuming, expensive, and can possibility expose the company to a civil suit if the prosecution fails. Thus, many career criminals take such threats of prosecution with a grain of salt. There is a similar problem in the legislation to prosecute terrorists. The federal government has been successful at gaining greater ability to prosecute terrorists in federal criminal court, but, due to various reasons, it is often not possible to prosecute the accused.

It is true that a number of accused suspects have been prosecuted and found guilty of terrorism-related charges. For example, in August 2003, a software engineer pleaded guilty to federal charges of aiding the Taliban.[103] In October 2003, an Ohio truck driver who admitted that he plotted with senior operatives of al-Qaida to destroy the Brooklyn Bridge was sentenced to 20 years.[104] The accused man pleaded guilty after prosecutors told him that he could be declared an enemy combatant and locked up indefinitely at Guantanamo Bay, Cuba.[105] In November 2003, three men were sentenced to prison for their roles in a Virginia jihad network that trained members to support a Pakistani terrorist group abroad.[106] The common factor in these and many other convictions for terrorism is that the accused pleaded guilty and they were relatively low-level terrorist operatives.

However, accused terrorists who plead not guilty have been difficult to prosecute. One of the greatest difficulties in prosecuting accused terrorists is the conflict between national security and the consitutional rights of the accused. When prosecuted in a criminal court, the accused has the constitutional right to confront the witnesses against him or her, to call witnesses in his or her defense, and to have access through the legal process known as *discovery* to the evidence amassed by the government. Often, the witnesses are secret informers or intelligence agents or the evidence against an accused terrorist is from classified intelligence sources that the government does not want to provide to the defendant or make public in the court trial. For example, the prosecution of Zacarias Moussaoui, an alleged terrorist linked to the September 11, 2001, attacks, has been hindered by the government's refusal to allow

Moussaoui to interview witnesses who he claims can provide proof of his innocence because the government fears it would reveal classified intelligence.[107] The witnesses are captured terrorists and the Justice Department has refused to allow Moussaoui to interview them on the grounds that their testimony may divulge national security secrets and interrupt the government's effort to interrogate them for information that might preempt terrorist attacks.[108] The Justice Department's refusal to permit the interviews has caused the court to make several rulings against the government's case that will make it more difficult to prosecute Moussaoui. Among those rulings is a prohibition against seeking the death penalty and a prohibition against any allegations that Zacarias Moussaoui was linked to the terrorist attacks on September 11, 2001.[109] Despite the government's argument that access to the witnesses would compromise national security, the court has ruled that Moussaoui's constitutional right to potentially favorable witnesses outweighs the national security concerns.[110]

Not only is it difficult to prosecute terrorists in criminal court in the United States but also the refusal of the United States to reveal classified information to foreign courts can hinder the prosecution of terrorists abroad. For example, In December 2003, a judge in Hamburg, Germany, released a Moroccan accused of aiding the September 11 hijackers because of the lack of U.S. cooperation in turning over evidence to the court.[111] Clearly, the prosecution of alleged terrorists can be a most difficult task. Although the government wants to prosecute and imprison the alleged terrorist, the fear that public testimony or access by the accused to intelligence data often compromise national security hinders the prosecution.

Even when accused terrorists are convicted in criminal court, they have the right to appeal their conviction. For example, the lawyers for three of four terrorists convicted in the 1998 embassy bombing of two U.S. embassies in Africa have asked a federal judge in Manhattan for a new trial, citing jury irregularities and other information that they contend could have affected the verdicts.[112] Thus, fighting terrorism though the criminal courts is fraught with loopholes and often lacks the finality that is promised by those who advocate that expanded law enforcement powers and legislation reduce the vulnerability to terrorism.

Conclusion: The Balance between Liberty and National Security

Throughout history when there have been perceived threats to national security, it was thought by some that national security would be enhanced if certain constitutional rights were suspended or new powers were bestowed on the government. Enhancing national security by legislating new powers and slighting constitutional rights has always proven to be controversial and opposed by civil libertarians on the grounds that it needlessly reduces the civil liberties of citizens and does not promote national security.

This chapter has illustrated how, on many occasions, the United States has adopted legislation aimed at improving national security at the expense of civil liberties. Whether it is the Sedition Acts of 1798 and 1800, the Ku Klux Act, the suspension of habeas corpus during the American Civil War, the Sedition Act of 1919, or the Red Scare, the government promised security in exchange for the concession of civil liberties.

One of the lessons of history is that the balance between liberty and national security is like a pendulum, swinging from one extreme to the other. Throughout history when civil liberties have been given up in the name of national security, after the threat passes the pendulum swings back and civil liberties are restored. For example, during World War II, the perceived threat from Japanese American people living on the West Coast was such that thousands of people of Japanese ancestry, many of them U.S. citizens, were forced to give up their land, possessions, careers, and freedom and were relocated to internment camps. However, after the war, the egregious violation of civil rights to these people was recognized and the U.S. government issued an apology and reparations were paid to those who were interned. Thus, there is a history of moving to reduce civil rights to enhance national security followed by a movement to restore civil rights after the threat has passed.

In looking at the bigger picture, civil rights have continued to expand in the United States. When a threat to national security subsides, not only are liberties restored but often they are also enhanced. The challenge posed by the war on terrorism is determining at what point the "war is won" and civil liberties can be restored. It has been more than four years since the September 11 terrorist attack and some think that it is time to recalibrate the balance between liberty and security.[113] However, there appears to be no movement by the U.S. government toward such recalibration. In fact, if anything, it appears that the government is pursuing even more powers and capitulation of civil liberties. The war against terrorism appears to be open-ended, with no end in sight. Former Attorney General Ashcroft, for example, certainly did not concede that there needed to be a reversing of the pendulum when he accused those opposed to the Justice Department's anti-terrorism proposals as "providing ammunition to America's enemies." He said, "To those who scare peace-loving people with phantoms of lost liberty, my message is this: your tactics only aid terrorists."[114] There appears to be no time soon when the pendulum will reverse.

Public opinion appears to be relatively tolerant of the new powers granted to law enforcement. A 2003 Monitor/TIPP poll reported that 38 percent of respondents were satisfied that the Bush Administration was honoring civil liberties and the USA Patriot Act was just right; 12 percent said the Patriot Act gave the government too little power; and only 28 percent said it gave the government too much power.[115] The Christian Science Monitor/TIPP poll also reported that 31 percent of the respondents were more concerned about the threat of terrorism, whereas only 17 percent of the respondents were concern about losing legal and privacy rights. The majority of respondents (62 percent) reported that they believed alleged terrorists should be tried in military tribunals rather than conventional criminal courts. The Justice Department website Preserving Life and Liberty asked the question, "Do you think the Patriot Act goes too far, is about right, or does not go far enough in restricting people's civil liberties to fight terrorism?" Of the people polled, 48 percent said that the Patriot Act was "about right"; 55 percent of the respondents agreed that the Patriot Act is a good thing for America; and 91 percent said that the Patriot Act has not affected their civil liberties. It appears that in the face of the threat of terrorist, at least for the present, the public is more concerned about the threat of terrorism rather than the loss of freedoms. Furthermore, Americans seem resigned to the curtailing of civil liberties, as a poll found that 51 percent of people believe it is necessary for average people to give up some individual freedom as part of the fight against terrorism.[116]

Chapter Summary

- Law has always been used as a strategy to enhance national security.
- Early legislation to promote national security includes the Alien Act, the Sedition Act, the Force Act, the Ku Klux Act, the Espionage Act, and the Sedition Act (1919).
- The Reagan Administration used classified presidential directives to develop a more effective response to terrorism. The administration first defined which agency was the lead agency in responding to various terrorist threats, focused on defending commercial civilian aviation from terrorist attacks, recognized the threat of state-sponsored terrorism, and established the nonconcession negotiation policy with terrorists.
- In the 1980s, congressional legislation was passed to reduce the nation's vulnerability to terrorism. This legislation provided for international cooperation, cut off funding to terrorist nations, promoted aviation security, and responded to the threat of biological attack by terrorists
- The Omnibus Counterterrorism Act of 1995 and the Anti-Terrorism and Effective Death Penalty Act of 1996 were the backbone of terrorism legislation until the passage of the USA Patriot Act.
- President Bush's Enemy Combatant Executive Order calls for the detention of "enemy combatants" captured and detained in the war on Afghanistan and al-Qaida. The act denies the prisoners prisoner-of-war status, access to civilian courts, and the right to an attorney, and allows them to be held indefinitely without charges. It provides for a trial by military tribunal with reduced civil rights. The Bush Administration has extended the jurisdiction of the executive order to U.S. citizens. The enemy combatant executive order has been appealed by critics to the United States Supreme Court as unconstitutional.
- The USA Patriot Act provides expanded powers to government agencies. It removes some civil liberty protections for those accused or detained under the Patriot Act. The investigative powers granted to the Federal Bureau of Investigation have been criticized as unconstitutional.
- The federal government strongly defends the need for expanded powers and curtailed civil liberties. It argues that essential constitutional rights are protected and the government can more effectively defend against attacks by terrorists.
- Prosecuting accused terrorists under the new laws is often difficult due to the conflict between national security and constitutionally protected rights. Some prosecutions have been hindered due to the government's concern over disclosure of information that would harm national security.
- The balance between national security and civil liberties is like a pendulum, swinging from one extreme to the other. Often, after the threat to national security has passed, there is a return to more emphasis on protecting civil liberties. With no end in sight to the war on terrorism, it is difficult to predict when the pendulum will swing toward protecting liberties.
- Public opinion is relatively tolerant of the new powers granted to law enforcement. Most people are willing to give up some individual freedom as a part of the fight against terrorism.

Terrorism and You _____

Understanding This Chapter

1. What have been the reasons cited for using legislation to promote national security?

2. What did the Alien Act and the Sedition Act (1798) prohibit? Why did Thomas Jefferson and James Madison criticize the act?

3. How did the Force Act and Ku Klux Act abridge the constitutional rights of citizens in the southern states after the Civil War? What was the purpose of the acts?

4. What did the Espionage Act (1918) and the Sedition Act (1919) prohibit? Why were these acts controversial?

5. Why was the decade of the 1980s a watershed in terrorism legislation and presidential directives?

6. What important National Security Decision Directives were issued by President Reagan and what were their contribution to the U.S. policy in responding to terrorism?

7. Discuss the importance of the Omnibus Counterterrorism Act of 1995 and the Anti-Terrorism and Effective Death Penalty Act of 1996 as strategies in fighting terrorism.

8. What are the provisions of the Enemy Combatant Executive Order issued by President Bush? How is the status of *enemy combatant* different from *prisoner of war* or *criminal defendant?* Why is the executive order criticized?

9. What are the provisions of the USA Patriot Act? Why is the law criticized? What is the defense of the government against these criticisms?

10. Why is it difficult to prosecute accused terrorists in criminal court?

Thinking about How Terrorism Touches You

1. Why are people willing to give up civil liberties during perceived threats to national security? What liberties would you be willing to give up to help fight terrorism? Why?

2. Legislation to protect national security has often been accused of impacting persons and rights not directly connected to national security. Do you agree with this criticism? Why or why not?

3. It is often said that if you have nothing to hide, you should have no fear of the powers granted to law enforcement agencies expanding their powers of search and seizure. Do you agree with this statement? Why or why not?

4. The Enemy Combatant Executive Order has been extended to apply to U.S. citizens on U.S. soil. Do you think it is a violation of the Constitution for the president to have the power to detain U.S. citizens in the United States indefinitely in military prison without providing them access to the courts, the right to an attorney, or the right to know the charges against them? Why or why not?

5. Does it bother you that the Federal Bureau of Investigation has the authority to demand that your college or university library provide them with a list of the books you have checked out

and that the library is never allowed to inform you that this information has been forwarded to the FBI? Why or why not?

6. Polls indicate that most people favor giving up liberties as a part of the fight against terrorism. Do you think these polls are accurate? Do you think that it is necessary to give up liberties to fight terrorism? Explain your answers.

7. This chapter concludes that the balance between personal liberties and national security is like a pendulum. It is said that after the national security crisis passes, the pendulum swings back to emphasis on the protection of constitutional rights. When do you think the pendulum will swing back to concern about individual rights—3 years, 5 years, 7 years, 10 years? Why?

Important Terms and Concepts

Act to Combat International Terrorism (1984)
Al-Qaida
Ali Saleh Kahlah al-Marri
Alien Act (1798)
Anti-Terrorism and Effective Death Penalty Act of 1996
Aviation Security Improvement Act of 1990
Biological Weapons Anti-Terrorism Act of 1989
Camp Delta
Camp X-Ray
Court Martial
Enemy Combatant
Espionage Act (1918)
Extraordinary Rendition
Force Act
Freedom of Information Act (FOIA)
Geneva Convention
Guantanamo Bay, Cuba
Habeas Corpus
John Ashcroft
Jose Padilla
Ku Klux Act
Library Awareness Program
Mahner Arar
Military Tribunal

National Security Decision Directive 179
National Security Decision Directive 180
National Security Decision Directive 205
National Security Decision Directive 207
National Security Decision Directives
No-Negotiations Policy
Omnibus Counterterrorism Act of 1995
Omnibus Diplomatic Security and Antiterrorism Act of 1986
Pen Registers
Presidential Decision Directives
Section 215 (USA Patriot Act)
Sedition Act (1798)
Sedition Act (1919)
Sneak-and-Peek
Taliban
Task Force on Combating Terrorism
Torture-by-Proxy
Trap and Trace
Uniform Code of Military Justice
United States v. Harris (1882)
USA Patriot Act
Weapons of Mass Destruction
Zacarias Moussaoui

Endnotes

1. Presidential Decision Directives 39, U.S. Policy on Counterterrorism, The White House, June 21, 1995, www.fas.org/irp/offdocs/pdd39.htm.

2. Dennis Jett, "Dirty Wars Cast Shadow on Virtues of Patriot Act," The Christian Science Monitor, www.csmonitor.com, September 29, 2003.

3. Ibid.

4. Adam Liptak, "U.S. May Fine Some Who Shielded Iraq Sites," New York Times Online, www.nytimes.com, August 14, 2003.

5. The Alien Act is officially entitled An Act Respecting Alien Enemies, and the Sedition Act is officially enti-

tled An Act in Addition to the Act, Entitled "An Act for the Punishment of Certain Crimes Against the United States."

6. The Avalon Project at Yale Law School, www.yale. edu/lawweb/avalon/statutes/alien.htm, October 5, 2003.

7. The Avalon Project at Yale Law School, www.yale. edu/lawweb/avalon/statutes/sedact.htm, October 5, 2003.

8. The Avalon Project at Yale Law School, www.yale. edu/lawweb/avalon/statutes/alien.htm, October 6, 2003.

9. Houghton Mifflin, "Great American History Fact-Finder—Force Act (Bill)," www.college.hmco.com/ history/readerscomp/gahff/html/ff_069100_forceact.htm, October 6, 2003.

10. "Ku Klux Klan," Britannica Online, http://search. eb.com/blackhistory/micro/329/99.html, October 6, 2003.

11. Ibid.

12. James A. Fagin, *Criminal Justice* (Boston: Pearson Education, 2005), p. 106.

13. Neil A. Lewis, "Canadian Was Abused at Guantánamo, Lawyers Say," New York Times Online, www. nytimes.com, February 10, 2005.

14. Raymond Bonner, "Detainee Says He Was Tortured While in U.S. Custody," New York Times Online, www.nytimes.com, February 13, 2005.

15. Gerog Mascolo and Holger Stark, Der Spiegel, "The U.S. Stands Accused of Kidnapping," New York Times Online, www.nytimes.com, February 14, 2005.

16. Carol D. Leoning, "U.S. Offers Judge Secret Evidence to Decide Case," *Washington Post,* February 12, 2005, p. B2.

17. Sara Kehaulani Goo, "Ban on Matches, Lighters Vexes Airports," *Washington Post,* February 15, 2005, p. A2.

18. Ibid.

19. Senate Bill 390, The Omnibus Counterterrorism Act of 1995, section 23.

20. Senate Bill 390, The Omnibus Counterterrorism Act of 1995.

21. American Civil Liberties Union, "Open Letter to President Clinton and Congressional Leadership: A Joint Letter from a Coalition of Diverse Organizations Concerned about Civil Rights, April 26, 1995, http://archive. aclu.org/news/n042695.html, November 11, 2003.

22. Statement by the President, The White House, April 24, 1996, http://clinton6.nara.gov/1996, November 11, 2003.

23. Ibid.

24. Deborah Orin, "Bush: Captured Terror Fighters Are Not POWs," *New York Post,* February 8, 2002, p. 12.

25. "Illegal Combatant," Wikipedia: The Free Encyclopedia, www.wikipedia.org, November 17, 2003.

26. Neil A. Lewis, "Six Detainees Soon May Face Military Trials," New York Times Online, www.nytimes.com, July 4, 2003.

27. "President Bush's Order on the Trial of Terrorists by Military Commission," *The New York Times,* November 14, 2001, p. B8.

28. Neil A. Lewis, "Rules on Tribunal Require Unanimity on Death Penalty," New York Times Online, www. nytimes.com, December 28, 2001.

29. William Glaberson, "Tribunal Comparison Taints Courts-Martial, Military Lawyers Say," New York Times Online, www.nytimes.com, December 2, 2001.

30. Ibid.

31. Neil A. Lewis, "Rules on Tribunal Require Unanimity on Death Penalty," New York Times Online, www. nytimes.com, December 28, 2001.

32. Associated Press, "ABA Panel Wants Tribunal Rules Changed," New York Times Online, www.nytimes. com, August 12, 2003.

33. Jonathan D. Glater, "ABA Urges Wider Rights in Cases Tried by Tribunals," New York Times Online, www. nytimes.com, August 13, 2003.

34. Ibid.

35. Elisabeth Bumiller and David Johnston, "Bush May Subject Terror Suspects to Military Trials," *The New York Times,* November 14, 2001, p. B1+.

36. William Glaberson, "Critics' Attack on Tribunals Turns to Law Among Nations," NYTimes Online, www. nytimes.com, December 26, 2001.

37. Elisabeth Bumiller and David Johnston, "Bush May Subject Terror Suspects to Military Trials," *The New York Times,* November 14, 2001, p. B8.

38. Ibid., p. B1+.

39. Elisabeth Bumiller and David Johnston, "Bush May Subject Terror Suspects to Military Trials," *The New York Times,* November 14, 2001, p. B1.

40. William Glaberson, "Critics' Attack on Tribunals Turns to Law among Nations," New York Times Online, www.nytimes.com. December 26, 2001.

41. Neil A. Lewis, "Try Detainees or Free Them, 3 Senators Urge," New York Times Online, www.nytimes. com.

42. John Shattuck, "Human Rights at Home," New York Times Online, www.nytimes.com, December 25, 2001.

43. Ted Conover, "In the Land of Guantanamo," New York Times Online, www.nytimes.com, June 29, 2003.

44. Linda Greenhouse, "Justices to Hear Case of Detainees at Guantanamo," New York Times Online, www. nytimes.com, November 11, 2003.

45. Ted Conover, "In the Land of Guantanamo," New York Times Online, www.nytimes.com, June 29, 2003.

46. David Stout, "Supreme Courts Takes First Case on Guantanamo Detainees," New York Times Online, www. nytimes.com, November 10, 2003.

47. Linda Greenhouse, "Justices to Hear Case of Detainees at Guantanamo," New York Times Online, www. nytimes.com, November 11, 2003.

47. Ibid.

49. David Stout, "Supreme Courts Takes First Case on Guantanamo Detainees," *New York Times Online,* www.nytimes.com, November 10, 2003.

50. Linda Greenhouse, "Justices to Hear Case of Detainees at Guantanamo," *New York Times Online,* www.nytimes.com, November 11, 2003.

51. Associated Press, "Feds Outline Plan on Enemy Combatants," *New York Times Online,* www.nytimes.com, December 17, 2003.

52. William Glaberson, "Judges Question Detention of American," *New York Times Online,* www.nytimes.com, November 18, 2003.

53. Ibid.

54. Eric Lichtblau, "Enemy Combatant Decision Marks Change, Officials Say," *New York Times Online,* www.nytimes.com, June 25, 2003.

55. FindLaw, www.findlaw.com, June 25, 2003.

56. "Enemy Combatant Charge Marks Policy Change," *TalkLeft: The Politics of Crime,* www.talkleft.com, June 25, 2003.

57. Ibid.

58. Eric Lichtblau, "Enemy Combatant Decision Marks Change, Officials Say," *New York Times Online,* www.nytimes.com. June 25, 2003.

59. Ibid.

60. "'Enemy Combatant' Sham," *New York Times Online,* www.nytimes.com, November 19, 2003.

61. William Glaberson, "Judges Question Detention of American," *New York Times Online,* www.nytimes.com, November 18, 2003.

62. Yasser Esam Hamdi is a U.S. citizen who was detained as an enemy combatant but he was captured on the Afghan battlefield.

63. Neil A. Lewis, "Six Detainees Soon May Face Military Trials," *New York Times Online,* www.nytimes.com, July 4, 2003.

64. Sarah Lyall, "Families of British Terror Suspects Alarmed by Tribunals," *New York Times Online,* www.nytimes.com, July 4, 2003.

65. Agence France Presse, "5 Pakistanis Freed from Guantanamo," *New York Times Online,* www.nytimes.com, November 23, 2003.

66. Alan Cowell, "4 Britons and an Australian to Be Freed at Guantanamo," *New York Times Online,* www.nytimes.com, January 12, 2005.

67. Pat M. Holt, "Driving Dangerously with the Patriot Act," *The Christian Science Monitor,* csmonitor.com, October 2, 2003.

68. Brian Knowlton, "Ashcroft Pushes Defense of Terror Law," *New York Times Online,* www.nytimes.com, August 19, 2003.

69. Dante Chinni, "Ashcroft on Tour and Unplugged," *The Christian Science Monitor,* www.csmonitor.com, August 26, 2003.

70. Warren Richey and Linda Feldmann, "Has Post–9/11 Dragnet Gone Too Far?" *The Christian Science Monitor,* www.csmonitor.com, September 12, 2003.

71. Warren Richey and Linda Feldmann, "Has Post-9/11 Dragnet Gone Too Far?" *The Christian Science Monitor,* www.csmonitor.com, September 12, 2003.

72. Al Gore, Freedom and Security, www.moveon.org/gore/speech2.html, November 10, 2003.

73. Pat M. Holt, "Driving Dangerously with the Patriot Act," *The Christian Science Monitor,* csmonitor.com, October 2, 2003.

74. Jim Hightower, "Locking Down Democracy to Keep America Free," *Common Dreams News Center,* www.commondreams.org, September 10, 2003.

75. Dante Chinni, "Ashcroft on Tour and Unplugged," *The Christian Science Monitor,* www.csmonitor.com, August 26, 2003.

76. Ibid.

77. Jennifer Nislow, "Portland Just Says 'No' to FBI," *Law Enforcement News,* November 30, 2001, p. 1,9.

78. Linda Feldmann, "Ashcroft's Lightning-Rod Role," *The Christian Science Monitor,* www.csmonitor.com, September 24, 2003.

79. Jim Hightower, "Locking Down Democracy to Keep America Free," *Common Dreams News Center,* www.commondreams.org, September 10, 2003.

80. Associated Press, "Poll: Terrorism Laws Could Erode Freedoms," *New York Times Online.* www.nytimes.com, September 11, 2003.

81. Warren Richey and Linda Feldmann, "Has Post–9/11 Dragnet Gone Too Far?" *The Christian Science Monitor,* www.csmonitor.com, September 12, 2003.

82. Philip Shenon, "Report on USA Patriot Act Alleges Civil Rights Violations," *New York Times Online,* www.nytimes.com, July 21, 2003.

83. Paul von Zielbauer, "Detainees' Abuse Is Detailed," *New York Times Online,* www.nutimes.com, December 19, 2003.

84. Warren Richey and Linda Feldmann, "Has Post–9/11 Dragnet Gone Too Far?" *The Christian Science Monitor,* www.csmonitor.com, September 12, 2003.

85. Darren Yourk and Drew Fagan, "Grahm Confirms Arar Deal," *The Globe and Mail,* www.globeandmail.com, January 13, 2004.

86. CBC News, "Despite U.S. Denials, Graham Believes Arar Was Tortured, Spokeswoman Says," www.cbc.ca/stories/200311/20/arar_ashcroft031120, November 21, 2003.

87. Matthew Clark, "Preventing 'Rendition': The US

and Canada Take Steps to Ensure 'Torture-by-Proxy' Doesn't Happen Again," The Christian Science Monitor, www.csmonitor.com, January 13, 2004.

88. Ibid.

89. Maher Arar, "Delivered into Hell by US War on Terror," Common Dreams News Center, www.commondreams.org/views03/1210-04.htm, January 22, 2004.

90. Bob Herbert, "Thrown to the Wolves," New York Times Online, www.nytimes.com, February 25, 2005.

91. Ibid.

92. Warren Richey and Linda Feldmann, "Has Post–9/11 Dragnet Gone Too Far?" The Christian Science Monitor, www.csmonitor.com, September 12, 2003.

93. Eric Lichtblau, "Ashcroft Blasts Efforts to Weaken Terrorism Law," New York Times Online, www.nytimes.com, August 20, 2003.

94. Brian Knowlton, "Ashcroft Pushes Defense of Terror Law," New York Times Online, www.nytimes.com, August 19, 2003.

95. "President's State of the Union Message to Congress and the Nation," New York Times Online, www.nytimes.com, January 21, 2004.

96. Don Van Natta, Jr., "Report Calls U.S. a Top Target for Terror Attack within a Year," New York Times Online, www.nytimes.com, August 17, 2003.

97. David Stout, "Bush Calls for Broader Police Powers to Fight Terrorism," New York Times Online, www.nytimes.com, September 10, 2003.

98. "President's State of the Union Message to Congress and the Nation," New York Times Online, www.nytimes.com, January 21, 2004.

99. Mike McIntire, "Terror Lesson Fading for Some, Ashcroft Says in Manhattan," New York Times Online, www.nytimes.com, September 10, 2003.

100. Eric Lichtblau, "Ashcroft Blasts Efforts to Weaken Terrorism Law," New York Times Online, www.nytimes.com, August 20, 2003.

101. "An Unpatriotic Act," New York Times Online, www.nytimes.com, August 25. 2003.

102. Dante Chinni, "Ashcroft on Tour, and Unplugged," The Christian Science Monitor," www.csmonitor.com, August 26, 2003.

103. Associated Press, "Oregon Man Pleads Guilty to Aiding the Taliban," New York Times Online, www.nytimes.com, August 7, 2003.

104. Eric Lichtblau, "Trucker Sentenced to 20 Years in Plot Against Brooklyn Bridge," New York Times Online, www.nytimes.com, October 29, 2003.

105. Ibid.

106. Associated Press, "Judge Sentences 3 to Prison for Roles in a Jihad Network," New York Times Online, www.nytimes.com, November 8, 2003.

107. Neil A. Lewis, "Terror Suspect Wins Ruling on Questioning Qaeda Figures," New York Times Online, www.nytimes.com, June 26, 2003.

108. Neil A. Lewis, "Bush Officials Lose Round in Prosecuting Terror Suspect," New York Times Online, www.nytimes.com, June 27, 2003.

109. Kirk Semple, "In Setback to U.S., Judge Refuses to Drop Moussaoui Case," New York Times Online, www.nytimes.com, October 2, 2003.

110. Associated Press, "Justice Dept. Defies Judge on Moussaoui," New York Times Online, www.nytimes.com, September 11, 2003.

111. Desmond Butler, "German Judge Frees Qaeda Suspect; Cites U.S. Secrecy," New York Times Online, www.nytimes.com, December 12, 2003.

112. Benjamin Weiser, "3 Seek Retrial in Bombing of Embassies," New York Times Online, www.nytimes.com, January 23, 2004.

113. Warren Richey and Linda Feldmann, "Has Post–9/11 Dragnet Gone Too Far?" The Christian Science Monitor, www.csmonitor.com, September 12, 2003.

114. Neil A. Lewis, "Ashcroft Defends Antiterror Plan and Says Criticism May Aid Foes," New York Times Online, www.nytimes.com, December 7, 2001.

115. Warren Richey and Linda Feldmann, "Has Post–9/11 Dragnet Gone Too Far?" The Christian Science Monitor, www.csmonitor.com, September 12, 2003.

116. Associated Press, "Poll: Terrorism Laws Could Erode Freedoms," New York Times Online, www.nytimes.com, September 11, 2003.

4

Terrorists on Main Street, USA

The realization that international terrorists may live next door to us and be plotting to attack the airplanes, subways, buildings, shopping malls, bridges, and tunnels that we use has alarmed many citizens. There is evidence that there are hundreds of terrorists living in the United States, plotting attacks.

The emergence of international terrorism within our borders has moved the front line of domestic security to Main Street, U.S.A. Faced with the realities of the September 11 attacks, the mission of protecting our homeland now entails "keeping our neighborhood safe" in the most literal sense. Safeguarding our Nation against the terrorist threat depends on our ability to marshal and project appropriate resources inward. Respect for the open, pluralistic nature of our society; the individual rights and liberties of our citizenry; and our federalist system of government define the framework within which security can be implemented.

—The National Strategy for the Physical Protection
of Critical Infrastructures and Key Assets, February 2003, p. 3

Chapter Outline

Learning Objectives

- After reading this chapter the reader will know what evidence suggests that terrorists are already in the United States and some are plotting or awaiting orders to strike U.S. targets.
- The reader will know why terrorists consider the United States their enemy and some facts and fictions regarding motivations of terrorists.
- The reader will know why some think the United States played an important role in creating terrorism.
- The reader will understand why bombs are the preferred weapon of terrorists.
- The reader will understand the difference between strategic targets and symbolic targets and why it is so difficult to defend symbolic targets.

Introduction: Nearer than You Think

What do Washington tourists, Rachel Packard, who was convicted of attempted murder, the University of California, Berkeley, and New York apartment residents have in common? The answer is terrorism. Following the 9/11 attacks, public tours of the White House and the National Archives, which houses the Declaration of Independence, the Bill of Rights, and the Constitution, were suspended. Public access was not allowed until September 2003. However, unlike the previous 20 million visitors a year who visited these attractions, tourists who want to visit the White House must now contact the office of a member of Congress and obtain a security clearance and reservations. Terrorism has closed or restricted many of the buildings on Main Street, USA.

Rachel Packard's trial for attempted murder of 75-year-old Geraldine Transue was held in district court in Stroudsburg, Pennsylvania, about 90 miles from New York City. Closing arguments for the trial concluded on the morning of September 11, 2001. After closing arguments the judge informed jurors in the case that terrorists had crashed airplanes into the World Trade Center and the Pentagon and that many people had died in the attack. Following that news the jury was sequestered for deliberations. Packard's defense attorney argued for a mistrial on the grounds that the news of the terrorist attack compromised the jury's deliberation and subsequent verdict of guilty, as many of the jurors were concerned that friends or relatives many have died or been injured in the attack.[1] The judge denied the motion for a mistrial. The defense protested that terrorists had not only destroyed the World Trade Center but they had also destroyed justice in the courtroom.[2]

Enrollment of graduate students from abroad at the University of California, Berkeley, has dropped by one-third since the 9/11 attacks. Most believe the reason for the drop in international students is due to the new immigration and visa controls adopted after 9/11.[3] Other universities are suffering the same decline in foreign students. A national survey of 125 universities showed an average of 18 percent decline in international students. The United States does not produce enough qualified persons with graduate degrees in science, engineering, and math to meet the demand of private industry. Thus, international students have been a significant source of scientists and engineers for U.S. industry. For example, international students are 18 percent of Berkeley's student body but account for 34 percent of the doctorates awarded in math and engineering.[4] Nationally, almost half of the international students who receive their degree from a U.S. university remain in the United States and go to work for private industry. The impact of international students on the progress in technology is seen in the fact that immigrants have founded one-third of the new technology companies in southern California.[5] In striving to keep terrorists out, United States immigration policy has also kept out those who would significantly contribute to the economic engine that drives the progress of Main Street, USA.

Finally, New York City apartment residents find that anti-terrorist security measures hit them where they live. Security measures adopted by high-rise buildings in New York City after 9/11 have disrupted the delivery of food, packages, and newspapers. In many buildings new security regulations prohibit vendors, delivery persons, packages, and food from going beyond the lobby.[6] If residents want pizza or Chinese food delivered, it can be delivered only to the lobby, where residents must come down and pick it up. Dry cleaning, flowers, and packages can no longer be delivered to the residents' doors. Dog walkers, nannies, and contractors cannot pass beyond the lobby without prior arrangements and security approvals. Open houses for real estate listings are becoming an endangered sales strategy, as strangers cannot just wander into the building to tour apartments for sale. Many residents have protested the security regulations. Some have been successful in forcing changes in the restrictions but most are resigned to the fact that high-rise buildings will never return to the days of open access.[7] Fear of terrorism has resulted in a new look and feel to Main Street, USA.

This chapter discusses the concern that terrorists are already living on Main Street, USA, and are ready to attack. It examines who these persons are, why they want to attack Main Street and Americans, what they want to attack, and why the bomb is the preferred weapon of the terrorist.

The Terrorists: Posed to Strike Main Street

One year after the 9/11 attacks a government report concluded, "The United States remains extremely vulnerable to a major terrorist attack."[8] Less than 18 months after the 9/11 attacks FBI Director Robert Mueller issued a statement that "nearly 100 terrorist attacks, some intended to take place on U.S. soil, have been thwarted since September 11, 2001. [But] . . . many potential terrorists remain at large in the United States."[9] He warned that there are several hundred people in the United States who are potential international terrorists. Two years after the 9/11 attacks the Department of Homeland Security and the State Department issued public warnings of possible terrorist attacks against U.S. citizens.[10] President Bush followed with a statement to the press that "there was a real threat of a new terror attack" by al-Qaida on the United States.[11] Several months later the Arabic television channel Al Jazeera broadcast an audiotape said to be from Dr. Ayman al-Zawahiri, a senior figure in the terrorist network al-Qaida, saying, "With God's help, we are still chasing Americans and their allies everywhere, including their homeland." Three years after the 9/11 attacks, in October 2004, a video surfaced that threatened to seek revenge on U.S. citizens. In the video a suspected al-Qaida spokesperson announced, "American streets will run with blood." The spokesperson proclaimed that Americans "will mourn because they will be unable to count the number of the dead." Given these warnings it is no surprise that many Americans do not consider their country to be safe. There is clear evidence that terrorists are living in the United States and are plotting to attack Main Street, USA.

Why Do They Hate Us?

Terrorism was the major campaign issue during the 2004 Bush-Kerry presidential election. During the election campaign President Bush declared that terrorists hate Americans because "they hate progress, and freedom, and choice, and culture, and music, and laughter, and women, and Christians, and Jews and all Muslims who reject their distorted doctrines." While this explanation is well received by those Americans who favor Mr. Bush's handling of the war on terrorism, it is rejected by the many non-Western nations. Although many Muslims and Arabs abroad like aspects of Western culture, they don't like the Middle East policies of the U.S. government.

Overseas there is a widespread vision of the United States as "an imperial power that has defied world opinion through unjustified and unilateral use of military force."[12] For example, a survey of people in Europe and the United States found Americans and Europeans agreeing on the nature of global threats but disagreeing sharply on how they should be handled. Whereas 84 percent of Americans supported force as a means of imposing international justice, only 48 percent of Europeans approved of force as a means of addressing international injustice.[13] Disapproval of U.S. policy and Americans has steadily increased since 2003. In some places disapproval has dropped sharply in recent years. For example, 61 percent of Indonesians reported a favorable impression of the United States in 2002 but that dropped to only 15 percent in 2003.[14]

The invasion of Afghanistan and Iraq has caused many countries to question the credibility of the United States. This skepticism of U.S. intentions extends not only to Middle East countries directly affected by U.S. policies but also to Europeans countries, including allies.[15] A 2003 Gallup poll found that 55 percent of citizens in Britain thought the United States "posed a threat to peace" and 25 percent of Canadians viewed the United States as a greater threat than al-Qaida.[16] Among countries with predominate Muslim populations, people's opinions toward the United States and Americans is even more critical. A June 2003 BBC survey found that 60 percent of Indonesians and 71 percent of Jordanians viewed the United States as a greater threat than al-Qaida.[17] The disdain for Americans in Indonesia is reflected by posters proclaiming, "People hate Americans."[18] A 2004 international poll reported "people in the Muslim-majority countries of Jordan, Morocco, Pakistan and Turkey are suspicious of the United States and think it is trying to dominate the world and control Middle East oil."[19]

The history of the United States is seen differently from a foreign perspective. Americans are much more likely to "forgive" the United States for "mistakes" or to attribute "good motives" when intended actions result in harm to foreign countries. For example, most Americans rarely think of the treatment of Native Americans in terms of terrorism. However, Native American activists describe the historical relationship in terms of racism, hatred, and violent attacks. Many Muslim-dominated societies can easily identify with that description. Various U.S. government agencies and the Central Intelligence Agency have alienated foreign opinion by supporting training for the military of brutal regimes, supporting corrupt and brutal governments because they were "anti-Communist," and supporting coups, military invasions, and covert wars aimed at toppling foreign governments of which the United States did not approve. Examples cited by those critical of U.S. policy include the support and then overthrow of Panama's Manuel Noriega, the training of the Contras in Nicaragua, the support of General Pinochet in Chile, and the 1961 failed invasion of Cuba to overthrow the Castro regime. Critics of U.S. policy stress how the United States has frequently supported corrupt and brutal governments and these governments have often had dismal human rights records.

Why Do They Attack Main Street?

It is one thing to dislike U.S. foreign policies but it is quite another to express that dislike by randomly killing innocent civilians. Why do terrorists engage in what is perceived by Americans as destructive violence, indiscriminate murder, and irrational hatred? One popular, but flawed, viewpoint is that terrorists are "senseless," "mindless," "insane," or "madmen." There are two flaws in this perspective.[20] This explanation of the violence used by the terrorists fails to give any credit to the perspective of the perpetrators as to the purpose and effectiveness of their actions. Also, this explanation can have the unintended effect of lulling Americans into thinking that the violent acts of the terrorists are unplanned, unpurposeful, and unlikely to be repeated in the future. Data from studies suggest that, compared with the general public, terrorists do not exhibit unusually high rates of clinical psychopathology, irrationality, or personality disorders.[21] Given the long-term planning and secrecy involved in terrorist attacks, most likely even the terrorists would exclude from their inner-cell membership those individuals who demonstrated signs of instability or personality disorders for fear that such persons would increase the risk of discovery. Studies of terrorists conclude there is no single or typical mentality and no evidence of a common pathology that defines a terrorist. Furthermore, these studies suggest that the evidence does not support the hypothesis that there is a "terrorist personality."[22] However, there are two characteristics that terrorists seem to have in common (1) terrorists are usually males between 15 and 30 years of age and (2) terrorists apparently find significant gratification in the expression of generalized rage.[23]

Poverty and Lack of Education Do Not Cause Terrorism.   Another flawed perspective advanced to explain the violence of terrorism is that poverty and lack of education are the major causes of terrorist acts and support for violence. A look at the data seems to support this theory. Of the 90 million Arab youth between the ages of 15 and 24, 14 million are unemployed. In some areas, such as the West Bank, the unemployment rate is significantly higher. Often this unemployment is accompanied by little hope that the situation will change. Also, Arab economies appear to be fixated on oil and lack entrepreneurship and innovation. For example, one of the measures of a country's educational quality, entrepreneurship, and innovation is the number of patents for inventions its produces. According to the 2003 Arab Human Development Report, between 1980 and 1999, the nine leading Arab economies registered only 370 patents in the Untied States for new inventions compared to the 16,328 patents registered by South Korea. Despite large oil revenues the per capita income of Arab economies is low, and for those countries and areas that lack income from oil, such as the West Bank, the per capita income is among the lowest in the world.

Assessments of the potential for economic development in the Arab world conclude that these countries are lacking the infrastructure, productivity, and education necessary for the development of high-tech jobs.[24] However, when the profile of the terrorist is examined, such poverty and economic distress do not seem to explain why someone becomes a terrorist. In fact, the data seem to suggest that terrorists are recruited from persons who have long-standing feelings of indignity and frustration that have little to do with economic circumstances. Terrorists have a commitment to the furtherance of the goals of the terrorist organization they join. Therefore, affluent, educated people may care more about the political goals of a terrorist organization than impoverished illiterates do.[25] The data suggest that "any connection between poverty, education, and terrorism is, at best, indirect, complicated, and probably quite weak."[26] Even suicide bombers do not seem to support the theory that terrorists come from the ranks of those with nothing to lose. A study of the characteristics of suicide bombers indicates that suicide bombers are less than half as likely to come from impoverished families than is the population as a whole and are more educated than the population as a whole.[27]

Terrorists Are Not Brainwashed. Another incorrect profile is that terrorists are "brainwashed" or "hypnotized attackers."[28] One argument against this theory is that the 9/11 hijackers were able to live among Americans for years without attracting attention, without being in a controlled environment normally required for "brainwashing," and remained focused and committed to their suicidal plan.

Islam and Violence—Jihad. Finally, some believe that Islam is a violent religion that promotes terrorism, religious war, and suicidal attacks against Jews, Christians, and political enemies. There are 1.2 billion followers of Islam in the world and over 7 million in the United States. If violence was a major tenet of the Islam religion, it would be expected that there would be much more violence. "Mainstream" followers of Islam reject viewpoints that characterize their beliefs as promoting violence. Followers of Islam point out that the Koran, the guiding spiritual guide for Islam, rejects suicide. Suicide is considered a serious sin similar to the philosophy held by the Roman Catholic Church. Also, the teaching of the Koran prohibits the killing of noncombatants in war. The Koran commands, "Do not kill any old person, any child or any woman. Do not kill the monks in monasteries. Do not kill people who are sitting in places of worship."

The concept of "jihad," or "holy war," is cited as another proof that Islam is the main reason for violent Muslims. Religious leaders of Islam claim that Western misunderstanding of jihad has been long-standing and pervasive.[29] The word *jihad* comes from the root word "jahada," which means to struggle.[30] Most religious leaders of Islam interpret jihad to mean the struggle for self-control and the pursuit of virtue and submission to God in all aspects of life. This interpretation is similar to the concept outlined in the Christian New Testament when the Christian is advised to reject the desires of the "flesh" and pursue "spiritual" goals. Although Islam does consider the struggle against tyranny, exploitation, and oppression ethical and justified, it does not condone the killing of innocent people in that struggle. One Islamic source declared, "Terrorizing the civilian population can never be termed as jihad and can never be reconciled with the teachings of Islam."[31]

"Mainstream" followers of Islam argue that those who justify terrorism and the murder of innocent people in the name of jihad are "a handful of Muslims."[32] In some cases they deny that those calling for jihad are believers of Islam, but rather assert that they have taken verses of the Koran pulled out of context to support their own personal ideology and political goals.[33]

Motivated by Revenge and Injustice. Data suggest that "one of the most common motivations for joining a terrorist organization is the desire for revenge or retribution for a perceived injustice."[34] Military response to terrorism seems to increase the terrorists' desire for revenge or retribution as it reinforces the terrorists' views of their enemies as the aggressors. Rather than extinguish terrorism, military response to terrorism may only make it easer for terrorist organizations to recruit new members.[35] For example, polls taken of Palestinians age 18 or older in the West Bank and Gaza indicate that support for attacks against Israeli targets ranges from 74 to 90 percent. Furthermore, 60 percent of the population surveyed reported they believed that "attacks against Israeli civilians have helped to achieve Palestinian rights in a way that negotiations could not have."[36]

Although it may be difficult to imagine that such "ordinary people" could be so callous to the violence they cause to "innocent" people, there are numerous studies to indicate that indeed "ordinary" people are capable of such violence. Psychologist Philip G. Zimbardo says that terrorists "embody creative evil at its worst."[37] He points out that numerous psychological research studies suggest that ordinary people can be recruited to engage in harmful behaviors against others with relative ease. For example, a study by Stanley Milgram demonstrated that ordinary college students participating in a study on obedience to authority could be persuaded to administer what they thought was a harmful or deadly electrical shock to peers participating in a "learning experiment." Studies have showed that elementary students can be quickly taught to discriminate against their peers based solely on eye color. Thus, it is not surprising to find that given the right circumstances, people can become disposed to disregard the humanity of those they hate and to discriminate against everyone they believe to belong to the group that is responsible for their downtrodden conditions.

When the actions and motivations of terrorists are viewed from the point of view of the perpetrator, one sees individuals who learn to use violence as a means of conflict resolution, and the cultural climate is such that there is a transfer of hostility. Transfer of hostility is when perpetrators believe their actions are justified and sanctioned because they see national leaders and other actors using violence as a means of conflict resolution. Once violence becomes accepted as a legitimate means of conflict resolution, a cycle of violence is created that feeds the development of terrorism. Psychologist Philip G. Zimbardo described this cycle of violence, saying, "Terrorists create terror; terror creates fear and anger; fear and anger create aggression; and aggression against citizens of different ethnicity or religion creates racism and, in turn, new forms of terrorism."[38]

Noam Chomsky, a vocal critic of U.S. policy, explained the spread of terrorism by reflecting on the viewpoint of the terrorist and the people supporting terrorism. According to Chomsky, the terrorist belongs to a population that sees U.S. politics as controlled by corrupt leaders motivated by greed. He asserts that the Bush Administration is seen by terrorists as "an unusually corrupt administration, kind of like an Enron administration, so there's a tremendous amount of profit going into the hands of an unusually corrupt group of gangsters."[39] Following this argument, Chomsky argues that as oppressed populations and nations realize they cannot resist the United States through conventional military strength, they find they must rely on terrorism, including weapons of mass destruction. He argues that U.S. "adventurism is just driving countries into developing weapons of mass destruction as a deterrent—they don't have any other deterrent. Conventional forces don't work, obviously, there's no external deterrent. The only way anyone can defend themselves is with terror and weapons of mass destruction."[40]

A 2003 interview with Syrians along the Iraq border illustrates Chomsky's point of view. In the interview local Syrian villagers complained that U.S. aircraft were firing randomly across the Syrian border, killing innocent Syrian citizens and firing on innocent Syrians who wandered by accident into the neutral zone that separates the Syrian and American positions.[41] Enraged by the killings, villagers cross the border and retaliate against U.S. targets in protest of the killings. Americans, in turn, detect and kill those Syrians who cross the border, further enraging the feelings of anger by the Syrians. This leads to further violence against Americans, which in turn leads to further U.S. military action. One villager interviewed summarized the situation by saying, "I never had a problem with the Americans but after what they did to my son, I hate them now."[42]

BOX 4.1 • *Up Close and Personal: Suicide Bombers*

Brian Jenkins, a terrorism expert, describes suicide attacks as "the benchmark of commitment for terrorists."[43] In the Middle East there have been more than 100 suicide bombings since November 2000. From May 2002 to May 2003, 54 Israelis were killed and 636 were wounded in suicide bombings.[44] There is no single profile of suicide bombers in the Middle East, as they include males and females and some are as young as age 16. The suicide bomber is the "low-tech, low-cost weapon of choice" for the contemporary terrorist organization. He or she has been described as the "poor man's F-16."[45] In Gaza many young people view the suicide bomber as an idol, similar to how American youth regard a movie star or singer. "There is a cult of the suicide bomber. There is no higher calling, no higher fashion statement, than the bomb around the belt. The martyr is worshipped. He is on walls and in windows."[46] Parents even dress their infants in "suicide bomber" outfits and proudly parade them or photograph them.

The suicide bomber was developed by Hezbollah in southern Lebanon in the 1980s and has been adopted as a routine strategy by Hamas and al-Qaida. In postwar Iraq the suicide bomber has proven to be an effective disruption of the efforts to rebuild Iraq.[47] The advantage of the suicide bomber is that the only qualification a person needs is "a moment of courage."[48] The suicide bomber does not need a lot of training nor does he or she have to have special physical capabilities. Suicide bombers are cost effective because they can inflict widespread death, destruction, and fear at a minimum cost.

Those who commit suicide or are willing to take their own lives are normally viewed as mentally ill in Western society, where the instinct for self-preservation is considered one of the fundamental foundations of mental health. It would appear on first examination that a similar view could be applied to suicide bombers. Many Islamic religious leaders denounce suicide bombers, citing the Koran as their authority as its teachings forbids suicide. However, studies of suicide bombers strongly suggest that the suicide bomber is not "crazy," "psychotic," or mentally ill.[49] Evidence

suggests that those who carry out suicide missions have usually seen what they view as "something terrible, some kind of atrocity" and see the suicide mission as a means of retaliation.[50]

The suicide bomber is not a "loner" or a depressed person but is someone who volunteers or is recruited by a larger terrorist organization. The suicide bomber is taught that in jihad the suicide bomber is a martyr. Being a suicide bomber is a way to be honored by one's society. The person is taught that the Koran does not teach that giving one's life in jihad is suicide. The belief is similar to that held in the United States regarding firefighters, police officers, and military soldiers who place their lives in jeopardy in the line of duty. A soldier who performs his duty when there are overwhelming odds of his survival or a police officer who risks her life to save others or to capture those who are considered a danger to others is not considered suicidal. Their actions are seen as heroism and a commitment to duty. Magnus Ranstorp, director of the Center for the Study of Terrorism and Political Violence at the University of St. Andrews, described the motivation of the suicide bomber as one spurred by honor and immortality. "In an instant you are propelled from being no one to someone who is glorified, and lionized with poems, and you live on in this historical chain of heroic martyrs, being remembered and saluted for longer than if you had not undertaken this kind of operation."[51]

Dr. Ariel Merari, head of the Center for Political Violence at Tel Aviv University, has extensively studied suicide bombings in the Middle East. He describes the process of a successful suicide bombing as one that involves numerous people and an extensive support group.[52] He observes that often suicide bombers are recruited by family members and undergo extensive preparation for their mission. Once recruited, the aspiring martyrs are told to write last letters to their families and friends. They are photographed in heroic poses and make videos that explain why they are becoming martyrs. The candidates are assured that their families will be taken care of by the sponsoring group after their death. Often the martyrs know or believe that their families will receive financial support not

(continued)

BOX 4.1 • Continued

only from the group but from other outside sup- porters. The suicide candidates are prepared for their missions and in the final stages are called "living martyrs."[53] Merari points out that at this time it is very difficult for a "living martyr" to change his or her mind without extensive loss of honor and shame.

Studies of suicide bombers suggest that the person is actually calm, even happy, during the carrying out of the bombing. Studies indicate that suicide bombers do not perceive themselves as "murderers." Despite the imminent threat of death, the bombers are convinced that they will receive great religious rewards for their actions and that their actions will advance the cause and secure retaliation for past injustices.[54] Interviews with suicide bombers whose missions failed due to defective detonators, or being intercepted by authorities before they could carry out their missions, report that they "never felt so calm in their life" and that they felt their actions "were the will of God." The calm state of the mind of the bomber during his or her attack is reflected by the description of the suicide bomber who drove a truck into the Marine barracks in Lebanon in October 1983. Marine guards said they were amazed that the driver was smiling.

Suicide bombers who fail to complete their mission do not attempt to kill themselves when captured and do not express regret for their suicidal

mission. Their primary reaction seems to be regret and depression because they failed to complete their mission. The unsuccessful suicide bomber is comforted by the teaching of jihad leaders that "whoever joins a holy war is considered a martyr and is worthy of entering Paradise even if he didn't accomplish his goal."[55]

Questions

1. It is reported that in the Middle East, for every suicide bomber "there are five who want to follow the bomber's example." There are a number of extremist groups such as Hamas in the United States but the United States has not experienced a wave of terrorist suicide bombers. Why do you think America has escaped such attacks?

2. Why do you think young people in the Middle East have taken to idolizing suicide bombers rather than condemning them?

3. Suicide bombers apparently believe their mission is motivated by duty and honor. Do you believe that the analogy comparing suicide bombers to military soldiers facing the threat of death in combat against overwhelming odds is a valid comparison? Discuss your answer.

4. What are your beliefs toward suicide bombers?

The U.S. Role in Creating Terrorists: Osama bin Laden and Al-Qaida

Osama bin Laden was born in Riyadh, Saudi Arabia, in 1957, the seventeenth of 53 children of Muhammad Awad bin Ladin, a wealthy businessman involved in construction and closely tied to the royal family of Saudi Arabia. Osama bin Laden's personal wealth has been estimated as high as $300 million but is thought to be closer to $25 million following the 9/11 attacks. Today, he is the leader of the al-Qaida terrorist network and is the alleged mastermind of the 9/11 attacks. He has a $50 million bounty on his head and is reported to be the "most wanted man in the world."

Osama bin Laden used his personal wealth and position to funnel money to support the Muslim guerrillas, known as the mujahedeen, in their fight against the Soviet Union in

Afghanistan. He formed his own group of "freedom fighters" in 1988, which the United States named "Qaida-al-Jihad," or the "base of the jihad." This group became known simply as al-Qaida.[56] Al-Qaida was instrumental in driving the Soviet Union out of Afghanistan. It is alleged that Osama bin Laden and al-Qaida were assisted by covert funding and training from the United States Central Intelligence Agency. The CIA allegedly funded and trained al-Qaida fighters because of their opposition to the Soviet Union. The CIA denies funding al-Qaida.

Following the withdrawal of the Soviet Union from Afghanistan, Osama bin Laden returned to Saudi Arabia and continued his support of al-Qaida and terrorism. He organized and funded training camps for terrorists, remained active in Afghanistan by providing support for the Taliban government, and allegedly engaged, funded, or masterminded numerous terrorist actions throughout the Middle East and the United States, including attacks in Somalia against U.S. troops, the 1993 World Trade Center bombing, the 1994 attempted assassination of Egyptian President Hosni Mubarak, the 1998 bombing of U.S. embassies in Kenya and Tanzania, and the 2000 *USS Cole* bombing. He was expelled from Saudi Arabia during the Gulf War for his outspoken rhetoric against the Saudi government for harboring U.S. troops and from Sudan in 1996 because of his terrorist activities. He returned to Afghanistan where he enjoyed the full protection of the Taliban government. In Afghanistan he organized terrorist training camps throughout the Middle East and continued his leadership and support of terrorism.

In February 1998, Osama bin Laden issued a fatwa (decree) calling for jihad (Holy War) against Americans. He asserted, "To kill Americans and their allies, civilians and military, is an individual duty of every Muslim who is able." The goal of al-Qaida is to work with allied Islamic extremist groups to destroy the state of Israel and to overthrow secular or Western-supported regimes and to establish a Caliphate, an Islam-based theocratic rulership, across the entire Islamic world. It is estimated that al-Qaida has more than 18,000 followers in more than 60 counties, including the United States.

Terrorism as a By-Product of the Cold War

A number of analysts blame the United States for the rise of Osama bin Laden and al-Qaida. As mentioned, the origins of the history of al-Qaida can be traced to the Afghanistan war of 1979–1992.[57] During this time the Soviet Union and the United States were engaged in a Cold War strategy that involved the use of surrogate groups to fight "communist-democracy" battles throughout the world. In these surrogate battles U.S.-backed forces would oppose Soviet-backed forces "for the hearts and minds" of the people of a nation. These proxy wars gave rise to a number of nationalist movements. In nations where the opposition was a guerrilla force, the CIA often provided training, weapons, and funding for the insurgent group.[58] This strategy has been characterized as a decision by the United States "to harness, or even to cultivate, terrorism in the struggle against regimes it considered pro-Soviet."[59]

The rise of al-Qaida is directly traced to the creation of a pan-Islamic front by the United States to fight the Soviets in Afghanistan. Furthermore, the skill and training of this group was largely underwritten by the CIA. It is estimated that 12,500 foreign fighters were trained in bomb making, sabotage, and guerrilla warfare tactics in Afghan camps that the CIA helped to set up.[60] After the end of the Afghan–Soviet War, elements from this pan-Islamic front migrated to Bosnia to fight alongside Bosnian Muslims against the Serbs.[61] In

2000, after the Bosnian conflict, these foreign Islamic extremists migrated throughout Europe.[62] Throughout the Middle East and Europe, al-Qaida was able to export its violent, now anti-Western militancy to dozens of like-minded regional terrorist groups.[63] This action created numerous "Qaida-ism" regional terror groups that were interconnected but distinct. One of the things they all had in common was that their principal enemy was the United States.[64]

After its role in various proxy wars during the Cold War, al-Qaida was able to reconstitute itself into an international network of Islamic extremist elements. Osama bin Laden had direct control of a relatively small portion of this network, but his influence and funding was extensive.[65] The Bush Administration attempted to link al-Qaida to Saddam Hussein, but a United Nations report found no evidence linking al-Qaida to Saddam Hussein's administration in Iraq.[66] However, following the U.S. invasion of Iraq, al-Qaida has claimed responsibility for various attacks against U.S. troops in Iraq.[67]

Europe as a Breeding Ground and Home Base for Terrorists

In October 2004, France's anti-terrorist police identified a young Frenchman killed while fighting the United States in Iraq. This is the first confirmed case of what is believed to be a growing stream of Muslims heading from Europe to fight what they regard as a new holy war.[68] It is suspected that this represents just one of hundreds of young militant Muslim men who have left Europe to fight in Iraq.[69] Furthermore, it appears that these terrorists all spent time in Bosnia, Afghanistan, or Chechnya for their training.[70] Intelligence data suggest that there may be approximately 1,000 young men from Europe and the Middle East who have been recruited to fight in Iraq. These radicals see themselves being victorious in Iraq in that they fully expect they will be able to force the United States out of Iraq in defeat, much the same as Osama bin Laden did the Soviet Union.[71] "These jihadists believe they can win by seizing cities and towns, killing American troops and destabilizing the country with attacks on the police, oil pipelines and reconstruction projects."[72] They have called for others to join them in jihad against the Americans, claiming that it is their religious duty to revenge "the torture at Abu Ghraib prison and rapes of Iraqi Muslim women."[73] The justification for the violence against Americans is justified by their claim that "the Americans are dishonoring our mothers and sisters. Therefore, jihad against America has now become mandatory."[74] The fear of European and U.S. governments is that after Iraq, these holy warriors will return to Europe or go to the United States.[75]

Terrorists on Main Street

Without a doubt the 9/11 attacks proved that terrorists have made it to Main Street, USA. They have arrived and they have the ability to carry out terrorist attacks on U.S. soil. Following the 9/11 attacks, the U.S. government has been concerned about "sleeper cells" of terrorists, terrorist supporters, and even U.S.-based training camps for terrorists. The number of terrorists, sleeper cells, and terrorist supporters in the United States is not known. An indication of the magnitude of the problem is the fact that following the 9/11 attacks, 240 visas were revoked because of concerns of possible links to terrorist organizations.[76]

One of the first major arrests of suspects alleged to be members of a sleeper terrorist cell was the arrest of a group of men from Lackawanna, New York, in September 2002. It was alleged by the prosecutor that the men went to Afghanistan to participate in a terrorist training camp and returned to New York to await orders to strike from al-Qaida.[77] Since then, numerous other al-Qaida terrorists or supporters have been arrested in the United States.

Other evidence suggests that terrorists were in the United States prior to the 9/11 attacks and remained in the United States after the attacks. This evidence includes documents found in association with the 2003 arrest of al-Qaida leader Khalid Shaikh Mohammed, al-Qaida's terrorist network operations chief. A search of documents resulted in the discovery of evidence identifying a dozen U.S.-based al-Qaida sympathizers.[78]

No Terrorist Profile Emerges. Those arrested in the United States for terrorism have come from varied backgrounds. Some of the alleged terrorists have lived in the United States for many years without attracting any attention. For example, Lyman Faris emigrated to the United States from Kashmir and lived in the United States long enough to become a naturalized American citizen. He was accused of being a terrorist awaiting orders to strike from al-Qaida. He was also accused of traveling to Afghanistan and Pakistan in 2000 to meet with Osama bin Laden and other al-Qaida leaders to plot an attack against the Brooklyn Bridge.[79] Faris returned to the United States in 2002 and lived and worked without attracting much attention. In fact, at his trial he was described as "a fairly ordinary person, not given to Middle Eastern attire and seemingly unmotivated by religion or politics."[80] Attorney General Ashcroft said, "On any given day, Lyman Faris appeared to be a hard-working, independent truck driver" but the truck driver's suburban life was a cover for his terrorist activities.[81]

Some alleged terrorists are U.S. citizens who have converted to Islam. For example, in June 2003, federal authorities charged 11 men in the Washington area and in Philadelphia with stockpiling weapons and conspiring to wage "jihad" against India in support of a terrorist group in Kashmir.[82] Nine of the 11 defendants are U.S. citizens and 3 spent time in the U.S. military. Justice Department officials emphasized how the arrests illustrate that terrorist threats can be close to home.

Some people arrested in the United States for alleged support of terrorism have been Islamic leaders. For example, one of the 11 men arrested in the previously mentioned example was Ali al-Timini, a well-known Muslim cleric and preacher in northern Virginia.[83] Another prominent Islamic leader arrested for terrorism was Abdurahman Alamoudi of Falls Church, Virginia. Alamoudi was arrested for making illegal trips to Libya and for accepting money from the Libyan government.[84] He is a former executive director of the American Muslim Council and president of the American Muslim Foundation. At one time he was authorized by the Pentagon to nominate candidates to be Muslim chaplains. He donated $1,000 to the campaigns of Hillary Clinton and George W. Bush and made a $2,000 donation to the campaign of Representative Cynthia A. McKinney, a five-term incumbent from Georgia.[85] (Both Clinton and Bush returned the donation.) The federal prosecutor alleges that Ali al-Timimi encouraged Muslims to take up violence against Americans.

Others alleged to support terrorism have included an international student studying at a university in Idaho who is accused of providing support for a terrorist website (he was found not guilty of the charges);[86] a 76-year-old New York jeweler who is alleged to engage in illegal money transfers connected to a scheme to provide terrorists with shoulder-fired missiles;[87] and a British citizen who is alleged to be an international arms dealer who offered to sell surface-to-air missiles to a U.S. undercover agent posing as an operative for al-Qaida.[88]

Not all of those accused of supporting terrorism have been foreign terrorists in the United States or members of sleeper cells. In fact, some of those charged with supporting terrorism in the Untied States illustrate how it is difficult to identify those in the United States who support terrorism. For example, Lynne F. Stewart, a well-known defense attorney in the United States, has been convicted of supporting terrorism by conspiring with a client who was a convicted terrorist being held in prison to aid him in communicating instructions related to terrorism with outside members.[89] Ms. Stewart's client was Sheik Omar Abdel Rahman, who was serving a life sentence for a failed plot to bomb New York City landmarks. The sheik is a blind Islamic fundamentalist cleric with a militant following in Egypt. Stewart met with Sheik Omar Abdel Rahman in prison and is alleged to have helped him smuggle secret messages out of prison. Stewart denies the charges and claims that she did not know of the sheik's ongoing terrorist activities.[90] She says she plans to appeal her conviction. Supporters accuse federal prosecutors of using Stewart as an example to intimidate attorneys who aggressively defend their clients accused of terrorism.

Another example of how those charged with crimes related to terrorism may not be easily identified as terrorists is the case of the Washington state National Guard member who was charged with attempting to supply intelligence of Army organizations and weapons systems to the al-Qaida terrorist network. Specialist Ryan G. Anderson, a U.S. citizen and Muslim convert, was charged as a result of a 2004 sting operation with aiding the enemy as he contacted what he thought were al-Qaida operatives and offered to transfer information about weaknesses in the military and "means of killing U.S. Army personnel and destroying U.S. Army weapon systems and equipment."[91] After his arrest those who knew Specialist Anderson were amazed at the charges. Some who knew him in high school and college described him as "a very active practicing Christian," "patriotic," and well informed about American government.[92]

Some who are charged with helping terrorists are difficult to distinguish from ordinary citizens because they are, for all appearances, ordinary citizens. For example, Susan Lindauer, a former journalist and congressional press secretary, was arrested in March 2004 on charges that she acted as an Iraqi spy before and after the U.S. invasion of Iraq. It appears that her motivation was monetary gain and not religious jihad.[93]

False Alarms—False Accusations.   Not all claims that terrorists are in the United States just waiting for orders from al-Qaida to strike or that truck drivers, taxi drivers, and lawyers are terrorist supporters have proven to be true. There have been several incidences where false alarms have been raised regarding the presence of terrorists in the United States who supposedly were ready to carry out attacks on U.S. soil. One of the most public of these false alarms was the nationwide manhunt in 2003 by the FBI for five terrorists who supposedly slipped across the Canadian border on Christmas Eve. The FBI issued a national alert, posted on its website the purported photos and names of the men, urged vigilance among law enforcement agencies, and advised the public to be cautious and cooperative in the manhunt. In early January the FBI called off the nationwide alert, stating that the information that initiated the search had proven to be incorrect.[94]

More serious than false alarms have been cases where innocent citizens have been falsely accused of being terrorists plotting against Americans. Karim Koubriti, a 26-year-old Moroccan immigrant, was accused of being a member of a sleeper operational combat cell

BOX 4.2 • *Case Study: Brandon Mayfield*

Perhaps the most egregious incident in the war on terrorism was the arrest of Oregon lawyer Brandon Mayfield when a faulty fingerprint analysis wrongly linked him to the deadly terrorist train bombings in Madrid, Spain, that killed 191 persons. He was taken into federal custody under a material-witness warrant. The statute authorizes such detentions under court supervision for "a reasonable period of time" in order to secure testimony. It has long been used with relatively little controversy in organized-crime cases.[95]

The FBI alleged that Mayfield's fingerprints were found on a bag containing detonators that were used in the bombing. He was arrested as a material witness but his treatment and press statements clearly indicated that the FBI considered him a co-conspirator. The warrant for his arrest was issued based on the government's argument that unless arrested, he would flee. The FBI based their arrest warrant on the fact that Mayfield was a Muslim convert, was married to an Egyptian-born woman, and had represented, in a child custody suit, one of the Portland Seven convicted terrorists. It appears that prior to his arrest he was subject to warrantless surveillance known as "sneak and peek" authorized by the Foreign Intelligence Surveillance Act (FISA).

Mayfield was arrested at his office on May 6, 2004, handcuffed, and led out to the media that had been notified in advance of his arrest. The FBI issued a statement that they had a 100 percent match of his fingerprints on the bag of detonators. Evidence of his guilt seem to be increased when another statement indicated that miscellaneous Spanish documents were found in a search of his house. (It turned out the Spanish language "documents" were Spanish language homework belonging to his children.)

The FBI arrested Mayfield on May 6 despite an opinion by Spanish authorities on April 21 that the fingerprints did not match those of Brandon Mayfield. Mayfield was detained for two weeks during which time numerous government-source leaks implied he was connected to the terrorists. During this time the Spanish government continued to release information that they rejected the

match. Finally the Spanish government issued a statement that the fingerprints in question matched that of Ouhnane Daoud, an Algerian living in Spain. On May 20 federal prosecutors petitioned the court for a dismissal of the arrest warrant on the basis of misidentification by the FBI of the fingerprint.[96] Due to the misidentification by the FBI of a fingerprint, the U.S. District Court issued the following rulings:

- The court orders the material witness proceeding dismissed.
- The court orders all property seized to be returned to the material witness and copies of any property retained by the government destroyed.
- The court's protective order is completely rescinded. All relevant pleadings previously filed are unsealed.
- The court orders all previously sealed minute orders be unsealed.
- The court orders the supervision of the material witness by Pretrial Services cancelled.
- The court will issue no further comment.
- The government is ordered to preserve all of the information it has obtained regarding the alleged fingerprint of Mr. Mayfield.

Not only was Mayfield released from jail, but the FBI issued a rare public apology, admitting it had erroneously matched his fingerprint to the latent print found on a bag of bomb detonators.[97]

Questions
1. That the government wrongly accused Brandon Mayfield is not questioned. The question is: Why was the FBI so eager to accuse him in light of the Spanish government's questioning of the fingerprint? Was it because Mayfield was Muslim? Samer Horani of the Islamic Center of Portland issued a statement, "If you are Muslim, you are suspect." Another source issued a statement, saying, "No Muslim is more than six degrees away from terrorism,"[98] Upon his release, Mr. Mayfield declared, "I have been

(continued)

BOX 4.2 • Continued

singled out and discriminated against." In the effort to arrest the terrorists on Main Street, USA, some errors might be made. Do you believe that, overall, the government's pursuit of terrorists in the United States has been bias free? Why or why not?

2. There was extensive negative media coverage of Mayfield's arrest. What should be the role of the media and the relationship be-

tween law enforcement and the media in the arrest of those charged with terrorism? If an innocent person is arrested and subject to negative media coverage, what are the harms? What are the remedies available to the person? Should the government owe compensation for wrongly accusing a person of terrorism and subjecting the person to media coverage? Support your answer.

and was convicted of material support of terrorism and document fraud charges in 2003.[99] He was first detained on September 17, 2001, when federal agents raided the apartment he lived in because a man on the terrorism watch list used to live there. Although the man on the terrorism watch list no longer lived in the apartment, agents found false identification papers and other evidence they believed were related to planned terrorist attacks. In October 2004, the charges against Koubriti were overturned and he was released from prison. When interviewed upon his release, Koubriti stated, "I thought it was a mistake or something and they would find out the truth. It took them too long to find out the truth. I'd feel better if it [his release] was 3, 6, or 30 months ago."[100]

Thus, although there is credible evidence and numerous arrests to demonstrate that there is serious threat posed by terrorists and supporters of terrorists who live and operate in the United States—often undetected and mingling with the tempo of everyday activities— there is also evidence to suggest that not all charges against alleged terrorists are legitimate. In the first half of 2004, the Justice Department received more than 1,600 complaints of civil rights and civil liberties abuses related to terrorism investigations by the Justice Department.

Preferred Weapon of the Terrorist: The Bomb

Knives and guns as weapons of destruction do not offer the advantages of bombs; therefore, the bomb has always been a preferred weapon of the terrorist. In the 1800s bombs were black power explosive devices with fuses that had to be lit by hand. Bombs were heavy, fuses were unreliable, and terrorists had to get within throwing distance of their targets to be effective. One of the keys to the increased deadliness of terrorist attacks is the advances in bomb technology. Heightened bomb technology has enabled terrorists to build smaller yet more powerful bombs with increasing control and reliability.

There are two important components to a bomb: the denotation device (fuse or trigger) and the explosive charge. The advances in these have revolutionized the deadliness of the bomb. The first fuses consisted of material impregnated with combustible material that was lit. When the lit fuse burned to the point that it contacted the explosive material, the bomb went off. The length of the fuse and the rate of the burn controlled the timing of the denotation. Generally, such fuses provided only seconds or a few minutes of time between the lighting of the fuse and the denotation of the bomb.

The next evolution of fuses was contact fuses that did not need to be lit. They were designed to initiate a small explosion upon physical contact. The small explosion would, in turn, detonate the primary explosive material. These bombs were more reliable, were easier to transport, and could be designed to explode without someone present to light the fuse. Thus, a contact fuse bomb could be set up so that when the contact fuse was released or was depressed by mechanical force, the bomb exploded.

Fuses

Modern fuses offer the bomber a wide variety of reliable ways to initiate a bomb explosion. These include radio-controlled fuses, timed fuses, altitude-sensitive fuses, pressure-sensitive fuses, heat-sensitive fuses, and motion-sensitive fuses. Today's fuses range from very sophisticated radio-controlled electronic devices to crude timed devices using a digital watch and a battery. These fuses allow the bomber to detonate a bomb from a great distance with remarkable reliability. Bombs can be planted at a site days, months, or even years in advance. For example, remote-detonated bombs can be planted in a building days before the planned explosion. When it is time to detonate the bomb, the bomber can accomplish this by merely pressing a button. Altitude-sensitive fuses allow bombs to be placed on airplanes and set to detonate only upon reaching a certain altitude. Thus, the bomb can be placed anywhere on the aircraft or in its baggage, but it will not explode until a predetermined altitude is reached. Bombs can even have multiple fuses. Multiple fuses can act as a backup detonation device to increase reliability or can act to make the bomb tamper-resistant. For example, a bomb with a motion-sensitive fuse, a timed fuse, and a temperature-sensitive fuse will be more difficult to remove safely from a public location and more difficult or impossible to defuse than a bomb with a simple timed fuse. With multiple fuses the bomb will explode if moved or if one attempts to neutralize it by freezing it. Most likely such a bomb will have to be detonated in place after evacuating people from the area before the timed device explodes.

Explosive Material

The second component of the bomb is the explosive material. Explosive materials can range from simple flammable-liquid bombs—a glass container filled with a flammable liquid and a fuse—to sophisticated military plastic explosives. The explosive power of the bomb has greatly increased and the size of the explosive material has grown smaller. A small quantity, as little as 4 ounces, of military plastic explosives can destroy a 747 aircraft in flight. If size is not an obstacle, large and powerful bombs can be made from commonly available—and relatively cheap—materials such as fertilizer and diesel fuel. The bomb that Timothy McVeigh used to destroy the federal building in Oklahoma was a homemade bomb using these materials. The wide range of explosive materials provides the terrorist with great flexibility in designing a bomb for a particular mission. Explosive materials can be mixed. A car or truck can be packed with an assortment of explosive materials to create a powerful destructive device.

If the mission requires a powerful but small explosive, military plastic explosives can be made so small that they can be sent through the mail, or they can be extremely difficult for authorities to detect as terrorists attempt to smuggle them onboard an aircraft. Because plastic explosives can be molded into different shapes they can be hidden in an unlimited number of ways—in electronic devices such as small radios, laptop computers, shoes, cans with false bottoms, and many other ways.

The Targets

Each year as the anniversary of the September 11th attacks draws near, the Department of Homeland Security has issued warnings that terrorists may attack the United States. The Department of Homeland Security, government intelligence agencies, and anti-terrorism experts all agree that, indeed, terrorists, specifically al-Qaida, continue to be determined to strike in the United States.[101] Intelligence agencies advise that the more time that passes without a terrorist attack since 9/11, the more desperate al-Qaida will be to carry off a successful attack. Desperation plays a role because al-Qaida fears it is losing its credibility.[102] Thus, as more time passes it is feared that al-Qaida will be motivated to achieve a "major spectacular attack."[103] What are the targets most likely to be attacked?

Understanding the Purpose of a Terrorist Attack

Terrorists fight from a position of military weakness and have no delusions that they are capable of causing the downfall of the United States through a military confrontation. What they count on is not so much the damage done by the attack as the widespread panic and public reaction as a result of the attack. Thus, the primary goal of any terrorist attack is not actual damage to the United States but widespread disruption of activities and public fear. The greater the disruption and fear, the more successful the attack.

Unlike government-sanctioned attacks using military forces, terrorists—both domestic and foreign—who attack the United States do not recognize the concept of "innocent civilians" and, thus, attack indiscriminately. The two most devastating terrorist attacks on the United States to date have been the bombing of the Alfred P. Murrah Federal Building in Oklahoma City by Timothy McVeigh and the September 11, 2001, attacks. In both of these examples the attacks resulted mostly in the death of what nearly everyone would consider "innocent civilians." For example, on the first floor of the federal building in Oklahoma was a day-care center. The bombing of the building occurred with complete disregard of the presence of these children.

Targets of terrorist attacks can be generalized into two types: strategic targets and symbolic targets. *Strategic targets* are targets that have strategic importance in the struggle for power, such as who controls the government, or geography. In Iraq, for example, insurgents and terrorists have attacked Iraq's national defense and police forces and buildings. They also attack power plants, oil pipelines, and businesses that collaborate with the U.S. forces. All of these targets can be considered strategic targets in that the terrorists hope that the damage inflicted by these attacks can impact the resources and resolve of the Iraqi people, U.S. allies, and the United States. In some cases evidence of the strategic value gained by the attack can be seen as nations withdraw their support of the United States in Iraq, as foreign contractors leave the country, and as Iraqi citizens become fearful of employment in the national defense and police forces.

The second general category of targets is called *symbolic targets*. The purpose of attacks on symbolic targets is to produce widespread fear, generate government overreaction, or persuade public opinion to change their support or actions against the cause of the terrorists. Symbolic targets may have some strategic value, but the purpose of attacking a symbolic target is significantly different from that of a strategic target. In a military campaign, strategic targets are important, as the end goal of the military campaign is to gain control of the government or geography. Terrorist attacks in the United States have focused on symbolic targets.

Symbolic Targets

The targets of the 9/11 attacks were considered symbolic targets by al-Qaida. It is believed the targets of the attacks were the World Trade Center Towers, the Pentagon, and Congress or the White House. Symbolically, these targets represent the business, the military, and the government of the United States. Although these attacks produced serious harm to the United States, it was not the strategic value of this harm that made these targets so attractive to al-Qaida but what they represented—symbols of American capitalism. Therefore, it is believed that al-Qaida will continue to focus on the same or similar symbolic targets. For this reason it is believed al-Qaida will continue to attempt to use aircraft as weapons of mass destruction and target major landmarks.[104]

Plans are underway to build a structure and memorial in place of the World Trade Towers. Officials have assured the public that the building will be built with greater structural strength, improved emergency escapes, and more flame-retardant materials than existed in the World Trade Center. The reason for this concern for increased strength and greater attention to structural engineering is that it is anticipated that this building will be an attractive symbolic target for future terrorist attacks. Given the focus on symbolic targets it is anticipated that al-Qaida will continue to consider a successful attack on the Freedom Tower as a significant statement of their power and ability. The 9/11 attack on the World Trade Center was the second attack. A 1993 bombing attack failed to produce the destruction anticipated. Thus, it is very realistic to anticipate that al-Qaida would consider a third attack.[105] It is likely that al-Qaida would even consider using aircraft to attack the building again. Although the building may be reengineered for great structural strength, the new generation of aircraft, such as the Airbus A380, will carry more than three times as much fuel as the 767 used in the 9/11 attacks.[106]

Symbolic targets are often referred to as "soft targets." This name refers to the fact that these targets often have little or no military or strategic value as compared to a military base, a nuclear power plant, or a hydroelectric dam and, thus, have few or no defenses against a terrorist attack. Often these targets have only minimum security and rarely is the security designed to provide a defense against a terrorist attack. Symbolic targets, or any target for that matter, that have defenses against terrorist attacks are referred to as a "hardened target." Soft, symbolic targets can be "hardened"—that is, defenses against terrorist attacks can make the target harder for terrorists to strike, but it is still a symbolic target. Strategic targets, by

BOX 4.3 • *Consider This: Politicians as Targets*

A major goal of terrorist attacks in the United States is to create widespread disruption. Politicians and political events are a prime target. The Department of Homeland Security issued warnings that the 2004 Democratic National Convention and the Republican National Convention might be targets for terrorist attacks. Suspecting the worst, each convention was designated "a national special security event." This designation put the Secret Service in charge of overall security planning for the event and made federal resources available for convention security. Thus, in addition to protection provided by the city and state, the conventions were protected by federal agents, military equipment, overhead flights by military aircraft, and constant radiation monitoring. Fortunately, nothing happened.

In addition to the conventions, it was feared that the 2004 presidential election might provoke a terrorist attack in the attempt to disrupt the elections. Prior to the elections, President Bush's national security adviser, Condoleezza Rice said that "terrorist groups could find the presidential elections too good to pass up." She indicated that appropriate measures were being taken to deter an attack seeking to influence the election's outcome.[107] Throughout May, June, July, and August, senior law enforcement and intelligence authorities made urgent public announcements warning that al-Qaida was ready to strike to disrupt the presidential elections.[108] On election day, terrorism command centers were activated in dozens of states and cities because of fears of an election-year terrorist attack. Many cities in the northeast had contingency plans in place to prevent a terrorist attack from causing widespread disruption of the voting process. Fortunately, again, nothing happened.

Congress itself has come under attack several times. It is believed that Congress (or the White House) was one of the 9/11 targets. Since the 9/11 attacks Congress has suffered two bio-terrorism attacks: one using anthrax and one using ricin, a deadly poison. A terrorist attack on Congress resulting in the widespread death of members of the House or the Senate could bring the U.S. government to a crisis. For Congress to do any official business, there must be a quorum of the members present—that is, a minimum of one-half of the members. Thus, if 50 members of the Senate were killed or incapacitated by a terrorist attack, the Senate would not be able to conduct any official business. If the Senate cannot conduct business, the government stops—bills cannot be passed, budgets cannot be approved, appointments cannot be ratified, and war could not be declared, as all of these require the approval of the Senate.

Fortunately, the Seventeenth Amendment provides that in the event of the death of a senator, the senator can be replaced temporarily by appointment (usually by governors). Likewise, a loss of a quorum in the House of Representatives would bring government to a standstill. However, unlike the Senate, members of the House can be replaced only by election. The death or incapacitation of half of the House of Representatives would paralyze government for months until special elections could be held to replace the lost members.

A new amendment would be needed to remedy this potential crisis in what is referred to as "continuity of government." So far, Congress has not made this a priority. The House has proposed a bill that would allow for special elections 45 days after a catastrophe if 100 or more of its members were killed.

Questions

1. Fears were raised of a terrorist attack disrupting the political conventions and the 2004 presidential election but nothing happened. Are fears that one-half or more of the members of the House of Representatives could be killed or incapacitated by a terrorist attack or other catastrophe reasonable? Should a new amendment be passed to provide for appointment or quick election of members of the House in the event of a catastrophe? Defend your answers.

2. Do you think the threat of an impending terrorist attack influences the political process and outcome regardless of whether there is such an attack? What influence, if any, do you think the video of Osama bin Laden released one week prior to the 2004 presidential elections had on the outcome of the election?

definition, almost always have defenses against terrorist attack, but their defenses can be improved or increased, Thus, even strategic targets can be "hardened" against a terrorist attack. Because almost anything, anyone, or any event can be a symbolic target for terrorists, it is impossible to harden all of the potential targets to detour terrorist attacks.

Targets Everywhere

The targets that could be selected by terrorists for attack are virtually unlimited. There is evidence to suggest that, indeed, terrorists have considered, even planned, attacking numerous symbolic targets in the United States such as raceways,[109] major sporting events,[110] and major landmarks in large cities.[111]

In fall 2004, the siege of a school in southern Russia by Chechen terrorists and the subsequent death of over 300 people, many of them children, caused great alarm in the United States. On the first day of school in Beslan, Russia, heavily armed fighters seized Middle School No. 1 and took up to 1,000 students, parents, and teachers hostage. The hostage takers placed explosives extensively throughout the school. Negotiations with Russian Special Forces broke down and an aggressive gun battle broke out with the hostage takers killing many of the hostages who tried to escape during the gun battle and the denotation of numerous bombs killed many others. The incident was so horrific that it has been referred to as Russia's "9/11."[112]

The alarm that the Beslan massacre caused in the United States was the discovery in October 2004 that a computer disk found in Iraq had diagrams and photographs of some U.S. schools. The disk had photographs and information about schools in California, New Jersey, Florida, Georgia, Michigan, and Oregon,[113] including transportation information for some of the schools. The Department of Homeland Security and the FBI said they did not believe the material indicated the existence of a serious threat by terrorists to U.S. schools.[114] However, the schools identified on the computer disk increased security and advised students and parents of the "potential terrorist threat."[115] One of the schools named on the computer disk was in Monmouth County, New Jersey, one of the wealthiest communities in the nation. The selection of this school would be consistent with the strategy of terrorists focusing on symbolic targets.

Domestic terrorists have also focused on symbolic targets. Animal rights groups have carried out attacks on research laboratories that use animals in testing. Eco-terrorists have executed arson attacks on businesses that they consider major threats to the environment. Car dealerships that sell large SUVs have been attacked. Pro-life terrorists have bombed abortion clinics and assaulted doctors and health workers who perform abortions.

Increased Threats to Infrastructure Targets

In August 2003, much of the eastern United States lost its power. Immediately the Department of Homeland Security investigated whether the widespread power failure resulted from a terrorist attack. Within an hour of the loss of power the Department of Homeland Security said it was confident that the power failure was not due to terrorism.[116] Although the strategy of al-Qaida terrorists has been to focus on symbolic targets, there is evidence that more and more terrorists are selecting infrastructure targets for attack. A successful attack on a vital infrastructure target can cause the widespread public disruption and fear desired by the terrorists and at the same time produce actual harm to the U.S. government, its economy, and its citizens. The primary infrastructure targets within the United States that have been or may be targeted by terrorists are bio-terrorism attacks on food and water and attacks on transportation systems other than aviation.

Food.   Much of the food consumed within the United States is imported from foreign countries. Many foreign nations, however, do not have as rigid control over possible contamination and bio-terrorism as U.S. food processors. Furthermore, in the transportation of the food from its nation of origin to the United States there are numerous opportunities for terrorists to introduce contaminants. To guard against bio-terrorism—and unintentional importation of contaminated food—the Department of Agriculture and the Department of Homeland Security inspect foreign food imports. Although a diligent attempt is made to detect any contaminated food or bio-terrorism, many fear that the resources to intercept and prevent such an attack are insufficient.[117]

Water.   Another concern is the possibility that al-Qaida terrorists might poison U.S. water reservoirs.[118] Water reservoirs for large cities are nearly always easily accessible to the public. In fact, many of these reservoirs are used for recreational purposes, thus ensuring open access to the public. The problem of protecting reservoir dams is complicated by the fact that many of the dams have roads that cross them and these roads are major transportation arteries. Although previous plots by domestic terrorists to contaminate the water supply of large cities have been discovered by law enforcement officials, no such plot by al-Qaida terrorists has been discovered. However, intelligence and communications among al-Qaida members indicate that such plans have been considered.[119] Plots to attack the water supply include poisoning the water as well as blowing up dams to disrupt the water supply and cause damage from the resulting flood.[120] As a result of this threat, many cities have taken steps to increase security of the water supply and dams. Some of these precautions include security patrols, closing access to dams and reservoirs, and prohibiting trucks and large commercial vehicles from crossing dams.[121] The purpose of banning trucks and large vehicles is the fear that these vehicles could contain explosives that could be detonated, thereby destroying the targeted dam.

Public Transportation.   In protecting the public transportation system, the United States has committed most of its anti-terrorism resources to aviation. As aviation targets have become "hardened," al-Qaida has shifted its attacks to other aspects of the public transportation system. Recent arrests of terrorists in the United States have revealed a growing threat of attack on the transportation system, including bridges, tunnels, and rail transportation. For example, in 2003, two men were arrested after police discovered them videotaping the Ambassador Bridge, the busiest United States–Canada border crossing.[122] In 2004, an alleged terrorist was arrested with blueprints for a Washington, D.C.-area overpass. Perhaps the alleged plot to destroy the Brooklyn Bridge received the most publicity. In June 2003, federal law enforcement officials announced they had uncovered a plot by operatives of al-Qaida to destroy the Brooklyn Bridge.[123] Lyman Faris, a 34-year-old naturalized American citizen from Kashmir living in Columbus, Ohio, pleaded guilty to supplying al-Qaida with information about how to destroy the Brooklyn Bridge by cutting the suspension cables.[124]

Faris, a truck driver, was described by Attorney General Ashcraft as a "sleeper agent" leading "a secret double life" and a man who supported al-Qaida's jihad against the United States while "freely criss-crossing the country making deliveries to airports and businesses without raising a suspicion."[125]

Rail security has lagged behind aviation security improvements since the 9/11 attacks. The Madrid, Spain, train bombing by al-Qaida on March 11, 2004, and the 2005 London bombings illustrate that the lack of security for rail transportation makes them a vulnerable target for terrorists. Trains and subways actually present a much more difficult target to defend than airports and airplanes. After the Madrid and London train bombing incidents, officials and intelligence agencies admitted that they were aware of the possible threat to rail transportation, but were resistant to undertaking airport-style security checks for rail passengers.[126] Even after the Madrid and London bombings made it clear that al-Qaida considers commuter trains and subway systems to be vulnerable targets, many security experts say it may be impossible to impose airport-type security for various forms of public transportation other than aviation. The sheer volume of public transportation using public transportation is one of the first obstacles. There are close to 2 million airplane boardings per day, but there are about 14 million people a day using public transportation, including buses, subways, suburban commuter trains, rail transportation, and ferries.[127]

In addition to the sheer volume of passengers, public transportation is very different in other ways. Public transportation is easily accessible. It is not necessary to present identification to purchase tickets, most passengers buy one-way tickets at the last minute, and trips can be as short as a few minutes. There is no checking of baggage or carry-on items and there is very little security training provided to public transportation workers.

Following the March 2004 train bombing that killed 191 people in Madrid, federal officials issued warnings to local police that terrorists might try to bomb buses or trains in U.S. cities.[128] As a result of this "wake-up call" new security efforts have been initiated for public transportation. Congress has provided funding to upgrade public transportation security and new security programs have been instituted around the country. Following the Madrid bombing, New York City took immediate steps to increase subway security. In July 2004, the Massachusetts Bay Transportation Authority became the first subway system in the nation to begin random searches of bags and packages on subway and commuter trains.[129] Riders who do not consent to allowing their belongings to be searched may be escorted off the subway. The most ambitious security enhancement for public rail transportation is the Transit and Rail Inspection Pilot, or TRIP, pilot program on Shore Line East commuter trains in Connecticut in summer 2004 to test a security system to provide for the X-raying of bags and the testing of passengers for potential traces of explosives. The pilot program is focusing on bombs, as there is minimum risk from hijacking or crashing trains into buildings.[130] Results from the pilot program will be used to design security enhancements to be applied to other public transportation.

The public reaction to enhanced security for public transportation is mixed. Surveys of passengers in general appear supportive of enhanced security but there is concern that delays and increased costs resulting from enhanced security could cause a drop in passengers.[131] Also, unlike airline pilots and flight crews who appear to universally support enhanced security measures, including the arming of pilots, public transportation workers seem less receptive to security training and prevention. One New Jersey Transit conductor who received additional training on responding to terrorism expressed the reservations of some employees. Commenting about these new security responsibilities New Jersey Transit is trying to persuade its employees to adopt, he said, "I'm a conductor, not a commando. For $24.11 an hour, I have no problem doing my job, but don't ask me to play Superman."

Conclusion

Main Street, USA, is not safe from terrorism. Both domestic terrorists and foreign terrorists have demonstrated their ability to carry out successful attacks. Hundreds of people have been arrested since the 9/11 attacks and charged with terrorism, plotting to attack U.S. targets, or support of terrorism. Those arrested have included truck drivers, taxi drivers, religious leaders, U.S. citizens, prominent defense attorneys, and spies. Studies suggest that contrary to popular opinion those who commit violent acts of terrorism are not "crazy" or psychotic. They seem to be motivated by revenge and a desire for justice. The United States is often perceived as the enemy.

International terrorists—as well as domestic terrorists—have focused on symbolic targets. These targets often have little defense against a terrorist attack because the sheer number of targets makes it difficult for the government to defend them. The preferred weapon of the terrorist in the United States is the bomb and the preferred target appears to be tunnels, bridges, overpasses, and public transportation.

Terrorists are among us. They live next door to us. They drive on the same roads we use. They photograph the bridges, tunnels, and overpasses we use as they plot to attack. They are determined in their purpose, hate the United States, and will attack whenever and wherever they can. These facts may alarm the public. They may cause some to change their behaviors, to alter their travel plans, or to be more vigilant when in public. These responses are justified given the threat. In fact, government officials encourage vigilance and reporting of suspicious persons and activities.

In the next chapter the extensive efforts of the government—at all levels—to protect Main Street, USA, are discussed.

Chapter Summary

- Terrorism has impacted the everyday lives of people throughout the United States, as there is clear evidence that there are hundreds of terrorists living in America, plotting attacks, and just waiting for orders to attack.
- Many in the world, especially terrorists, disapprove of the policies and practices of the United States. They see the United States as an aggressor and a global threat.
- Evidence suggests that terrorists are not "crazy" or psychotic. The actions of the terrorist, as seen from the perspective of the terrorist, are purposeful and effective.
- Evidence suggests that lack of education and poverty is not the primary reason people become terrorists.
- Evidence suggests that terrorists are not brainwashed or hypnotized.
- Data suggest that the most common motivator for becoming a terrorist is the desire for revenge or retribution for a perceived injustice.

- The use of "proxy wars" by the United States during the Cold War may have contributed to the creation of terrorism. Evidence suggests that it played a strong role in the development of al-Qaida and the role of Osama bin Laden.
- Numerous terrorists have been arrested in the United States and major terrorists attacks have been uncovered.
- Those arrested for terrorism or support of terrorism in the United States come from widely varied backgrounds, including truck drivers, "sleeper agents," lawyers, Islamic religious leaders, and spies.
- The destructiveness and reliability of the bomb makes it the preferred weapon of terrorists. It is a low-tech weapon and it takes little training to instruct someone how to use a bomb. Often the bomber needs only "a moment of courage."
- The variety of means to detonate a bomb and the variety of explosives make it very cheap and reliable as a weapon. It is easy to obtain the materials necessary to build a bomb. Very powerful bombs can be built using only materials that can be legally purchased by anyone.
- Terrorists in the United States have focused on attacking symbolic targets rather than strategic targets. Symbolic targets, or soft targets, include sporting events, schools, commercial buildings, government buildings, and so on.
- The Beslan (Russia) massacre has caused increased concern about the possibility of a terrorist attack on schools in the United States.
- It is impossible to defend all of the symbolic targets in the United States.
- Many recent plots have focused on infrastructure targets such as bridges, tunnels, overpasses, and reservoirs.
- The Madrid (Spain) train bomb has caused increased alarm regarding the security of public transportation in the United States.

Terrorism and You

Understanding This Chapter

1. How have terrorist attacks and the threat of terrorist attacks affected everyday life in the United States?

2. Why do terrorists hate the United States?

3. What motivates terrorists to want to attack on American soil?

4. Why do some consider the United States responsible for the creation of al-Qaida?

5. What kind of people have been arrested for terrorism in the United States?

6. What targets in the United States have terrorists plotted against?

7. Why is it more difficult to defend trains, subways, and buses than it is to defend airplanes and airports?

Thinking about How Terrorism Touches You

1. Has the discovery of terrorist plots against public transportation, bridges, tunnels, and similar targets caused you to change your behavior or attitude? Explain your answer.

2. Do you think there is a serious threat that terrorists would attack a school in the United States as they did in Beslan, Russia? Why or why not? If so, does that cause you to fear for your safety or the safety of friends and family?

3. When you use public transportation, attend large sporting events, or do other activities that may be symbolic targets for terrorists, are you more vigilant that you were before the 9/11 attacks? Why or why not?

4. Do you believe the threat of terrorism played an important role in the 2004 presidential elections? Support your answer.

5. Do you believe the enormous amount of money that is being spent on prevention, such as security for the political conventions, security on election day, and security for public transportation, is worth it?

Important Terms and Concepts

Al-Qaida
Beslan Massacre
Brandon Mayfield
Continuity of Government
Infrastructure Targets
Lyman Faris
Madrid Train Bombing
Martyr
National Special Security Event
Osama bin Laden

Proxy Wars
Sleeper Cells
Soft Targets
Strategic Targets
Suicide Bombers
Symbolic Targets
Timothy McVeigh
Transfer of Hostility
Transit and Rail Inspection Pilot (TRIP)

Endnotes

1. William Doolittle, "'Tainted' Deliberations May Lead to New Trial," *Pocono Record,* September 11, 2003, p. A3.

2. William Doolittle, "New Trial Likely for Attempted Murderer," *Pocono Record,* January 13, 2003, p. A1.

3. Samuel G. Freedman, "Grad School's International Glow Is Dimmed by Security Concerns," New York Times Online, www.nytimes.com, October 27, 2004.

4. Ibid.

5. Ibid.

6. David W. Chen, "In Many Co-ops, Ordering IN Becomes 'Go Fetch,'" New York Times Online, www.nytimes.com, April 10, 2003.

7. Ibid.

8. James Dao, "Terrorism Panel Says U.S. Is Still Unready," New York Times Online, www.nytimes.com, October 25, 2002.

9. Associated Press, "FBI Director Says Nearly 100 Attacks Thwarted Since 9/11," *Pocono Record,* December 15, 2002, p. A5.

10. Philip Shenon, "Government Issues New Terror Warning," New York Times Online, www.nytimes.com, July 30, 2003.

11. Brian Knowlton, "Bush Acknowledges 'Real Threat' of Terrorism," New York Times Online, www.nytimes.com, July 30, 2003.

12. Richard Bernstein, "Foreign Views of U.S. Darken Since Sept. 11," New York Times Online, www.nytimes.com, September 11, 2003.

13. Ibid.

14. Ibid.

15. Tom Regan, "Growing Anti-US Sentiment in Europe," *Christian Science Monitor,* www.csmonitor.com, March 17, 2004.

16. Samantha Power, "'Hegemony or Survival': The Everything Explainer," New York Times Online, www.nytimes.com, January 4, 2004.

17. Ibid.

18. Doug Bandow, "American Carefree Tourists, Beware," *Christian Science Monitor,* www.csmonitor.com, October 6, 2003.

19. Associated Press, "Poll: U.S. Faces Suspicion in

Terror War," New York Times Online, www.nytimes.com, March 17, 2004.

20. Philip G. Zimbardo, "Opposing Terrorism by Understanding the Human Capacity for Evil," *Monitor on Psychology,* Volume 32, No. 10, November 10, 2001.

21. Scott L. Plous and Philip G. Zimbardo, "How Social Science Can Reduce Terrorism," *The Chronicle of Higher Education,* Volume 51, Issue 3, p. B9.

22. Ibid.

23. Ibid.

24. Thomas L. Friedman, "War of Ideas, Part 6," New York Times Online, www.nytimes.com, January 25, 2004.

25. Alan B. Krueger and Jitka Malackava, "Seeking the Roots of Terrorism," *The Chronicle of Higher Education,* June 6, 2003, p. B11.

26. Ibid.

27. Ibid.

28. Mark Clayton, "Reading into the Mind of a Terrorist," Christian Science Monitor, www.csmonitor.com, October 30, 2003.

29. "What Does Islam Say about Terrorism?" http://whyislam.org/877/Services/Literature/22.asp.

30. Ibid.

31. Ibid.

32. Ibid.

33. Mark Clayton, "Reading into the Mind of a Terrorist," Christian Science Monitor, www.csmonitor.com, October 30, 2003.

34. Scott L. Plous and Philip G. Zimbardo, "How Social Science Can Reduce Terrorism," *The Chronicle of Higher Education,* Volume 51, Issue 3, September 10, 2004, p. B9.

35. Ibid.

36. Alan B. Krueger and Jitka Malackava, "Seeking the Roots of Terrorism," *The Chronicle of Higher Education,* June 6, 2003, p. B11.

37. Philip G. Zimbardo, "Opposing Terrorism by Understanding the Human Capacity for Evil," *Monitor on Psychology,* Volume 32, No. 10, November 10, 2001.

38. Ibid.

39. Norm Chomsky, "U.S. Is a Leading Terrorist State," www.sf.indymedia.org, December 30, 2002.

40. Ibid.

41. Dexter Filkins, "Conflict on Iraq-Syria Border Feeds Rage Against the U.S.," New York Times Online, www.nytimes.com, July 15, 2003.

42. Ibid.

43. Don Van Nata, Jr., "The Terror Industry Fields Its Ultimate Weapon," New York Times, Online, www.nytimes.com, August 24, 2003.

44. "Mind of the Suicide Bomber," www.bsnews.com/stories/2003/05/23/60minutes/main555344.shtml, November 5, 2004.

45. Spencer S. Hsu and Sari Horwitz, "Impervious Shield Elusive Against Drive-By Terrorists," *Washington Post,* August 8, 2004, p. A1.

46. "Mind of the Suicide Bomber," www.cbsnews.com/stories/2003/05/23/60minutes/main555344.shtml, November 5, 2004.

47. Don Van Nata, Jr., "The Terror Industry Fields Its Ultimate Weapon," New York Times Online, www.nytimes.com, August 24, 2003.

48. Ibid.

49. "Mind of the Suicide Bomber," www.cbsnews.com/stories/2003/05/23/60minutes/main555344.shtml, November 5, 2004.

50. Don Van Nata, Jr., "The Terror Industry Fields Its Ultimate Weapon," New York Times Online, www.nytimes.com, August 24, 2003.

51. Ibid.

52. "Mind of the Suicide Bomber," www.cbsnews.com/stories/2003/05/23/60minutes/main555344.shtml, November 5, 2004.

53. Ibid.

54. Ibid.

55. Ibid.

56. The names of Osama bin Laden and al-Qaida are transliterations of the Arabic and as such there are many variations, including al-Qaeda, al-Qa'ida, al-Quaida, Al-Qaida, el-Qaida, and al Qaeda. Osama bin Laden and al-Qaida followers normally do not refer to their group by any of these names. They call it by such names as "The Base," "Islamic Army," "World Islamic Front for Jihad Against Jews and Crusaders," "Islamic Army for the Liberation of the Holy Places," "Osama bin Laden Network," "Osama bin Laden Organization," "Islamic Salvation Foundation," and "The Group for the Preservation of the Holy Sites." Likewise, Osama bin Laden is a transliteration from Arabic and there are several commonly used forms of his name, including Usama bin Laden, Ussamah Bin Ladin, and Oussama Ben Laden.

57. Brendan O'Neill, "How We Trained al-Qa'eda," *The Spectator,* www.spectator.co.uk/article.php3?2003-09-13&id=3499, September 6, 2003.

58. Hugh Eakin, "When U.S. Aided Insurgents, Did It Breed Future Terrorists?" New York Times Online, www.nytimes.com, April 10, 2004.

59. Ibid.

60. Brendan O'Neill, "How We Trained al-Qa'eda," *The Spectator,* www.spectator.co.uk/article.php3?2003-09-13&id=3499, September 6, 2003.

61. Ibid.

62. Ibid.

63. Don Van Natta, Jr., "A World Made More Dangerous as Terrorism Spreads," New York Times Online, www.nytimes.com, April 18, 2004.

64. Ibid.

65. Timothy L. O'Brien, "Al Qaeda Remains a Global

Threat, U.N. Report Says," New York Times Online, www. nytimes.com, June 26, 2003.

66. Timothy L. O'Brien, "U.N. Group Finds No Hussein-Al Qaeda Link," New York Times Online, www. nytimes.com, June 27, 2003.

67. Reuters, "New Group Says It Strikes G.I.'s," New York Times Online, www.nytimes.com, July 14, 2003.

68. Craig S. Smith and Don Van Natt, Jr., "Officials Fear Iraq's Lure for Muslims in Europe," New York Times Online, www.nytimes.com, October 23, 2004.

69. Ibid.

70. Ibid.

71. Daniel Benjamin and Gabriel Weimann, "What the Terrorists Have in Mind," New York Times Online, www. nytimes.com, October 27, 2004.

72. Craig S. Smith and Don Van Natt, Jr., "Officials Fear Iraq's Lure for Muslims in Europe," New York Times Online, www.nytimes.com, October 23, 2004.

73. Ibid.

74. Ibid.

75. Ibid.

76. Rachel L. Swarns, "30 Linked to Terrorism Stayed in U.S., Report Says," New York Times Online, www. nytimes.com, June 19, 2003.

77. John Kifner, Susan Sachs, and Marc Santora, "After 3 Days of Testimony, Some Gaps Are Unfilled," New York Times, September 23, 2002, p. A11.

78. Toni Locy and Kevin Johnson, "Suspects Listed in al-Qaeda Materials," USA Today, March 6, 2003, p. 4A.

79. Monica Davey and Eric Lichtblau, "Qaeda Operative's Ex-Wife Says Charges Sickened Her," New York Times Online, www.nytimes.com, June 20, 2003.

80. Ibid.

81. Ibid.

82. Eric Lichtblau, "Group of Muslims Charged with Plotting Against India," New York Times Online, www. nytimes.com, June 28, 2003.

83. Neil A. Lewis, "3 Plead Guilty as Terror Investigation in Virginia Expands," New York Times Online, www. nytimes.com, August 27, 2003.

84. "U.S. Charges Islamic Leader Who Met Bush," New York Times Online, www.nytimes.com, September 30, 2003.

85. Ibid.

86. Timothy Egan, "Computer Student on Trial for Aid to Muslim Web Sites," New York Times Online, www. nytimes.com, April 27, 2004.

87. Ronald Smothers, "New York Jeweler Pleads Guilty to Handling Money for Missiles," New York Times Online, www.nytimes.com, March 31, 2004.

88. Richard Lezin Jones and David Johnston, "Arms Dealer Held without Bail in Missile Case," New York Times Online, www.ntyimes.com, August 13, 2003.

89. Julia Preston, "Terrorist's Lawyer Denies Working to Deceive U.S.," New York Times Online, www.nytimes. com, October 27, 2004.

90. Ibid.

91. Sarah Kershaw, "Guardsman Charged with Trying to Spy for Al Qaeda," New York Times Online, www. nytimes.com, February 19, 2004.

92. Ibid.

93. Associated Press, "U.S. Woman Charged with Giving Secrets to Iraq," New York Times Online, www. nytimes.com, March 11, 2004.

94. Associated Press, "FBI Calls Off Search for Five Men, Says Tip Was False," Pocono Record, January 8, 2003, p. A5.

95. "Arresting Witnesses," Washington Post, www. washingtonpost.com, May 22, 2004, p. A26.

96. A copy of the court order can be found at www. ord.uscourts.gov/Mayfield/mayfield.htm.

97. Dan Eggen, "Justice to Probe FBI Role in Lawyer's Arrest," Washington Post, September 14, 2004, p. A5. The FBI's statement can be viewed at www.fbi.gov/pressrel/ pressrel04/mayfield052404.htm.

98. Daniel Pipes, "If You Are Muslim, You Are Suspect," New York Sun, June 1, 2004, viewed at www. danielpipes.org/article/1853.

99. Danny Hakim, "Defendant Is Released in Detroit Terror Case," New York Times Online, www.nytimes.com, October 13, 2004.

100. Ibid.

101. David Johnston, "Antiterrorism Experts Warn More Attacks May Be Coming," New York Times Online, www.nytimes.com, August 5, 2003.

102. Bill Gertz, "Al Qaeda Seen Planning for 'Spectacular' Attack," Washington Times, www.washingtontimes. com, September 21, 2004.

103. Ibid.

104. David Johnston, "Antiterrorism Experts Warn More Attacks May Be Coming," New York Times Online, www.nytimes.com, August 5, 2003.

105. Daniel Benjamin, "The 1,776-Foot-Tall Target," New York Times Online, www.nytimes.com, March 23, 2004.

106. Ibid.

107. David E. Sanger, "Election Could Tempt Attack by Terror Groups, Rice Says," New York Times Online, www.nytimes.com, April 19, 2004.

108. Ibid.

109. Catherine Rodriguez, "Terrorists Might Have Interest in Army Depot, Raceway," Pocono Record, March 20, 2003, p. A4.

110. Reuters, "Sports Events Could Be Targets," New York Times Online, www.nytimes.com, July 24, 2004.

111. Judith Miller, "U.S. Received Tip on Qaeda Threats Against Landmarks," New York Times Online, www.nytimes.com, August 13, 2002.

112. Jim Bencivenga, "Putin's Response," *Christian Science Monitor,* www.csmonitor.com, September 8, 2004.

113. Nick Madigan, "Schools, on Alert, Step Up Security Measures," New York Times Online, www.nytimes.com, October 9, 2004.

114. Ibid.

115. Ibid.

116. Philip Shenon, "Agency Quickly Concludes No Terrorists Were Involved," New York Times Online, www.nytimes.com, August 15, 2003.

117. Elizabeth Becker, "Meat Inspections Declining, Impact of Policy Is Contested," New York Times Online, www.nytimes.com, July 10, 2003.

118. Associated Press, "U.S. Water Supplies May Be Next on al-Qaida Hit List," *Pocono Record,* May 30, 2003, p. A5.

119. Ibid.

120. Robert D. McFadden, "Citing Security, City Closes Reservoir Road," New York Times Online, www.nytimes.com, March 4, 2003.

121. Ibid.

122. Associated Press, "Two Arrested Near Detroit–Canada Bridge," New York Times Online, www.nytimes.com, April 21, 2003.

123. Eric Lichtblau, "U.S. Cites Al Qaeda in Plan to Destroy Brooklyn Bridge," New York Times Online, www.nytimes.com, June 20, 2003.

124. Ibid.

125. Ibid.

126. Patrick E. Tyler and Don Van Natta, Jr., "New Security Worries for Europe's Sprawling Rail System," New York Times Online, www.nytimes.com, March 12, 2004.

127. Eric Lichtblau and Sarah Kershaw, "Bombings Lead U.S. to Raise Security for Trains," New York Times Online, www.nytimes.com, March 13, 2004.

128. Eric Lichtblau, "Warning of Possible Attacks on Big-City Buses and Trains," New York Times Online, www.nytimes.com, April 3, 2004.

129. Associated Press, "Mass. Starts Random Searches on Trains," New York Times Online, www.nytimes.com, July 22, 2004.

130. Matthew L. Wald, "Train Station Set as Test Site for Screening of Passengers," New York Times Online, www.nytimes.com, April 16, 2004.

131. Alison Leigh Cowan, "Small Rail Line to be Focus of Security Test," New York Times Online, www.nytimes.com, July 16, 2004.

5

Defending Main Street, USA

Prevention of terrorist attacks rather than responding to terrorist attacks after the fact is considered critical for public safety and national security. Self-examination indicates that citizens, cities, and government are at risk. Responding to the need to enhance our ability to prevent terrorist attacks is transforming intelligence, agencies, and public spaces.

Preventing and responding to terrorism is all the more complex because no agency can do it alone. The "readiness" of any one agency . . . is insufficient in the face of the potential threat. For more than 125 years, American law enforcement has been organized around the principles of independence and decentralization. Some 18,000 local, state and federal agencies operate as autonomous entities, often unconnected to those in neighboring jurisdictions or at different levels of government. The threat of terrorism in America's cities and towns, however, has revealed the critical need for improved coordination and resource sharing—whether personnel, equipment or information—to develop a formidable strategy to counter future acts of terrorism.

—Gerald R. Murphy and Martha R. Plotkin,
Protecting Your Community from Terrorism:
The Strategies for Local Law Enforcement Series
(Washington, DC: U.S. Department of Justice, 2003), p. 1.

Chapter Outline

Introduction: A Nation in Danger

Defending Main Street: Intelligence and Prevention

Intelligence
Post-9/11 Changes in Intelligence
New Intelligence Agencies: Connecting the Dots
Intelligence and Local and State Law Enforcement
The Need for Federal-Local Partnerships
    Up Close and Personal: Citizen Reporting

Prevention: Who Protects Main Street?
Federal Agencies
Local and State Agencies
Volunteer and Self-Defense Groups
    Case Study: Surveillance of Main Street

Prevention: What Is Being Done?
Prevention of Truck Bombs
Physical Security: The Last Line of Defense
    Consider This: Would a National ID Card Help Fight Terrorism?
The Transformation of Public Spaces
Nonvehicle Suicide Bombers

Conclusion: Will It Be Enough?

Chapter Summary

Terrorism and You
Understanding This Chapter
Thinking about How Terrorism Touches You

Important Terms and Concepts

Endnotes

Learning Objectives

- After reading this chapter the reader will understand why local, state, and federal agencies need to change to defend against future terrorist attacks.
- The reader will understand why intelligence and physical security are the keys to defending against future terrorist attacks.
- The reader will know what key federal agencies play an important role in defending against future terrorist attacks.
- The reader will know what the role of state and local agencies is in defending against future terrorist attacks.
- The reader will understand why suicide bombers are considered the most likely terrorist threat and what is being done to defend against such attacks.

Introduction: A Nation in Danger

On the third anniversary of the 9/11 attacks a number of editorials proclaimed that U.S. policies concerning the war on terrorism had not made the world a safer place.[1] President Bush issued a press release on September 11, 2004, warning that "our country is safer than it was on September the 11th, 2001, yet, we're still not safe. . . . We are a Nation in danger." To what extent is America a nation in danger? Some senior Central Intelligence Agency counterterrorism officials suggest that rather than make the world and the United States safer, the invasion of Iraq has helped to fuel Islamic terrorism by inflaming anti-American sentiment.[2] Such statements provoke a number of questions: Are we safe? How much danger are we in? Who is responsible for keeping America safe and what is being done to keep our country safe?

The Police Executive Research Forum has concluded that one of the critical obstacles in responding to terrorism is that the United States does not have the necessary infrastructure in place that is necessary to protect Main Street, USA, from terrorism.[3] Their report declares that September 11, 2001, was a turning point for American law enforcement because immediately following the attacks, local, state, and federal law enforcement agencies faced service demands, problems, and issues that they had never seen before. In examining the collective response and capacity of the various government agencies, the demoralizing conclusion is that prior to the 9/11 attacks, the United States simply was not prepared for major attacks by terrorists. Law enforcement agencies were not prepared to detect such an attack, prevent such an attack, nor respond to such an attack. Furthermore, there was no government agency that was prepared to and capable of responding to such a challenge in absence of state and local law enforcement.

American law enforcement has inherent organizational and legal obstacles that preclude it from preventing future attacks by international terrorists. Local, state, and federal law enforcement agencies are primarily designed to "respond to" rather than be proactive. By design, the criminal justice system is not a system at all, but a group of loosely connected, independently operating organizations.[4] The founding fathers of the nation were suspicious of centralized authority and established a system based on independence and decentralization. As a result of this organizational mission and culture, the 18,000 municipal, state, and federal law enforcement agencies do not have the ability to share information and resources or to engage in cooperative planning. Without these abilities, the skill to respond effectively to serious international terrorists attacks is compromised. There is no "quick fix." Analysis of the prevention and response capacity of the various government agencies clearly indicates that no one agency has the power to prevent and respond to terrorist attacks. Effective prevention and response is going to require a strategy based on coordination, cooperation, and new patterns of response to future acts of terrorism.

The *National Strategy for Homeland Security* identifies the three goals of homeland security as (1) preventing terrorist attacks within the United States, (2) reducing America's vulnerability to terrorism, and (3) minimizing the damage and recovering from attacks that do occur.[5] This chapter and the next two chapters will discuss the first two goals identified by the *National Strategy for Homeland Security.* Chapter 8 will examine the response to the third goal.

This chapter examines how terrorism literally impacts us where we live. It affects our neighborhoods, our daily actions, our taxes, and what we worry about. The 9/11 attacks have changed how we view the police and fire departments in our communities and what we expect from our local, state, and federal government. Terrorism is no longer just a foreign policy concern, an overseas military problem, or something that happens elsewhere in the world. Terrorism now happens were we live, work, and play. And, we expect someone to do something about it. This chapter examines the various agencies that have the responsibility of responding to terrorism, the challenges facing these agencies, and the response of the government and Americans to the threat of future acts of terrorism.

Defending Main Street: Intelligence and Prevention

The keys to responding to future terrorist attacks are intelligence and prevention. The report of the *National Strategy for Homeland Security* concluded, "Our society presents an almost infinite array of potential targets that can be attacked through a variety of methods."[6] The United States does not have the resources to provide security for every potential target. Thus, it is necessary to choose which targets to protect and to decide to what degree they will be protected. Some of these targets are referred to as *key assets* and *high-profile events*. "Key assets and high-profile events are individual targets whose attack—in the worst-case scenarios—could result in not only large-scale human causalities and property destruction, but also profound damage to our national prestige, morale, and confidence."[7] It is these targets that represent the highest priority in the war on terrorism. In assessing which targets to protect and what resources should be committed to their protection, "the level of investment in security reflects implicit risk-versus-consequence tradeoffs, which are based on: (1) what is known about the risk environment; and (2) what is economically justifiable and sustainable in a competitive marketplace or in an environment of limited government resources."[8] The primary factors in making this decision are intelligence and preventive action. These factors are interrelated because often the decision as to the degree and type of preventive action is influenced by information gleaned from intelligence data.

Intelligence

Executive Order 12333 states, "Timely and accurate information about the activities, capabilities, plans, and intentions of foreign powers, organizations, and persons and their agents, is essential to the national security of the Untied States. All reasonable and lawful means must be used to ensure that the United States will receive the best intelligence available." Despite the current preoccupation with intelligence data and agencies, the United States is a relative newcomer to the intelligence world. The United States did not have a permanent intelligence office of any sort until 1882, when the Office of Naval Intelligence was created. The first permanent national intelligence office was the Central Intelligence Agency (CIA), which was not created until 1947. Prior to the 9/11 attacks the mission of the CIA focused on gathering intelligence related to the so-called Cold War. It focused on perceived Soviet aggression, possible nuclear attack, and counterintelligence. Middle East groups and states were only of concern as they related to the Cold War.

There have always been shortcomings in intelligence data. George J. Tenet, former director of Central Intelligence said, "By definition, intelligence deals with the unclear, the unknown, the deliberately hidden. What the enemies of the United States hope to deny, we work to reveal." However, there are limitations to what intelligence can provide. The assistant director of the Central Intelligence for Analysis and Production listed three limitations:[9]

- First, intelligence is, at the end, an intellectual process. Regardless of the means by which intelligence is collected, the ultimate product is the result of smart people pondering what is known, what is unknown and trying to determine what it all means.
- Second, the need to deal with incomplete, insufficient and often conflicting bits and pieces of intelligence is constant.
- Third, we [the intelligence community] do not make predictions. Fortune-tellers do; we do not. Rather, we write estimates, attempts to portray one or more possible outcomes based on varying amounts of concrete intelligence.

Prior to the 9/11 attacks intelligence focused on the Communist threat. Thus, the primary intelligence targets and sources were counties such as the Soviet Union, North Korea, China, Cuba, and Soviet-bloc nations. Middle East intelligence primarily concerned Israel. Little attention was focused on those countries and groups that are considered the primary threat to the United States today. For example, the CIA lacked even the basic ability to read documents from these groups because few CIA agents were proficient in Dari, Pushtu, or other languages of the Middle East.

Post-9/11 Changes in Intelligence

Prior to September 11, 2001, the Central Intelligence Agency was responsible for foreign intelligence assessing threats to the United States, and the Federal Bureau of Investigation was (and is) responsible for domestic intelligence, and the two agencies did not share intelligence. The report of the 9/11 Commission investigating the 9/11 attacks was extremely critical of the gathering, management, and distribution of intelligence by the intelligence community. The commission attributed deficiencies in intelligence as one of the contributing factors to the success of the September 11 attacks. The 9/11 Commission called for extensive restructuring of the intelligence gathering and sharing among agencies. Some government leaders critical of the CIA, which many believed to be the key agency responsible for intelligence failures that made the 9/11 attacks possible, have called it "dysfunctional."[10]

Despite the call for reorganization, progress has been slow due in part to the extensive political sensitivity involved in major changes to a covert organization. In November 2004, President Bush made some changes in the administrative leadership of the CIA, but the radical changes recommended by the 9/11 Commission will require extensive political persuasion as these changes go to the question of oversight of the CIA, funding, and accountability. The 9/11 Commission recommended a new organizational structure for the CIA. However, the organizational changes recommended would diminish the Pentagon's control over the CIA and its budget. As a result, both the CIA and Congressional CIA Oversight Committees have opposed these changes. In November 2004, President Bush appointed Porter J. Goss as the new chief of the CIA. Goss has initiated several changes in the operations of the CIA aimed at a major overhaul of the agency to address shortcomings that have become evident with intelligence failures related to the September 11, 2001, attacks and prewar assessments of Iraq.[11] These changes have been met with criticisms, resignations of top CIA officials, and opposition from both within and outside the CIA.[12]

The FBI is the key agency responsible for domestic intelligence. Prior to the 9/11 attacks there was a "bright line" dividing foreign intelligence and domestic intelligence. This meant that the CIA and the FBI did not share intelligence. In fact, the FBI and the CIA were forbidden by law from sharing intelligence. Intelligence gathered by the CIA was fed primarily to the President, various federal government agencies, and the Pentagon and various military units. Virtually no intelligence gathered by the CIA was funneled to local, state, or federal law enforcement agencies. The 9/11 Commission criticized this lack of communication, citing it as one of the reasons that the United States failed to "connect the dots" and piece together the intelligence information that would have enabled action to prevent the 9/11 attacks. Following September 11, 2001, Congress passed legislation allowing the CIA to share intelligence data with domestic federal agencies, specifically the Federal Bureau of Investigation and the Department of Homeland Security.

New Intelligence Agencies: Connecting the Dots

In 2003, President Bush said, "All our successes in the war on terror depend on the ability of our intelligence and law enforcement agencies to work in common purpose. In order to better protect our homeland, our intelligence agencies must coexist like they never had before."[13] Acting on this principle, a new joint intelligence agency was created to allow the FBI and the CIA counterterrorism analysts to work together. This intelligence agency is called the Terrorist Threat Integration Center (TTIC). The TTIC is unique in the history of United States intelligence gathering in that the new center will "merge and analyze terrorist-related information collected domestically and abroad in order to form the most comprehensive possible threat picture."[14] As a result, the TTIC will have "unfettered access to all terrorist threat intelligence information, from raw reports to finished analytic assessment, available to the U.S. government."[15] Both the FBI and the Department of Homeland Security will share intelligence gathered by the CIA. Furthermore, the FBI and the Department of Homeland Security are expected to disseminate this terror-related intelligence to the public, private industry, and state and local governments as appropriate.[16]

The mission of the Department of Homeland Security (DHS) is to reduce the vulnerability of the United States to terrorism and to detect, prevent, and respond to terrorist attacks. Intelligence is a critical strategy in accomplishing this mission. Thus, in addition to the TTIC, the DHS has its own intelligence directorate: Information Analysis and Infrastructure Protection (IAIP). The IAIP responsibilities are to coordinate the gathering of intelligence from all possible sources, both public and covert, to assess the scope of terrorist threats to the homeland from the intelligence gathered, and to respond appropriately by disseminating this information to those agencies that are responsible for providing security against terrorist attacks. The IAIP and the TTIC are complementary and collaborative and both share the same goal of preventing terrorism.

One of the main uses the Department of Homeland Security makes of its intelligence gathering and analysis is the dissemination of color-coded terrorist threat levels. These warnings are issued to state, local, and private sector authorities as well as the general public. There are five threat levels: low (green), guarded (blue), elevated (yellow), high (orange), and severe (red). The Homeland Security Advisory System can place specific geographic regions or industry sections on a higher alert status than other regions or industries, based on specific threat information. For example, based on intelligence received from al-Qaida informants and documents, the financial services sector in New York City, northern New Jersey, and Washington, D.C., was raised to "high" (orange) for approximately three months in 2004 while the rest of the nation was at "elevated" (yellow).

The value of the threat advisories of the DHS has been questioned. In a survey by the General Accounting Office,* agencies receiving the DHS threat advisories reported that "the warnings were often vague and inadequate, and had 'hindered their ability to determine whether they were at 'risk' and what protective measures to take in response."[17] Critics have warned that the public is at risk for "threat fatigue" if the DHS advisory warning system is not improved.[18] At times the DHS and the FBI have issued conflicting advisory warnings.[19] Elevated advisory warnings can be costly for state and local governments and private sector businesses because often as a result of elevated warning threat advisories additional security measures are put in place. The three-month "high" threat advisory warning for the northeast financial services sector cost businesses and law enforcement agencies millions of dollars in additional security expenses. In some cases when the threat advisory level is raised to "high," high-risk security events are cancelled, resulting in inconvenience to the public or loss of business income. The frustration with the vague nature of the warning and the appearance of "ambiguity" of the threat advisory warnings could result in loss of public trust and confidence in the warning system. The DHS has indicated that it will evaluate the need to change the threat advisory warning system.

Director of National Intelligence: Connecting the Dots.   The 9/11 Commission strongly criticized the failure of the intelligence community to analyze the threat information the various agencies had received and to "connect the dots" to uncover the 9/11 plot. The 9/11 Commission asserted that the failure to "connect the dots"—that is, to put the various pieces of intelligence data together and see the threat that emerged—was primarily due to the lack of sharing of intelligence among the intelligence agencies. Responding to the recommendations of the 9/11 Commission for more oversight of the various federal intelligence agencies, Congress passed and President Bush signed into law in December 2004 the Intelligence Reform and Terrorism Act of 2004. The act has been called "the biggest restructuring of the intelligence-gathering system since the CIA was created in 1947."[20]

One of the key provisions of the Intelligence Reform and Terrorism Act is the creation of a director of national intelligence to oversee the top 15 intelligence agencies. In February 2005, President Bush appointed John Negroponte as the first Director of National Intelligence. In making the appointment President Bush said, "The Director's responsibility is straightforward and demanding. John will make sure that those whose duty it is to defend America have the information we need to make the right decisions." The responsibilities of the Director of National Intelligence include:

- Serving as the principal advisor to the president on intelligence matters
- Being responsible for ordering the collection of new intelligence
- Ensuring the sharing of information among agencies

---

*Until 2004, GAO was an abbreviation for General Accounting Office. After July 2004 the GAO was renamed Government Accountability Office.

- Establishing common standards for the intelligence community's personnel
- Determining the annual budgets for all national intelligence agencies and offices
- Directing how intelligence agencies spend their funds

The Director of National Intelligence is not a cabinet-level position. Thus, each intelligence agency will retain its own command and control structure but the director will have oversight power over all the agencies.

Upon accepting the nomination Negroponte, who was serving as ambassador to Iraq and has an extensive background of experience, said this assignment would be the most challenging in his more than 40 years of government service. In public statements he promised he would transform the culture of the intelligence community from one where intelligence is carefully guarded from other agencies, a culture he described as a "need to know culture," to one where intelligence is shared or what he called "a need to share" culture. If successful, the transformation may go a long way in allowing the intelligence community "to connect the dots" as it gathers intelligence data to prevent the next major terror attack.

Intelligence and Local and State Law Enforcement

Prior to the 9/11 attacks few local and state law enforcement agencies had intelligence units. Those that did were very restricted in the information they could gather. Local and state law enforcement agencies were forced by law, court rulings, and regulations to disband their intelligence units in the 1960s and 1970s due to civil rights and privacy abuses.[21] Thus, in the post-9/11 era, where intelligence is considered to be a key strategy in preventing future terror attacks, local and state law enforcement agencies find themselves dependent on federal agencies for intelligence information. However, local and federal law enforcement agencies have been critical of federal agencies for failing to share intelligence data. It is their perception that information flow between federal and local agencies is "one way." Locals give more to the federal agencies than they get in return.[22] Two proposals have been advanced to enhance the intelligence available to local and state law enforcement agencies: (1) joint local-federal terrorism tasks forces and (2) reengineering the intelligence function of local law enforcement agencies.

Although local law enforcement agencies are organized along lines of geographical responsibility by city, county, and state, terrorists know no such boundaries and freely move about in the United States. In fact, information gathered from terrorist cells operating in the United States indicates that they are extremely mobile. This mobility is a critical obstacle for local law enforcement agencies, which are often unable to gather intelligence to uncover future planned attacks because of the mobility of the terrorists. Also, few local law enforcement agencies have full-time personnel dedicated to counterterrorism. The combination of limited jurisdiction and limited personnel presents a major obstacle to effective counterterrorism response.

To overcome this obstacle, joint local-federal task forces (JTTFs) can be an effective "force multiplier as it provides additional personnel to focus on counter-terrorism activities and it can make intelligence from federal agencies available to local agencies." One of the first joint terrorism task forces began in 1980, in New York City with 11 New York police department officers and 11 FBI special agents. On September 11, 2001, there were 35 JTTFs in operation. By 2003, the number nearly doubled to 66 and continues to rise.[23]

For local agencies, JTTFs provide a "fix," but many local departments are critical of JTTFs and do not believe JTTFs are a viable long-term solution.[24] The main argument is that federal agencies, and this criticism is aimed primarily at the FBI, often "do not draw on the full capabilities" of local law enforcement, and local law enforcement agencies "often get little back from their investment" in the JTTF.[25]

Given these limitations, many local departments argue that an alternative solution is to reconfigure the intelligence function of local agencies. Local intelligence units of the past were focused on traditional crimes, not domestic terrorist threats.[26] Furthermore, law enforcement personnel do not receive the training necessary to prepare them to gather and analyze terror-related intelligence data. Detectives and investigators may possess valuable information without knowing it.[27] Recent arrests of alleged terrorists within the United States have emphasized the need for law enforcement to be trained in terrorism intelligence. For example, local law enforcement officers have arrested several alleged terrorists for videotaping bridges. It is alleged that under the guise of being a tourist, terrorists have videotaped structural support details of bridges for possible future attack. Only the alert action of local and state police officers, who recognized the activity as "suspicious" and stopped to interrogate those doing the videotaping, revealed the underlying threat of this "innocent" activity. However, it must be remembered that law enforcement officers have had little, if any, training in recognizing suspicious terrorist activity, as most of their training has focused on recognizing criminal activity.

This lack of training can result in two harms: (1) innocent people being suspected and apprehended for plotting terrorist attacks when in reality they are only tourists taking pictures of what they think is an interesting bridge and (2) failure to recognize suspicious activity and/or failure to collect and share patterns of suspicious behavior. Both shortcomings can be harmful. The first deprives people of their civil rights and perhaps subjects them to racial profiling and the second could result in a successful terror attack if the terrorists can avoid detection by authorities.

The Need for Federal-Local Partnerships

The FBI and the Department of Homeland Security will continue to be the primary conduit for homeland intelligence analysis and exchange. Local law enforcement agencies will never have the intelligence-gathering resources and authority of these agencies. However, local agencies are going to have to continue to improve their intelligence-gathering analysis and sharing. It will be necessary for local agencies to develop effective partnerships with federal agencies, including the FBI, Department of Homeland Security, Secret Service, Internal Revenue Service, Immigration agencies, and others. Also, local law enforcement agencies will need to improve their local-to-local intelligence sharing and become more proficient in sharing intelligence with other local and state agencies. Not all of the problems in intelligence sharing are local-to-federal problems. Many local agencies have numerous barriers that prevent them from sharing intelligence with neighboring agencies or local agencies with state agencies. Some of these barriers include internal polices and practices, lack of cross-jurisdictional agreements, and incompatible technology.

The training of local personnel to perform these new intelligence responsibilities will present a significant challenge. Law enforcement is taking on a function it has never performed before, so there is no model to guide individuals as they seek to combat

BOX 5.1 • *Up Close and Personal: Citizen Reporting*

No one likes a person who tells on others. Stool pigeons are portrayed as disloyal comrades. Experience has demonstrated that citizens who witness crimes in progress are reluctant to report them to the police even when they can do so anonymously and without endangering themselves. Thus, it is not surprising that following the 9/11 attacks, when the Justice Department proposed a program to recruit citizens to report suspicious activities, there was a firestorm of protest. The program, known as TIPS (for Terrorism Information and Prevention System), would encourage and facilitate various persons such as truck drivers, gas and electric company employees, taxi drivers, bus drivers, port workers, meter readers, letter carriers, and others to report suspicious activities. Representative Dick Armey said the program "promotes citizens spying on one another."[28] Representative Bob Barr (GA) called it a "snitch system." He said the program "smacks of the very type of fascist or Communist government we fought so hard to eradicate in other countries in decades past."[29] Laura W. Murphy of the American Civil Liberties Union said TIPS is a "government-sanctioned peeping Toms" program.[30] Senator Orrin Hatch (UT) said it could create "a '1984' Orwellian-type situation."[31]

Despite these criticisms, cities, states, and federal agencies have continued to develop programs to encourage citizens to report suspicious activity they think may be related to terrorism. Many agencies have developed web-based reporting systems. For example, one can report suspected terrorism-related activities to the Philadelphia Police Department using their Internet "Suspected Terrorism Tip Form" (www.ppdonline.org/ppd2_terrorism_tipform.htm). The person submitting the tip to the Philadelphia Police Department Counter-Terrorism Bureau can remain anonymous.

The FBI has an extensive web-based appeal for citizens to report suspicious activities (www.fbi.gov/page2/aug04/preventterror080204.htm). The FBI website advises citizens, "This is a message that bears repeating, **no matter where you live in the world:** Your assistance is needed in preventing terrorist acts." The FBI website lists suspicious activities that may indicate terrorist activity that should be reported. The website asks people to report if they observe any of the following:

- *Surveillance:* Are you aware of anyone video recording or monitoring activities, taking notes, using cameras, maps, binoculars, etc., near key facilities/events?
- *Suspicious Questioning:* Are you aware of anyone attempting to gain information in person, by phone, mail, email, etc., regarding a key facility or people who work there?
- *Tests of Security:* Are you aware of any attempts to penetrate or test physical security or procedures at a key facility/event?
- *Acquiring Supplies:* Are you aware of anyone attempting to improperly acquire explosives, weapons, ammunition, dangerous chemicals, uniforms, badges, flight manuals, access cards or identification for a key facility/event or to legally obtain items under suspicious circumstances that could be used in a terrorist attack?
- *Suspicious Persons:* Are you aware of anyone who does not appear to belong in the workplace, neighborhood, and business establishment or near a key facility/event?
- *"Dry Runs":* Have you observed any behavior that appears to be preparation for a terrorist act, such as mapping out routes, playing out scenarios with other people, monitoring key facilities/events, timing traffic lights or traffic flow, or other suspicious activities?
- *Deploying Assets:* Have you observed abandoned vehicles, stockpiling of suspicious materials, or persons being deployed near a key facility/event?

Persons are advised to contact the Joint Terrorist Task Force or law enforcement/counterterrorism agency closest to them if they observe such activities. The website advises them, "Your tip could save the lives of innocent people, just like you and yours."

BOX 5.1 • Continued

Questions

1. Would you report any of the mentioned "suspicious" activities to the FBI? If not, why? Do you think *most* people would report "suspicious" activities to law enforcement? Why or why not?
2. Why do you think there is such strong criticism of programs to encourage and to enable people to report "suspicious" activity to law enforcement?
3. What are potential abuses that could occur as a result of programs that encourage persons to report "suspicious" activity to law enforcement?

terrorism.[32] Training will be required for both local law enforcement officers and executives. It will be necessary to build trusting relationships among agencies that for some have had long-standing distrust and suspicions of each other. Most likely, this training will need to be directed by federal agencies such as the FBI and the Department of Homeland Security. It is also reasonable to assume that the federal government will need to underwrite the cost of much of this training.

Prevention: Who Protects Main Street?

The responsibility of protecting Main Street, USA, is shared by federal, state, and local agencies. Numerous federal agencies have a role in preventing and responding to terrorism in the United States. A small number of agencies have a primary role and devote significant or most of their resources to counter terrorism.[33] Among the key agencies are the Department of Justice, the Federal Bureau of Investigation, and the Department of Homeland Security.

Federal Agencies

Department of Justice. The Department of Justice advises on legal aspects of dealing with terrorism and coordinates legislative proposals. The agency spearheaded the adoption of the USA Patriot Act and other legislation that has expanded federal intelligence-gathering powers and provided new powers to federal law enforcement agencies. The Department of Justice is also responsible for prosecuting suspects accused of terrorism.

Federal Bureau of Investigation. The Federal Bureau of Investigation has the primary responsibility for the investigation, prevention, and detection of terrorist activities. The FBI emerged as a federal law enforcement agency in the twentieth century, and during its relatively short history has been asked to perform a wide range of problems. Initially the FBI had limited responsibility related to the enforcement of federal law and domestic intelligence. As previously discussed, the FBI's mission expanded during the "Red Scare" when the FBI was the primary law enforcement agency charged with protecting the United States from Communist subversives. Ever since World War II the FBI had a major role in domestic intelligence and protecting the United States from foreign enemies within the United States. However, additional responsibilities eroded the focus of the FBI on domestic intelligence and defending against foreign agents. For example, during the 1960s the FBI assumed responsibility for civil rights enforcement and during the 1980s the FBI assumed additional responsibilities for drug and violent crimes.

Prior to the 9/11 attacks the FBI was the lead federal law enforcement agency responsible for investigation of domestic terrorism. However, this was not the FBI's *primary* focus, as there were few acts of domestic terrorism prior to 2001. During the 1980s and 1990s the resources of the FBI became strained as it assumed more responsibility for providing law enforcement services similar to local police and other federal law enforcement agencies.[34] As acts of domestic terrorism committed by Middle Eastern groups like al-Qaida increased, the FBI lacked the ability to respond adequately to these terrorist threats due to the wide range of new responsibilities the FBI had assumed. Prior to the 9/11 attacks internal assessments of the FBI's ability to respond to acts of domestic terror by international terrorists reported that the FBI lacked the ability to respond adequately to the increasing problem.[35] These internal assessments concluded that the FBI was not processing information in a timely manner that would provide the agency with the ability to prevent terror attacks. Furthermore, the FBI's request for increased funds to enhance their counterterrorism and intelligence abilities were turned down.[36] The vulnerability of this shortcoming was clearly demonstrated when, in the summer of 2001, the FBI received warnings that Arabs who were being monitored for possible terrorist ties were taking flight training in Arizona and that followers of Osama bin Laden might be coming to the United States for aviation training. The FBI did not follow up on this information before the 9/11 attacks.[37]

Following the 9/11 attacks the FBI underwent major organizational changes, refocused its priorities, and received new resources. The primary mission of the FBI shifted to fighting terrorism. The FBI reengineered its structure and operations to enhance its ability to prevent terrorist attacks, to process domestic intelligence, and to combat cyber-crime–based attacks and other high-technology crimes. FBI agents were shifted from traditional crime fighting to counterterrorism and domestic intelligence. New agents were recruited who had Middle East foreign language skills. As a result of this reorganization following the 9/11 attacks the number of FBI agents working narcotics cases dropped 45 percent, bank fraud cases dropped 31 percent, and bank robbery investigations dropped 25 percent.[38]

It was difficult for the FBI to shift focus from a decades-long focus on solving traditional federal crimes such as bank robberies, drug trafficking, and kidnapping to counterterrorism and intelligence.[39] Assessing the transformation of the FBI, Senator Charles E. Grassley (R-IA) remarked in 2002, "Old habits die hard at the F.B.I. The days of Bonnie and Clyde are over."[40] Following the 9/11 attacks and its new charge, the FBI shaped its workforce, developed new intelligence capacities, and received new authority to fight terrorism. Some of these new authorities included much needed reforms such as authorizing the FBI to gather intelligence by monitoring the World Wide Web. Prior to the 9/11 attacks FBI agents were not allowed to use the World Wide Web unless they had probable cause or authorization. Agents were prohibited from doing what any citizen could do—"surf the Web" to glean information. Other new powers were more controversial. New legislation authorized the FBI to monitor political groups, libraries, and religious organizations, including mosques.

Today, the FBI has embraced its new counterterrorism mission. Since September 11, 2001, nearly 200 suspected terrorist associates have been charged with crimes in the United States and the FBI claims credit for breaking up as many as 100 terrorist attacks or plots.[41] The FBI is uniquely situated to achieve its counterterrorism mission as it is the only agency with both domestic intelligence and law enforcement capabilities. For example, the FBI has four intelligence and analysis offices:

1. The Office of Intelligence is a new office that works with the CIA to upgrade its analytical and intelligence capabilities focused on international terrorism. Information from this office is shared with other agencies fighting terrorism.
2. The Counterterrorism Watch (CT Watch) is the FBI's 24-hour global command center for terrorism prevention operations. It is the focal point within the FBI for gathering and managing all domestic and international terrorism threats. The CT Watch evaluates the credibility of all terrorism threats. Also, it produces daily terrorism threat briefing materials and intelligence reports that are distributed to the president, key national security policymakers, and members of the intelligence and law enforcement communities.
3. The College of Analytical Studies provides training to intelligence analysts.
4. The Document Exploitation (DocEX) Working Group works with the Central Intelligence Agency, National Security Agency, and Defense Intelligence Agency to analyze the massive amount of paper documents, electronic media, and video and audiotapes seized in military and intelligence actions overseas.

Legislation such as the USA Patriot Act and federal court decisions now allows the FBI to share the information it gathers through intelligence with the law enforcement community and allows the FBI and CIA to share information. New legislation even permits intelligence gathered for the purposes of identifying foreign agents and terror plots in the United States to be used in the prosecution of certain criminal offenses not related to terrorism. Previously such use of intelligence was strictly prohibited.

The FBI points out that this dual ability gives the agency the ability to discover threats through intelligence and surveillance and to act against these threats through investigation and arrest.[42] Thus, the FBI is the primary federal law enforcement agency responsible for protecting Main Street, USA.

Department of Homeland Security. The Department of Homeland Security has one of the most complex roles in protecting the United States. Its mission is to provide the unifying core for the vast national network of organizations and institutions involved in efforts to secure homeland security. The Department of Homeland Security has six strategic goals. They are:

1. *Awareness:* Identify and understand threats, assess vulnerabilities, determine potential impacts, and disseminate timely information to homeland security partners and the American public.
2. *Prevention:* Detect, deter, and mitigate threats to the homeland.
3. *Protection:* Safeguard people and their freedoms, critical infrastructures, property, and the economy of our nation from acts of terrorism, natural disasters, or other emergencies.

4. *Response:* Lead, manage, and coordinate the national response to acts of terrorism, natural disasters, or other emergencies.
5. *Recovery:* Lead national, state, local, and private sector efforts to restore services and rebuild communities after acts of terrorism, natural disasters, or other emergencies.
6. *Service:* Serve the public effectively by facilitating lawful trade, travel, and immigration.

The Department of Homeland Security, a new federal agency formed after the 9/11 attacks, has significant responsibilities for aviation security, border security, and protection of infrastructure targets such as bridges, tunnels, buildings, and transportation systems. The role of the Department of Homeland Security in aviation security is discussed in Chapter 6. The role of the Department of Homeland Security in border protection will be discussed later in Chapter 9.

Other Federal Agencies.   There are other federal agencies that have significant responsibilities in defending Main Street, USA. The Federal Aviation Administration (FAA) is responsible for responding to terrorist incidents involving aircraft in flight or under flight conditions. (The FBI and the FAA have a clear understanding to clarify possibly overlapping responsibilities and to foster close cooperation.) The Department of Energy has responsibilities and expertise regarding nuclear weapons.

The Department of the Treasury has several bureaus involved in anti-terrorism. The Secret Service is responsible for protection of Heads of State or Heads of Government visiting the United States; the Bureau of Customs is involved in controlling international movement of weapons; and the Bureau of Alcohol, Tobacco, Firearms and Explosives has legal responsibilities and expertise concerning illegal weapons and explosives.

There are a number of federal agencies that play a significant but indirect role in protecting Main Street, USA. These include the Central Intelligence Agency, the State Department, and the Armed Forces. Their role is described as indirect in that their primary mission is focused on terrorist threats outside the United States. (The cooperative role of the CIA and the FBI in domestic terrorism has already been discussed in this chapter.)

Finally, the Federal Emergency Management Agency (FEMA) has the primary responsibly for minimizing damage as a result of a terror attack (or any other national emergency) through its efforts to rebuild and restore the community and infrastructure. The role of FEMA will be discussed in Chapter 8.

Local and State Agencies

The Department of Homeland Security recommends that local law enforcement agencies should recognize that there is a need for prevention planning and actions and that prevention is critical to a jurisdiction's preparation for terrorism. For example, DHS recommends that local police agencies use community policing initiatives, strategies, and tactics as a basis to identify suspicious activities related to terrorism.[43] Local and state agencies are frequently referred to as "first responders" and they play an essential role in defending Main Street, USA, against future terrorist attacks. The FBI and the Department of Homeland Security are responsible for many aspects related to preventing future terror attacks but local and state agencies provide the day-to-day patrolling of Main Street and in the event of a terrorist attack, local police and fire departments will be the first to respond.

Following the 9/11 attacks many states and cities did take steps to enhance their first-response capability and to establish counterterrorism and response agencies and plans. Generally, state anti-terrorism agencies have worked to coordinate the responsibilities of the various state and local agencies in the event of a terrorist attack and coordination between the state and federal agencies. State anti-terrorism agencies play a significant role in channeling federal grants to state agencies, establishing interagency radio communication capabilities, establishing planning commission, and recommending changes to enhance domestic security. However, states and local governments lack the resources of the federal government and as a result some of their counterterrorism agencies and response plans have been criticized as ineffective.[44] Another criticism of state and local agencies is that sometimes the staffing of the agencies has been by political patronage, resulting in unqualified persons occupying administrative positions.[45]

Police and Fire Departments. Police and fire departments are considered the most important "first responders" in defending our country. Police departments play a role in both prevention and response. The primary role of the fire department is reactive. Often it is local or state police officers who are first alerted to suspicious behavior or respond to the scene of a terrorist attack. Responding to terrorism is a new duty for police and fire departments. Although trained and equipped to respond to traditional criminal assaults, fires, and hazardous incidents, police and fire personnel often lack the training, equipment, and resources to respond to a significant terrorist attack. Police and fire union leaders often express the opinion that their members are unprepared to respond to a major terrorist attack.[46] Fire departments complain that they lack both the training and the equipment to respond to terrorist attacks involving hazardous, biological, or nuclear materials.[47]

State and city governments have tried to respond to these complaints but often the cost is more than they can afford. As a result, plans to rectify the deficiencies will take years to implement or will be implemented only to a limited degree. For example, some police departments have complained that the firearms they carry, usually a medium-powered semiautomatic pistol and perhaps a 12-gauge shotgun, are inadequate to respond to an armed attack by terrorists, as it is suspected that the terrorists would be equipped with fully automatic or high-powered weapons. Some cities, such as New York City, have responded to this criticism and now issue new high-powered weapons such as the MP5 submachine gun and the mini-14 assault rifle to officers.[48] However, the cost of the weapons is such that only a small number of New York police officers will receive the new weapons.

Firefighters face the same challenge of lack of money to properly equip themselves for responding to counterterrorism. For example, citing the lack of air masks to protect firefighters from hazardous materials such as nerve agents and other dangerous chemicals, New York City agreed to purchase 1,500 new air masks.[49] However, the plan to enhance New York City's fire department's ability to respond to future terrorist attacks will take two years to implement. During the two-year implementation period, the fire department will have to "make do" in the event of a terrorist attack using hazardous, biological, or nuclear materials.

A significant problem in coordinating an effective response of "first responders" to a terrorist incident is the problem of command and control. Fire departments and police departments often come in conflict when responding to an incident as to who is in charge. In some extreme incidents, police officers have even arrested firefighters on obstruction charges as police and fire personnel disagree over who has the final authority to give orders and make decisions. Fire department personnel express the opinion that in incidences involving chemical, biological, radiological, and nuclear incidents, the fire department should have the primary responsibility in responding to the incident. Police personnel by their actions have often assumed primary responsibility for controlling access to the scene and directing actions of emergency personnel. Police officials argue that the incident is a crime scene and that it is necessary to take steps to preserve evidence at the scene that can be gathered and analyzed so that the perpetrators can be discovered and prosecuted. The police argue that firefighters destroy valuable evidence in their emergency response. Firefighters argue that the primary goal of saving lives and preventing injury to people should be given priority. New York City has implemented protocols that establish the police department as the controlling agency in responding to certain future terrorist attacks wherein both the police and fire department respond to the scene.[50] Fire department officials criticize the primacy of the police department, arguing that the police have little training, knowledge, or experience in responding to such incidents.[51]

New Threats—New Needs.   In considering their preparedness for responding to future terrorist attacks, some local agencies have discovered what they consider serious shortcomings and have taken innovative measures to prepare for their new anti-terrorism duties. For example, the Alameda County (CA) Sheriff's Department was concerned with protecting Alameda County's 26 miles of coastline, which includes some of the West Coast's busiest shipping lanes, and the Port of Oakland, the fourth-busiest container port in the country. By writing grant proposals, cutting costs, and establishing an information campaign to convince supervisors and local anti-terrorism officials of the need, Sheriff Charles C. Plummer was able to raise the money necessary to buy a 31-foot patrol boat equipped with two machine guns.[52]

Another example of local action is New York City, where law enforcement officials wanted to be able to see "beyond the horizon" to detect potential terrorist threats before they were within close proximity to the harbor. To enhance harbor and water security, a new surveillance camera and radar was developed and installed. The new system works similar to air traffic control radar in that not only does it detect objects as small as a raft 30 miles away but it can also provide automatic computer identification for commercial ships. The automatic identification system provides Coast Guard computers with information on the name, cargo, course, and speed of the ship. The Department of Homeland Security says this advance look at ships and information will enable the various agencies responsible for harbor and sea security to make informed decisions quicker and with more confidence.[53]

Some problems associated with new anti-terrorism duties have required local police departments to work with a number of other agencies for a solution. For example, New York City's police department personnel were concerned about their legal authority to enforce a quarantine and isolation in the event of a terrorist attacking using biological agents. Working with city officials, health officials, and federal agencies, the New York City's health code was changed to allow the city to detain anyone health officials suspect of having being exposed to a deadly infectious pathogen.[54] Also, the police department developed plans that would allow the department to house and feed thousands of police officers who may be required to work continuously in the aftermath of a catastrophic attack.

Strains on Local Agencies.   Two of the most significant problems impacting the ability of local police to defend Main Street, USA, against future terrorist attacks are (1) the call-up of military reserve units and (2) the additional security duties required when the alert level is raised. The Police Executive Research Forum reported that 44 percent of 976 law enforcement agencies it surveyed between September and November 2003 reported losing personnel to reservist duty.[55] Some departments report losing 10 percent of their officers. The call-up of reserve units has forced law enforcement departments to make up for missing officers by paying more overtime, transferring officers to ensure essential services are covered, borrowing officers from other agencies, and using more police volunteers on the streets.[56] Small police departments have been especially hard hit by the activation of military reserve units.[57] Many of these departments do not have officers to replace those doing specialized duty. For some small departments the call-up has wiped out the police department as the department had only two, three, or four officers total.[58] Many of the nation's governors have complained to senior Pentagon officials that their cities face severe manpower shortages in guarding prisoners, fighting wildfires, preparing for hurricanes and floods, and policing the streets because of the largest call-up since World War II.[59]

Additional security duties during times of high alert has strained some local resources to the point that they can no longer provide "routine" services. During the Republican National Convention, all hearings and trials were suspended in New York City courts because police officers had to devote their time to convention security.[60] In addition to security duties, local resources are strained as new anti-terrorism responsibilities are added to local law enforcement officers.

One of the most controversial of these duties is the move to deputize local law enforcement officers as federal immigration agents. The purpose of this strategy is to tighten U.S. borders against terrorists. Deputized local officers would have the authority to detain and start deportation proceedings for suspects who do not have proper documentation. Local law enforcement officials argue that they do not have the resources to perform these additional duties and even if they did, these duties would be counterproductive to the performance of their traditional duties.[61] Local law enforcement officers can already alert federal authorities about a suspect's immigration status. However, law enforcement officials argue that immigrants are more likely to be victims of crime rather than terrorists. Law enforcement officials argue that the perceived threat of deportation will make illegal immigrants less likely to report crime or to provide testimony if they witnessed a crime. Also, the threat of deportation would make them less likely to report criminal victimization. As a result, this group of people would become more silent, fearful, and vulnerable if local law enforcement officers also served as immigration officers.[62]

Volunteer and Self-Defense Groups

Historically, self-help groups have been a prominent strategy in defense against attack. Self-defense is rooted in the tithing system of England where voluntary citizen groups performed local policing. Sir Robert Peel, who was the founding father of the modern policy system,

BOX 5.2 • *Case Study: Surveillance of Main Street*

What would you do to fight terrorism with a $5 million grant from the Department of Homeland Security? The city of Chicago bought cameras. In September 2004, the city started an 18-month project to connect over 2,000 cameras into a single surveillance system monitored by 911 personnel. These cameras will use existing surveillance systems and another 250 cameras for what have been defined as high-risk areas, most of them downtown. Existing camera systems will include Chicago public schools, the Central Transit Authority, city colleges, the park district, government buildings, court houses, the Chicago Housing Authority, and O'Hare International Airport. Private business will also be able to send their video feeds from surveillance cameras into the system. The 911 personnel will have the ability to manipulate the cameras and magnify images up to 400 times to watch suspicious people and follow them from one camera's range to another's.

One of the innovative aspects of Chicago's surveillance system will be software that will automatically identify "suspicious behavior" and alert control center personnel. This software will "fix" one of the biggest problems with video surveillance. Studies have found that monitoring video surveillance is so boring and mesmerizing that even trained and motivated persons cannot provide the vigilance necessary to pay attention to the video screens for suspicious activities and crimes after just 20 minutes.[63] To overcome this shortcoming, the software will be programmed to alert control center personnel to suspicious activities, such as someone leaving a suitcase in a stairwell, or if activity appeared to indicate an assault on a person.[64]

Chicago will be the first U.S. city to install such an extensive network of surveillance cameras. However, Chicago was not the first in the world to use video surveillance and surveillance of public spaces. In fact, the inspiration for the surveillance project is based on London's video surveillance network.[65] The United Kingdom has been using video surveillance in London and other cities for over 10 years to deter terrorism by the Irish Re-

publican Army. Throughout the United Kingdom there are more than four million video surveillance cameras. Many other foreign cities have adopted extensive video surveillance of public places. St. Petersburg, Russia, for example, has 50,000 security cameras around the city.

Video surveillance of public activities has been steadily growing in the United States. The initial use of video surveillance was to promote safety and serve as an anti-crime measure. Video surveillance has been used extensively by businesses to monitor their premises. Casinos have elaborate video surveillance to scan for criminal activity. Cameras monitor ATM machines, parking garages, shopping malls, and national parks. Law enforcement agencies use cameras to scan intersections for motorists who run red lights or stop signs. Video cameras and radar have even been used to issue speeding tickets automatically to those offenders captured on video.

Studies indicate that despite the public perception that video cameras are effective crime-fighting tools, the evidence suggests that surveillance is not as effective in preventing crime as most people may believe. The United Kingdom has found that video surveillance did little to deter terrorism by the Irish Republican Army. Video surveillance appeared to have some impact on low-level street crimes, such as vandalism, property crime, car thefts, burglaries, shoplifting, fraud, and arson, but they are much less effective in deterring violent crimes, such as rapes or assaults.[66] When compared to other crime-prevention measures, video surveillance was not as effective in crime reduction. Studies of London-based crime reduction found that video surveillance reduced crime by 3 to 4 percent, while better street lighting led to a 20 percent reduction in crime.[67] Other studies suggest that video surveillance may not reduce total crime but may simply move criminal activity from one place to another where there are no video cameras.[68]

The use of video surveillance has had mixed results. In 1997, the city of Tampa, Florida, used video surveillance combined with facial recogni-

BOX 5.2 • Continued

tion to identify criminals on the street. It abandoned the effort after two years because it never identified a wanted criminal.[69] However, New York City adopted video surveillance of public housing projects and claimed a 40 to 60 percent decline in housing project crime.[70] Also, gambling casinos strongly believe in the value of cameras to detour crime.

Also, there appears to be little objection to the constitutionality of video surveillance of public places. Even the American Civil Liberties Union concedes that there is no expectation of privacy on public streets, buildings, parks, airports, and government offices. Chicago Mayor Daley dismissed any constitutional objection to the surveillance project, saying, "We are not inside your home or your business. The city owns the sidewalk. We own the street and we own the alley."[71]

Whether effective or not, it looks like the public favors video surveillance of public places. One poll of the British citizenry found that 90 percent approved of its expansive surveillance system.[72] Chicago officials report that they cannot keep up with the demand by citizens for installation of video surveillance of public places. As a result, video surveillance cameras are appearing everywhere. Even the Washington Monument has been transformed into an observation platform equipped with banks of surveillance cameras recording activity on the mall.

Video surveillance of public places has become so common that citizens are photographed many times during the course of the day by various surveillance cameras. One estimate is that by the year 2008, citizens of all industrial nations will be under constant video surveillance by government or businesses.

Questions

1. Are you aware of the extent to which your daily public activities are watched by surveillance cameras? When you are aware that surveillance cameras monitor your activities does it cause you to change your behavior? Why or why not?

2. What is your reaction to Chicago's aggressive video surveillance network project? Do you think it will have an impact on terrorism or crime? Explain.

3. What are the abuses that may be associated with video surveillance of citizens in public places?

said, "The police are the public and the public are the police; the police being only members of the public who are paid to give full-time attention to duties which are incumbent on every citizen." In the fight against terrorism this philosophy was clearly demonstrated on September 11, 2001, with the passengers of hijacked United Airlines Flight 93 who took it upon themselves to terminate the suicide mission of the terrorists who took control of the plane. Their actions resulted in the crash of the airplane in rural western Pennsylvania before it could complete its suspected mission of crashing into the Capitol.

President Bush introduced the idea of a volunteer-based group of "ordinary" citizens to engage in protecting the United States from terrorist attacks and helping out in future catastrophes. His idea of a Citizen Corps was presented during his State of the Union address in January 2002. In the same year, President Bush created by executive order a new umbrella organization called USA Freedom Corps. This organization includes three existing organizations: the Peace Corps, the Senior Corps, and AmeriCorps. The Citizen Corps "creates opportunities for individuals to volunteer to help their communities prepare for and respond to emergencies by bring together local leaders, citizen volunteers and a network of first responder organizations. Their goal is to have all citizens participate in making their communities safer, stronger, and better prepared for preventing and handling threats of terrorism, crime, and disasters of all kinds."[73] Local Citizen Corps consist of citizen-organized volunteer groups that are networked and supported by the federal agency Citizen Corps.[74] Citizen Corps members do not have any official law enforcement or intelligence authority but are encouraged to form community partnerships to observe and report suspicious behaviors. Citizen Corps members are provided training to assist with disaster support services. This training would allow Citizen Corps volunteers to assist local or federal agencies in responding after a catastrophic terrorist attack or other national disaster, such as hurricane, flood, tornado, or fire. Citizen Corps has an active educational campaign to inform citizens how to prepare for a national emergency and what planning should be done in advance to prepare for an emergency and what supplies should be kept on hand. In 2003, the federal government provided $25 million to support emergency response training for Citizen Corps groups.[75]

The Department of Homeland Security has started a critical new initiative to support citizen involvement called "Homeland Security from the Citizens' Perspective." The initiative is a citizen-centered effort focused on citizens' concerns about health, safety, transportation, and economic viability. The two principal operating groups of the initiative are "Town Halls" and "Working Groups." Town Halls are a series of pubic meetings in several locations across the country "to understand and map citizens' concerns and to engage local and state leaders regarding the protection and safety of our communities and the nation."[76] Working Groups are meetings with "key representatives from business academia, civic organizations, and government to help develop integrated enterprise-wide recommendations, guided by public input from the Town Halls."[77]

In addition to government-organized and -sponsored self-defense groups, individual citizens have been motivated to engage in self-defense against terrorists attacking Main Street, USA. Although the government provides protection against many terrorist threats, there are some threats that the government can offer little protection to the individual citizen. For example, in June 2004, it was revealed that al-Qaida operatives were plotting to blow up a Columbus, Ohio, shopping mall.[78] Had the plot been carried out, those shoppers unfortunate enough to be present in the mall when it was attacked would have had to rely on their own resources for protection.

Many citizens are feeling fearful of being a victim of a terrorist attack and are taking personal measures to enhance their self-defense. Two measures of the extent of this fear and feeling for the need for self-defense are the increased sales of armored cars and guns. Since 1995 the sale of armored cars has risen from 5,000 to 22,000. Sales of armored cars rose by 20 percent in each year following September 2001. Bulletproof and bombproof armored cars run about $150,000 and cars that can be sealed against chemical and biological attacks cost about $300,000.[79] For those who cannot afford armored cars, many citizens are turning to personal firearms. Gun and ammunition sales across the country have risen sharply since the 9/11 attacks. In the three months following 9/11 gun sales rose nearly 22 percent.[80] Many gun dealers report an increase in first-time buyers and an increase in the sale of small handguns that are easy to carry and shotguns and assault rifles that can be used for home defense. Gun manufacturers are promoting purchases based on fear of terrorist attacks, as evidenced by such gun models as the Beretta 9mm pistol "United We Stand," the Henry Repeating

Arms Company's "U.S. Survival Rifle," and the Ithaca Gun Company's "Homeland Security" model.

Also, private citizens are enrolling in counterterrorism self-defense classes. For example, one four-hour self-defense class costing $60 is taught by retired police personnel. The four-hour class provides citizens the opportunity to recognize the signs of a chemical attack, what to do if a grenade lands in their midst, how to stop a knife-wielding or box-cutter–wielding terrorist, and how to use improvised weapons such as a soft-drink can or a sock full of quarters. Participants are even taught how to take back an airplane from hijackers.[81]

One of the goals of terrorism is to promote fear among the citizenry. One of the countermeasures of the citizenry is to engage in self-defense actions that make them feel safer. Citizens are engaging in many different strategies of self-defense in an effort to feel safer. For example, New York neighborhood associations are offering nine-week courses by the city's Office of Emergency Management to train civilians to provide help during catastrophes or national disasters until emergency services arrive.[82] Also, New York City doormen are being trained to observe and report suspicious persons and behavior to authorities. Some of the self-defense measures taken by citizens may provide only a false sense of safety. Other measures, such as firearms in the home or carrying a firearm, may actually increase the danger to the citizen rather than promote safety.

Prevention: What Is Being Done?

In May 2004, the FBI issued a warning to law enforcement agencies to be on the alert for the possibility that suicide bombers may attempt to strike inside the United States.[83] The warning advised that suicide bombers may disguise themselves in stolen military, police, or firefighter uniforms, or even as pregnant women. Experts warn that the next terror attack in the United States may be a "truck bomb" using ammonium nitrate fertilizers and fuel oil.[84] In fact, U.S. analysts are at a loss to explain why the homeland has thus far escaped such attacks, since a number of extremist groups who have used this strategy extensively in the Middle East have a sizable presence here.[85] In the last five years almost 90 percent of terrorist attacks against Americans have involved improvised explosives.[86] Both the 1993 World Trade Center attack plotted by Ramzi Yousef with 1,200 pounds of chemical explosives tied to Casio watch timers in a rented Ford van and the 1995 bombing by Timothy McVeigh of the Alfred P. Murrah Federal Building in Oklahoma City with a 5,000-pound mixture of ammonium nitrate and fuel oil involved truck-size batches of ammonium nitrate/fuel oil "homemade" bombs. Ammonium nitrate/fuel oil bombs are low-cost, low-tech weapons that have the capacity to produce explosions equivalent to over 4,000 pounds of dynamite.

Terrorists need little training and resources to construct such deadly explosive devices. The Terrorist Explosive Device Analytical Center (Tedac), a FBI forensic investigation unit that became operational in December 2003, studies forensic evidence to analyze improvised explosive devices. Their analysis indicates that Islamic militant bomb builders have used the same designs for car bombs in Africa, the Middle East, and Asia. This fact leads experts to conclude that there is a "global bomb-making network."[87] It is suspected that terrorists may share a common bomb-making design that enables members of local terror cells to assemble a car bomb or truck bomb with minimum skill other than following the instructions, while larger, more deadly bombs, are assembled by more skilled builders. Of course, terrorists do not even need to know how to construct a bomb from improvised materials, for it is always possible to hijack a tractor-trailer carrying thousands of gallons of gasoline or some other deadly chemical cargo and use it as an improvised weapon.

Prevention of Truck Bombs

The Bush Administration has focused primarily on two areas: aviation security and bioterrorism. Truck bombs are not a Bush Administration priority. Indeed, there are few regulations and monitoring that could effectively stop a truck bomber.[88] There are millions of vehicles in the United States. It is difficult to conceive of vehicle ownership regulations that would prevent members of terrorist cells from acquiring a vehicle. Even if it were possible to draft and enact such regulations, terrorists could simply steal a vehicle. Over 1 million vehicles are stolen each year; it would be impossible to know which, if any, of these were stolen by terrorists planning to use it to deliver a car bomb or truck bomb.

Preventing terrorists from having access to explosive materials necessary to construct a car bomb or truck bomb is equally difficult. The Safe Explosive Act and various federal and state laws require criminal background checks and proof of identification for most explosives. Access and possession of high-powered military-type explosives are strictly regulated. The problem is that the materials commonly used for a high-power car bomb or truck bomb are legal and easily obtainable by any person. The primary ingredients are ammonia nitrate–based fertilizer and fuel oil, diesel fuel, or gasoline. Nearly 5 million tons of ammonium nitrate fertilizer are sold each year in the United States and none of it is regulated.[89] Farmers commonly use it for legitimate purposes. Not only do they use it as fertilizer but also its explosive properties are well known and the law permits farmers to mix it with fuel oil for personal demolition uses.

The fertilizer industry has opposed federal regulations requiring buyers to show identification. Only Nevada and South Carolina have state laws requiring tracking fertilizer purchases. Even if there were laws requiring identification to purchase ammonium nitrate fertilizer, such actions would be virtually useless, as the fertilizer is frequently stored by businesses in large quantities with minimum or no security measures to prevent theft. Several educational campaigns have been attempted to encourage manufacturers, distributors, and retailers to prevent and report theft.

For the most part, the primary reason that terrorists might have difficulty obtaining large quantities of ammonium nitrate fertilizer is that most retailers are located in rural areas and the sales personnel know their customers. A stranger attempting to purchase several thousand pounds of ammonium nitrate fertilizer would be suspicious. Law enforcement officers have visited thousands of businesses that sell fertilizer to alert them to report such suspicious activity.

Besides improvised car bombs or truck bombs using fertilizer and fuel oil, a terrorist could inflict significant damage by hijacking a tractor-trailer carrying explosive or hazardous materials. There are 23.8 million trucks used for business purposes and 70 million more in personal use. There are 600,000 trucking companies, which have 2.6 million tractors, 3.1 million big-rig drivers, and 5 million trailers.[90] Such an armada of trucks is nearly impossible to regulate. The problem is compounded by the fact that unlike commercial aviation that is regulated by the FAA, motor vehicles are registered and regulated by each of the states.

There is some regulation of truck drivers licensed to transport hazardous materials. Such drivers are required to be licensed by the state to transport hazardous, explosive, or toxic materials. New federal regulations effective January 2005 require states to collect fingerprints from "hazmat" (hazardous materials) drivers and for applicants to undergo FBI background checks. The effectiveness of registration of hazmat drivers to prevent terrorist attacks is questionable. Persons alleged to be members of al-Qaida terrorist cells have been arrested with valid commercial drivers licenses, including validations for the transportation of hazardous and toxic materials.

If a terrorist were to hijack a tractor-trailer carrying explosive, toxic, or hazardous materials and the hijacking was detected by law enforcement, how could such a vehicle be safely stopped? Without a way to stop the vehicle, the terrorist could drive right down Main Street, USA, and detonate the vehicle at the target of his or her choosing. The Department of Homeland Security has submitted a proposal to the Federal Motor Carrier Safety Administration, which regulates truck safety, to require federal regulations for trucks to be equipped with truck-stopping devices that would allow law enforcement to stop a suspect truck.[91]

Growing concerns about truck bombs have prompted the authorities in California to look with new interest at an invention designed in 2001 to disable big rigs hijacked by terrorists.[92] The truck-stopping device was developed at Lawrence Livermore Laboratories. The mechanism, mounted at the rear of a truck, activates the emergency brakes when triggered by taps from a pursuing vehicle's bumper or by a remote control signal.[93] The California Trucking Association opposes legislation that would require the device, saying that "the device was created by people who didn't understand terrorism and didn't understand trucking."[94] Officials of the trucking industry fear that the device would actually make it easier for terrorists to hijack a truck by activating the device. Also, they fear that it could be accidentally activated when a truck backs into a loading dock. Finally, they fear that if trucks were equipped with such devices, motorists might engage in trucking stopping as a mischievous activity.[95]

Physical Security: The Last Line of Defense

Federal agents acknowledge that the United States has virtually no defense against a terrorist barreling down the street with a truck bomb.[96] A Bureau of Alcohol, Tobacco, Firearms and Explosives official warned, "If a person doesn't care about dying, [he or she] can pull right up to a building, push a button and the building would go."[97] The prevention of future attacks by terrorists using truck bombs and improvised weapons depends primarily on intelligence and preventive security measures to "harden" potential targets. The United States has spent more than $1 billion on efforts to stop the explosion of a car bomb or truck bomb at a government installation or other structure.[98] However, an ATF agent said, "The only true defense is to shut the road down."[99]

BOX 5.3 • *Consider This: Would a National ID Card Help Fight Terrorism?*

More than 100 nations have some kind of national identification card. The United States and Great Britain are not among these nations. However, in November 2004, the British government announced plans to introduce national identity cards for the first time since the World War II era.[100] The British plan is to require compulsory national identification cards by 2008. Queen Elizabeth II, on behalf of the government, said national identification cards were needed because Britons "live in a time of global uncertainty with an increased threat from international terrorism and organized crime."[101] Conservatives and liberal democrats assailed the plan as "politics of fear" and "an enormous threat to privacy and liberty." In the United States, a similar conflict is occurring over national identification cards for America.

For some countries, providing fake passports is a thriving industry. However, it is not necessary to travel abroad to obtain counterfeit identification documents. Simply go to www.google.com and request a search for "fake id." You will get hundreds of thousands of hits. Many of the websites advertise "Best effective fake photo IDs available," "Best quality, fastest delivery, lowest price!," "Most effective fake id cards available anywhere," and "All our fake ID cards go through strict quality control."

No wonder federal authorities and the Government Accountability Office concluded obtaining fake licenses by using counterfeit documents is "relatively easy." In investigations testing the system, some investigators were able to obtain an official state driver's license or a state identity card from the Virginia motor vehicle department, where five of the September 11 hijackers had illegitimately obtained driver's licenses. One test of the system indicated that one state motor vehicle department had issued licenses and identity cards to 41 people who used names of people listed as deceased in the Social Security Administration's master death file.[102]

Following the 9/11 attacks there was an immediate call for mandatory national identification cards,[103] especially as a proposed solution to address airport security. Most of the proposals for a national identification card envision an identification card with biometric and photographic data. Critics argue that a national identification card would not have any impact on fighting terrorism but would significantly increase government control and surveillance over persons. Civil rights libertarians protest the adoption of mandatory national identification cards. The American Civil Liberties Union (ACLU) said national identification cards would be "impractical and ineffective." The ACLU argues that national identification cards would only "threaten our right to privacy and foster new forms of discrimination." The ACLU also believes that just as "the Social Security Act originally contained strict prohibitions against use of the Social Security card for unrelated purposes, over the past 50 years those prohibitions have been ignored or legislated into oblivion . . . restrictions on a national I.D. card would follow the same path."[104] According to the ACLU, a national identification card would become "an internal passport" and failure to carry a national identification card would likely be viewed as a reason for search, detention, or arrest of minorities.[105]

Despite protests that national identification cards would lead to the loss of personal liberties, the United States seems to be moving toward the adoption of a national identification card or an identification system regulated by the federal government. The U.S. public is becoming more and more agreeable to the idea, leaning toward security as opposed to civil liberties in the fight against terrorism. Some are referring to a national identification card as a "fundamental issue" in the war on terrorism.[106] The 9/11 Commission called identification cards "the last opportunity to ensure that people are who they say they are and to check whether they are terrorists."[107]

The Department of Transportation, acting on instructions from Congress, has begun work with states to develop electronically smarter driver's licenses with a standardized format and biometric data that can be checked for validity across the country. The "standardized smart-driver's license" would not be a national identification card, but it would the next closest document to it.[108] It

BOX 5.3 • Continued

would actually be a part of a new nationwide network that would link all drivers' licenses to a central database. A standardized smart-driver's license would contain digital information about a person's identity, address, and "digital watermark" that would make tampering detectable. If adopted, the information and "look" of the standardized smart-driver's license would be determined by the Department of Homeland Security.[109] A standard "look" is considered an important tool in helping law enforcement and security personnel to identify valid driver's licenses. With each state issuing its own driver's licenses and each state's licenses different from the others, the task of identifying a valid license is extremely difficult. The proposed legislation also would allow the Department of Homeland Security to mandate a "standardized look" and decide what information to include on the driver's licenses. Furthermore, legislation would allow the Department of Homeland Securi-

ty to require that travelers show this identification card when using "any mode of transportation."[110] The American Civil Liberties Union said the new standards set by the Homeland Security and Transportation departments would be a "back door" for licenses to become the de facto national identification card.[111]

Questions

1. What do you think about requiring national identification cards for everyone in the United States? Do you think it would help in the war on terrorism? Why or why not?

2. What abuses could occur if everyone was required to have a national identification card?

3. Do you think a standardized smart-driver's license is a "back door" to a national identification card? Explain your answer.

Terrorists can use cars, vans, limousines, trucks, or tractor-trailers to blow up buildings, bridges, and tunnels, or as anti-personnel bombs. Blast walls, barricades, and setbacks are the last line of defense against such attacks. The problem is securing buildings and infrastructures without impeding normal life and commerce.

Sometimes it is impossible to provide both security and freedom of movement. For example, in August 2004, when the New York City police department received a federal alert about possible terrorist plots, the only option to ensure the safety of the city was to ban trucks and vans using the various bridges and tunnels providing access to and from Manhattan. After three days the ban was partly lifted on some bridges and tunnels and trucks were allowed to enter Manhattan subject to inspection. The prohibition and inspection of truck traffic caused significant traffic congestion and disruption of commerce but was considered necessary in light of the threat. Also, during the Republican National Convention any truck passing within proximity of Madison Square Garden was stopped and inspected for hazardous or destructive materials at checkpoints by barriers strong enough to stop a large truck if it tried to break through.

Cities considered to be likely targets by terrorists are being transformed by roadblocks, checkpoints, and barriers. When a national alert was announced naming the financial institutions of the Northeast as targets, metal barricades and trucks were used to block intersections. Parking spaces near potential targeted buildings were closed and checkpoints stopped traffic for inspections. The sidewalk by the Morgan Stanley building was transformed into 700 feet of pen-like enclosure. New York Governor George Pataki called the physical security protecting the New York financial district "obtrusive, obnoxious security measures."[112]

City officials in Washington, D.C., object to the fact that the proliferation of concrete barricades and checkpoints is making "this place feel like Fortress Washington."[113] Road-blocks and checkpoints create a maze that is intrusive and backs up traffic. Closed parking spaces have cost the city $100,000 a month in parking revenue.[114] What is considered to be excessive street closures in the name of security has prompted D.C. officials to threaten to sue the federal government in the event that additional streets are closed on 15th Street NW east of the White House and Treasury building in response to a heightened security alert. Local officials say, "Closing streets wreaks havoc on traffic and tourism and damages the city's sense of well-being without eliminating the threat of terror attacks."[115]

The threat of car bombs and truck bombs has reshaped the cityscape. The most effective preventive measure to minimize the damage from a car or truck bomb is distance. Therefore, "Jersey barriers" are appearing everywhere. Jersey barriers are the long concrete slabs used as a traffic barrier. They were developed by the New Jersey State Highway Department and are commonly used to redirect traffic in highway construction projects. They are easy to erect and effective in diverting traffic but they are ugly. Jersey barriers can provide a barrier to car bombs and truck bombs but they can also "psychologically subvert their own purpose. When you put Jersey barriers in, it proclaims the need for them, which makes people uneasy. . . . You exacerbate the sense of danger."[116]

The Transformation of Public Spaces

The advent of powerful car and truck bombs driven by suicidal assailants has made enhanced security measures unavoidable. There appears to be no end to the potential threat on public building and infrastructure targets. Recognizing that enhanced physical security will be a permanent requirement to protect against terrorist attacks, many cities and businesses are beginning to transform the look and nature of public spaces to achieve the security needed to defend Main Street, USA, against suicide bombers and at the same time provide a sense of security and aesthetics. Jersey barriers are being replaced with permanent barriers that provide the same positive control of pedestrian and traffic but forms a layered line of defense through which pedestrians can travel easily and confidently.[117] Retractable metal posts known as *bollards* are replacing Jersey barriers. In some places officials and architects are working to construct more aesthetically pleasing yet just as effective physical security barriers. For example, randomly stacked, rough-edged granite slabs replaced Jersey barriers at the Warren E. Burger Federal Building and United States Court House in St. Paul, Minnesota. The granite slabs provide physical security and at the same time people can sit on them and skateboard on them. Architects are working on ways to transform everyday urban objects, such as park benches, bicycle racks, planters, and lampposts, into security devices that would be capable of stopping a truck bomber.[118] Washington, D.C., officials are exploring plans to build a tunnel under the White House complex as a way to divert potential truck bombers away from this sensitive area but at the same time avoid the feeling of a fortress.

Knowing that physical security to minimize the damage from truck bombs will be a permanent need, Washington, D.C., is working to strike a balance between security and openness. One of the strategies to achieve this balance is the creation of pedestrian plazas at Washington landmarks. By permanently redirecting traffic away from the landmarks, public spaces can be both secure and welcoming.[119] One of the first of these pedestrian plazas was opened in November 2004. The street between the White House and Lafayette Square was closed due to security concerns. This street connected the White House and the Capitol and the three branches of government. It was rebuilt at a cost of $23 million as a pedestrian plaza and opened to the public.

Checkpoints and inspection for car and truck bombs are becoming more common and performed in more locations than ever before. For example, vehicular traffic is being stopped at the United Nations building and inspected by bomb-sniffing dogs. The Department of Homeland Security has deployed a mobile X-ray truck that takes X-ray pictures of unoccupied vehicles as they are loaded onto the ferry from New Jersey to New York. The project was started in October 2004 and is considered a pilot program. During the pilot stage X-ray scanning will be voluntary. Drivers who agree to have their car scanned will be asked to leave their cars and to remove pets. However, if the pilot is considered successful as a deterrent against car and truck bombs, the Department of Homeland Security will consider a decision to make the inspections compulsory and to use it at other locations. A spokesperson for the Department of Homeland Security said the "ferry scanning program was part of an effort to use advanced technology in the government's crime prevention and anti-terrorism efforts."[120] The spokesperson indicated that X-raying of vehicles might become a common preventive measure, just as airports have adopted various advanced technologies to verify the identities of workers and travelers.

Major public events are also being transformed by the threat of bombings. For example, major sports events could be opportunistic targets for terrorist bombers so security officials have taken significant actions to enhance security. Sports domes are being equipped with video surveillance equipment, parking garages attached to sports complexes are being closed, and street parking surrounding stadiums has been restricted to minimize the threat of car bombs. At some major sports events the National Guard joins state and local police in providing security, and the use of metal detectors has become commonplace.[121]

Fearing what is called the "Madrid factor," the influence the Madrid train bombing had on national elections in Spain, local and federal governments have placed greater emphasis on physical security during times when a terrorist attack could impact the actions or policies of the government or the outcome of an election. Thus, security was enhanced at polling places during the 2004 presidential elections and President Bush's second inauguration was protected by unprecedented physical security including barriers, checkpoints, metal detectors along the parade route, and 2,500 law enforcement officers and 4,000 combat troops.[122]

New standards for government buildings have been adopted that will transform the look of and access to government buildings and will incorporate new post-September 11 security standards. The primary focus of these new standards is to make buildings less vulnerable to explosives, as car bombs or other explosives are considered the most likely form of attack.[123] The level of physical security required varies by the size and purpose of the building. Large federal buildings and federal buildings housing law enforcement agencies and day-care facilities will require higher physical security. Among other requirements, depending on the size and purpose of the building, the new standards could require:[124]

- A deep setback of the entrance from the street—30 to 50 feet
- The building to be constructed of precast concrete reinforced with steel to withstand the pressures of an explosion
- "Progressive collapse avoidance structural engineering" that will prevent the building from pancaking in the event of structural failure
- A lobby that is "expendable" in the case of a blast to confine causalities to that area
- Garages that are separate hardened structures so that if a bomb goes off underground, the impact will not be felt elsewhere in the building
- Air intake equipment located on the roof to protect occupants from chemical or biological attacks
- Blast-resistant windows
- Access control for entrances and parking lots

Obviously, these new physical security standards will increase the cost of federal buildings. Some question whether the new standards will tend to move federal buildings into suburban office parks to avoid high-rise building or whether new security standards may ban nongovernment tenants and businesses. Even if nongovernment tenants were permitted in the building, there is concern that many customers would find the enhanced security and access control too intimidating, which could impact the success of the business.

Nonvehicle Suicide Bombers

In Israel 77 percent of Palestinian suicide bombers carried the bomb on their bodies rather than used cars or trucks. In nearly all of the suicide bombings involving bombs carried on the body, the target was to inflict damage to people surrounding the bomber rather than to cause damage to infrastructure targets or targets with strategic value. In Israel over 90 percent of suicide bombers exploded their bomb at a place where there was a large concentration of people. The most often targets selected were at a shopping mall (38 percent), while using public transportation (30 percent), or at a bus or railway station (23 percent). The choice of targets clearly illustrates that the prime purpose of the suicide bomber is to cause widespread fear and panic among the general population.

The United States has escaped the wave of suicide bombers wearing bomb jackets whose aim is to detonate it in a crowded public place in order to kill innocent men, women, and children. Domestic terrorists have extensively used bombs, including car and truck bombs, but there are few incidences of suicide bombers among domestic terrorists groups such as right-wing extremists, animal rights groups, and hate groups. In those incidents involving domestic terrorist suicide bombers, it seems they are "loners" more motivated by suicide than homicide. On the other hand, the primary objective of Middle East suicide bombers is the killing of civilians.

Experts have hypothesized that the instinct for self-preservation appears to have moderated the development and spread of the suicide bomber among domestic terror groups. However, among Middle East terrorist groups there appears to be a willingness of certain followers of Middle East radical groups, including al-Qaida and Hamas, to volunteer—to be eager—to advance the cause of their group by becoming a suicide bomber.

Authorities have asked why the homeland has thus far escaped such attacks by Middle East suicide bombers.[125] One theory is that moderate Muslim donors in America are seen as a source of significant financial support and such suicide bombings would change their willingness to support Middle East groups. Another theory is that U.S. domestic terrorists and U.S. converts to Middle East-related terrorist groups still have an intrinsic value that defines suicide as "mental illness" and are less likely to become suicide bombers. Finally, it is hypothesized that although there are numerous followers in the Middle East who would be willing to come to America as suicide bombers, they simply cannot get visas to enter the United States.[126]

Numerous physical security measures have been taken to counter car and truck bombs, but the transformation of pubic buildings, spaces, and transportation to protect against suicide bombers carrying bombs on their bodies would require extensive resources and would be very intrusive. There are very limited options when it comes to stopping a suicide bomber who is wearing a bomb jacket. Usually the bomb is designed to explode when the person releases the trigger, rather than presses the trigger. This design means that even if the bomber is killed or disabled, the bomb will still blow up when the trigger mechanism is released due to death or unconsciousness. Intervention by law enforcement, security, or other personnel is extremely hazardous to both the person intervening and bystanders. For example, once a suicide bomber wearing a bomb jacket or carrying a bomb entered a large shopping mall, it would be virtually impossible to disable the bomber before he or she could activate the bomb. Early detection by alert security personnel may minimize the damage if the bomber is forced to detonate his or her bomb prior to the planned target, but an explosion anywhere inside the mall would be deadly. If Americans lose confidence in their safety in malls, public buildings, buses, subways, and public places, the psychological and economic impact of widespread fear would be devastating to the economy and to confidence in the government.

Although there have been no incidences of suicide bombers carrying bombs on their person into crowded public places and detonating them, the sheer number of suicide attacks in the Middle East require that U.S. authorities should be engaged in groundwork to prevent possible attacks. The American culture is not prepared for dealing with the concept of a suicide bomber, especially young male and female bombers. However, suicide bombers are a tool in the terrorist's arsenal that is frequently used elsewhere in the world. Often its use is quite effective in causing widespread fear. The migration of such tactics to the United States is more probable than not. The belief that "since it has not occurred here, it will not" is shortsighted and potentially exposes Main Street, USA, to significant risk.

Conclusion: Will It Be Enough?

A report assessing preparation for future terrorist attacks asked the question, "American law enforcement is working diligently to prevent the next terrorist attack. Will it be enough?"[127] Defending the homeland against terrorist attacks is a new challenge that has never been faced by local, state, and federal governments. Many changes have occurred since the 9/11 attacks to prevent future attacks. The Department of Homeland Security and new intelligence agencies have been created. The Federal Bureau of Investigation has reorganized. The firewall between the Central Intelligence Agency and domestic law enforcement agencies has been removed. Building, public spaces, and cities are being transformed to enhance physical security. However, it is impossible to provide 100 percent protection against future terrorist attacks.

Throughout history small groups of dedicated radicals have been able to cause widespread fear throughout great civilizations because terrorism is so difficult to defend against. The terrorists can choose from an infinite number of targets and can choose to strike at a time of their own choosing using the weapons of their choice. There simply are not enough local and federal resources to protect against such an enemy. Thus, it becomes necessary for governments to use their resources wisely. Governments must identify those targets most vulnerable, those targets that if attacked would cause the greatest harm, and those targets that if attacked would have the greatest psychological repercussions. Government must identify these targets and then develop strategies to defend them against future terrorist attacks with the resources available.

Governments must also identify agencies that are not optimally organized to defend the homeland and make changes to them. Since the 9/11 attacks local and federal governments have made significant changes, created new anti-terrorism agencies, and provided resources and funding to new programs. Often these changes have been stressful on government. In some cases changes to enhance one anti-terrorism program has detracted from another program as both compete for the same resources and personnel.

This chapter has focused on protecting Main Street, USA. Protecting Main Street against the threats discussed in this chapter is a formidable challenge but it is not the most difficult of the challenges facing the homeland. The next two chapters address the challenge of defending aviation from terrorism and the disquieting challenge of defending against an attack using a weapon of mass destruction.

Chapter Summary

- Questions as to whether the nation is safer from terrorism have resulted in counterterrorism plans and actions.
- The key strategies in being prepared to respond to future terrorist attacks are intelligence and prevention.
- The division between domestic intelligence and international intelligence is blamed in part for the failure to prevent the September 11, 2001, attacks. As a result, post-9/11 changes in intelligence have removed the firewall between these two. There has been an overhaul of the intelligence community. The Department of Homeland Security and the Federal Bureau of Investigation have assumed new intelligence responsibilities.
- Local law enforcement officers play an essential role in preventing terrorist attacks but lack critical intelligence to perform their mission.
- Various local, state, and federal agencies have key roles in preventing and responding to future terrorist attacks. The key federal agencies are the Department of Homeland Security and the Federal Bureau of Investigation. Local police and fire departments are first responders. Feeling that government cannot provide for their safety, many citizens have turned to volunteer and self-defense groups.
- Suicide bombers using large truck and/or car bombs are seen as likely future terrorist attacks. The best line of defense against such an attack is physical security. As a re-

sult, public spaces are being transformed to defend against and minimize damage from suicide bombers.

Terrorism and You

Understanding This Chapter

1. Why does the traditional organizational structure of U.S. law enforcement create barriers to responding to future terrorist attacks?

2. Why are intelligence and prevention the two key strategies for responding to future terrorist attacks?

3. What is the difference between the roles of the CIA and the FBI in counterterrorism?

4. What changes have been made in international and domestic intelligence?

5. What new intelligence agencies have been created to fight terrorism?

6. Why is there a need for federal-local cooperation in intelligence gathering, analysis, and dissemination?

7. What federal agencies have primary roles in responding to terrorism?

8. What is the role of local and state agencies in responding to terrorism?

9. Why are truck and car bombs a significant threat to homeland security?

10. How has the threat of truck and car bombs transformed public spaces?

Thinking about How Terrorism Touches You

1. How much information should local and federal law enforcement and intelligence agencies be permitted to gather about persons suspected of terrorism? Do you believe your local law enforcement agency is properly trained to recognize suspicious activities?

2. While in public places and in federal and local government buildings are you fearful of suicide bombers? Have you noticed any physical security changes aimed at stopping truck and car bombs?

3. Have you joined a volunteer group or sought self-defense information to prepare yourself for a terrorist attack? Do you think such actions are effective? What do you think about the use of personal firearms to protect against homeland terrorists attacks?

4. Were you concerned that terrorists might execute a major attack during the 2004 presidential elections in an effort to influence the elections?

5. If a national identification card or a standardized smart-driver's license were mandatory, how could the uses for such a card evolve? Could it replace the use of one's social security number as an identification number? Could it be used as an ATM card? Could it be required for employment, helping to eliminate the problem of illegal aliens working without work permits?

6. The American Civil Liberties Union (ACLU) says the primary purpose of a national identification card is to provide for legislation that would enable law enforcement to stop anyone

simply to demand to see his or her identification card. The ACLU believes law enforcement could abuse such power to randomly stop minorities and persons of color. Do you agree with this criticism of national identification cards?

Important Terms and Concepts

American Civil Liberties Union (ACLU)
Ammonium Nitrate/Fuel Oil Bombs
Central Intelligence Agency (CIA)
Citizen Corps
College of Analytical Studies
Color-Coded Terrorist Threat Levels
Command and Control
Counterterrorism Watch (CT Watch)
Department of Homeland Security (DHS)
Department of Justice
Document Exploitation Working Group (DocEX)
Federal Bureau of Investigation (FBI)
First Responders
High-Profile Events
Homeland Security from the Citizens' Perspective

Information Analysis and Infrastructure Protection
    (IAIP)
Jersey Barriers
Joint Local-Federal Task Forces (JTTFs)
Key Assets
Madrid Factor
National Identification Card
Office of Intelligence
Suicide Bombers
Terrorism Information and Prevention Systems
    (TIPS)
Terrorist Threat Integration Center (TTIC)
Truck Bombs
USA Freedom Corps

Endnotes

1. Tom Regan, "Global Opinion: World Is Not a Safer Place," *Christian Science Monitor,* www.csmonitor.com, September 6, 2004.

2. Douglas Jehl, "Intelligence Report to Assess Threat Posed by Terrorists," New York Times Online, www.nytimes.com, October 28, 2004.

3. Gerald R. Murphy and Martha R. Plotkin, *Protecting Your Community from Terrorism: Strategies for Local Law Enforcement, Volume I: Local-Federal Partnerships.* Washington DC: U.S. Department of Justice, 2003, p. 1.

4. Ibid., p. 61.

5. *The National Strategy for the Physical Protection of Critical Infrastructures and Key Assets.* Washington, DC: Office of Homeland Security, February 2003, p. 1.

6. *National Strategy for Homeland Security.* Washington, DC: Office of Homeland Security, July 2002, p. vii.

7. *The National Strategy for the Physical Protection of Critical Infrastructures and Key Assets,* February 2003, p. viii.

8. Ibid., p. xi.

9. United States Intelligence Community, "The Role of Intelligence in the United States Today," www.intelligence.gov/0-role_intell.shtml, November 12, 2004.

10. Faye Bowers, "An Internal War at the CIA," *Christian Science Monitor,* www.csmonitor.com, November 16, 2004.

11. Douglas Jehl, "2 Top Officials Are Reported to Quit C.I.A.," New York Times Online, www.nytimes.com, November 25, 2004.

12. Ibid.

13. Eric Lichtblau, "F.B.I. and C.I.A. Set for a Major Consolidation in Counterterror," New York Times Online, www.nytimes.com, February 15, 2003.

14. George W. Bush, "Fact Sheet: Strengthening Intelligence to Better Protect America," www.whitehouse.gov/news/release/2003/01/print/20030128-12.html, January 28, 2003.

15. Associated Press, "Details of Counterterror Center Unveiled," New York Times Online, www.nytimes.com, February 14, 2003.

16. George W. Bush, "Fact Sheet: Strengthening Intelligence to Better Protect America," www.whitehouse.gov/news/release/2003/01/print/20030128-12.html, January 28, 2003.

17. Eric Lichtblau, "Report Questions the Value of Color-Coded Warnings," New York Times Online, www.nytimes.com, July 13, 2004.

18. Ibid.

19. Eric Lichtblau, "F.B.I. Issues and Retracts Urgent

Terrorism Bulletin," New York Times. www.nytimes.com, May 29, 2004.

20. David Stout, "Bush Signs Bill to Revamp U.S. Intelligence Community," New York Times Online, www.nytimes.com, December 17, 2004.

21. Gerald R. Murphy and Martha R. Plotkin, *Protecting Your Community from Terrorism: Strategies for Local Law Enforcement, Volume I: Local-Federal Partnerships.* Washington DC: U.S. Department of Justice, 2003, p. 53.

22. Ibid., p. 9.

23. Ibid., p. 31.

24. Ibid., p. 1.

25. Ibid., p. 32.

26. Ibid., p. 54.

27. Ibid., p. 53.

28. Adam Clymer, "Worker Corps to be Formed to Report Odd Activity," New York Times Online, www.nytimes.com, July 26, 2002.

29. Ibid.

30. Ibid.

31. Ibid.

32. Gerald R. Murphy and Martha R. Plotkin, *Protecting Your Community from Terrorism: Strategies for Local Law Enforcement, Volume I: Local-Federal Partnerships.* Washington DC: U.S. Department of Justice, 2003, p. 72.

33. *The Inman Report: Report of the Secretary of State's Advisory Panel on Overseas Security,* www.fas.org/irp/threat/inman/part08.htm, July 5, 2003.

34. Gerald R. Murphy and Martha R. Plotkin, *Protecting Your Community from Terrorism: Strategies for Local Law Enforcement, Volume I: Local-Federal Partnerships.* Washington DC: U.S. Department of Justice, 2003, p. 41.

35. James Risen and David Johnston, "F.B.I. Was Warned It Could Not Meet Terrorism Threat," New York Times Online, www.nytimes.com, June 1, 2002.

36. Ibid.

37. Ibid.

38. Eric Lichtblau, "F.B.I. Officials Say Some Agents Lack a Focus on Terror," New York Times Online, www.nytimes.com, November 21, 2002.

39. Ibid.

40. Ibid.

41. Federal Bureau of Investigation, "War on Terrorism," www.fbi.gov/terrorinfo/counterrorism/waronterrorhome.htm, November 12, 2004.

42. Ibid.

43. Office for Domestic Preparedness, *The Office for Domestic Preparedness Guidelines for Homeland Security: Prevention and Deterrence.* Washington, DC: U.S. Department of Homeland Security, June 2003, p. 7.

44. Al Baker and Marc Santora, "First Steps and First Controversies for State Security Agency," New York Times Online, www.nytimes.com, February 17, 2004.

45. Robert F. Worth, "Questions about the Fitness of

Rowland's Security Chief," New York Times Online, www.nytimes.com, February 12, 2004.

46. Kevin Flynn, "New York City Officials Defend Counterterror Training," New York Times Online, www.nytimes.com, February 14, 2003.

47. Michelle O'Donnell, "2-year Fire Depart. Plan Girds for Terrorism," New York Times Online, www.nytimes.com, March 30, 2004.

48. Richard Lezin Jones, "500 Officers to Be Issued High-Powered Weapons Used by Elite Unit," New York Times Online, www.nytimes.com, December 16, 2001.

49. Jennifer Steinhauer, "Bloomberg Defends Changes to Fire Dept." New York Times Online, www.nytimes.com, May 28, 2004.

50. William K. Rashbaum, "Plan to Define Agencies' Roles in Emergencies Is Criticized," New York Times Online, www.nytimes.com, June 16, 2004.

51. Ibid.

52. Dean E. Murphy, "Armed for Terrorists, in Case Kindness Doesn't Work," New York Times Online, www.nytimes.com, February 8, 2004.

53. Diane Cardwell, "New System to Extend Harbor's Surveillance Beyond Horizon," New York Times Online, www.nytimes.com, February 26, 2003.

54. William K. Rashbaum and Judith Miller, "New York Police Take Broad Steps in Facing Terror," New York Times Online, www.nytimes.com, February 15, 2004.

55. Associated Press, "War Deployments Drain Police Departments," New York Times Online, www.nytimes.com, February 19, 2003.

56. Ibid.

57. Associated Press, "Small Town Feels Void After Call-Ups," New York Times Online, www.nytimes.com, March 12, 2003.

58. Jennifer Lee, "Thin Work Force of North Dakota Gets Thinner as Residents Go to War," New York Times Online, www.nytimes.com, April 3, 2003.

59. Sarah Kershaw, "Governors Tell of War's Impact on Local Needs," New York Times Online, www.nytimes.com, July 20, 2004.

60. Thomas J. Lueck, "Convention to Delay Some Cases in City Courts," New York Times Online, www.nytimes.com, July 21, 2004.

61. "To Serve and Deport," New York Times Online, www.nytimes.com, November 9, 2003.

62. Ibid.

63. Vicki Haddock, "Public Eye: Hundreds of Thousands of Surveillance Cameras Across America Track Our Behavior Every Day," *San Francisco Chronicle,* www.sfgate.com/cgi-bin/article.cgi?f=/c/a/2004/10/17/ING3Q98R2A1.DTL, October 17, 2004.

64. Debbie Howlett, "Chicago Plans Advanced Surveillance," *USA Today,* September 10, 2004, p. 3A.

65. Stephen Kinzer, "Chicago Moving to 'Smart' Sur-

veillance Cameras," New York Times Online, www. nytimes.com, September 21, 2004.

66. Dawn Turner Trice, "Despite Threats, We Must Keep Eye on Cameras," Chicago Tribune Online Edition, www.chicagotribune.com, September 13, 2004.

67. Ibid.

68. Vicki Haddock, "Public Eye: Hundreds of Thousands of Surveillance Cameras Across America Track Our Behavior Every Day," *San Francisco Chronicle,* www. sfgate.com/cgi-bin/article.cgi?f=/c/a/2004/10/17 /ING3Q98R2A1.DTL, October 17, 2004.

69. Debbie Howlett, "Chicago Plans Advanced Surveillance," *USA Today,* September 10, 2004, p. 3A.

70. Vicki Haddock, "Public Eye: Hundreds of Thousands of Surveillance Cameras Across America Track Our Behavior Every Day," San Francisco Chronicle, www. sfgate.com/cgi-bin/article.cgi?f=/c/a/2004/10/17/ ING3Q98R2A1.DTL, October 17, 2004.

71. Stephen Kinzer, "Chicago Moving to 'Smart' Surveillance Cameras," New York Times Online, www. nytimes.com, September 21, 2004.

72. Vicki Haddock, "Public Eye: Hundreds of Thousands of Surveillance Cameras Across America Track Our Behavior Every Day," San Francisco Chronicle, www. sfgate.com/cgi-bin/article.cgi?f=/c/a/2004/10/17/ ING3Q98R2A1.DTL, October 17, 2004.

73. George W. Bush, "Fact Sheet: A Better Prepared America: A Year in Review," www.whitehouse.gov/news/ releases/2004/05/print/20040525-4.html, May 25, 2004.

74. Information about Citizen Corps can be found at www.citizencorps.gov.

75. Dan Barry, "Citizen Corps? Hang on, New York," New York Times Online, www.nytimes.com, April 9, 2003.

76. "Homeland Security from the Citizens' Perspective," www.citizensecure.org.

77. Ibid.

78. Associated Press, "Man Charged in Alleged Plot on Ohio Mall," New York Times Online, www.nytimes.com, June 14, 2004.

79. Earle Eldridge, "Dealerships Sell Armored Cars," USA Today, March 31, 2003, p. 3B.

80. Al Baker, "Steep Rise in Gun Sales Reflects Post-Attack," New York Times Online, www.nytimes.com, December 16, 2001.

81. Dana Candey, "Floridians Take War on Terror into Own Hands," New York Times Online, www.nytimes. com, January 1, 2002.

82. Sam Knight, The Day After Tomorrow (or Soon), They'll Be Ready if Disaster Strikes," New York Times Online, www.nytimes.com, June 20, 2004.

83. Elaine Shannon-Washington, "FBI Issues Homeland Suicide Bomber Warning," *Time,* May 20, 2004,

www.time.com/time/nation/printout/0,8816,640684,00. html.

84. Andrew C. Revkin, "Few Measures Exist to Avert Truck Bombs, Experts Say," New York Times Online, www.nytimes.com, August 3, 2004.

85. Elaine Shannon-Washington, "FBI Issues Homeland Suicide Bomber Warning," *Time,* May 20, 2004. www.time.com/time/nation/printout/0,8816,640684,00. html.

86. David Johnston, "U.S. Agency Sees Global Network for Bomb Making," New York Times Online, www. nytimes.com, February 22, 2004.

87. Ibid.

88. Spencer S. Hsu and Sari Horwitz, "Impervious Shield Elusive Against Drive-By Terrorists," *Washington Post,* August 8, 2004, p. 1.

89. Ibid.

90. Ibid.

91. Dean E. Murphy, "California Looks Anew at a Truck-Stopping Device," New York Times Online, www. nytimes.com, August 6, 2004.

92. Ibid.

93. Ibid.

94. Ibid.

95. Ibid.

96. Spencer S. Hsu and Sari Horwitz, "Impervious Shield Elusive Against Drive-By Terrorists," *Washington Post,* August 8, 2004, p. 1.

97. Ibid.

98. Ibid.

99. Ibid.

100. Alan Cowell, "Citing Terror Issues, Britain Plans ID Cards," New York Times Online, www.nytimes.com, November 24, 2003.

101. Ibid.

102. Jennifer Lee, "Fake Licenses Are Still Seen as Easy to Obtain," New York Times Online, www.nytimes.com, September 9, 2003.

103. Jennifer Jones, "Sept. 11 Attacks Stir National ID Card Debate," *InfoWorld*, www.infoworld.com/articles/hn/ xml/01/09/25/010925hnidcard.html, September 25, 2001.

104. American Civil Liberties Union, "National Identification Cards: Why Does the ACLU Oppose a National I.D. System?" www.aclu.org/news/NewsPrint.cfm?ID= 9938&c=22, March 12, 2002.

105. Ibid.

106. Leslie Miller, "National ID Card Suggested," *The Detroit News,* www.detnews.com/2004/politics/0408/17/ a04-244103.htm, August 17, 2004.

107. Matthew L. Wald, "A Smarter License: What Can It Tell? New York Times Online, www.nytimes.com, October 27, 2004.

108. Frank Pellegrini, "The National ID Card That Isn't,

Yet," *Time,* www.time.com/time/nation/printout/0,8816, 191857,00.html, January 8, 2002.

109. Mathew L. Wald, "Congress Close to Establishing Rules for Driver's Licenses," New York Times Online, www.nytimes.com, October 11, 2004.

110. Ibid.

111. Audrey Hudson, "National ID Cards Feared in License Standards," *The Washington Times,* http://washtimes.com/national/20041007-123853-6683r.htm, October 7, 2004.

112. David W. Dunlap, "Financial District Security Getting New Look," New York Times Online, www.nytimes.com, November 27, 2003.

113. Rachel L. Swarns, "Is Anti-Terrorist Anti-Tourist?" New York Times Online, www.nytimes.com, October 31, 2004.

114. James Dao, "Federal Roadblocks and Checkpoints Creating Capital Maze," New York Times Online, www.nytimes.com, August 7, 2004.

115. Debbie Wilgoren, "D.C. May Sue Government if 15th Street Is Closed," *Washington Post,* August 7, 2004, p. A2.

116. David W. Dunlap, "Envisioning a Safer City Without Turning It into Slab City," New York Times Online, www.nytimes.com, April 17, 2003.

117. Ibid.

118. Ibid.

119. Manny Fernandez, "America's Main Street Revisited," *Washington Post,* November 10, 2004, p. A1.

120. Iver Peterson, "In Test, X-Rays Scan Cars as Part of Antiterror Effort," New York Times Online, www.nytimes.com, October 22, 2004.

121. Associate Press, "At Superdome, Security Is Bolstered for Sugar Bowl," New York Times Online, www.nytimes.com, January 2, 2004.

122. Sari Horwitz and Spencer S. Hsu, "Unrivaled Security Planned for Inauguration," *Washington Post,* November 7, 2004, p. A10.

123. Terry Pristin, "U.S. Landlords Face Post-9/11 Standards," New York Times Online, www.nytimes.com, February 11, 2004.

124. Ibid.

125. Elaine Shannon-Washington, "FBI Issues Homeland Suicide Bomber Warning," *Time,* www.time.com/time/nation/printout/0,8816,640684,00.html, May 20, 2004.

126. Ibid.

127. Gerald R. Murphy and Martha R. Plotkin, *Protecting Your Community from Terrorism: Strategies for Local Law Enforcement, Volume I: Local-Federal Partnerships.* Washington DC: U.S. Department of Justice, 2003, p. 77.

6

Defending Aviation from Terrorism

The threat to the aviation industry from terrorists is a relatively new phenomenon. As a result, there have been many major changes in aviation security in a very short time. The government continues to explore new strategies to stop terrorist attacks against the aviation industry.

> *Before September 2001, GAO's work in transportation security focused largely on aviation security. . . . This work often demonstrated the existence of significant, long-standing vulnerabilities in aviation security. . . . The Departments of Transportation and Homeland Security face long-term transportation security challenges. . . . The enormous size of the U.S. airspace alone defies easy protection, and no form of travel can ever be made totally secure.*
>
> —Gerald L. Dillingham, *Transportation Security:*
> *Post-September 11th Initiatives and Long-Term Challenges*
> (Washington, DC: GAO), 2003, pp. i, 2.

Chapter Outline

Learning Objectives

- After reading this chapter the reader will understand why aviation security is a modern problem and why the aviation industry did not focus on aviation security during its formative years.
- The reader will understand how aviation security underwent a dramatic transformation after 9/11.

- The reader will know the major priorities of the government to improve aviation security.
- The reader will know how the government is tightening security regarding passenger identification and immigration controls.
- The reader will understand the reasons that some government aviation programs, such as CAPPS II and the No-Fly List, were rejected or criticized by the public.
- The reader will understand TSA's role in passenger screening.
- The reader will understand the difficulties of defending aircraft against portable surface-to-air missiles.
- The reader will know the major in-flight security strategies that have been implemented to counter hijacking.
- The reader will understand the limitations of the government in addressing all threats to aviation security.

Introduction: Aviation—The Sleeping Threat

The Wright brothers' first flight was in 1904. The aircraft carried a single passenger and its maximum range was measured in feet and minutes. Hijacking the aircraft was impossible. Even as the aviation industry developed, criminal and terrorist attacks on aircraft were relatively uncommon during the formative years of aviation. Airport security and in-flight security were minimum.[1] Friends and relatives could accompany air travelers to their gates and in some incidences passengers were even allowed to visit with the pilot while in flight. Because there were very few criminal or terrorist attacks on early aviation, security was not a major concern. The limitations of early propeller-driven aircraft made them unsuitable as weapons of mass destruction and few civilians had the ability to pilot the aircraft. The limited destructive power of early aircraft as "flying missiles" was demonstrated when on July 28, 1945, a U.S. Army B-25 bomber accidentally crashed into the seventy-ninth floor of the Empire State Building. The crash caused about a million dollars in damage to the building, killed 14 people and injured 26 people, but it did not cause any threat to the structure of the building.[2]

One hundred years after the Wright brothers' first flight, airplanes can transport hundreds of passengers at speeds in excess of 500 miles per hour and commercial flights span continents. Today, international aircraft and airports have become high-profile targets of terrorist groups.[3] Terrorists have successfully commandeered aircraft in flight, attacked passengers and personnel at airports, and exploded bombs in flight. As a result, aviation security has become a major concern of government, the airlines, and passengers.

The threat of jet aircraft as weapons of mass destruction has been awakened. This chapter will examine the threat posed to U.S. air travel by terrorist groups, the changes in aviation security that have occurred since the September 11 attacks, and the challenge of ensuring safe air travel without unacceptable infringements on passenger privacy and rights. The discussion will focus primarily on attacks and preventive measures on aircraft, passengers, and property in the continental United States.

The Emergence of Aviation Security

The Regulation of Commercial Aviation

Legislation addressing the regulation of civil aviation did not emerge until the Air Commerce Act of May 20, 1926. Prior to this legislation, aviation was virtually unregulated. The Air Commerce Act charged the Secretary of Commerce with "fostering air commerce, issuing and enforcing air traffic rules, licensing pilots, certificating aircraft, establishing airways, and operating and maintaining aid to air navigation."[4] The Aeronautics Branch of the Department of Commerce was renamed the Bureau of Air Commerce in 1934. In 1938, a newly created independent agency, the Civil Aeronautics Authority, assumed the powers of the Bureau of Air Commerce, but its primary mission continued to focus on economic regulation and governance of the airline industry. In 1940, responsibility for regulation of aviation was split between two agencies: the Civil Aeronautics Administration (CAA) and the Civil Aeronautics Board (CAB). Both agencies were still part of the Department of Commerce and concerned primarily with safety, development, accident investigation, and economic regulation.

The introduction of jet airliners and the new problems associated with high-speed jet travel resulted in the creation of a new independent body in 1958, the Federal Aviation Agency, which took over the responsibilities of the previous agencies. In 1966, the cabinet-level Department of Transportation (DOT) was created. The DOT was charged with combining major federal transportation responsibilities, including aviation. The Federal Aviation Agency was placed under the DOT and renamed the Federal Aviation Administration (FAA). Some of the accident investigation functions of the former CAB were transferred to the DOT's new National Transportation Safety Board. The primary mission of the FAA continued to be defined in terms of regulation and safety.

The Origins of Aviation Security: Bombs and Hijacking

The absence of emphasis on aviation security was due primarily to the lack of demonstrated need. The first recorded hijacking occurred in May 1930, when Peruvian revolutionaries seized a Pan American mail plane with the aim of dropping propaganda leaflets over Lima. No other hijacking was recorded until 1947. Between 1947 and 1958, 23 hijackings were reported, mostly committed by eastern Europeans seeking political asylum in the West.[5] The first major act of criminal violence against a U.S. airliner did not occur until November 1, 1955, when Jack Graham, seeking to collect his mother's life insurance policy, placed a bomb in luggage belonging to her and killed all 44 people on board a Denver-bound plane.[6] It was not until five years later that another bombing of an aircraft in flight occurred when a heavily insured suicide bomber killed all aboard a National Airlines plane. After this incident baggage inspection assumed an important role in aviation security.

During the 1960s and into the early 1970s, hijacking was one of the most serious security problems facing aviation. After Fidel Castro came into power in Cuba in 1959, a number of hijackings occurred to and from Cuba. In May 1961, the first American airliner was hijacked from the United States and diverted to Cuba. Legislation was passed in the United States, making air piracy (hijacking) a felony punishable by a minimum of 20 years imprisonment up to the death penalty. Additionally, international agreements were signed with the intent to discourage hijacking by requiring the prompt return of hijacked aircraft and passengers and criminalizing hijacking.[7] The hijackings abated until 1968. From 1968 to 1972, hijacking again became a serious security threat.

The public and government demanded increased security measures when eight airliners were hijacked to Cuba in January 1969. Responding to the demand for increased aviation security, the FAA created the Task Force on the Deterrence of Air Piracy. The Task Force developed a hijacker "profile," and required the use of metal detectors (magnetometers) in screening passengers.[8] The first deaths related to air piracy did not occur until March 1970, when a copilot was killed and a pilot and hijacker seriously hurt during a hijacking. The first passenger death in a U.S. hijacking occurred in June 1971.

The first hijacking of a U.S. aircraft flying outside the Western Hemisphere occurred when terrorists diverted an Israel-bound TWA aircraft to Syria in August 1969. Other overseas terrorists incidents included a hijacking by Arab terrorists in September 1970, during which four airlines were blown up. The escalating use of violence in air piracy in the early 1970s resulted in greater demand for aviation security. In response to this demand, on January 1, 1973, the FAA required the mandatory inspection of carry-on baggage and the scanning of all passengers before boarding. These measures appeared to have an impact, as the number of hijackings in the United States significantly diminished.

From February 1991 to September 11, 2001, there were no airline hijackings in the United States. However, bombings became the new bane of aviation security. In March 1972, bombs were discovered on three airliners. Two fatal bombings occurred in 1974 and 1975. A bomb exploded in September 1974 on a U.S. plane bound from Tel Aviv to New York, killing all 88 persons aboard. Another bomb exploded in a locker at New York's La-Guardia Airport in December 1975, killing 11.[9] On December 21, 1988, a bomb destroyed Pan American Flight 103 over Lockerbie, Scotland, killing all 259 people aboard the London-to-New York flight. In response to these incidents, new security measures were adopted requiring new equipment to detect bombs and weapons, the banning of certain hazardous materials from passenger airplanes, improvements in the effectiveness of screening personnel at airports, better controls of airport identification cards, the matching of passengers and their baggage, and the X-ray or search all checked baggage.

The impact of these measures appeared quite promising as the number of incidents of bombings abated. Although attacks of this kind were front-page headlines, there actually were relatively few such attacks on commercial aviation in the United States. Most of the major terrorist attacks on commercial aircraft originated at foreign airports. As late as 1999, the Federal Bureau of Investigation was downplaying the threat to commercial aviation in the United States. A special retrospective report by the FBI on 30 years of terrorism reported that the United States "remained largely untouched by serious acts of international terrorism."[10]

Prior to the September 11 attacks, aviation security was primarily concerned with bombs being placed on aircraft and hijacking by domestic terrorists, criminals, or mentally ill individuals. It was thought that these attacks were fairly well controlled by the passing of anti-hijacking legislation, the adoption of baggage and passenger screening, and better security at the gate. The response of the government and the airlines to these threats effectively "hardened" commercial aviation as a target of attack. Thus, despite sensational headlines throughout the later twentieth century, air travel was one of the safest modes of transportation per passenger mile.

The Crisis in Public Confidence

Public confidence in the ability of the FAA and airliners to provide adequate aviation security was shattered with the hijacking and subsequent use of the airliners as flying missiles on September 11, 2001. Major changes quickly occurred in aviation security following the September 11 terrorist attacks. The use of commercial civilian aircraft loaded with thousands of gallons of aviation fuel as flying missiles to attack the World Trade Center and Pentagon resulted in a complete reassessment of the adequacy of aviation security in the United States.

The extent of the resulting fear of terrorist attack by the public was indicated by the massive economic impact on the airlines as air travel plummeted to record lows. The drop in passenger travel crippled airlines and many, including some of the largest airliners, were unable to avoid bankruptcy. The economic impact caused by the fear of terrorism spread far beyond just the airline companies, as related businesses, such as crop dusting, were crippled due to fear that crop dusters could become weapons for terrorist to spread bio-chemical agents.[11] Airports were closed or demolished, as cities feared they could not provide protection against terrorists using the airfield to launch an attack.[12] Even entire cities suffered economic damage caused by the impact on aviation. The aircraft industry was one of the major economic sources of Wichita, Kansas, "The Air Capital of the World." Following September 11, 11,000 aircraft workers in Wichita were laid off, unemployment doubled, and food stamp cases rose 38 percent.[13] The crisis in public confidence in the security of air travel resulted in the complete overall of aviation security.

The Aviation Security Revolution

Prior to September 11, 2001, the Federal Aviation Administration and the individual airline carriers shared civil aviation security functions jointly. The FAA, under the authority of the Department of Transportation, was charged with the economic regulation of the airline industry, safety, and accident investigation. It gave little attention to the threat of terrorism.

On the morning of September 11, 2001, four commercial civilian aircraft were hijacked from airports in the continental United States. The hijackers crashed two of the jets into the twin towers of the World Trade Center; one was crashed into the Pentagon; and one crashed in a field in rural Pennsylvania as passengers, alerted to the fate of the other hijacked aircraft, stormed the cockpit to prevent the hijackers from using the fourth aircraft as a flying missile. The death toll from the four hijackings and crashes was nearly 3,000 people. The twin towers of the World Trade Center were completely destroyed. This attack was unprecedented both in the number of aircraft hijacked on United States soil and in the death toll. As a result of this single act of aviation piracy, there was an immediate and drastic heightening of air transportation security and a complete reorganization of the agencies responsible for air transportation security.

The success of the FAA and airlines, as measured by the absence of any bombings or hijackings of a U.S. commercial civilian aircraft for a decade prior to 9/11, bolstered the belief that the principles underlying the strategy for aviation security were valid. In hindsight, the strategy underlying aviation security suffered from a cascading series of misjudgments about the nature of terrorist threats to commercial aviation.[14] The universal assumption was that explosives were the main threat to commercial aviation.[15] Hijacking was seen as a secondary threat but was viewed in the same paradigm as earlier hijackings: It was assumed that the hijacker was not suicidal.[16]

The Failure to Anticipate New Terrorist Strategies

Airliners and their contractors, who were responsible for aviation security but at the same time had to keep in mind any adverse impact on business, attempted to fulfill their responsibility by adopting a computerized system in 1998 to speed the search for explosives. Believing the computerized screening for bombs addressed the primary threat, manual searches of hand luggage were considered less important. The policy adopted by airlines emphasized a "common-sense" approach to hand luggage searches that has been described as "incredibly porous."[17] Warnings from the General Accounting Office and the Department of Transportation's inspector general failed to produce any changes in aviation security procedures.[18]

The threat to aviation security in the United States from terrorist hijackers simply was "not on the radar screen" of those charged with protecting the flying public. For example, the government did not share intelligence data about al-Qaida with the FAA. As a result, the FAA's "no-fly" list of people regarded as too dangerous to be allowed to fly without rigorous inspection was wholly independent of the State Department's Tipoff list, a roster of suspected terrorists.[19] Prior to the September 11 attack, the no fly list had only about 20 names on it, compared to the thousands of names on the Tipoff list.[20]

The New Aviation Security Model: Government Control

In 2005, the aviation industry could claim that there have been no successful hijackings of a commercial airliner in the United States since September 11, 2001. Officials say this record is attributed to the new vigilance regarding aviation security. Although the government agencies charged with the oversight of commercial civilian aviation and the airliners had always taken steps to ensure aviation security, past efforts were deemed inadequate with the reality of the September 11 terrorist attacks. A new tougher standard has become the norm. New government oversight agencies, such as the Department of Homeland Security and the Transportation Safety Administration, have undertaken to "harden" commercial civilian aviation as a terrorist target. Four areas have been the primary focus of efforts to improve aviation security in a post-September 11 world:

- Airport security
- Passenger identification and screening
- Airport proximity security: Aircraft security during take off and landings
- In-flight security

Airport Security

Airports were initially designed as public spaces. Post-September 11 security measures have transformed public access to airports. Airport security has evolved to the standard concentric circle security design whereby the outer circle begins the screening process and only authorized persons are allowed to proceed to the next secure area. By the time one reaches the boarding gate only ticketed passengers and authorized airport personnel are allowed in this area. Access to nonpublic areas is strictly controlled and only authorized airport personnel are allowed in these areas. This strategy of concentric circles of secure areas was initiated in 2002 as airports began prohibiting passengers without tickets from proceeding beyond central checkpoints. Prior to these new security procedures the public had access to nearly all public areas of the airport up to the gate. Even parking has been affected by this strategy: During the height of the aviation terrorism scare, public parking within 300 feet of an airport terminal was banned. This action closed some prime parking areas at airports as these "close" spots often commanded a premium fee for parking.[21]

Since airports were originally designed without regard to the post-September 11 security standards that are now in place, an obvious suggestion for the improvement of airport security is to build the security into the design of new airports. That is exactly what Los Angeles International Airport, one of the nation's busiest airports, has proposed. The airport is 75 years old and the post-9/11 environment has spurred Los Angeles airport planners to propose a major modernization of the airport building in new concentric rings of security, with the passenger terminals being a secure inner core.[22] This plan calls for doing away with passenger pick-ups and drop-offs at the airport. Passengers would check in for their flights and board trains to their planes at a new facility a mile east of the terminals. Concessions such as rental cars would be moved off-airport and connected by "people-mover" trains. The radical design would produce a secure inner core at the passenger terminals where only screened, ticketed passengers and authorized personnel would be allowed. The safety of this design is praised, but some critics have expressed concern that the concentration of all passengers at a central check-in location may actually create a greater risk because such a design would increase the number of casualties in a terrorist attack.[23] If approved, the redesign will take more than a decade and is not expected to be completed until around 2015.

One of the unintended effects of restricting public access in the effort to promote security is that many airports have suffered economic loss due to forfeited parking revenue and decreased sales revenue from airport shops and businesses. Prior to September 11 many airports were designed as mini-shopping centers. The Pittsburgh International Airport, for example, has a 100-store shopping mall. The businesses in the shopping mall have suffered a drop in business because only ticketed passengers can reach it.[24] Motivated by the desire to improve the business economy of the airport shops, Pittsburgh International Airport has asked to become the nation's first major airport to be allowed to abandon the federal government's post-September 11 rule that lets only ticketed passengers proceed past security checkpoints to the gate.[25]

Passenger Identification and Security Screening

The pre-9/11 partnership of shared responsibility for air transportation security with the airlines and the government was terminated in November 2001, as the Aviation and Transportation Security Act (Public Law 107-71) gave the federal government direct responsibility for airport security screening. The act also created a new federal agency, the Transportation Security Agency (TSA), to oversee security in all modes of travel.[26] Congress passed the Homeland Security Act of 2002 that President Bush signed into law on November 25, 2002. On March 1, 2002, the Department of Homeland Security assumed command of the Transportation Security Agency. The primary goals of the new TSA were to increase the effectiveness and efficiency of (1) identifying passengers who were potential threats and (2) screening passengers and luggage for potential weapons and explosives.

Passenger Identification: Immigration Controls

One of the major strategies to counter a terrorist attack on an aircraft is to positively identify the passenger and determine if the passenger is a suspected or known terrorist prior to allowing him or her to board the aircraft. The identification of foreign passengers who may be a threat to aviation safety was one of the major recommendations of the 9/11 Commission. The commission recommended more effective tracking of foreign visitors to the United States. The gravity of this recommendation was emphasized by the fact that four of the 9/11 hijackers had expired visas. The General Accounting Office estimates the number of visa overstays at 2 million.[27] Recognizing the need for more effective screening and monitoring of foreign visitors, the United States has new visa requirements, new high-tech passport requirements, and the United States Visitor and Immigration Status Indicator Technology, or US VISIT, program.

New visa requirements enacted in 2003 require passengers from all but 27 nations, most of them in western Europe, to have visas for the briefest of stays in the United States. In addition, these new regulations eliminated the waiver of visas for passengers who layover in the United States when they connect from one international flight to another while traveling to other countries. The new visa requirement has caused protest and retaliation by some countries, especially Latin and South American nations, whose citizens used to be able to travel to the United States without visas.

The United States has notified those nations whose citizens are permitted to travel to the United States with visas that it will be necessary in the near future for them to issue to their citizens high-tech passports that have computer chips to provide facial recognition, fingerprints, and biographical information.

The most comprehensive and controversial immigration control program is the US VISIT program initiated in 2004. The purpose of the US VISIT program is to track foreign visitors' entry into and exit from the United States. The program will track an estimated 24 million foreign visitors each year. The entry and exit of foreign visitors will be tracked not only at airports but also at ports and land crossings between Mexico and the United States and Canada and the United States. As mentioned, the US VISIT program initially exempted visitors from 27 countries, including Britain, France, Germany, Spain, and Japan, from being fingerprinted and photographed. However, in April 2004, the program was revised and the visa requirement was extended to nearly all foreign visitors. One of reasons for this change was that Zacarias Moussaoui, the only suspect charged in the terrorist attacks of September 11, 2001, traveled to the United States on a French passport, and at least two of the people arrested in the March 2004 trains bombings in Madrid carried Spanish passports.[28]

Upon exit from the United States foreign travelers must have their travel documents scanned and repeat the fingerprint process. Tracking when and who exits the United States has historically been a very ineffective process, and the US VISIT program is expected to greatly improve the ability to track visitors who overstay their visas. Mark Krikorian, executive director of the Center for Immigration Studies in Washington, claims that "a third to a half of all those in the United States illegally came in legally and overstayed their visas."[29]

Passenger Identification: Computer-Assisted Passenger Prescreening System

At the heart of aviation security is the ability to identify not only foreign air travelers but all persons who are a potential threat and to keep such people from flying. Since the September 11 terrorist attacks this strategy has been aggressively pursued by checking lists of passengers against lists of known or suspected terrorists kept by the TSA, FAA, and the State Department. The origins of this strategy were in the attempts to detour hijacking in the 1970s when airline companies developed "hijacker profiles" that were used in screening passengers. This early strategy was very unscientific and the profile consisted primarily of a male passenger who bought a one-way ticket for cash for a short flight. In 1996, Northwest Airlines developed a refined system called Computer-Assisted Passenger Prescreening System, or CAPPS. The system was operated by the airlines and based on their computer records about passengers. It did not compare passenger names to lists of potential terrorists kept by the State Department. In 1998, other airlines began to use CAPPS, as recommended by the White House Commission on Aviation Safety and Security.

In 1999, CAPPS was no longer used to select passengers and their carry-on luggage for additional screening but was used only to subject their checked luggage to additional screening. After September 11 CAPPS was again used to screen passengers for additional security screening but was still not connected to State Department watch lists. The data used by CAPPS to select passengers for additional security screening did not accurately discriminate between passengers who were potential security risks and those who were not. As a result, CAPPS flagged about 50 percent of the passengers for additional security screening in short-haul flights.[30]

CAPPS II. The failure of CAPPS to provide any alert of the hijackers on September 11 and its poor record in discriminating between potential hijackers and ordinary passengers resulted in Congress authorizing the creation of a new system for determining who should receive additional security screening at airport checkpoints. The replacement system, known as CAPPS II (the original CAPPS is now referred to as CAPPS I) was to be operated by the Department of Homeland Security.

The goal of CAPPS II was to authenticate all travelers' identities and perform risk assessments to detect individuals who may pose a terrorist-related risk or who have outstanding federal or state warrants for crimes of violence. CAPPS II worked by using data from the "Passenger Name Record" (PNR) generated by the airline when a passenger makes a reservation or purchases a ticket and data from the State Department, law enforcement computer systems and more than 50 commercial databases such as credit reports, voter registration, real estate transactions, and driving records. Under CAPPS II the data gathered about the traveler was compared against government and commercial databases to authenticate the identity of the passenger. In addition to government and commercial databases, intelligence data from the Department of Homeland Security was to be incorporated into CAPPS II screening. For example, if intelligence data provided specific information on the character-istics of a suspected terrorist incident, such as the target airport or any distinctive char-acteristics or behaviors of the suspected terrorists, these data could be programmed into CAPPS II and passengers would be screened against this profile.

After CAPPS II performed this identity check, the traveler was to be assigned a color-coded recommended screening level that was to be encrypted onto their boarding passes. Green meant the traveler was categorized as no risk. Yellow meant the risk level of the trav-eler was unknown or elevated. The traveler would be subject to additional interrogation, the traveler and his or her baggage may be extensively searched, and the traveler may not be al-lowed to fly. Red meant the traveler was high risk and could not fly at all. Not only would the traveler be detained, he or she may be arrested or taken into custody by law enforcement. The Transportation Security Agency (TSA) claimed the average passenger "will notice lit-tle change in the check-in process. Many will actually see improvements. CAPPS II will im-prove aviation security."[31]

Initially, the TSA advised the public that the information gathered by CAPPS II would be used only to track terrorists. However, it was quickly proposed that CAPPS II would also be an excellent method to track criminals who attempted to fly. Furthermore, the initial pro-posal would have allowed CAPPS II to retain passenger data for 50 years. The public reac-tion was extremely critical of the initial proposed scope of CAPPS II based primarily on concerns that CAPPS II would be a serious intrusion into the privacy of innocent travelers, would provide little oversight and correction of misidentification of passengers, and may be less effective than promised. In response to initial critical reviews the TSA quickly revised the scope of CAPPS II and indicated that it would be used to screen only for terrorists and travelers with outstanding arrest warrants for violent crimes.

To test the effectiveness of passenger screening through data mining with such pro-grams as CAPPS II, the nation's largest airlines, including American, JetBlue, Northwest, and United, secretly provided the FBI with data on more than 10 million passengers.[32] This secret turnover of data sparked complaints of privacy violation, lawsuits, and warnings of in-fringement on privacy rights by various civil rights watchdogs, including the American Civ-il Liberties Union. Also, passenger data were sought from European countries. The European Union expressed concern that their laws may prohibit the turnover of such data to the United States but yielded under pressure of threatened fines and denial of landing rights.[33]

CAPPS II was criticized as being not only a significant intrusion into privacy rights but also as being ineffective in screening for terrorists. Several categories of travelers who are not terrorists or criminals were likely to be flagged as needing additional scrutiny by se-curity. These included: (1) travelers who had moved and had not updated their address on their driver's license and/or with their creditors, (2) travelers who did not have driving or credit records, and (3) young travelers who had not established records in the various data-bases. The TSA claimed that CAPPS would identify approximately 3 to 4 percent of pas-sengers for further screening due to the extensive cross-checking of data records. Despite this claim the Government Accounting Office (GAO) found that in initial testing, CAPPS II fell short on seven out of eight criteria set by Congress for system integrity and functional-ity.[34] Critics also pointed out that terrorists could simply circumvent detection by CAPPS II by identity theft. A terrorist traveling with someone else's stolen identity may be cleared by the system, as it does not confirm the traveler is actually who he or she claims to be. Also, it was argued that CAPPS II could be used by terrorists to develop "passenger profiles" that are not subject to additional security inspection by having a number of terrorists repeatedly board flights to see which ones are flagged by CAPPS II and which ones are not. CAPPS II could actually become a tool for the terrorists to assess airport security.

CAPPS II was scheduled for implementation in Fall 2004. Apparently the criticisms and shortcomings of CAPPS II tipped the balance and Congress and the Department of Homeland Defense canceled the CAPPS II program. Privacy concerns and "mission creep" appear to be the major reasons for canceling the implementation of CAPPS II. Congress directed the Transportation Security Administration to halt implementation of the program until the numerous privacy issues are addressed, the Government Accounting Office certifies to Congress the reliability of the system, and the reliability of using commercial databases was proven.[35] Although a noble public safety goal, the proposed expanded use of CAPPS II to screen for other than potential terrorists did not resonate well with the public. Proposed language that would have allowed for the screening of criminals, persons with arrest warrants, and violent offenders was too vague to satisfy the public that innocent people would not become ensnared through inaccurate information or for minor past criminal activity.[36]

Secure Flight

In the same statement announcing that CAPPS II would not be implemented, the Department of Homeland Security announced that it was developing "Secure Flight," a new airline screening system.[37] TSA had over $100 million invested in the development of CAPPS II, so it is not surprising to find the government reluctant to completely abandon the project. Preliminary details of Secure Flight indicate that it would narrowly focus on screening for potential terrorists and would not screen passengers wanted for violent crimes. Secure Flight would rely primarily on government databases rather than commercial databases for its data mining, but would make some use of the latter.

To test the effectiveness of Secure Flight, TSA requested a federal mandate for airlines to turn over all passenger records for every passenger carried domestically in June 2004. The TSA is seeking not only data about a passenger's identification, such as name, address, and telephone number, but also data about any aberrant behavior of the passenger, traveling companions, meal preference, and information about the passenger's method of payment and how and when the flight reservation was made. (Meal preference can be used to infer the religious beliefs of the passenger.) Given the protest by both the public and the airlines over access to passenger data sought for CAPPS II, TSA chose to seek a legal order to compel airlines to supply the passenger data. Also, a legal order to turn the data over to TSA provides the airlines with protection against lawsuits for violation of privacy rights. Like CAPPS II, the goal of Secure Flight is to create an effective computer-assisted passenger screening system to verify each person's identity and match passenger names against lists of known or suspected terrorists. If effective, Secure Flight would reduce the number of passengers selected for more intensive screening and the need for random searches and increase the chances of identifying people on government watch lists. In the meantime, TSA is relying on official identification, such as a valid driver's license confirmed by a commercial data service to establish the identity of passengers.

Racial Profiling

Passenger screening systems such as CAPPS (both I and II) and Secure Flight should not be confused with racial profiling. Computer-assisted passenger screening programs are not based on racial profiling and do not use racial profiling to identify passengers who may be potential threats to aviation. The Department of Homeland Security, TSA, and the airlines have repeatedly stated their opposition to screening passengers based on racial profiling. Numerous arguments support their position. Among these are the fact that race is often confused with ethnicity, racial profiling would result in a great number of passengers screened needlessly, racial profiling could result in mistreatment and abusive security screening of innocent passengers, and there is no evidence that racial profiling would be effective in screening for potential terrorists.

Other Passenger Identification Systems

CAPPS and Secure Flight should not be confused with (1) voluntary traveler registration programs, (2) the use of technology to screen passengers and passenger travel documents, and (3) the government's no-fly list. These programs are independent of CAPPS and Secure Flight.

Registered Traveler. A number of voluntary programs are being developed for passenger screening. One of these programs, "Registered Traveler," was initiated in Summer 2004. The pilot Registered Traveler program offers frequent travelers the option of an expedited security screening check-in procedure in return for providing the airlines with biometrics such as a fingerprint and/or eye scan and data including name, home address, phone number, and date of birth. The Registered Traveler program uses this information to confirm the identity and security threat level of the passenger. Qualifying passengers are issued identification cards and may use expedited screening gates at their home airport. Registered travelers are not exempt from screening by metal detectors or X-raying of carry-on baggage. If the pilot program proves successful and is implemented as a permanent program, participants may have to pay a fee to enroll in the Registered Traveler program. Another pilot program is testing to see if passenger security screening can be relaxed for chartered flights used by professional sports teams. The Washington Redskins is one of the sports teams being used in this pilot project.

Machine-Readable Document Screening. A number of airports are using advanced technology to screen passengers and their travel documents. The goal of this security screening is to create assurance that the identification documents that passengers present are valid both in terms of not being falsified and actually belonging to the traveler. Logan International Airport (Boston) was one of the first airports to adopt the advanced document scanning technology.

Intelligence-Based Passenger Screening: The No-Fly List

The no-fly list is the government's secret list of passengers who are not allowed to board a commercial aircraft or who must go through extensive screening before boarding. It differs from the CAPPS-type screening programs in that it uses government databases and intelligence data from federal law enforcement and intelligence agencies to compile a list of names. This list is forwarded to the Transportation Security Administration where airline passenger names are compared against the names on this list. The government does not disclose how many people are on the lists or how people qualify to get on or off the list. Nor does it confirm any names on the lists.[38] The government claims that disclosure of information about how the list is developed may reveal critical information about how intelligence data are gathered and would compromise national security.

The reliability of the no-fly list has been called into serious question as hundreds of innocent citizens have found their name on the no-fly list and discover there is little they can do to prove they are not a security risk and little chance of removing their names from the list. One of the flaws of the no-fly list is that the list is often just that—a list of names with little or no other information to identify the person named. The list may contain other identifying information but for some common names the information is not sufficient to distinguish the innocent traveler. Thus, the inclusion of a common name on the list could impact hundreds or thousands of people with the same name. Perhaps one of the most convincing examples of the flaws of the no-fly list was when the name Ted Kennedy was placed on the list. In August 2004, Senator Ted Kennedy of Massachusetts found that he was denied permission to board an airplane because his name matched a name on the no-fly list. Senator Kennedy was able to get his name removed from the list by placing a call to Tom Ridge, the Secretary of Homeland Defense. Most average citizens who find they are banned from flying because their name matches a name on the list do not have the political clout of Senator Kennedy and often find they are repeatedly delayed at airports by intensive security screening or are prohibited from boarding their flight.[39]

Because the government will not disclose why a name has been placed on the no-fly list, controversy is often generated when a publicly known person is identified as on the list who many do not believe should be. For example, in September 2004, the Department of Homeland Security ordered a United Airlines jet flying from London to Washington rerouted to Bangor, Maine. The Department of Homeland Security was concerned that a passenger, Yusuf Islam, who was on the no-fly list, had been permitted to board the airplane. Yusuf Islam is more commonly known as the musician Cat Stevens. Despite the fact that Yusuf Islam or Cat Stevens, a British citizen, had just traveled to the United States in May 2004, he was isolated and deported upon his arrival. Yusuf Islam disavowed any association with terrorism and many criticized the government's decision, declaring he was an example of Muslin moderation and an advocate against terrorism.

ACLU Challenges the No-Fly List.   In April 2004, the American Civil Liberties Union (ACLU) filed a lawsuit challenging the no-fly list as a violation of passenger rights. The ACLU is asking the court to declare that the list violates airline passengers' constitutional rights to freedom from unreasonable search and seizure and to due process of law under the Fourth and Fifth Amendments. The suit also seeks corrective procedures for those innocent persons whose name matches a name on the no-fly list.[40] In response to the lawsuit, the Department of Homeland Security changed the procedure for reviewing passenger names. Under the new procedures the airlines will provide the Department of Homeland Security with passenger lists and government officials will check those names against classified government watch lists to flag potential passengers for screening or denial of boarding.[41]

However, the government continues to refuse to reveal any details regarding why names are placed on the no-fly list or the information about how the government determines who should be barred from flying and how people mistakenly put on the list might be able to get off.[42] Some innocent travelers who have discovered their names match that of a name on the no-fly list have found that the solution to getting off the list may be as simple as altering the name used to purchase the airline ticket. Thus, if the name Robert Smith is on the no-fly list, an innocent passenger by the name of Robert Smith may avoid the no-fly list by flying under the name Bob Smith or by using his middle initial and flying under the name Robert A. Smith. Critics argue that this indicates the ineffectiveness of the list and the negative impact of the no-fly list on innocent travelers.

Passenger Security Screening

Shortly after assuming responsibility for aviation security, the TSA hired and deployed over 55,000 federal passenger screeners, hired and deployed more than 20,000 baggage screeners, implemented 100 percent screening of all checked baggage, and implemented screening of all cargo carried aboard commercial passenger aircraft. It would be assumed that these actions would directly address the problem of screener performance in the detection of potential weapons—now recognized as one of the primary threats to aviation security. Secretary of Transportation Norman Y. Mineta made the following remarks on the occasion of the handover of passenger security screening to the TSA: "Creating TSA was by far the toughest, most challenging, and most satisfying endeavor I've ever undertaken. . . . Not only have we improved security for the traveling public, but [we] have also cut waiting times at checkpoints, fulfilling our promise of delivering world-class security and a world-class customer service."[43] The performance of government-employed TSA screeners does not appear to have lived up to Secretary Mineta's praise.

Prior to federal government-employed TSA personnel assuming responsibility of aviation security, airline employees performed security passenger screening. The FAA issued several reports critical of the ability of these airline employee screeners to prevent passengers from boarding with potential weapons and explosives. Tests of airline-employed passenger screeners conducted in 1987 revealed that screeners missed 20 percent of the potentially dangerous objects that the FAA used in its test data. Follow-up tests of screeners' proficiency in detecting potential weapons in 1991 and 1999 showed declining ability to detect potential weapons rather than improvement.[44] Furthermore, as the screening tests were made more realistic, screeners' performance declined significantly.[45] The FAA characterized this level of performance as unsatisfactory. The principal causes of screeners' performance problems were identified as (1) the skill of the persons who applied for the job, considering the low wages and limited benefits; (2) the repetitive, monotonous nature of the work; (3) rapid turnover (over 100 percent a year at most large airports); and (4) insufficient training.

TSA Assumes Responsibility for Passenger Screening.   To improve the performance of screeners, the government turned over the responsibility of passenger screening to the TSA. The TSA sought to improve the performance of passenger screeners by adopting new hiring standards for government-employed TSA screeners. However, some of these standards have drawn criticism as being only marginally related to job performance. The most criticized job requirement is that checkpoint screeners must be U.S. citizens and speak English. The

BOX 6.1 • *Up Close and Personal: Air Travel in the Twenty-First Century—10 New Rules*

In the post-9/11 environment, air travelers must be must more aware of the impact that security regulations may have on them and the potential liability for violating security regulations and/or engaging in suspicious behavior. These new regulations affect everyone, as the Department of Homeland Security, the TSA, and the airlines have adopted a zero-tolerance policy for suspicious behavior and weapons. Former Department of Homeland Security Secretary Tom Ridge said that although there is no evidence to prove conclusively that the new aggressive security procedures have prevented a hijacking, "my gut tells me that we probably did."[46] Given the determination of the government and airlines to prevent another 9/11-type incident, air travelers are finding that they are subject to much more security screening. Given the fact that the government thinks that these security measures are effective, it is logical to expect that this emphasis on aviation security will not change in the near future. Therefore, to minimize inconveniences, promote security, and avoid potential civil and criminal penalties, air travelers need to adapt to the new rules of air travel.

The 10 New Rules of Air Travel

1. *Security regulations apply to everyone.* Whether you are the President of Fisk University and the former Secretary of Energy, a passenger playing with your cigarette lighter, or just a passenger who takes too long to obey the flight crew, you could be considered a terrorist. For example, when the plane Hazel R. O'Leary, President of Fisk University and former Secretary of Energy, was on was delayed, she used her cell phone to book another flight. However, the flight crew denied her permission to get off her delayed plane so that she could take the other flight. The flight crew reported she became frustrated and attempted to enter the cockpit. (She denied that she did this). As a result, the President of Fisk University and the former Secretary of Energy was removed from the plane by the police and questioned for approximately three hours to determine if she was a terror threat.[47]

Another example of how to get in trouble is when, in April 2004, a Delta fight from Los Angeles to New York made an emergency landing at Salt Lake City because a man "acting strangely" with a butane lighter alarmed the flight crew.[48] Gurdeep Wander found himself under arrest and facing a possible 20-year prison term when the fight crew became alarmed at his behavior when he failed to take his assigned seat and later did not leave the restroom when repeatedly ordered to do so by the flight attendant. He protested his innocence and accused the airlines of racial profiling but ultimately agreed to a court order diversion plea and fine.[49]

Children are not exempt from security screening. TSA cited in defense of this policy the fact that they discovered a loaded pistol concealed inside a teddy bear carried by a child who tried to pass through the metal detector. Parents should realize and accept the fact that their child will be screened. Parents should take similar actions with their child as they do with themselves to assure that he or she is not identified for further screening. No matter who you are, it is important to follow the rules and instructions of the flight crew—regardless of whether you agree with the rules or feel they are "fair"—or face potential arrest and fines.

2. *First impressions make a difference.* Clearing the metal screener and screening for explosives on the first try is an important landmark in passing through security. Passengers who fail to clear the metal detector or screening for explosives are automatically subject to additional security inspection. Passengers may be subject to search, questioning, delay that could result in missing their flight, and/or being denied permission to board the airplane. There are several important actions you can take to improve your chances of clearing security screening on the first try. Post-9/11 shoes are recommended—that is, slip-ons with no metal. Shoe manufacturers advertise certain models of their shoes as "airport security friendly." Although passengers may not be asked to remove their shoes prior to passing through security screening, it is a good practice to do so and send them through the

BOX 6.1 • Continued

X-ray machine. Get rid of all metal, including jewelry, watches, PDAs, coins, keys, and glasses, before passing through the metal detector. Have space in your carry-on luggage to place these items until after you have cleared the metal detector. Any clothing with metal, including jackets with metal buttons and underwire bras, can trigger the metal detector. Dress accordingly—it may be easy to pass your sports jacket through the X-ray machine but it's another matter if the offending object is your underwire bra. Body piercing may also cause you to fail the metal detector. It might be necessary to remove your body piercing or be subject to a search to confirm the reason for the alarm by the metal detector.

3. *Cleanliness is important.* Explosives technology is extremely sensitive and produces many false positives. A false positive may be triggered by explosive screening technology because of contact with fertilizer, black power gun powder, certain petroleum products, and hand lotions with glycerin. Avoid contact with these products prior to your flight. Avoid the use of hand creams with glycerin, as it may transfer a chemical signature to your baggage or boarding pass that will cause a false positive reading. Remember that many golf courses commonly use large amounts of fertilizer and if you are coming from the golf course to the airport, you may have picked up enough of the fertilizer to cause a false positive alarm. The screener cannot tell a false positive from a genuine indicator that you are carrying explosive materials and will treat you accordingly. If you trigger a false positive, you will be subject to additional security screening and delay. You could miss your flight or be denied permission to board.

4. *No guns, no knives, no excuses.* New security regulations have banned sharp objects such as knives, scissors, razor blades, box cutters, meat cleavers, ice picks, and swords. Martial arts weapons, including nunchakus and throwing stars, are prohibited in carry-on luggage. In addition, regulations prohibit golf clubs, baseball bats, and certain tools. Explosives (including black power) and firearms are also banned. This includes flare guns,

starter guns, gun lighters, pellet guns, and realistic replicas of firearms. Passengers who attempt to board with these objects may be subject to civil fines up to $10,000 and imprisonment. This prohibition applies to everyone. For example, when the head of Los Angeles Police Department's counterterrorism bureau attempted to board a flight at Los Angeles International Airport with a loaded handgun in his carry-on luggage, he was detained, his gun was confiscated, and he was subject to a fine up to $3,000. Although authorized to carry the handgun, he failed to declare it as required before attempting to board the flight.

Some passengers may fail to recognize the prohibited nature of their contraband, such as when the middle-aged female passenger attempted to bring leftover holiday fireworks on board in her carry-on luggage. She claimed it did not occur to her that the fireworks might be prohibited. In such incidences TSA says it is not accepting ignorance as an excuse.

TSA will carefully screen all liquids under the assumption that they may be explosives or flammable. It is common for TSA personnel to ask passengers to drink from the container to demonstrate that it is not a threat. If you refuse, you will not be allowed to board and may be subject to additional security screening. Liquid bleach and chlorine for pools is prohibited both as carry-on and checked baggage.

5. *Medical devices may target you for additional screening.* Certain medical prosthetic devices and implants, although allowable, may target you for additional security screening. If you have a medical implant such as a pacemaker or any metallic medical device, including an insulin pump, it will be necessary for TSA personnel to verify that this device is the reason for the metal detector alarm. You may be required to expose the part of your body with the implant or device for visual inspection. Documentation from a doctor may be a good thing to have to speed you through security screening. Diabetes-related supplies and equipment are allowed but regulated as to how such items may be carried. Oxygen equipment to help those pas-

(continued)

BOX 6.1 • Continued

sengers with difficulty breathing may be more problematic.

6. *Locking your luggage may be hazardous to your bag. Leaving them unlocked may be hazardous to your bag.* Your baggage may be inspected. If you lock your bags TSA personnel are authorized to break the lock, even if it results in permanent damage to your bag, to gain access to the bag. There are TSA "accepted and recognized locks." These bags and locks can be opened by TSA without damage. If you want to lock your bags, you should use only TSA "accepted and recognized" products.

Many passengers do not have TSA accepted and recognized products and must leave their luggage unlocked. Unlocked luggage has proven to be a significant problem for travelers. Although TSA has proclaimed a zero-tolerance policy for criminal activity by baggage screeners, the Transportation Security Administration will pay more than $1.5 million to some 15,000 airline passengers who claim that items in their checked baggage were stolen or damaged in 2003–2004.

7. *Be alert when traveling, as there is a certain degree of risk in air travel.* A 2004 study by the Rand Corporation entitled *Near-Term Options for Improving Security* at Los Angeles International Airport concluded that security screening may actually provide terrorists a potential target. The study indicated that as a result of security screening, passenger density in the terminal area has increased. The report concluded that a crowded terminal area could provide terrorists the opportunity to explode a bomb in the vicinity, resulting in a large number of deaths and injured people. Also, the report concluded that in the event of even a minor terrorist attack, a crowded terminal area promotes the possibility of death or injury. The Rand report recommended that immediate steps be taken to shorten security screening and flight check-in lines.

Travelers to foreign airports should be aware that they may be at greater risk due to a number of factors, including lax security and greater terrorist and criminal activity. Overseas business travelers need to be aware that in many countries they are prime targets for kidnapping, and demands for bribes and protection money.

8. *Photographic equipment is not safe.* Both the X-rays used to screen carry-on luggage and the checked baggage is harmful to photographic film. The equipment used to screen checked baggage is even more harmful to photographic equipment than that used to screen checked baggage. Even a single scanning by checked baggage equipment may harm photographic film. The rule of thumb is that photographic film will not be harmed if screened less than five times by carry-on screening X-rays.

9. *Some people will be more inconvenienced than others.* Politicians and residents of Alaska and Hawaii are more inconvenienced than the average air traveler. What they have in common is that they purchase one-way tickets on short notice more often than most travelers and, therefore, are subject to additional security. The purchase of a one-way ticket is one of the characteristics of the hijacker profile. The use of this profile characteristic seems to assume that hijackers are either ignorant of this widely known fact or are incapable of figuring out that if they purchase a round-trip ticket they will avoid this screening.

Certain geographical areas are more disadvantaged than others by the new security regulations. Airlines in Alaska and Hawaii are used as a common means of travel similar to the way one might travel by bus on the mainland. Prior to 9/11, air passengers in Hawaii, for example, could buy airline flight coupons good for any flight between the islands. The airlines had hourly flights between the islands and the passenger could simply show up at the airport without reservations, fill out the coupon with his or her name and destination, and board the flight. Likewise, in Alaska many residents use air travel to get from place to place due to fact that travel by land is difficult, dangerous, or impossible. Again, they use one-way tickets purchased on short notice more frequently than the average traveler. Also, politicians find that they

BOX 6.1 • Continued

purchase one-way tickets on short notice to accommodate the demands of their office or the necessity of campaigning.

10. *Check with www.tsatraveltips.us.* This TSA website provides information for the air traveler, including tips for the screening process, passenger rights, screening procedures and policies, lists of prohibited items, how to transport hunting and fish-

ing equipment, general screening considerations for religious or cultural needs, and security checkpoint wait times. Security checkpoint wait times provide the traveler with wait time information based on historical factors (not real-time data) so the traveler can anticipate how much time is needed to catch his or her flight.

citizenship requirement disqualified 30 percent of previous airport security workers nationwide from reapplying for their jobs under TSA administration.[50]

On the other hand, some new TSA hiring standards appear to be screening out potential security risks. TSA hiring standards required valid social security numbers and background clearance checks for all baggage handlers, luggage screeners, security guards, and aircraft mechanics. As TSA assumed responsibility for checking that employees met these standards, the agency found numerous airport workers without valid social security numbers or with a criminal record. Over 900 workers at major U.S. airports were arrested or indicted in 2002 as a result of background checks.[51] The TSA discovered that prior to the handover of responsibilities, workers who had to be cleared to receive security badges were not routinely fingerprinted and social security numbers were not verified. Some previous employers simply took applicants at their word when they said they had no criminal history.[52]

Since TSA personnel have assumed responsibility for checkpoint screening, numerous potential weapons have been detected. During the Thanksgiving weekend of 2002, security screeners seized 15,982 pocketknives, 98 box cutters, 6 guns, and 1 brick. At the nation's 38 busiest airports, 1,072 clubs or bats were confiscated, 3,242 banned tools, 2,384 flammable items, 20,581 sharp objects, and a toy cannon capable of firing live ammunition were seized.[53] TSA checkpoint screeners continue to detect potential weapons, including an eight-inch dagger concealed in a hollowed-out compartment of a sneaker,[54] a land mine,[55] and a loaded .22-caliber handgun inside a teddy bear carried by a 9-year-old boy.[56] In 2003, after a year of checkpoint screening the TSA reported intercepting 1,437 firearms, 2 million knives, and 49,331 box cutters.[57]

Evaluation of Passenger Security Screening by TSA

Despite this impressive record of intercepted potential weapons, criticisms of TSA personnel and efficiency continues. Some of the failures of TSA personnel are personnel centered, as when a security screening supervisor at the Atlanta airport was fired after failing to find a loaded gun while searching a passenger's carry-on bag.[58] Other potential security flaws are more widespread, such as the case of the Newark-based security company charged with failing to do required background checks on employees who guarded area airports and with bribing officials to help them keep their contracts.[59]

BOX 6.2 • *Consider This: Security Screening Vigilantes*

An interesting phenomenon related to checkpoint security has been the emergence of people who feel it is their duty to demonstrate the security flaws of the system by smuggling weapons aboard aircraft and then revealing their accomplishment to the public. For example, Nathaniel T. Heatwole, a 20-year-old junior at Gilford College in Greensboro, found himself the center of attention after smuggling box cutters, small bottles of bleach, and modeling clay aboard lavatories on two Boeing 737s in New Orleans and Houston. The bleach and modeling clay were meant to simulate explosive materials.[60] Prior to placing the items aboard the aircraft, Heatwole sent email messages to government officials warning that such items would be left on a half-dozen airlines as an act of civil disobedience and to demonstrate weaknesses in airport security procedures.

When apprehended by the Federal Bureau of Investigation, Heatwole told them the purpose of his actions was "to improve public safety for the air-traveling public."[61] Some fellow students praised Heatwole at his college for pointing out flaws in aviation security.[62] Bruce Schneier, a security expert, dismissed the praises of Heatwole, comparing the act to that of computer hackers who break into computer networks "to see if they can."[63] Schneier stated that such behavior has the ability to make some folk heroes and to be praised by others, but it is illegal and can cause inadvertent harm.[64]

In part to discourage such vigilante actions and to promote awareness of the seriousness of attempting to board an airplane with a prohibited item, the penalties for such actions have been increased. Characterizing passengers who attempt to board with contraband as "a sleeping population," the Transportation Security Administration warned, "I forgot I had a gun in the bag" is not an acceptable excuse.[65] The new guidelines provide for fines up to $250 for a knife and $10,000 for an explosive device. Aggravating facts such as "attitude" and "artful concealment" can result in an increase in the fine. Under the new guidelines airline passengers carrying banned items can be prosecuted either for civil or criminal violations.

One of the concerns is that the increased fines and penalties may prove to be ineffective due in part to the few convictions that prosecutors have been able to secure in airport security cases. For example, of 900 airport employees who were arrested in 2002 for security violations, federal prosecutors are having difficulty winning convictions.[66] Many of the cases brought to trial are being dismissed or jurors are finding the accused not guilty. Some civil liberties lawyers argue that many of the arrests seem aimed mostly at public relations and ignore the cost to the people selected as examples.[67] Most of those arrested—as probably will be the case for those charged with attempting to board with scissors, nail files, cigarette lighters, and countless other prohibited items—have absolutely no connection of any kind to terrorists. Many are just ordinary people who forgot or who did not realize the item was prohibited. It will be difficult to convict such persons, as many jurors will be sympathetic to the defendant because they can easily imagine themselves doing the same.

The most serious criticisms arise from an internal investigation by the Department of Homeland Security and another security review by the General Accounting Office. An internal investigation by the DHS found that the hiring of tens of thousands of airport screeners by the TSA was so haphazard that many screeners had criminal records or failed other employment requirements.[68] TSA fired more than 1,900 screeners after background checks found criminal records, deceptions on applications, and other problems. However, many of the employees were not fired until months after the discovery that they had failed their criminal background check.[69] Some of the screeners were discovered to have criminal convictions or arrests on charges including manslaughter, rape, and burglary. The TSA issued a statement responding to the report, saying the deficiencies in the background checks involved less than 2 percent of TSA employees and the TSA has taken steps to correct this flaw.[70]

A more critical report of the performance of TSA checkpoint screeners is a report issued by the General Accounting Office. In 1,164 tests between September 2002 and February 2004, the GAO tried to get weapons past screeners at 127 airports. Screeners missed approximately 20 percent of the test weapons.[71] This performance is the same as tests conducted by the GAO prior to the TSA assuming responsibility for checkpoint security. Furthermore, the tests showed that both federal and private screeners performed equally poorly.[72] The GAO report concluded that the Transportation Security Administration continues to face challenges in hiring, deploying, and training its screener workforce and that TSA is overly bureaucratic.[73]

The Use of Technology to Detect Weapons and Explosives

Increasingly the TSA is moving toward the use of advanced technology to assist in passenger security screening. The focus of this technology has been the screening of passengers and baggage for explosives and weapons. TSA uses chemical testing to screen all passengers' luggage, including carry-on luggage.

Another security screening technology used to detect explosives has been adopted by Reagan National Airport. Starting in 2004, passengers identified for additional security screening will have their boarding passes checked for traces of explosives by document-scanning machines. These machines are sensitive enough to scan the boarding pass handled by the passenger to determine if he or she has handled any chemical associated with explosives that have then been transferred to the boarding pass.

Another method of scanning passengers for explosives is the use of technology to detect microscopic particles of chemicals used in explosives that may be on the passenger or their clothing. Several airports have adopted "people-sniffers" or "people-puffers" to perform this screening. People-puffers are high-tech machines that isolate the person in a controlled environment and direct a strong current of air into the environment to dislodge microscopic particles from the person and their clothing. The machine then performs a chemical analysis on these microscopic particles to determine if any are associated with explosives. The process is quick and more effective than X-ray machines or metal detectors in detecting explosives. The disadvantage of the technology is that its accuracy is influenced by environmental factors such as temperature and humidity. Thus, the machine must be located in a climate-controlled environment. Also, the technology falsely identifies passengers who have been in contact with common chemicals that may be associated with explosives, such as fertilizer. The machines are much more sensitive than bomb-sniffing dogs both at detecting the presence of explosives and in the number of different explosive compounds that they can identify.

Search of Passengers.   The search of passengers for weapons or explosives is a controversial security strategy. The use of metal detectors to screen passengers for potentially dangerous weapons has near universal acceptance among the flying public. However, technology is a double-edge sword in that as new machines become more capable of

BOX 6.3 • *Case Study: Checkpoint Security Failures*

Checkpoint security has been one of the primary defenses in the war on terrorism. Despite the numerous changes in checkpoint security, the securing of airports, gates, and restricted access space continues to be a challenge. Despite the best efforts to provide a secure environment at the airport, flaws in the system can compromise this security. In a post-September 11 environment, when airport security is thought to be compromised, the result is often the evacuation of the airport terminal and the rescreening of all passengers. Such a response is caused by a breach in security when it is suspected that a person or potentially dangerous item has passed though a security checkpoint.

The cause of such a security breach can be as simple as the inattentiveness of security personnel, such as when a baggage screener was found sleeping on the job at Seattle-Tacoma International Airport.[74] The screener was discovered napping and as a result the concourse was evacuated, searched, and checked with explosive-sniffing dogs before passengers were allowed back into the concourse. The security lapse delayed flights for about two hours.[75]

Also, airport security can be thought to be compromised when a screener spots a suspicious item, contraband, or a suspicious person but loses sight of the item or person before screening. For example, a concourse at El Paso International Airport was evacuated for about two hours after an airport screener spotted a suspicious item and lost track of it before it was screened.[76] To ensure that there had not been a breach of security it was necessary to search the concourse and to rescreen all passengers in the area, including taking people who had boarded off planes and rescreening them. A terminal at John F. Kennedy International Airport was evacuated and all departing flights were delayed for several hours when a man reportedly breached security.[77] Evacuations and delay of flights is not only costly and inconvenient but it is also a potential danger to passengers. For example, when bomb threats caused the evacuation of passengers at the Seattle-Tacoma International Airport some passengers became concerned for their personal safety when the exodus of the anxious crowd created the potential for some to be injured in the rush of the crowd.[78]

detecting potential threats, technology makes new threats possible. One of the areas where this conflict is seen is in the use of the metal detector. Although metal detectors are very useful in detecting potential weapons made of metal, they are not effective in detecting new weapons made of ceramic or plastic. Neither do they detect hidden objects on the body such as dangerous or flammable liquids. It is also very difficult to detect military-grade explosives with a metal detector. As little as 4 ounces of military-grade plastic explosives is sufficient to destroy an airplane in flight. Such a small quantity of nonmetallic substance concealed on a passenger is very difficult to detect. TSA is turning to the use of technology to detect such threats.

A new security device that bounces a low-energy X-ray beam off the human body remedies this shortcoming. The new scanner is similar to what one may expect in a science fiction movie in that it "sees through the clothes" of the person being scanned and displays an anatomically correct naked image of the person. This image provides the screener with sufficient detail to be able to detect any object hidden on the passenger.

The problem with the use of this technology is its ability to accurately render an anatomically correct, detailed image of the passenger. It essentially has the ability to perform an electronic strip search and display a clearly recognizable naked image of the person.

While this technology is superior to current technology used to detect potentially dangerous concealed objects, some object to the introduction of this new technology because of the loss of privacy.

A low-tech "pat-down search" may yield similar results in the ability to detect hidden nonmetal objects, but it appears that more people object to TSA personnel performing a pat-down search than to being scanned by a machine. There have been many complaints that TSA personnel have been unprofessional in performing pat-down searches, especially searches of female travelers.[79]

However, it may be that technology will help sort out this dilemma, as it is possible through the use of technology to transform the detailed anatomically correct naked image of the person scanned into a sexless, nondescript mannequin with areas concealing potential weapons marked on the mannequin image.[80] This image would not be as intrusive and it is hoped that the public will find this more acceptable.

Airport Proximity Security: Aircraft Security during Takeoffs and Landings

When a commercial jet aircraft is in flight it is approximately five to six miles above the ground. At that distance, short of a sophisticated military surface-to-air missile, it is not subject to attack from the ground. However, while the aircraft is on the ground or taking off or landing, there are several threats to commercial aviation. Some threats are as simple as high-powered .50 caliber sniper rifles with armor-piercing incendiary ammunition.

Sniper Rifles

The .50 caliber sniper rifle weights about 35 pounds and the ammunition it uses is capable of destroying an aircraft. A Rand Corporation report identified the weapon as a potential threat to parked aircraft. However, the Transportation Security Administration discounts the threat to aircraft from such weapons.[81] Furthermore, the ability of a terrorist to use such a rifle to shoot down an aircraft while landing or taking off is minimized because of the difficulty in hitting a moving target. Given the range at which the rifle would have to be fired, the use of a scope would be required. However, because a gunman would have to "lead the target" (that is to say he would have to aim ahead of the aircraft, to take account of gravity's effect on the bullet as it traveled and the motion of the aircraft), the airplane would not be visible in the scope. Although there are attempts to ban such weapons and ammunition, present laws do not ban the sale of such to qualified civilians.

The Threat from Portable Surface-to-Air Missiles

Of much more serious concern to low-flying aircraft are man-portable surface-to-air missiles known as SAMs or MANPADs (man-portable air defense systems). In late 2002, terrorists fired surface-to-air missiles at an Israeli airliner departing from Mombassa, Kenya. This incident was the first time such a weapon had been used to attack a commercial aircraft in a noncombat zone. Portable surface-to-air missiles are a significant threat because they are easily transportable and concealable, require minimum training, are relatively inexpensive (less than $1,000 to $250,000), and are widely available on the black market.[82] The United States Government Accounting Office has cited the lack of study of the threat to commercial aviation from such weapons and the lack of any effective defense against such weapons.[83]

Surface-to-air missiles are widely available because of their extensive use throughout the world in regional conflicts, including the Soviet-Afghanistan conflict. As a result, numerous nonstate groups are believed to possess significant quantities and access to SAMs, including al-Qaida, the Armed Islamic Group, Hizbullah, Palestinian Authority, Popular Front for the Liberation of Palestine-General Command, and the Taliban.[84] It is estimated that terrorists already possess approximately 5,000 to 150,000 SAMs.[85] No commercial aircraft has been attacked with SAMs in the continental United States but alleged Islamic terrorists have been arrested in the United States on charges of trying to buy shoulder-fired missiles from an FBI undercover sting operation.[86]

The Department of Homeland Security has issued a statement that there is no evidence to suggest that there is an imminent threat to commercial aviation from SAMs, but at the same time the government and airlines have embarked on a security campaign to deal with this deadly threat.

Protecting against Portable Surface-to-Air Missiles

Surface-to-air missiles are effective anti-aircraft weapons; the odds of an aircraft surviving a direct hit with a SAM are very low. There are two ways to reduce the threat from SAMs. The first is to ensure that airport perimeter security is effective in preventing SAMs from being deployed during the time that the aircraft is vulnerable—that is, during takeoff and landing. SAMs have an effective range of 2 to 5 miles and many of the older style SAMs must be fired from behind the aircraft (the sight-tracking device depends on the heat-signature of the aircraft's engines); thus, commercial aircraft are most at risk during takeoff and landing. During this period of time, a successful attacker would have to be within 2 to 3 miles of the airport runway and would most likely have a window of opportunity of only 20 to 30 seconds to fire the SAM. Thus, if the airport can secure its perimeter, especially the runway paths, the threat of the use of portable surface-to-air missiles can be greatly reduced. Major airports in the United States have already adopted enhanced perimeter security to achieve this goal.

The second approach is to equip aircraft with anti-missile technology. Such technology already exists and military aircraft are already equipped with anti-missile technology to protect them against SAMs. However, to equip commercial aircraft with anti-missile technology would be expensive and there are several significant obstacles in transferring the technology from military to commercial aircraft.

It is estimated that it would cost $11 billion or more to equip the 6,800 commercial aircraft in the U.S. fleet with anti-missile technology equipment. Furthermore, once installed, the maintenance cost of such equipment would be about $2.1 billion per year. At a time when many air carriers are facing serious economic challenges it is nearly impossible to imagine that they would be able to afford this expense. Air carriers have engaged in discussions with the Department of Homeland Security and other government agencies to ask that the government consider paying for the installation of anti-missile devices on commercial aircraft. Such a program could cost billions of dollars, but a single successful SAM attack on a commercial airliner in the continental United States would most likely cripple the entire air transportation industry.

Besides the cost of equipping commercial aircraft with anti-missile technology, another problem is that the current technology used by military aircraft is not suitable for commercial aircraft. Older SAM technology, the type most commonly available to terrorist groups, depends on a heat-seeking or infrared guidance technology. A common counter-defense for these missiles is the deployment of flares. However, the deployment of such high-heat incendiaries over populated areas would pose extreme risks to innocent persons and property when these devices fell to the ground.

Newer SAM guidance technology uses command line-of-sight and laser beam technology to guide the missile to its target. This technology is more difficult to defeat, and present anti-missile technology results in a large number of false warnings. Because this guidance technology is not affected by the heat-signature of the aircraft, a common defense is missile-avoidance corkscrew maneuvers by the aircraft. The sensitivity of the military anti-missile technology is such that it produces numerous false warnings. Such false warnings require the military pilot in a combat zone to engage in extreme-avoidance maneuvers but such maneuvers are well within the tolerance of the pilot and aircraft. It is not reasonable to expect that large commercial jets loaded with hundreds of passengers could perform similar maneuvers except in the most extreme cases and even then the commercial jet mostly likely would not be able to achieve the performance necessary to avoid the missile. Given the large number of false warnings produced by the present technology, this would require numerous jets to engage in avoidance maneuvers. This simply is not feasible.

The Department of Homeland Security has embarked on a program plan for developing an anti-missile device for commercial aircraft. The goal is to develop an effective FAA-approved anti-missile technology by 2006 that would be economically feasible for use by commercial aviation and safe to persons and property on the ground. However, the 2005 Rand Report, *Protecting Commercial Aviation Against the Shoulder-Fired Missile Threat*, does not recommend the installation of anti-missile technology until such technology is more appropriate to civilian aircraft. The Rand report recommends the pursuit of other alternatives to reduce the threat from MANPADs, such as reducing the availability of missiles.

In-Flight Security

If a terrorist manages to board an airplane, once the plane is airborne there are very few security procedures to prevent the terrorist from hijacking the aircraft. There are basically four security measures designed to counter in-flight hijacking and/or the use of the aircraft as a destructive missile, as in the 9/11 attacks: reinforced cockpit doors, armed pilots, air marshals, and the Pentagon's domestic air-defense command.

Reinforced Cockpit Doors

Following the 9/11 hijackings, the FAA ordered all commercial passenger airlines to install reinforced cockpit doors. The purpose is to prevent hijackers from gaining access to the cockpit to take control of the aircraft. This change was quickly adopted by the airlines and created little if any controversy. More controversial are the security measures that allow airline pilots to carry pistols during the flight and the placing of armed air marshals on selected flights.

Armed Pilots

Attached to the bill creating the Department of Homeland Security (signed into law November 25, 2002) was a provision that would require the Undersecretary of Transportation for Security to deputize qualified volunteer pilots as federal law enforcement officers to defend the cockpits of commercial aircraft in flight against acts of criminal violence or air piracy. The law allows pilots who complete a training program to carry handguns in their cockpits as a last-ditch defense against hijackers. Although not the first time that pilots of some commercial flights are allowed to carry handguns, this is the most comprehensive program to date for arming pilots. One prediction is that by 2008 as many as one-third of U.S. pilots could be carrying weapons on the flight deck.[87]

Reactions by pilots and the public to the program have been mixed. Many pilot associations have lobbied for armed pilots even before the 9/11 attacks. They point out that many of the civilian pilots have extensive military backgrounds with previous training in the use of firearms. In the event a hijacker attempts to take control of the cockpit, the pilot is the last defense. They argue that an armed pilot would have a much greater chance of successfully defending against a hijacker than an unarmed pilot.

However, some pilots and passengers object to armed pilots. They feel that the presence of a handgun in the cockpit could result in the accidental discharge of the firearm, the loss of control of the gun to the hijacker, or the accidental loss of the gun with it ending up in a passenger's hand. They also argue that if the weapon is fired while defending the cockpit, there is the chance that the bullet would injure a passenger or cause structural damage to the aircraft. Others simply argue that they do not feel safe giving some pilots the right to carry a handgun.

Air Marshals

Despite reservations expressed by the public over the arming of pilots following the 9/11 attacks there was strong public demand for more armed air marshals on flights. Armed marshals have been used on U.S. flights since 1961. In 1961, President John Kennedy initiated the first U.S. Sky Marshal program as a deterrent to the increase in hijackings of U.S. aircraft to and from Cuba. Security reforms quickly reduced the number of Cuban hijacking attempts and the number of sky marshals deployed was reduced to a minimum.

As a result of September 11, 2001, the president and the Congress decided to rapidly expand the armed marshal program and to eventually transfer it from TSA to the Office of U.S. Immigration and Customs Enforcement (ICE) under the Department of Homeland Security in 2003. Between October 2001 and July 2002, TSA received nearly 200,000 applications for federal air marshal positions and more than 10,000 applicants were added to the service.[88] The Federal Air Marshal Service provides armed agents on about 5 percent of U.S. commercial flights.

Although the U.S. flying public views armed air marshals in positive terms, foreign air carriers and citizens have mixed views of armed air marshals. Some foreign airlines, such as Israel, Germany, and Switzerland, have been using armed air marshals since the 1970s; however, many foreign carriers have voiced their opposition to armed marshals on flights. Air carriers from Portugal, South Africa, Denmark, Sweden, Norway, Finland, and France have said in public statements that they would not use armed marshals on their flights.[89] The importance of foreign opposition to armed air marshals is the fact that new U.S. security measures adopted in 2004 require international air carriers in certain cases to place armed law enforcement officers on flights to or over the United States. Initially, some foreign air carriers from Britain, Sweden, Portugal, and France said they would cancel fights rather than place armed marshals on the flight. In January 2004, a number of international flights originating from Mexico, France, and Britain were denied landing in the United States because of security concerns. Thus, despite protests of unilateral "unacceptable use of government authority," foreign carriers quickly realized that their choices were limited—cancel flights or put armed marshals on board—and conceded to the security requirement.[90]

Between September 15, 2001, and September 16, 2003, federal air marshals responded to 2,083 mission-related incidents.[91] Nearly half (48 percent) of these incidents involved responding to a suspicious person, suspicious activities by a person, or a suspect item or object. Although federal air marshals have not been credited with defeating a hijack attempt and certain improvements have been suggested in the Federal Air Marshal program, evaluations of the Federal Air Marshal Service strongly endorse its continued use as a security measure against aviation terrorism.[92]

Domestic Air Defense

One of the most controversial and draconian defenses against the use of hijacked aircraft as destructive missiles, as in the 9/11 attacks, is the shooting down of the hijacked aircraft. There are two ways that a hijacked aircraft can be downed: (1) by missiles or (2) by the Pentagon's domestic air-defense command known as North American Aerospace Defense Command (NORAD). Perhaps only the White House and the Capital Building are protected by the use of ground-to-air missiles to down a hijacked aircraft. In the event that a hijacked aircraft appears to be on course to crash into either of these targets, it is believed that both are protected by a missile defense system capable to downing the airliner before it could crash into its intended target. Following the 9/11 attacks the Pentagon has established a military headquarters, the Joint Forces Headquarters for the National Capital Region, with the mission to defend the nation's capital and to assist the civil authorities in responding to a terrorist attack. Further details regarding the capacity, type of defenses, and placement of security defenses is classified.

Air defense is the responsibility of the North American Aerospace Defense Command. NORAD is a joint military partnership between Canada and the United States to provide air sovereignty and defense of the United States and Canada against attack from all enemies, both foreign and domestic. Prior to 9/11 the primary mission of NORAD was to protect North America against air attack from foreign (e.g., the former Soviet Union) military aircraft. The 9/11 attacks demonstrated the need for NORAD to reevaluate their mission and capacity.

The commission investigating the September 11 attacks concluded that NORAD's air defenses were in an outdated Cold War posture and did not reflect the new generation of threats—such as the use of hijacked passenger planes as missiles. The commission's investigation revealed that there was confusion and delay in the FAA reporting to NORAD the potential threat of the hijacked aircraft in the 9/11 attacks. As a result, there is conflicting opinions as to whether NORAD could have been able to protect the Pentagon from attack or intercept Flight 93 over western Pennsylvania. Although an emergency order from Vice President Dick Cheney authorized NORAD to shoot down the hijacked aircraft, this order did not reach the NORAD interceptor pilots until after the last of the four hijacked aircraft had crashed.[93]

One of the findings to come out of the investigation was that prior to 9/11 NORAD had no existing protocol for the shooting down of a hijacked commercial airliner. Following the 9/11 attacks NORAD has adopted new rules of engagement that acknowledge the threat that may be posed by domestic aircraft. NORAD partnered with the Transportation Security Administration and the Federal Aviation Administration to develop the capacity to monitor and respond to the potential threat of commercial and private aircraft.

Today, in the event an aircraft is identified as a potential threat, a NORAD military jet fighter will intercept the aircraft to assess the threat level. In the event the NORAD interceptor determines there is a potential threat, it dispenses flares. These flares signal the pilot of the aircraft: (1) Pay attention, (2) Contact Air Traffic Control immediately on the local frequency or 121.5/243.0, (3) Follow the interceptor's visual ICAO signals, and (4) Noncompliance may result in the use of force.

Since 9/11 NORAD has sent military fighter jets to respond to more than 1,500 incidences. NORAD has forced several of these intercepted suspicious aircraft to land or have escorted the plane until it has landed. In addition to intercepting suspicious aircraft, NORAD also provides protective air patrols with both armed and unarmed aircraft over major cities during times of an elevated alert level.

To enhance their mission performance, NORAD pilots who fly missions that could be ordered to down hijacked jets are specially certified and trained for their mission.[94] NORAD conducts regular weekly exercises in shooting down a domestic airplane and air defenses in the national capital area. Their goal is to be able to respond to a potential air threat within eight minutes. The president or someone delegated by the president is the person authorized to issue the order to shoot down an airliner.

The Tip of the Iceberg

In a sense, the government and airlines have responded to only the most immediate aviation targets—the tip of the iceberg. Given the speed at which changes have been initiated in aviation security and the cost of these changes, many aspects of aviation security have not been addressed. The government has chosen by necessity to focus on the most immediate security threats. For example, four significant areas that have not been the focus of the priority efforts to defend against possible terrorist attacks are (1) general aviation—that is, privately owned and recreational airplanes; (2) corporate and nonpassenger (cargo) airlines; (3) oversight of FAA air traffic control (ATC) computer systems and navigational aids; and (4) the security of U.S. aircraft operating at foreign airports. These factors of aviation safety have been called "the backdoor of airports."[95] There have been incidences that suggest these aspects of aviation have demonstrated their potential vulnerability to attack but there has been limited response given the limited resources and the ability of the government and airlines.

There are about 214,000 general aviation planes registered in the United States. The sheer volume and diversity among owners of private planes presents an almost impossible task of propagating effective anti-terrorist policies while still allowing private pilots access to airports and air space. Corporate air travel has been called a "soft target" because most corporate airlines perform little or no screening of its passengers. The travelers are exempt from the security screening and metal detector screening required of commercial air travelers. In September 2003, one humorous but sobering illustration of the laxness in cargo security was when a New York man successfully shipped himself by airfreight to Dallas, Texas. In September 2004, a failure of ATC computers resulted in the loss of ability to communicate with aircraft in the Los Angeles airspace. This communications failure grounded hundreds of flights and resulted in several incidences where ATC controllers were concerned about the safety of aircraft in flight because air traffic controllers were not able to issue instructions to maintain safe distances between airplanes. The communications failure was not caused by terrorist attack, but the impact of the failure clearly illustrated the potential threat to air travel in the event of a successful terrorist attack on ATC computer systems or navigations aids.

Finally, although domestic aviation security has been significantly improved, officials at the Department of Homeland Security have expressed concerns about aviation security at a number of airports in Europe and Asia.[96]

Conclusion: "The Fear of God"

In many aspects the war on terrorism in the United States has focused on aviation.[97] Airports, passengers, and airplanes are the focal point. Despite improved security measures that have significantly improved aviation security, it is reported that al-Qaida continues to study potential weaknesses in America's aviation security net, looking for ways to strike again through the air.[98] Regardless of the increasing difficulty of carrying off a successful aviation terrorist attack, an aviation attack continues to have appeal to the terrorist mind. The reason for the continued popularity of an aviation terrorist attack is that such an attack would "strike the fear of God in the public" and it would generate lots of coverage.[99]

Despite the hardening of aviation targets, terrorists continue to identify attacks on aviation as a high-priority objective. The government, airlines, and travelers have undergone tremendous transformation in attitudes, behaviors, and policies since September 11, 2001, but there is no end in sight to the diligence that is required to thwart terrorist attacks on air travelers.

Chapter Summary

- Hijackings and bombings were not a concern for aviation during its formative years.
- Early regulation of aviation focused on commerce regulation and safety, not security.

- The "Cuba problem" resulted in new air piracy laws, passenger screening, and the development of the hijacker profile.
- Serious concern about aviation security emerged in the 1970s as hijackings and bombings increased. The initial concern was for aviation security at foreign airports.
- Prior to 9/11 the primary concern of aviation security was bombs. Suicidal hijackers were not a concern of aviation security plans.
- The 9/11 attacks resulted in a complete and radical overhaul of aviation security. The focus of this overhaul was on airport security, passenger identification and screening, airport proximity security, and in-flight security.
- After 9/11 airports restricted public access.
- After 9/11 more emphasis was placed on passenger identification and immigration controls. The US VISIT program tracks foreign visitors' entry into and exit from the United States. Nearly all foreign visitors are required to be photographed and fingerprinted.
- The Department of Homeland Security attempted to improve and expand the computer-assisted passenger prescreening system (CAPPS) that was in place before 9/11. Public protest concerning the use of commercial databases to gather extensive information on passengers and concerns about privacy rights resulted in the program being canceled. However, the Department of Homeland Security continues to develop computer-assisted passenger prescreening programs.
- The government maintains a secret no-fly list of persons who are prohibited from boarding an aircraft. Controversy surrounds the accuracy of the list and the rights of "innocent passengers" who claim they are mistakenly placed on the list. The ACLU has filed a lawsuit challenging the no-fly list.
- After 9/11 the Transportation Security Agency assumed responsibility for airport security and passenger screening. Evaluation reports tend to suggest that TSA personnel are not more effective than the private screeners they replaced.
- New technology is being deployed at airports to screen passengers for weapons and explosives.
- The threat of .50 caliber sniper rifles to aircraft is minimal but there is serious concern about the potential threat of the use of portable surface-to-air missiles by terrorists to down an airplane during take-off or landing. Equipping commercial aviation with anti-missile technology is complicated and expensive.
- In-flight security strategies include reinforced cockpit doors, armed pilots, federal air marshals, and NORAD. NORAD has been revamped to train for the possibility of shooting down a hijacked civilian airliner.
- Because of limitations of technology, time, and resources, many potential aviation security risks are not receiving priority attention. These include general aviation, corporate and cargo aviation, FAA air traffic control computer systems and navigational aids, and the security of U.S. aircraft operating at foreign airports.
- Much of the war against terrorism is an "air war" and despite the hardening of aviation targets intelligence suggests that terrorists continue to study potential weaknesses in U.S. aviation, looking for ways to strike again through the air.

Terrorism and You

Understanding This Chapter

1. Why was aviation security not a serious problem during the formative years of aviation (i.e., prior to the introduction of the jet aircraft)?

2. What were the primary security concerns during the pre-9/11 era? How did the government and airlines address these concerns?

3. Why did the airlines and government fail to anticipate an event such as the 9/11 hijackings?

4. What security measures have been implemented to prevent another 9/11 incident?

5. How has the government attempted to establish the identity and threat level of air travelers?

6. Why is it difficult to transfer military anti-missile technology to civilian aircraft?

7. What in-flight security measures have been implemented to counter hijacking?

8. What are the "backdoor" threats to aviation?

Thinking about How Terrorism Touches You

1. Has your opinion about how safe it is to fly changed as a result to 9/11 and all the focus on aviation security? Do you feel that the changes that have been made make travel safer? Why or why not?

2. If it is necessary to add additional taxes and security charges to the cost of an airline ticket to pay for new security technology, how much more are you willing to pay for an airplane ticket before you question the need for such expenses?

3. Do you feel that computer-assisted passenger identification that would check a traveler's identification against government and commercial databases is a serious concern to personal privacy? Support your answer.

4. How much information would you voluntarily supply to the airline company if it would expedite your passage through securing screening?

5. How do you feel about the anti-hijacking policy that would allow NORAD to shoot down a civilian aircraft?

Important Terms and Concepts

Al-Qaida
American Civil Liberties Union (ACLU)
Aviation and Transportation Security Act (Public Law 107-71)
Computer Assisted Passenger Prescreening System (CAPPS and CAPPS II)
Department of Homeland Security
Department of Transportation (DOT)

Federal Air Marshal Service
Federal Aviation Administration (FAA)
Hijacker Profile
Machine Readable Document Screening
MANPADS (Manportable Air Defense Systems)
No-Fly List
North American Aerospace Defense Command (NORAD)

Pan American Flight 103
Passenger Name Record (PNR)
People-Sniffers
Racial Profiling
Registered Traveler
Secure Flight

Surface-to-Air Missiles (SAMS)
Task Force on the Deterrence of Air Piracy
Transportation Security Agency (TSA)
United States Visitor and Immigration Status
     Indicator Technology (US VISIT)

Endnotes

1. "Aviation Security," U.S. Centennial of Flight Commission, www.centennialofflight.gov, April 25, 2004.

2. "ESB in the News," Empire State Building: Official Internet Site, www.esbnyc.com, April 25, 2004.

3. Counterrorism Threat Assessment and Warning Unit National Security Division, *Terrorism in the United States 1996*. Washington, DC: Federal Bureau of Investigation, 1997, p. 24.

4. "The Federal Aviation Administration and Its Predecessor Agencies," U.S. Centennial of Flight Commission, www.centennialofflight.gov, April 24, 2004.

5. "Aviation Security," U.S. Centennial of Flight Commission, www.centennialofflight.gov, April 24, 2004.

6. Ibid.

7. Some of the international conventions include the Tokyo Convention, or the Convention on Offenses and Certain Other Acts Committed on Board Aircraft, 1963; the Hague Convention, or the Convention for the Suppression of Unlawful Seizure of Aircraft, 1971; and the Montreal Convention, 1973.

8. "Aviation Security," U.S. Centennial of Flight Commission, www.centennialofflight.gov, April 24, 2004.

9. Ibid.

10. Counterrorism Threat Assessment and Warning Unit National Security Division, *Terrorism in the United States 1999*. Washington, DC: Federal Bureau of Investigation, 2000, p. 16.

11. Associated Press, "FBI Checking Crop-Dusting Planes and Pilots," *Pocono Record,* April 23, 2004, p. A5; Associated Press, "Crop Duster Industry Changed by 9/11," New York Times Online, www.nytimes.com, September 9, 2002.

12. John W. Fountain, "Chicago Mayor Bulldozes a Small Downtown Airport," New York Times Online, www.nytimes.com, April 1, 2003.

13. Peter T. Kilborn, "Slump in Plane Travel Grounds Wichita," New York Times Online, www.nytimes.com, April 16, 2003.

14. "Holes in Aviation Security," New York Times Online, www.nytimes.com, April 20, 2004.

15. Ibid.

16. Ibid.

17. Ibid.

18. Ibid.

19. Ibid.

20. Ibid.

21. Matthew L. Wald, "New Rule to Limit Boarding Passes from Gate," New York Times Online, www.nytimes.com, December 10, 2002.

22. Nick Madigan, "$9.6 Billion Plan Announced for Redesign of Los Angeles Airport to Thwart Terrorists," New York Times Online, www.nytimes.com, July 10, 2003.

23. Ibid.

24. Associated Press, "U.S. Ponders Easing 9/11 Airport Rule," New York Times Online, www.nytimes.com, April 20, 2004.

25. Ibid.

26. "Aviation Security," U.S. Centennial of Flight Commission, www.centennialofflight.gov, April 24, 2004.

27. Kris Axtman, "New Tracking System to Safeguard Borders," *Christian Science Monitor,* www.csmonitor.com/2004/0106/p03s01-usfp.html, January 6, 2004.

28. Rachel L. Swarns, "Millions More Travelers to U.S. to Face Fingerprints and Photos," New York Times Online, www.nytimes.com, April 3, 2004.

29. Kris Axtman, "New Tracking System to Safeguard Borders," *Christian Science Monitor,* www.csmonitor.com/2004/0106/p03s01-usfp.html, January 6, 2004.

30. Paul Rosenzweig and Ha Nguyen, "CAPPS II Should be Tested and Deployed: Backgrounder #1683," The Heritage Foundation, www.heritage.org, August 28, 2003.

31. U.S. Department of Homeland Security, Transportation Security Administration, *TSA Fact Sheet Law & Policy: CAPPS at a Glance,* February 20, 2004.

32. John Schwartz and Micheline Maynard, "F.B.I. Got Records on Air Travelers," New York Times Online, www.nytimes.com, May 1, 2004.

33. Thomas Fuller, "Europe Agrees to Let U.S. Get Passenger Data," New York Times Online, www.nytimes.com, May 18, 2004.

34. American Civil Liberties Union, "Passenger Threat-Ranking System Rated 'Red' for Stop by Congressional Investigators," www.aclu.org/capps, February 12, 2004.

35. Matthew L. Wald, "Government Is 'Reshaping' Airport Screening System," New York Times Online, www. nytimes.com, July 16, 2004.

36. Matthew Wald and John Schwartz, "Expansion Sank Terror Screening Program, Officials Say," New York Times Online, www.nytimes.com, September 19, 2004.

37. Sara Kehaulani Goo and Robert O'Harrow Jr., "New Airline Screening System Postponed," *Washington Post,* www.washingtonpost.com, July 16, 2004, p. A02.

38. Associated Press, "7 Join in Suit to Overturn 'No Fly' List Set by Agency," New York Times Online, www. nytimes.com, April 7, 2004.

39. Ibid.

40. "American Civil Liberties Union, "ACLU Files First Nationwide Challenge to 'No-Fly' List, Saying Government List Violates Passengers' Rights," www.aclu.org/SafeandFree/SafeandFree.cfm?ID=15430&c=272, April 6, 2004.

41. Rachel Swarns, "Government to Take Over Watch-List Screening," New York Times Online, www.nytimes.com, August 2004.

42. Eric Lichtblau, "Judge Scolds U.S. Officials Over Barring Jet Travelers," New York Times Online, www.nytimes.com, June 16, 2004.

43. Dale Grinder, "The United States Department of Transportation Office of the Historian," http://isweb.tasc.dot.gov/Historian/historian.htm, May 1, 2004.

44. Gerald L. Dillingham, "Transportation Security: Post-September 11th Initiatives and Long-Term Challenges." Washington, DC: United States General Accounting Office GAO-03-616T, April 1, 2003, p. 3.

45. Ibid.

46. Philip Shenon, "Ridge Asserts Action Halted Terror Attack," New York Times Online, www.nytimes.com, February 5, 2004.

47. Associated Press, "Fisk Univ. President Escorted Off Flight," New York Times Online, www.nytimes.com, July 23, 2004. Matthew L. Wald, "When Can You Deplane Early?" New York Times Online, www.nytimes.com, September 5, 2004.

48. Associated Press, "L.A. Flight to New York Diverted to Utah," New York Times Online, www.nytimes.com, April 27, 2004.

49. Edward Wong, "Bound for Las Vegas, 2 Men Take a 9/11 Detour to Jail," New York Times Online, www.nytimes.com, September 20, 2002.

50. Associated Press, "Would-Be Screeners Must Be Citizens," New York Times Online, www.nytimes.com, August 28, 2002.

51. Andy Newman, "127 Airport Workers Face Charges of Hiding Past," New York Times Online, www.nytimes.com, November 20, 2002.

52. Ibid.

53. Associated Press, "Confiscated at Airports: Knives, Guns and a Brick," New York Times Online, www.nytimes.com, December 4, 2002.

54. "Knife in Shoe Is Found at Newark Airport," New York Times Online, www.nytimes.com, October 8, 2003.

55. Associated Press, "Land Mine Is Found in Passenger's Luggage," New York Times Online, www.nytimes.com, January 10, 2004.

56. Joe Sharkey, "Gun Inside a Teddy Bear," New York Times Online, www.nytimes.com, July 22, 2003.

57. "Knife in Shoe Is Found at Newark Airport," New York Times Online, www.nytimes.com, October 8, 2003.

58. Associated Press, "Airport Screening Supervisor Fired," New York Times Online, www.nytimes.com, August 27, 2002.

59. Ronald Smothers, "Security Firm Charged with Bribing Company Executives," New York Times Online, www.nytimes.com, February 4, 2004.

60. Robert D. McFadden, "Day in Court for Suspect in Breaches of Security," New York Times Online, www.nytimes.com, October 20, 2003.

61. Peter T. Kilborn and Gary Gately, "College Student Is Charged with Hiding Hazards on Jets," New York Times Online, www.nytimes.com, October 21, 2003.

62. Ibid.

63. John Schwartz, "Hacking Into Airline Security, Box Cutters and All," New York Times Online, www.nytimes.com, October 26, 2003.

64. Ibid.

65. Associated Press, "New Guidelines for Airline Security Breaches," New York Times Online, www.nytimes.com, February 22, 2004.

66. William Glaberson, "Few Convictions in Airport Security Cases," New York Times Online, www.nytimes.com, March 7, 2003.

67. Ibid.

68. Philip Shenon, "Report Faults Lax Controls on Screeners at Airports," New York Times Online, www.nytimes.com, February 6, 2004.

69. Ibid.

70. Ibid.

71. "Better Airport Security Checks," *Christian Science Monitor,* www.csmonitor.com/2004/0426/p08s02-comv.html. April 26, 2004.

72. Ibid.

73. Ibid.

74. Associated Press, "Seattle Airport Concourses Evacuated," New York Times Online, www.nytimes.com, January 6, 2003.

75. Ibid.

76. Associated Press, "El Paso Airport Terminal Evacuated," New York Times Online, www.nytimes.com, December 2, 2002.

77. Associated Press, "JFK Terminal Evacuated, Flights Delayed," New York Times Online, www.nytimes.com, September 9, 2002.

78. Associated Press, "Seattle Airport Concourses Evacuated," New York Times Online, www.nytimes.com, January 6, 2003.

79. Joe Sharkey, "Shoe Inspections Leave Passengers Fit to Be Untied," New York Times Online, www.nytimes.com, June 24, 2003.

80. Jeffrey Rosen, "Naked Terror," New York Times Online, www.nytimes.com, January 4, 2004.

81. Matthew L. Wald, "Citing Danger to Planes, Group Seeks Ban on a Sniper Rifle," New York Times Online, www.nytimes.com, January 31, 2003.

82. *Missile Protection for Commercial Aircraft.* Washington, DC: United States General Accounting Office GAO-04-341R, January 2004.

83. Ibid.

84. Christopher Bolkcom, Bartholomew Elias, and Andrew Feicket, "Homeland Security: Protecting Airliners from Terrorist Missiles." Washington, DC: Congressional Research Service, November 23, 2003, pp. 5–6.

85. Ibid., p. 4.

86. Eric Lichtblau and James C. McKinley, Jr., "2 Mosque Leaders Are Arrested in Plot to Import Missile and Kill Diplomat," New York Times Online, www.nytimes.com, August 6, 2004.

87. Associated Press, "Pilots Finishing Cockpit Gun Training," New York Times Online, www.nytimes.com, April 18, 2003.

88. *Aviation Security: Federal Air Marshal Service Is Addressing Challenges of Its Expanded Mission and Workforce, But Additional Actions Needed.* Washington, DC: United States General Accounting Office, November 2003, p. 6.

89. Alan Cowell, "Pilots in Europe Look Askance at Marshals," New York Times Online, www.nytimes.com, January 25, 2004.

90. Heather Timmons, "Pilots and Officials in Europe Balk at Push for Guns on Gets," New York Times Online, www.nytimes.com, January 6, 2004.

91. *Aviation Security: Federal Air Marshal Service Is Addressing Challenges of Its Expanded Mission and Workforce, But Additional Actions Needed.* Washington, DC: United States General Accounting Office, November 2003, p. 39.

92. Office of Inspections, Evaluations, & Special Reviews, *Evaluation of the Federal Air Marshal Service.* Washington, DC: Department of Homeland Security, August 2004, pp. 6–7.

93. Philip Shenon, "Panel Investigating 9/11 Attacks Cites Confusion in Air Defense," New York Times Online, www.nytimes.com, June 16, 2004. "Excerpts from Report on Orders to Shoot Down Planes on Sept. 11," New York Times Online, www.nytimes.com, June 18, 2004. (Excerpts from Staff Statement No. 17 prepared for the Commission on Terrorist Attacks.)

94. Eric Schmitt, "Military Practices Downing Hijacked Airliners, General Says," New York Times Online, www.nytimes.com, October 2, 3003.

95. Carl Hulse, "Lawmakers Cite Air Safety Flaws," New York Times Online, www.nytimes.com, August 9, 2003.

96. Eric Lichtblau, "U.S. Wants to Place Its Own Inspectors at Airports Abroad," New Times Online, www.nytimes.com, March 2, 2004.

97. Walter Kirn, "Winging It," New York Times Online, www.nytimes.com, January 18, 2004.

98. Associated Press, "Al-Qaida Said Studying Aviation Security," New York Times Online, www.nytimes.com, December 23, 2003.

99. Ibid.

7

Defending the Homeland

Weapons of Mass Destruction

The worst-case scenario of a terrorist attack involves the use of a weapon of mass destruction. The destructive potential poses such a great threat that the government has taken extraordinary efforts to prevent such an attack.

The expertise, technology, and material needed to build the most deadly weapons known to mankind—including chemical, biological, radiological, and nuclear weapons—are spreading inexorably. If our enemies acquire these weapons, they are likely to try to use them. The consequences of such an attack could be far more devastating than those we suffered on September 11—a chemical, biological, radiological, or nuclear terrorist attack in the United States could cause large numbers of casualties, mass psychological disruption, contamination and significant economic damage, and could overwhelm local medical capabilities.

—Office of Homeland Security, *National Strategy for Homeland Security,* July 2002, p. ix

Chapter Outline

Learning Objectives

- After reading this chapter the reader will understand why weapons of mass destruction make a terrorist group of any size a serious threat to the United States.
- The reader will know the most common scenarios for a nuclear attack by terrorists.
- The reader will appreciate why the lack of access to highly enriched uranium (HEU) is the major obstacle for terrorists who would attack the United States using a high-yield nuclear bomb.
- The reader will understand what targets would be chosen by terrorists for nuclear attack.
- The reader will know the role of the Nuclear Regulatory Commission (NRC) in preventing terrorist attacks, radiological sabotage, or diversion of NRC-licensed materials.
- The reader will understand the difference between biological weapons and chemical weapons and know the most common weapons terrorists might use.
- The reader will appreciate the state of preparation of the United States in the event of a nuclear, biological, or chemical terrorist attack.

Introduction: Trump Card—Weapons of Mass Destruction

To some degree modern terrorists continue to use predominantly the same weapons of violence as they have traditionally used: the bomb and the gun. However, modern technology has provided new weapons that have increased the damage that terrorists can inflict on society. New weapons with great destructive power, such as nuclear weapons, biological and chemical agents, and compact but powerful explosives, are commonly referred to as *weapons of mass destruction* (WMD). The term refers to the great harm that can be inflicted on very large numbers of people. These weapons give the terrorist an ultimate advantage—a trump card. Regardless of the size, motivation, extremism, or ideology of the terror group, a terrorist group with a weapon of mass destruction must be taken with deadly seriousness.

Every generation has had to endure the assault of violence by terrorists, but the contemporary terrorist has at his or her disposal an arsenal of weapons that has greatly increased the potential of his or her violence. The power a terrorist group lacks to achieve political and social change through legitimate means can be offset by the use of intimidation and blackmail made possible through the modern technology of nuclear weapons, biological and chemical toxins, and powerful sophisticated explosives. Despite the repulsiveness of these weapons of mass destruction to the average person, terrorists have actively engaged their use with an alarming degree of success.

This chapter will discuss the challenge of defending the United States against the use of weapons of mass destruction by terrorists. This discussion will focus on the following threats by terrorists: (1) nuclear, (2) biological and chemical, and (3) explosives. It will close with a discussion of the unique problems associated with responding to these threats.

Nuclear Threat from Terrorists

Concerns that terrorists may pose a nuclear threat have been voiced since the 1980s.[1] Today one of the most deadly scenarios imaginable is a terrorist attack involving the use of a nuclear weapon or radioactive material. Unfortunately, such an attack is possible, if not probable. Some experts predict that barring radical new anti-proliferation steps, a terrorist nuclear strike somewhere in the world is more likely to happen than not to happen in the next 10 years.[2]

If or when, depending on which report one relies on, there is a nuclear attack by terrorists on the United States the three most common threat scenarios are: (1) an attack on a population center using a nuclear weapon or radioactive material; (2) an assault by terrorists on an existing nuclear facility, such as an electric generating plant, and the subsequent release of radioactive material into the environment; and (3) an attack on nuclear materials in transit or storage.

BOX 7.1 • *Up Close and Personal: Got Security?*

How many people know what to do in the case of a chemical attack by terrorists? Only about 19 percent of the respondents of a 2003 survey knew the correct answer. Furthermore, only 4.4 percent of the people in the survey indicated that they knew where to obtain information about planning for a terrorist attack. The Department of Homeland Security has found that although the U.S. public is fearful of terrorist attacks, there is a distinct lack of knowledge about what to do in the likely event of future emergencies. Just as other industries turn to advertising to inform the public, the Department of Homeland Security has initiated a major advertising campaign to promote public awareness of the preparations the public can and should take to prepare for a terrorist attack. Working with the Ad Council (www.adcouncil.org) and the America Prepared Campaign (www.americaprepared.org), the Department of Homeland Security has created public service announcements and informational material to inform individuals about specific actions they can take to protect themselves and their families.

The scope and magnitude of a terrorist attack using weapons of mass destruction make it impossible for the government and local authorities to provide individuals the protection and resources needed to minimize the dangers of such an attack. In the event of a terrorist attacking using nuclear, biological, or chemical weapons, it will be necessary for individuals to know what to do and to have prepared supplies in advance for such an emergency.

The Department of Homeland Security is promoting the campaign in schools as well as a public media campaign. The focus of the plan is to get Americans to prepare an emergency plan and to have supplies for a emergency. The recommended supplies include

- Water and food for three days
- First-aid kit
- Special needs items for babies, adults, seniors, and people with disabilities
- Portable kit including supply items essential for survival such as a transistor radio, batter-

ies, whistle, can opener, flashlight, pliers, and so on.
- Items to protect against airborne contaminants such as a dust mask, plastic sheeting, and duct tape
- A supply checklist to help quickly assemble clothing, bedding, tools, and other basic supplies necessary for an emergency situation

In addition to lacking knowledge about the proper actions to take in case of a terrorist attack, over 60 percent of the people surveyed indicated they did not have an emergency kit, supplies for three days, or a first-aid kit.

Information on the proper response to a terrorist attack and the emergency supplies considered essential to be prepared for such an attack can be found at www.ready.gov.

Questions

The America Prepared Campaign website has a quiz to test one's knowledge of what to do in case of a terrorist attack. Here is a sample of the questions asked:

1. True or False: You are in the vicinity of an explosion. It is a good idea to cover your nose and mouth with a cotton t-shirt or dust mask as soon as possible.

2. If you are outside and see people suddenly getting violently ill, or choking or passing out (which are signs indicating a chemical attack), which of the following is the FIRST thing you should do?
   a. Leave the area as fast as possible.
   b. Stop, look wherever you can to find a dust mask or cotton fabric to cover your mouth and nose, and then run away as fast as possible.
   c. Run into the basement of the closest building and seal all the doors and windows.
   d. Put a cotton fabric or dust mask over your nose and mouth, and wait for emer-

BOX 7.1 • Continued

gency personnel to arrive so that you don't spread the contaminate.

3. You should shelter as high as possible in a building for some emergencies and as low as possible, such as in a basement or a cellar, for others. Should you shelter HIGH or LOW during a BIOLOGICAL incident?
   a. HIGH
   b. LOW

4. You should shelter as high as possible in a building for some emergencies and as low as possible, such as in a basement or a cellar, for others. Should you shelter HIGH or LOW during a CHEMICAL incident?

   a. HIGH
   b. LOW

5. You should shelter as high as possible in a building for some emergencies and as low as possible, such as in a basement or a cellar, for others. Should you shelter HIGH or LOW during a RADIOLOGICAL incident?
   a. HIGH
   b. LOW

The correct answers are: (1) true, (2) a, (3) a, (4) a, and (5) b.

Nuclear Attack on a Population Center

There are two possible scenarios involving a nuclear attack by terrorists on a population center: (1) the use of a military-type nuclear weapon and (2) an attack using a radiological dispersal device (RDD) or "dirty bomb." Military-type nuclear weapons are extremely powerful weapons of mass destruction but they are also very sophisticated and carefully guarded. Radiological dispersal weapons use conventional explosives to spread radioactive material. The technology to build an explosive device to spread the radioactive material is commonly available and, unfortunately, it is relatively easy to obtain radioactive material.

The explosion of a military-style nuclear weapon by terrorists is considered a remote possibility; however, the threat should not be dismissed. A report issued by the Congressional Research Service reported that evidence suggests that terrorists have tried to obtain nuclear weapons and that the United States should implement a "suitable level of effort, safeguarding foreign nuclear material, improving port security, and mitigating economic effects of an [nuclear] attack."[3]

High-Yield Nuclear Weapon of Mass Destruction.   A terrorist group could obtain a nuclear weapon of mass destruction from one of the approximately 16 countries possessing such weapons or build their own nuclear device. Although about 16 countries have such nuclear weapons, the most common scenario for a terrorist attack using a military-type nuclear weapon is for the terrorists to obtain a nuclear weapon from Russia.

There are two types of military-type nuclear weapons terrorists may obtain: strategic nuclear weapons and tactical or "battlefield" nuclear weapons. *Strategic nuclear weapons* are long-range, high-yield nuclear weapons. These are the type of weapons that were the focus in the nuclear escalation between the United States and the former Soviet Union.

Tactical or "battlefield" nuclear weapons are mobile, short-range, lower-yield weapons intended for battlefield use.

Strategic nuclear weapons most likely would come from Russia, as other countries do not have the capacity to build high-yield strategic nuclear weapons. Fortunately, Russian strategic weapons are reportedly well guarded and there is a very low probability that terrorists could obtain such a weapon.[4] The mostly likely source of a strategic nuclear weapon, other than the former Soviet Union, would be the United States. The level of security for strategic nuclear weapons in the United States is redundant and considered close to fail-safe.

By one estimate, a 10- to 20-kiloton strategic nuclear weapon detonated in a major seaport or Washington, D.C., would kill 50,000 to 1 million people and would result in direct property damage of $50 to $500 billion, losses due to trade disruption of $100 billion to $200 billion, and indirect costs of $300 billion to $1.2 trillion.[5] Thus, although the probability of such an attack is considered very low, the magnitude of such an attack would be devastating. Nearly all experts believe that the most dangerous threat terrorists pose to the United States would be an attack using a strategic nuclear weapon. As a result, considerable security efforts are directed at preventing terrorists from obtaining strategic nuclear weapons and from bringing such weapons into the United States.

Tactical Nuclear Weapons Less Secure.   The level of security for Russia's and Pakistan's tactical nuclear weapons is considered more vulnerable. The Congressional Research Service reported that there are thousands of Russian tactical nuclear weapons stored at sites that apparently lack inventory controls and have porous security.[6] One of the reasons for the great gap in the level of security of strategic versus tactical weapons is that while strategic weapons were the subject of many treaty negotiations between Russia and the United States, tactical nuclear weapons were off the table. Tactical nuclear weapons generally have a range of 300 to 400 miles and an explosive yield of between 0.1 and 1,000 kilotons. (The bomb that destroyed the Federal Building in Oklahoma City had an explosive yield of 0.002 kilotons.)[7] Tactical weapons lack the massive destructive power of strategic nuclear weapons but what they lack in destructive power they make up for in their portability. It is their smaller size and portability that make them attractive weapons of choice for terrorists. They are easier to steal, easier to conceal, and easier to transport.

It is estimated that there are 22,000 tactical nuclear weapons in the world. As previously mentioned, these weapons were not subject to treaty or nuclear weapons reductions agreements so their distribution, storage, security, and verification is uncertain. There have been hundreds of reported serious incidents of attempts to obtain such weapons. Russia alone has reported to have broken up 601 attempted thefts of tactical nuclear weapons since 1998 and lists up to 200 terrorist organizations it believes may be trying to obtain nuclear weapons or materials.[8]

Build Your Own Nuclear Weapon.   Another possibility is that the terrorists could (1) build a crude "Hiroshima-type" atomic bomb or (2) build a "dirty bomb." A Hiroshima-type bomb is the simplest type of nuclear weapon. Many experts believe that a terrorist group having access to a mass of uranium highly enriched in the isotope 235 (highly enriched uranium, or HEU) and the requisite skills, but without the resources available to a nation, could build such a weapon.[9] It would take considerable scientific knowledge and sophisticated manufacturing capacity to build an atomic bomb, but it is assumed that if a terrorist group obtained the necessary HEU, most likely the same source that provided the HEU would assist in the design and manufacture of the weapon.

In 2004, to demonstrate the validity of this argument a group of U.S. scientists built an explosive nuclear weapon within a few months and presented it to Senator Joseph Biden, chairman of the senate Foreign Relations Committee. The weapon was built with "off-the-shelf technology" and without doing anything illegal. The only thing missing from the weapon was the HEU fissionable material.[10]

The Importance of HEU.   The most significant obstacle to a terrorist group building a bomb is not the lack of scientific expertise and equipment but the lack of HEU. For this reason the United States has placed great emphasis on the control of HEU. The United States will spend $450 million to retrieve nuclear materials that the United States and the former Soviet Union originally sent to various countries for research purposes. Called the Global Threat Reduction Initiative, the goal of the program is to have unused and new uranium of the type suitable for bombs that originally was distributed under the Atoms for Peace program returned. However, some of the fuel is not considered recoverable.[11]

The ability of a "rogue" nation to develop the means to produce a sufficient quantity of HEU necessary for the manufacture of an atomic bomb is why the United States has expressed great concern regarding the nuclear capacity of North Korea and Iran. North Korea has provided conflicting information about its nuclear capacity. Many believe that under the guise of developing civilian nuclear power plants for the generation of electricity, North Korea has developed the capacity to produce bomb-grade HEU.[12] North Korea has both declared it has nuclear weapons and denied it has nuclear weapons.

Similar fears are expressed about Iran's pursuit to build "civilian nuclear reactors."[13] Despite Iran's protests that the purpose of its nuclear program is to develop nuclear power plants, world opinion is doubtful that a nation rich in oil would find a nuclear power plant a viable economic alternative power source. In defiance of a resolution passed by the United Nation's International Atomic Energy Agency, Iran has confirmed that it has begun processing uranium to prepare it for enrichment.[14] Although the HEU could be used for nuclear weapons, Iranian officials have declared repeatedly that Iran, as a member of the nuclear Non-Proliferation Treaty, does not intend to use the HEU to develop a nuclear weapon.[15]

Concerns over Iraq's nuclear capacity have been controversial; in fact, allegations that Iraq posed an imminent nuclear threat was one of the justifications used by President Bush to justify the invasion of Iraq. An October 2002 Central Intelligence Agency report on Iraq's weapons of mass destruction programs concluded that the acquisition of sufficient fissionable material is Iraq's principal hurdle in developing a nuclear weapon. The report concluded that Iraq most likely had the indigenous capacity to produce weapons-grade material for a nuclear weapon within eight years but may have acquired uranium enrichment capabilities that would substantially shorten the amount of time necessary to make a nuclear weapon. Postwar investigations have concluded that Iraq did not have nuclear weapons but that it indeed did have an ongoing nuclear development program. One of the concerns is that after the U.S. invasion of Iraq, much of the nuclear-related equipment in Iraq was removed by exports working systematically over an extended period of time.[16] Statements by the International Atomic Energy Agency expressed concern that the high-precision nuclear production equipment would end up in the hands of "rogue governments or terrorist groups interested in making nuclear weapons."[17]

Another potential source of HEU are college and private reactors in the United States. Although commercial nuclear plants and government sources of HEU are well protected, there is a growing concern about the security of HEU used by college and private reactors. According to the Government Accountability Office, 66 research reactors around the world use weapons-grade uranium rather than low-enriched uranium. In the United States there are six campus reactors and two industrial reactors that use HEU.[18] Each of the reactors contains less HEU than is needed to make a nuclear weapon but it is feared that the security at these reactors is "far less rigorous than that imposed by the government for its own bomb-grade uranium stockpiles."[19] Proposals to convert these reactors to low-enriched uranium have been delayed due to the estimated cost of $5 million to $10 million apiece to make the conversion.

"Dirty Bomb."   A "dirty bomb" is not a nuclear or atomic bomb; rather, it is a conventional explosive device whose purpose is to disperse radioactive material. Such weapons are known as radiological dispersal devices or RDD. The threat of RDD is not the devastating killing power or geographically involved area of the weapon but the panic, economic disruption, and psychological impact that would occur if terrorists exploded such a weapon. A radiological dispersal device would have no more explosive power that the conventional explosives used in other bombs. Outside the initial area destroyed by the blast of the explosion, the catastrophic effect of an RDD would be the dispersion of radioactive material by the device. An RDD detonated in the air could spread radioactive material for miles. A RDD detonated on the surface or in a building could contaminate approximately 15 square miles. RDDs could scatter radioactive materials that can chemically bind to concrete and asphalt or become lodged in crevices on the surfaces of buildings and streets. Anyone coming in contact with this contaminated area would develop radiation sickness or die if exposed to a lethal level of radiation.

An RDD does not have to be large or extremely powerful, as the purpose of the explosive device is to disperse a radioactive material such as powdered cesium-137, cobalt-60, americium, strontium-90, iridium-192, or plutonium.

Unlike HEU, there are millions of devices in the United States that use these radioactive materials. Materials with the potential for serious attacks are used in hundreds of medical, industrial, and academic applications. Some of these devices not only have lax security but are actually abandoned. Incidences in the former Soviet Republic of Georgia in January 2001 and in Brazil in 1987 where radioactive materials were accidentally spread among the civilian population illustrate the fact that such radioactive materials are readily available. In June 2003, authorities in Thailand arrested a man for trying to sell 66 pounds of cesium-137 on the black market.[20] Only a few ounces of cesium-137 are needed for a "dirty bomb."

Since the materials to build RDDs require only conventional explosives and radioactive material that is easily acquired from tens of thousands of facilities in the United States, the use of an RDD by terrorists is much more probable than the use of a high-yield nuclear weapon. The use of a "dirty bomb" by terrorists is considered a serious threat. In January 2003, the British Broadcasting Corporation reported that Osama bin Laden's al-Qaida terrorist network successfully built a crude "dirty bomb." U.S. officials denied the allegation, saying, "We have no evidence to substantiate that he's built such a device."[21]

Targets for Nuclear Attack.   Major seaports are highly vulnerable to nuclear attacks for several reasons. First, building a weapon of mass destruction using HEU within the United States would increase the risk of detection. Monitoring of people, equipment, and radioactive signatures by various government agencies would pose a significant risk that the project would be detected before the bomb was complete. Smuggling a nuclear bomb into the United States actually poses less risk of detection than trying to build a bomb in the United States.

Second, other than a seaport the only other strategy would be to smuggle a nuclear weapon into the United States from Mexico or Canada. This would add the additional risk of first building or smuggling the weapon into the country before transporting it across the border into the United States.

Finally, a major seaport is most vulnerable because the front-line ability of seaport officials to detect a nuclear device entering the United States by ship each year is a serious challenge.

The most probable strategy for smuggling a nuclear weapon into a seaport is for terrorists to load it in a sea container and ship it. A sea container is a truck trailer body, usually about 50 feet in length, that can be detached from the chassis of the truck and loaded onto a ship or rail car. The size of the container makes it easy to hide a nuclear weapon within the container. The number of containers entering the United States each year, approximately 6 million, makes it difficult to impose rigorous customs inspections. Only about 2 percent of all containers are inspected.[22] These containers are stackable; thus, a great many can be efficiently and conveniently loaded by using cranes. The fact that they are stackable adds to the difficulty of screening the containers for nuclear weapons. The container's door is part of the container's structure, so once the container is stacked it is impossible to open its door for inspection. If the door *is* opened, the weight of the stacked containers may crush the container and could cause a catastrophic collapse of the stack. Furthermore, it is possible to use lead shielding within the container to shield the nuclear weapons from discovery by radioactive detectors.

Once the nuclear weapon arrived in port, it would not even be necessary to unload and transport it. The weapon could be detonated on the ship while in port. The geographical and demographic characteristics of large seaports make them ideal nuclear targets. Ports are usually flat terrain, near large population centers, and contain a large amount of volatile and explosive material in the immediate vicinity, such as gasoline, oil, and petroleum products. An explosion of a nuclear weapon in a large harbor area such as New York, Boston, or Philadelphia would have devastating consequences.

A major population center is the most likely target for terrorists using an RDD. Because of the limited blast area of an RDD, exploding an RDD onboard a ship in a seaport would not be as effective as exploding the device in a populous center-city area. The destructive power of an RDD depends on its ability to contaminate an area with radioactive material. Exploding an RDD within the hull of a ship may contain the spread of radioactive material. The resulting environmental harm to the sea may be significant, but such an explosion would not generate as much panic and psychological impact as an explosion in downtown Manhattan, Los Angeles, Washington, DC, Chicago, or Philadelphia. Because it would be easier to build and transport an RDD, it would not be necessary to smuggle one aboard a ship at a large seaport. Thus, any large city could be a suitable target for such an attack.

Attack on an Existing Nuclear Facility or Nuclear Material in Transit or Storage

Two types of nuclear facilities are of particular concern in defending against terrorist attack: (1) nuclear research and weapons facilities and (2) nuclear power plants. There are three major nuclear weapons laboratories in the United States: Sandia and Los Alamos in New Mexico and Lawrence Livermore in California. The fear is not that terrorists would directly attack these laboratories but there are concerns over national security and espionage. There is a concern by some that security at these laboratories is lax and that nuclear weapons-related secret technology may be obtained by enemy governments or agents. Revelations of security breaches in 2003[23] and 2004[24] have raised concern among some congressional members.[25] In response to these concerns a spokesperson for the National Nuclear Security Administration, a part of the Energy Department, said, "Security at our weapons labs is the highest priorities of N.N.S.A. and the secretary of energy. We have multiple and redundant means at each facility to ensure that our secrets and materials are not at risk."[26]

Safeguarding Nuclear Power Plants.   It is important to safeguard nuclear weapons laboratories, but there is only a remote possibility that such laboratories would be directly attacked by terrorists. Government and regulatory agencies provide the primary safeguards and security for these facilities. However, of much greater concern to both the government and the public is the safety of nuclear facilities such as power plants.

There are 104 commercial nuclear reactors in the United States. These nuclear power plants produce about 20 percent of the electricity used by the country. Nuclear power plants were designed to be well protected by physical security and to be extremely resilient to environmental threats such as hurricanes or earthquakes. In fact, nuclear power plants have been described as the "best protected private sector facilities in the Nation."[27]

Since 1975 the Nuclear Regulatory Commission (NRC) has had oversight responsibility for nuclear facilities. Following the September 11, 2001, terrorist attacks the NRC reviewed and revised the nation's nuclear power security policy. The focus of the NRC was to enhance security against (1) terrorist attack on a nuclear power plant, (2) radiological sabotage, and (3) theft or diversion of NRC-licensed materials.[28]

The NRC is concerned about (1) whether nuclear power plants could withstand a 9/11-style attack by airplane and (2) whether they have adequate security and safeguards to withstand a direct assault by terrorists on the plant facilities in an effort to take over control of the plant. At the time the nuclear power plants were built in the United States there was no consideration given to conducting a vulnerability assessment of an intentional aircraft attack on a nuclear power plant.[29] However, evaluations were performed to evaluate the vulnerability to accidental crashes during the licensing of nuclear power plants located relatively close to airports. Since 9/11 the NCR has reviewed the structural integrity of nuclear facilities and concluded that a 9/11-style airplane attack on a nuclear facility would not result in the failure of the structure that protects the nuclear reactor.[30] There are critics who dispute the conclusions of the NRC but most seem satisfied that a reactor-containment building would not be vulnerable to such an attack.[31]

Another concern of the NRC and the public is that a group of heavily armed terrorists may attempt to assault a nuclear power plant for the purposes of radiological sabotage. Many nuclear power plants are located away from metropolitan areas but some are near densely populated metropolitan areas. A nuclear meltdown of a nuclear reactor located near a metropolitan area could result in tens of thousands of deaths and result in the area being uninhabitable for centuries. Even if radioactive material were not released by the terrorists, "widely held misconceptions of the potential consequences of an attack on a nuclear facility could have significant negative impact."[32]

Stricter Security Precautions.   The NRC has always required nuclear power plants to be well protected by physical barriers, armed guards, access controls, and sophisticated anti-intrusion technology. Following 9/11 the NRC ordered nuclear power plant owners to increase physical security to defend against "a more challenging adversarial threat."[33] The NRC has specifically directed power reactor licensees to enhance security and improve their capabilities to respond to a terrorist attack.

Prior to 9/11 the security forces of nuclear power plants were designed primarily to respond to a conventional sabotage attack. Once every eight years the plant was required by the NRC to perform mock exercises to assess the ability of the nuclear plant to respond to such an attack. These exercises were called force-on-force exercises. After 9/11 these exercises were suspended until February 2003. During this time the NRC required power plant licensees to enhance training and qualification programs for security personnel and to adopt new enhanced physical security standards. Today, power plants must conduct force-on-force exercises every three years.

When these force-on-force mock attacks were resumed in 2003, the Government Accountability Office criticized the realism of the exercises, reporting the "attackers in security exercises were often under-trained and under-armed, while the defenders were unrealistically overstaffed."[34] In response to this critique the NRC employed the services of Wackenhut, a private security company. The new force-on-force exercises include additional weaponry, more complex tactical approaches, and increased realism. The goal of NRC is to develop an adversary team that is credible, well trained, and consistent from exercise to exercise.[35] One of the concerns is that Wackenhut also provides security personnel for many nuclear power plants. Some critics express concern that in situations where Wackenhut attackers face Wackenhut defenders the confidence in the outcome of the testing would be undermined.[36]

The effect of this focus on increased realism and competence of the adversary team testing the security of the nuclear power plant most likely will not be public knowledge. Prior to 9/11 the NRC posted security evaluations on a website. Since 9/11 the NRC has removed this information. The Government Accountability Office will review the performance of nuclear power plants in force-on-force exercises and their report will be one of the few sources of authoritative information regarding the impact of these changes and the effectiveness of Wackenhut.

Attack on Nuclear Material in Transit.   One of the by-products of nuclear power plants is highly enriched uranium. These spent fuel rods can be processed and converted into HEU

BOX 7.2 • *Consider This: Is It Justified to Suspend Civil Rights?*

Government and law enforcement officials have thought about the worst-case scenario for a terrorist attack using nuclear, biological, or chemical weapons. The worst-case scenario would involve a strategic nuclear weapon hidden in a container and brought into the United States by ship to a large seaport such as New York City or Philadelphia. (The East Coast is considered a more likely target than the West Coast.) This nuclear weapon would be detonated on board the ship while in the harbor. The resulting nuclear explosion is estimated to kill tens of thousands, destroy the ecology of the harbor for decades, and cause a cessation of sea freight and possibly rail and land freight because of the fear of other attacks. This would cripple the U.S. economy and most likely would cause the collapse of some foreign nations due to economic distress given their dependence on U.S. imports and exports. Recovery could be measured in decades.

If U.S. intelligence had credible evidence that such an attack was in progress and that evidence would lead to the capture of terrorists in the United States who had knowledge of what ship the nuclear bomb was on and when and where it was to arrive, what measures would be justified in extracting this information from these suspects?

Questions

1. Would it be justified for interrogators to use "truth drugs" against the suspects' will?
2. Would it be justified for interrogators to torture the suspects to obtain the information?
3. Would it be justified for interrogators to kill some of the suspects to cause fear in the others and obtain confessions by the remaining suspects?
4. In a case like this, would it be justified to suspend any and all civil rights of the suspects and use the most brutal interrogations methods imaginable to obtain information that would prevent this disaster?

usable in a nuclear weapon. For this reason the control and reprocessing of spent nuclear fuel is highly controlled in the United States. Spent nuclear fuel is stored in spent fuel pools (wet storage) or in geological repositories, or reprocessed into low-yield uranium. The security guarding these nuclear storage sites, the Nuclear Regulatory Commission, has declared that its vulnerability assessments indicate that stored spent nuclear fuel is not at risk from ground assault or a 9/11-type assault using a large aircraft.[37]

There are approximately 3 million shipments each year involving radioactive material and about 50 of these involve shipment of spent nuclear fuel. The typical radioactive material package weights about 125 tons and is shipped using multiple security precautions and a great degree of secrecy. Although it may not be possible for terrorists to hijack such a shipment, the NRC has considered the possibility that terrorists could attempt to sabotage these shipments.

The NRC has evaluated the potential vulnerability of radioactive material transportation packages to various terrorist weapons and explosives. It has concluded that the various ground packages used to ship spent nuclear fuel are not vulnerable to explosives or radiological sabotage.[38] Also, NRC works closely with the Department of Homeland Security to ensure security. If there are specific threat advisories or if the threat advisory is elevated to the point that there could be a risk in transporting spent fuel rods, the NRC suspends shipping of radioactive material.

Biological and Chemical Threats

In addition to nuclear weapons of mass destruction, terrorists can use biological and chemical weapons of mass destruction. "Biological weapons are living organisms, whatever their nature, or infected material derived from them, which are used for hostile purposes and intended to cause disease or death in man, animals and plants, and which depend for their efforts on the ability to multiply in the person, animal or plant attacked."[39] They tend to be agents made up of organisms that rely on their highly contagious properties and their ability to reproduce to achieve their potentially catastrophic effect.[40] Chemical weapons are highly toxic liquid and gaseous substances that can be dispersed in bombs, rockets, missiles, artillery, mines, grenades, spray tanks, and other means.

Bio-terrorism and bio-warfare have a long history dating back to the sixth century B.C. when Assyrians poisoned the wells of their enemies with rye ergot. During the 1400s attacking armies would hurl plague-ridden dead bodies over the walls of cities under siege. In 1767, during the French and Indian War, the English general, Sir Jeffrey Amherst, gave blankets laced with smallpox to Indians loyal to the French. During the American Civil War confederate soldiers poisoned ponds by dumping the carcasses of dead animals into them. Mustard gas was used on the battlefields of Europe during World War I and the Japanese used plague bacteria and biological bombs during World War II.

Biological Weapons of Mass Destruction

In evaluating the potential harm of biological and chemical weapons, biological weapons are much more potentially devastating as weapons of mass destruction. The 2002 report of the Office Homeland Security, *National Strategy for Homeland Security,* identified defense against bio-terrorism as one of the four priority areas for additional resources and attention in the upcoming years.[41] The foreword, written by President George W. Bush, declared that it is necessary to create a comprehensive plan so scientists are "better able to fight Mother Nature's deadliest diseases." In fact, the destructive power of biological weapons is such that they are called the "poor man's atomic bomb." For example, if approximately 220 pounds of anthrax spores were dispersed into the air over a metropolitan area, it would cause more deaths than a hydrogen bomb.[42] Biological weapons are relatively cheap to produce, do not require high-technology laboratories, are difficult to detect, and are very difficult to defend against—the perfect profile for use by terrorists.

Biological weapons of mass destruction are outlawed by international treaties and within the United States by the USA Patriot Act of 2001. However, unlike nuclear weapons of mass destruction that have never been used to attack the United States, the United States has come under attack by the use of biological weapons. The most common scenarios for modeling the use of biological weapons of mass destruction include scenarios involving the use of (1) anthrax, (2) smallpox, (3) plague, and (4) botulinum toxin.

Anthrax. Anthrax is the top choice for use as a biological warfare agent. Anthrax is a life-threatening disease caused by *Bacillus anthracis,* a bacterium that forms spores. Naturally occurring anthrax spores are common in the rural soil throughout Asia, Africa, Texas, Oklahoma, and the Mississippi Valley. Anthrax spores can remain dormant in the soil for decades.

For centuries, anthrax has caused disease in animals. Humans can become infected with anthrax when grazing animals ingest them and become infected with the disease. Anthrax can be spread from animal to human but there are no reported cases where anthrax is known to spread from one person to another. Anthrax spores are invisible, tasteless, and odorless. The early symptoms of exposure resemble the common cold or flu and most likely would not be detected by routine health care providers unless they were highly suspicious that the patient was exposed to anthrax spores.

The fatality rate for exposure for anthrax spores is from 20 to 90 percent, depending on the type of exposure. There are three types of anthrax: (1) skin (cutaneous), (2) digestive (gastrointestinal), and (3) lungs (inhalation). Skin contact is the least fatal, followed by ingestion. Inhalation anthrax is about 90 percent fatal. Very little of the bacterium is necessary to be deadly. Less than one ounce of airborne anthrax spores could result in over 100,000 deaths. Anthrax spores are stable, are difficult to decontaminate, have a long life, can be dispersed in numerous ways, can be safely transported until ready for use, and are nearly impossible to detect by any present technology until released into the environment. The technology to manufacture anthrax spores is available on the open market. The cost to produce crude anthrax spores is very cheap—about $50 per kilogram. Such a quantity would be sufficient to wipe out the population of a major metropolitan area.

Amerithrax.   The United States has already been attacked using anthrax. The attack is commonly called "Amerithrax." From October 4 to November 2, 2001, the first 10 confirmed cases of inhalation anthrax caused by intentional release of *Bacillus anthracis* were identified in the United States. Epidemiologic investigation indicated that the outbreak, in the District of Columbia, Florida, New Jersey, and New York, resulted from intentional delivery of *Bacillus anthracis* spores through mailed letters or packages.[43] The spore-laden letters were mailed in prestamped envelopes to the offices of Senators Thomas A. Dashle (D-SD) and Patrick J. Leahy (D-VT) and to media outlets in Florida and New York.

The first anthrax-contaminated letter appeared seven days after the September 11 attacks. By November, there were seven confirmed and four probable cases of cutaneous anthrax; all survived. Eleven people contracted inhalational anthrax. Of those 11 people, 5 died. Other damage caused by the attack included the closing of the U.S. Senate mailroom, parts of the U.S. Senate building, and major United States Postal letter-processing centers. The mail-sorting center was not decontaminated until a year later. The $24 million Florida building of the tabloid that received anthrax spore-contaminated letters was deemed "worthless" due to the anthrax contamination.[44]

The person(s) responsible for the attack has not been caught despite an ongoing investigation that has included 5,280 interviews, more than 4,480 grand jury subpoenas, and thousands of hours of laboratory work to identify the spores.[45] Because no terrorist group claimed responsibility for the attack and the anthrax spores have been identified as virtually indistinguishable from a type of anthrax strain called Ames that was produced by the U.S. military, it is suspected that the person(s) responsible for the attack was not a foreign-based terrorist. The Federal Bureau of Investigation has focused its investigation on two "persons of interest," both U.S. citizens who have been involved with the government in bioterrorism–related research.[46] Both individuals have proclaimed their innocence and charged the FBI with professional misconduct. One has filed a lawsuit against the Justice Department, claiming his situation is similar to the Richard Jewell case in which the FBI falsely identified Jewell as a suspect in the 1996 Olympics bombing in Atlanta.[47]

The anthrax attack demonstrated the vulnerability of the United States to bio-terrorism. No confirmed bio-terrorism attacks have been confirmed since 2001, but thousands of fraudulent attacks have persisted ever since. Numerous city officials, public figures, judges, news media, and corporations continue to receive envelopes containing an unknown white powder. Some are accompanied by threatening letters and others contain only powder. Law enforcement has been successful in prosecuting some of the offenders, but given the ease at which such letters can be mailed, discovery of the perpetrator is often difficult and unsuccessful.

Targets: Water and Air.   Two likely targets of bio-terrorism are a city's water supply and the air-conditioning system of high-rise buildings. For example, in 1972, members of the right-wing "order of the Rising Sun" were arrested in Chicago. They possessed 30 to 40 kg of typhoid cultures that they intended to use to poison the water supply in Chicago, St. Louis, and other midwest cities. In 1982, the Los Angeles Police Department and the FBI arrested a man who was preparing to poison the city's water supply with a biological agent. The air-conditioning systems of high-rise buildings are attractive targets because of the closed nature of the air return system in these buildings. A biological agent introduced into the air system of the building would be circulated throughout the building. Such an attack could cause thousands of deaths.

Smallpox.   When smallpox was a common and dreaded disease, nearly everyone in the United States was inoculated against it. Smallpox was eradicated worldwide in 1980 and since that time people in the United States are no longer routinely inoculated against the disease because of the risks associated with inoculation. In the absence of the threat of small-pox, the benefit of the vaccination program was not considered worth the risks, including death, from the vaccination dose.

The lack of widespread immunity, the ease with which smallpox spreads from person to person, and the potential health risks associated with smallpox, including death, raises concern that smallpox could be used in a bio-terrorism attack.[48] As a result of this concern that a terrorist attack might use smallpox as a biological weapon, a vaccination program was initiated in 2003 for at-risk persons. About 493,000 people, mostly military personnel, were vaccinated before the program was stopped due to adverse side effects.[49] Health officials considered the vaccine too dangerous. Thus, the primary defense against smallpox as a bio-logical weapon is a coordinated and quick response time to this public health threat.

Plague.   In A.D. 541, the first recorded plague pandemic began in Egypt and swept across Europe, killing between 50 and 60 percent of the population in North Africa, Europe, and central and southern Asia. The second plague pandemic, also known as the *black death,* began in 1346 and eventually killed 20 to 30 million people in Europe, one-third of the European population.[50] There is little published information indicating that the use of plague is a serious bio-terrorism threat. However, the willingness of terrorists to do whatever will cause mass destruction suggests that the United States needs to be alert to the possibility of a bio-terrorism attack using plague. The most likely agent would be *Yersinia pestis.* It is estimated

BOX 7.3 • *Case Study: One Man's Terrorist Is Another Man's Artist*

Artist Steve Kurtz found his wife of 20 years dead from apparent heart failure. He phoned 911. The paramedics responded to his call, but it is unlikely that he anticipated the outcome. He found himself charged with biological terrorism under the Patriot Act.

Kurtz, an art professor at the University of Buffalo, founded the Critical Art Ensemble, an artists' collective that produces artwork to educate the public about the politics of biotechnology. His nontraditional art has involved blending elements of biology with agricultural issues. His 2002 exhibit, titled "Molecular Invasion," was a statement against genetically modified crops. His biotech themed artwork tends to be "tactical media" or multimedia presentations rather than artwork that one hangs on the wall. It was his artwork that got him indicted for possession of prohibited biological agents.

When Kurtz phoned 911, the paramedics who arrived at his home noticed biological laboratory equipment and biological samples. They were alarmed by the presence of the biotech equipment in his home and alerted law enforcement authorities. FBI agents responded with hazardous-material suits and spent two days searching his home for evidence of bio-terrorism agents, confiscating his equipment and biological material used in his artwork. They even confiscated his artwork. His current project involved the use of E. coli bacteria. After the search the FBI declared Mr. Kurtz's home "not a danger to public health" and the E. coli bacteria was a "harmless" transgenic or genetically modified form of E. coli bacteria. His wife's death did not appear to be due to natural causes and not related to any biological agent. However, the FBI continued the investigation of Kurtz's possible ties to any terrorism links. The funding of his artists' collective was investigated, people who knew him were interviewed, and his colleagues were subpoenaed to testify before a grand jury. In the end, he was charged with four counts of wire fraud and a mail fraud indictment by a federal grand jury. His charge was a result of a statute expanded and strengthened by the Patriot Act. It prohibits the possession of "any biological agent, toxin, or delivery system of a type or in a quantity that, under the circumstances, is not reasonably justified by a prophylactic, protective, bona fide research, or other peaceful purpose."

Kurtz's attorney called the charges "a real stretch" and accusations that amount to nothing more than a complaint of "petty larceny." Colleagues of his have called the criminal charges "a total, paranoid overreaction." Fellow artists call the indictment censorship and invasions of their freedom. John Curr II, assistant director for the Buffalo chapter of the American Civil Liberties Union, said the initial response of the hazmat team was justified, but then calls the follow-up investigation and charges "overreacting."

Although Kurtz is confident he has done nothing wrong, he has retained the services of lawyer Paul J. Cambria, who represented Larry Flynt, the *Hustler Magazine* publisher, in his Supreme Court case on censorship. They plan to use a First Amendment defense, arguing that the bacteria was harmless and there is no evidence to suggest that Kurtz intended anything other than the use of the bacteria for a "peaceful purpose."

Questions

1. Should artists be allowed to use biological agents in their artwork? Would it make a difference if the "harmless" biological agents could be changed to harmful agents? Defend your answers.

2. Many critics of the Patriot Act used this example to call for the repeal of the Patriot Act. They claim the prosecution of Kurtz demonstrates that the Patriot Act is too broad and prohibits actions that should not be criminal. The federal government defends the Patriot Act as "the best defense against terrorists looking to kill as many Americans as possible." What do you think should be the crite-

BOX 7.3 • **Continued**

ria that should be used to balance protection against nuclear, biological, and chemical	weapons and the First Amendment rights of privacy and self-expression?

Note: Information for this case study was obtained from Carolyn Thompson, "Artist's Biological Props Spur Terror Probe," *Boston Globe*, www.boston.com, June 6, 2004; David Staba, "Use of Bacteria in Art Leads to Federal Inquiry," New York Times Online, www.nytimes.com, June 7, 2004; Tom Regan, "Artist Falls Afoul of Patriot Act," *Christian Science Monitor*, www.csmonitor.com, June 7, 2004; and Mel Gussow, "Professor Is Indicted Over Procuring Biological Materials for Art," New York Times Online, www.nytimes.com, July 1, 2004.

that if 50 kg of *Yersinia pestis* were released as an aerosol over a city of 5 million, pneumonic plague could occur in as many as 150,000 persons, 36,000 of whom would be expected to die.[51]

The United States has little experience or knowledge of plague as a biological warfare weapon, as the country has restrained from such research. The former Soviet Union, on the other hand, has engaged in an active research program to produce quantities of plague organisms sufficient to use as an effective weapon.[52] Thus, the response of the United States to plague as a bio-terrorism weapon would chart new ground for the government and the nation's medical services. One of the challenges if plague were used as a bio-terrorism weapon would be infection control. Plague is readily spread by person-to-person contact, so isolation of infected persons would be a major priority. Environmental decontamination would not pose the same problem as in the use of anthrax. *Yersinia pestis* is estimated to be a health threat as a plague aerosol for about one hour after dispersion. *Yersinia pestis* is very sensitive to the action of sunlight and heating and does not survive long outside the host. There would be no need for environmental decontamination of an area exposed to an aerosol of plague.[53]

Botulinum Toxin.   Terrorists have already attempted to use botulinum toxin as a biological weapon.[54] Botulinum toxin is the most poisonous substance known. A single gram of crystalline toxin, evenly dispersed and inhaled, would kill more than 1 million people.[55] The 1972 Biological and Toxin Weapons Convention prohibits offensive research and production of biological weapons. However, botulinum toxin has legitimate medical purposes, so it is manufactured as a licensed substance. It is known that the former Soviet Union engaged in the development of botulinum toxin for use as a weapon, and Iraq has admitted to the United Nations inspection team to having produced enough botulinum toxin for military use to kill the entire human population.[56]

The disadvantage of botulinum toxin is that it is difficult to stabilize the toxin for aerosol dissemination. Also, despite it power as a poison, it is easy to destroy the toxin. Intact skin is impermeable to botulinum toxin. However, terrorists may choose to use it as a biological weapon to contaminate the food supply to produce an outbreak of botulism rather than as an aerosol to affect an entire city.

There is a least one incident of such use. In 1984, the Rajneeshee cult, an Indian religious cult, contaminated salad bars of the Dalles, Oregon, and Wasco County, Oregon, restaurants with Salmonella typhimurium. Over 750 people were poisoned and 40 were hospitalized. The purpose of the attack was to influence the outcome of a local election. The attack was not only successful in the number of people affected but also the outbreak was not recognized as a terrorist attack until a year later when members of the cult turned informants. The Japanese cult, Aum Shinrikyo, has attempted to disperse botulinum toxin as a biological weapon in downtown Tokyo, Japan, and at U.S. military installations in Japan. These attempts have not been successful but the reasons for the failure were defective equipment and faulty microbiological technique. Despite its limitations, botulinum toxin poses a major biological weapons threat.

Chemical Weapons of Mass Destruction

Chemical weapons are highly toxic liquid and gaseous substances that can be dispersed in bombs, rockets, missiles, artillery, mines, grenades, and spray tanks. According to the *Weapons of Mass Destruction Reference Guide,* there are four basic types of chemical agents: (1) blister agents that destroy exposed skin tissue, such as mustard gas and lewisite; (2) blood agents that, when inhaled, block oxygen circulation within the body, such as hydrogen cyanide and cyanogens chloride; (3) choking agents that inflame the bronchial tubes and lungs, possibly causing asphyxiation, such as phosgene and chlorine; and (4) nerve agents that cause the nervous system to overload, resulting in respiratory failure and death, such as tabun, sarin, soman, and VX.[57]

Chemical weapons were used in World War I; their use was considered cruel and indiscriminate by many nations. This experience led to the banning of the use of poisonous gases and certain other chemical weapons in war by the Geneva Protocol in 1928. This ban did not prohibit nations from continuing to develop chemical weapons, however, and many countries continued to pursue chemical programs. Today, the former Soviet Union has the world's largest chemical weapons stockpiles and development program. The United States has its own respectable stockpile of chemical weapons, too. Authorities in the United States believe the stockpile of chemical weapons possessed by the United States is safeguarded by adequate security but fear that similar security may not protect the vast stockpile of chemical weapons in the former Soviet Union. In 1996, the United States and the Soviet Union agreed to the Chemical Weapons Convention, which prohibits the development, production, acquisition, stockpiling, retention, transfer, and use of chemical weapons. (The agreement has been signed by 145 nations.) The United States has agreed to the destruction of 45 percent of its chemical weapons stockpile by 2004 and its entire stockpile by 2007. Current progress suggests that the United States will not meet this goal.

The concern that terrorists could obtain chemical weapons from the vast stockpile of chemical weapons possessed by the former Soviet Union has resulted in the United States entering into a cooperative agreement with the former Soviet Union to help finance the destruction of Soviet chemical weapons. Like the United States, it appears that the former Soviet Union will not meet its deadlines for the destruction of chemical weapons, even with assistance from the United States.

Terrorists could also obtain chemical weapons from nonsignatory nations to the Chemical Weapons Convention such as Libya, North Korea, and Syria. All three are thought to have chemical weapons capabilities. Prior to the U.S. invasion of Iraq, Iraq demonstrated its chemical weapons capabilities by the use of such on insurgent Kurds. After the U.S. invasion, a vast amount of chemical weaponry remains unaccounted for.

Also, terrorists could manufacture their own chemical weapons. The manufacture of many chemical agents requires only the minimum of laboratory facilities, technical knowledge, and expense. The reality of this source of weapons is demonstrated by the release of sarin nerve gas in the Tokyo subway system in 1995 by the cult group Aum Shinrikyo. It is believed they manufactured the sarin nerve gas used in the attack.

Ricin, the deadly poison for which no antidote exists, used in the 2004 attacks on Capital Hill, can be easily manufactured from bean-like seeds of the castor plant with a minimum of technical skills and equipment. The average person can legally obtain all of the resources needed to manufacture ricin. Recipes for ricin can be found on the Internet and have been alleged to have been found among captured al-Qaida documents. Until 1962, an Army patent for making weapons-grade ricin was available on a public computer at the United States Patent Office. Although the webpage has been closed, the military's recipe is still available elsewhere on the Internet.[58]

Finally, terrorists in the United States could effect a chemical weapons attack simply by hijacking any one of the millions of trucks and trains transporting commonly used industrial chemicals that, if released, would pose a deadly threat. Such chemicals are transported with minimum security. If terrorists sabotaged a train carrying chlorine, a common industrial chemical and deadly poisonous gas, the derailment and release of the chlorine gas would endanger everyone within miles of the site. There have been accidental derailments of trains carrying chlorine that have demonstrated the dangers of chlorine gas.

Although a chemical attack by terrorists would not be as deadly as a nuclear or biological attack, the potential for destruction and negative psychological impact is great. Also, concern for defending against such an attack is high, as the United States has already suffered several attacks involving ricin. On October 15, 2003, a vial of low-grade ricin was found in a Greenville, South Carolina, post office. Also, a letter enclosed with the ricin threatened to poison public water supplies with ricin. In November 2003, a letter with ricin enclosed addressed to the White House was intercepted at the offsite White House mail facility. On February 3, 2004, powdered ricin was found in the office suite of Senate majority leader Bill Frist. The discovery caused the evacuation of about 6,200 people from Senate office buildings. No one was injured in any of these attacks, but the ability of terrorists to deliver deadly agents to public officials and buildings continues to illustrate the vulnerability of the United States to such attacks. After the 2001 anthrax attacks on Capital Hill, irradiation machines were installed to kill bacterium such as anthrax for all first-class mail bound for Washington government offices. However, irradiation machines have no effect on poisons such as ricin.

Domestic Terrorists and Bio-Terrorism. An interesting observation about the ricin attacks is that it appears that domestic terrorists rather than international terrorists may have been responsible for the attacks. No international group claimed responsibility. Also, letters accompanying the ricin addressed to the White House and those found at the airport mail office in Greenville, South Carolina, were signed by "Fallen Angel." The letter threatened contamination of the public water supplies with ricin if changes were not made to the federal trucking regulations limiting the number of hours that a driver could remain on the road. It is more likely that such a demand was issued by a domestic terrorist rather than an international terrorist.

Whereas the United States has focused consideration attention to remain vigilant against terror attacks by international terrorists, the ricin attacks and several other incidents emphasize the fact that attacks from domestic terrorists cannot be ignored. It should be remembered, for example, that the second most destructive terrorist attack in the United States (the first being the 9/11 attacks) was the bombing of the federal building in Oklahoma City by Timothy McVeigh, an act of domestic terrorism.

It is not uncommon for law enforcement personnel to uncover planned bio-terror attacks by domestic terror groups. For example, in January 2004, law enforcement officials in Texas reported finding nearly two pounds of cyanide compound and other chemicals that could create enough poisonous gas to kill everyone inside a space as large as a department store or a small-town civic center. Also, the cache included 60 pipe bombs, remote-controlled bombs disguised as briefcases, machine guns, nearly half a million rounds of ammunition, and pamphlets on how to make chemical weapons. These destructive weapons were not seized from suspected international terrorists but from William Krar and Judith Burey. Krar had ties to white supremacist and anti-government militia groups.[59] Critics have accused the United States Justice Department of ignoring the violent potential of domestic terrorist groups as it focuses upon international terrorism.[60]

Problems in Defending the Homeland against Nuclear, Biological, and Chemical Threats

Assessments of the U.S. ability to respond to terrorists using nuclear, biological, and chemical threats suggest there is a continuing lack of preparedness by federal and local governments.[61] A planning exercise in 2001, called "Dark Winter," which involved the simulated release of smallpox virus, showed there were too few resources, a lack of training by first responders, a lack of knowledge by critical public health officials, and a lack of coordination among the various agencies involved in responding to the threat.[62] A five-day exercise in May 2003 in Chicago and Seattle, known as "Topoff 2," tested the response of federal agencies and local governments to nearly simultaneous terrorist attacks using biological agents and a dirty bomb.[63] The unclassified summary of the report released to the public concluded, "A continuing lack of preparedness by federal and local governments would result in unnecessary deaths in the event of a major terrorist attack.[64] The conclusions of a classified report on the 2001 anthrax attacks identified weaknesses in "almost every aspect of U.S. biopreparedness and response."[65] An analysis of New York City hospitals concluded its hospitals lacked important protective clothing, decontamination facilities, and essential drug supplies that could be needed to respond to a biological, chemical, or nuclear strike.[66] Surveys of other hospitals came to the same conclusion. Hospital officials indicated that although much had been done to prepare for a terrorist attack, they were poorly prepared, lacked essential equipment, and lacked essential response information and plans. Some hospitals reported spending $20 million to install trauma and decontamination facilities, but in the event of a serious attack the number of people needing health care could easily exceed the capacity of the hospitals.[67]

Federal and local government agencies have responded to these reports of vulnerability. However, defending the United States against nuclear, biological, and chemical weapons poses a unique set of challenges. Unlike previous threats, the threat of attack by terrorists using nuclear, biological, and chemical weapons requires a level of preparedness that has never been required before. To better respond to a terrorist attack using nonconventional weapons starting in 2004, the Department of Homeland Security will conduct a national risk assessment every two years on new biological threats. In addition, the Department of Homeland Security will perform a biological "net assessment" every four years to evaluate the effectiveness of existing bio-defenses and to remedy vulnerabilities.[68]

Public Opposition to Counteract Bio-Terrorism Strategies

Aggressive strategies are being adopted to better prepare for a terrorist attack. However, some of the strategies have proven to be fraught with unforeseen problems. For example, when the military attempted to require military personnel to be vaccinated against anthrax without their consent, protests by military personnel led to a court injunction against the program. Despite the government's assurance that the anthrax vaccination was safe and had minimum risk of serious adverse reactions, some military personnel refused to comply.

Even research projects aimed at enhancing the ability of the United States to respond to a nonconventional attack have come under attack by critics as posing a public danger. The federal government has approved $5.6 billion to help prepare for possible germ or chemical attacks on U.S. soil for "Project BioShield." However, critics express concerns that research to defend against germ or chemical attacks may pose serious risks to the public. One of the concerns is that an "accident" involving the world's deadliest pathogens may create a grave threat to the public. Indeed, there have been accidents in bio-terrorism research. For example, a worker at a military biological research facility contracted a contagious, potentially fatal, disease in 2000, after handling laboratory equipment without gloves. The worker failed to report the incident after he became ill and continued to work for six weeks until he was forced to seek hospitalization due to illness. Many cite this incident as an example of the risk to which the general population is exposed. Although it did not happen, it is possible to conceive that under different circumstances the contaminated worker could have spread deadly pathogens to the general population.

In addition to the dangers posed by workers who may be accidentally contaminated, there is concern over the safety procedures at research facilities studying bio-terrorism threats. For example, a security review of New York's Plum Island Animal Disease Center revealed numerous security flaws and safety concerns.[69] The mission of the Plum Island facility was to study the threat of biological terrorism to America's food supply. However, a 2003 study by the General Accounting Office reported that the facility itself posed a threat to public health. The report expressed concerns that there were inadequate controls to prevent the loss or accidental release of pathogens.[70]

In the war on bio-terrorism, the federal government has approved $2.5 billion to build laboratories across the United States to study deadly biological weapons. Citizens and political action groups have questioned the safety measures used by these laboratories. Many of the research laboratories are located near populated cities such as San Francisco; Davis, California; Boston; Long Island, New York; and Atlanta, Georgia. Citizen groups have charged that these bio-research facilities have been rushed into existence without sufficient consideration as to how to deal with a major disease outbreak or environmental damage in the event of an accident.[71]

Another charge is that biological research may inadvertently provide information or agents that may be useful to terrorists. For example, when scientists announced they had created a highly lethal virus in an effort to develop stronger protections against supervirulent forms of smallpox that terrorists might turn on humans, some scientists expressed concern that terrorists could use the research to produce deadlier kinds of biological weapons.[72] To help safeguard biological research, the federal government plans to establish an advisory board to counsel agencies on safeguarding biological research that could inadvertently be useful to terrorists. The board will be managed by the National Institutes of Health and made up of experts in molecular biology, infectious diseases, and food production, among other fields. It will recommend specific strategies for the oversight of federally financed biological research.[73]

Other Problems in Responding to Nuclear, Biological, and Chemical Terrorism

There are some unique problems associated with defending the United States against terrorists using nuclear, biological, and chemical weapons. An attack using these weapons would require that first responders—such as police, fire, and health personnel—have adequate protection against the nuclear, biological, or chemical threat. Few agencies have such equipment in sufficient quantity to allow for a response to a serious attack.

The cost of protecting nuclear power plants from a comprehensive number of possible terrorist attacks exceeds what power plants can afford. Many nuclear power plants are privately owned and must make a profit from the sale of electrical power. Few if any of these privately owned power plants could afford an unlimited budget to staff and train personnel and to install expensive anti-intrusion technology and remain in business. It is accepted by most authorities that to adequately ensure nuclear power plants are not at risk to terrorist attack or sabotage, the federal government will have to assume partial or significant financial responsibility for enhanced security.

Nearly all reports suggest that the U.S. health system does not have the capacity to respond to a nuclear, biological, or chemical attack. Studies suggest that public health officials may not even be able to detect a biological threat in time to provide early intervention. Public health services are decentralized and it would take time for officials to realize the magnitude and scope of a biological threat.

The U.S. public is not prepared for a nuclear, biological, or chemical attack. Studies indicate that few persons have the supplies, including food and water, recommended to prepare for a possible nuclear, biological, or chemical attack.[74] Most residents in large metropolitan areas have no escape plan or area where they would be safe from such attack. Furthermore, despite the 9/11 attacks and subsequent anthrax and ricin attacks, there seems to be little progress in this area. Most people profess they lack information about how they should prepare for or respond to such an attack. In the event of a serious terrorist attack using nuclear, biological, or chemical weapons, panic, confusion, and pandemonium would most likely follow.

Finally, the average citizen and local and state governments have little control over many of the important security initiations related to nuclear, biological, and chemical weapons. America's safety depends to a large measure on international treaties, use or threat of the use of military force, global economic sanctions, covert international actions, intelligence, and the ability to fund billion-dollar programs. Thus, many citizens and local and state governments feel they can do little to contribute to national security. As a result, the federal government, particularly the Department of Homeland Security, must continue to emphasize the importance of the actions of individual citizens, the need for individual preparations, and the cooperative role between the federal government and local and state governments.

Conclusion: Thinking Outside the Box

Despite the passionate warning of the government that a terrorist attack using nuclear, biological, or chemical weapons is not only possible but probable unless a high degree of diligence is maintained, some critics downplay such threat.[75] They argue that the government is deliberately using fear tactics for political advantage. They maintain that although there is a threat from international terrorists, including al-Qaida, there is not "a huge terrorist organization run by a small man with a beard in a cave."[76] One critic discounted the ability of a dirty bomb "to kill anybody," saying, "The most exposed individual would get a fairly high dose of radiation, not life-threatening."[77] These critics argue that having committed tremendous resources to countering another terrorist attack on Untied States soil, the government has exaggerated the threat.

Despite these counterclaims, the government continues to affirm the reality of the threat of another terrorist attack on United States soil. The 2003 report, *The National Strategy for the Physical Protection of Critical Infrastructures and Key Assets,* concluded,

> The September 11 attacks demonstrated our national-level physical vulnerability to the threat posed by a formidable enemy focused on mass destruction. The events of that day also validated how determined, patient, and sophisticated—both in planning and execution—our terrorist enemies have become. The basic nature of our free society greatly enables terrorist operations and tactics, while, at the same time, hinders our ability to predict, prevent, or mitigate the effects of terrorists acts. Given these realities, it is imperative to develop a comprehensive national approach to physical protection.

However, the task of preparing a comprehensive national approach to counter terrorist attacks appears overwhelming. For example, using such simple items as yeast, infant formula, sugar, Epsom salts, cheesecloth, blenders, masks, and gloves, terrorists with minimum training could set up a laboratory to make chemical and biological weapons. If terrorists, foreign or domestic, within the United States lack the necessary knowledge to manufacture bio-terrorism weapons, they can buy old declassified government documents for as little as $15 that provide the information needed to manufacture anthrax and other biological and germ weapons. If the United States fortifies its major seaports, terrorists could attack a smaller seaport. If all seaports were 100 percent screened for nuclear, biological, and chemical weapons—an impossible proposition—terrorists could smuggle weapons in by land or make a weapon in the United States.

In summary, terrorists already possess the motive to attack the United States using nuclear, biological, and chemical weapons, and it appears that the means and availability of technology and materials necessary to carry out such an attack are not lacking. Furthermore, terrorists have virtually an unlimited number of targets to attack. Since terrorists do not distinguish between "military" targets and "civilian" targets, any target that produces headlines, panic, and fear will do. Whether they attack the White House, a major financial building, a sports event, a school, or the corner store makes little difference to the terrorist and, to a large degree, achieves the same goal of using violence to further the cause of the terrorist.

To achieve a comprehensive security strategy it will be necessary to be innovative and flexible. For example, many schools have weather stations that gather data used by the students for class exercises or private contractors such as TV forecasters. Linking these school weather stations it is possible to create a monitoring system for a fraction of the cost if it were necessary to replicate the system that could provide key information for predicting how and where nuclear, chemical, or biological threats might spread.[78] Other innovative detection systems might include using centralized computer programs and data systems used by veterinarians and animal hospitals. Animals respond to biological agents in much the same way as humans. Using data from these centralized databases, it would be possible to develop a early warning system to detect anthrax, plague, or other threats.[79]

In fact, many adaptations are being made to promote flexibility and innovativeness in responding to nuclear, biological, and chemical threats. For example, the Food and Drug Administration has adopted regulations that will allow some drugs and vaccines designed to counter biological, chemical, and nuclear terrorism to be approved without being tested in people to prove they work.[80] Although the Food and Drug Administration acknowledges the risk in approving drugs not tested on people, it also acknowledges the unique circumstances that are involved in countering such a threat. Also, the federal government has been more proactive in publishing advice for state and local governments on how to react to terrorist attacks using weapons of mass destruction.[81] This action is necessary, as the lack of information has been consistently cited as a major weakness in responding to nuclear, biological, and chemical threats.

Many of the preparations to enhance national security against nuclear, biological, and chemical threats will be very expensive but necessary. In 2003, the Department of Homeland Security installed Project Biowatch. Biowatch is a $60 million sensor network that monitors the air in 31 cities to detect bio-terrorism threats. Biowatch monitors New York, Washington, Chicago, Houston, San Francisco, San Diego, Boston, and other metropolitan areas to provide early detection of traces of any biological threat. Such early warning could save tens of thousands of lives.[82] New York City has opened a $16 million high-security Biosafety Level 3 laboratory to help detect bio-terrorism threats such as anthrax. This facility gives New York City one of the most elaborate disease surveillance operations in the country.[83] Other cities may find it necessary to invest in similar facilities to ensure against bio-terrorism.

If the United States is to maximize its ability to enhance national security and preserve the principles of democratic government and liberty consistent with a free society, it will be necessary to think outside the box. It is not possible to depend on scrutiny by law enforcement, restrictions of personal liberties, and military operations as the sole or even primary response to the threat of terrorism. To enhance national security, it will be necessary to give consideration to a wide variety of options and innovative strategies.

Chapter Summary

- Weapons of mass destruction make a terrorist group of any size a serious threat to the United States.
- The most common scenarios for a nuclear attack by terrorists are an attack on a population center using a dirty bomb, an attack on an existing nuclear facility, or an attack on nuclear materials in transit or storage.
- The lack of access to highly enriched uranium (HEU) is the major obstacle for terrorists who would attack the United States using a high-yield nuclear bomb.
- If terrorists use a dirty bomb, they would most likely attack a population center. If terrorists use a nuclear weapon, they would most likely attack a major seaport.
- The Nuclear Regulatory Commission (NRC) has oversight responsibility for nuclear facilities and they strive to enhance security against a terrorist attack, radiological sabotage, or diversion of NRC-licensed materials.
- Biological weapons are living organisms intended to cause disease or death.
- Biological weapons are called the "poor man's atomic bomb" because of their destructive power.
- The most likely biological weapons to be used by terrorists are anthrax, smallpox, plague, and botulinum toxin. The United States has already been attacked using anthrax, ricin, and botulinum toxin.
- Chemical weapons are highly toxic liquid and gaseous substances that can cause harm or death.
- Studies indicate that the United States is not adequately prepared to respond to a biological attack.
- Preparing to respond to a nuclear, biological, or chemical attack will require extensive planning, innovative strategies, and expensive preparations.

Terrorism and You

Understanding This Chapter

1. Why is the modern threat of terrorism significantly different from the threat of terrorists experienced in the past?

2. What are the two types of nuclear military-type weapons and why does one type present a greater threat than the other type?

3. If terrorists used a dirty bomb, what would be the most likely target? Why?

4. Why is the security of highly enriched uranium so important?

5. What agency is charged with oversight responsibility of the security of nuclear power plants? What is being done to enhance the safety of nuclear power plants?

6. Which is a greater threat: biological weapons or chemical weapons? Why?

7. What are the most common biological weapons terrorists could use in an attack against the United States?

8. Why is anthrax the biological weapon of choice of terrorists?

9. Why must the threat of international terrorism not detract the United States from the threat of domestic terrorism?

10. What have studies of the level of preparedness of the United States against nuclear and biological weapons suggested?

Thinking about How Terrorism Touches You

1. Most preparations for attacks by terrorists using nuclear, biological, and chemical weapons have focused on major metropolitan population centers. Do you think medium-sized cities and rural towns should be concerned about a terrorist attack using weapons of mass destruction? Why or why not?

2. If anthrax or smallpox vaccinations were made available to the general public, would you get vaccinated? Why or why not? If you were in the military and required to be vaccinated against anthrax, would you consent? Why or why not?

3. Nuclear power generating plants are becoming more popular in light of the world's demand for fossil fuel energy. Do you think the risk posed by nuclear power plants are worth the benefit derived from them? Why or why not?

4. Government authorities and experts believe that one of the reasons a dirty bomb would be harmful is the great fear by the public of anything "radioactive." It is believed that public panic would exceed the actual threat posed by a dirty bomb because of this fear and ignorance. Do you agree? Why or why not?

5. Attacks against the United States using anthrax, ricin, and botulinum toxin most likely were carried out by domestic, not international, terrorists. Is the focus on international terrorism causing the government to give inadequate attention to domestic terrorism? Remember that prior to 9/11, the FBI considered domestic terrorists the major threat to the United States.

Important Terms and Concepts

Anthrax	Dark Winter
Aum Shinrikyo	Dirty Bomb
Biological Weapons	Force-on-Force Exercises
Biowatch	Highly Enriched Uranium (HEU)
Blister Agents	Nerve Agents
Blood Agents	Nuclear Regulatory Commission (NRC)
Botulinum Toxin	Plague
Chemical Weapons	Radiological Dispersal Device (RDD)
Choking Agents	Ricin

Smallpox
Strategic Nuclear Weapon

Tactical Nuclear Weapon
Topoff 2

Endnotes

1. James A. Fagin, "The Impact of Technology and Communications upon International and Transnational Terrorism," *International Journal of Comparative and Applied Justice,* Vol. VI, No. 1, Spring 1982.

2. Nicholas D. Kristof, "An American Hiroshima," New York Times Online, www.nytimes.com, August 11, 2004.

3. Jonathan Medalia, "Terrorist Nuclear Attacks on Seaports: Threat and Response," CRS Report for Congress. Washington, DC: Congressional Research Service—The Library of Congress, August 13, 2003, p. 1.

4. Ibid., p. 2.

5. Ibid., pp. 1–2.

6. Ibid., p. 2.

7. *Weapons of Mass Destruction Reference Guide—Protecting America: Nuclear, Biological, and Chemical Threat Reduction.* Washington, DC: Nuclear Threat Reduction Campaign, nd.

8. Ibid.

9. Jonathan Medalia, "Terrorist Nuclear Attacks on Seaports: Threat and Response," CRS Report for Congress. Washington, DC: Congressional Research Service—The Library of Congress, August 13, 2003, p. 3.

10. Peter Slevin, "Report Urges Tighter Nuclear Controls: White House Not Doing Enough to Secure Weapons Materials, Analysts Say," *Washington Post,* www.washingtonpost.com, May 24, 2004, p. A02.

11. Matthew L. Wald and Judith Miller, "Energy Department Plans a Push to Retrieve Nuclear Materials," New York Times Online, www.nytimes.com, May 26, 2004.

12. David E. Sanger, "C.I.A. Said to Find North Korean Nuclear Advances," New York Times Online, www.nytimes.com, July 1, 2003. David E. Sanger, "North Korea Says It Has Made Fuel for Atom Bombs," New York Times Online, www.nytimes.com, July 15, 2003. David E. Sanger and Thom Shanker, "North Korea Hides New Nuclear Site, Evidence Suggests," New York Times Online, www.nytime.com, July 20, 2003.

13. Felicity Barringer, "Traces of Enriched Uranium Are Reportedly Found in Iran," New York Times Online, www.nytimes.com, August 27, 2003.

14. Matthew Clark, "Iran Prepares Uranium for Enrichment," *Christian Science Monitor,* www.csmonitor.com, October 5, 2004.

15. Scott Peterson, "A Push for Candor on Iran Nukes," *Christian Science Monitor,* www.csmonitor.com, September 19, 2003.

16. George Jahn, "Diplomats Say Removal of Nuclear Equipment from Iraq Was Well-Organized," www. boston.com/dailynews/288/world/Diplomats_say_removal_of_nucle:..shtml, October 14, 2004.

17. Ibid.

18. "Bomb Materials at Campus Reactors," New York Times Online, www.nytimes.com, August 19, 2004.

19. Ibid.

20. Philip Shenon, "Police in Thailand Seize Radioactive Material," New York Times Online, www.nytimes.com, June 14, 2003.

21. Associated Press, "BBC: Al-Qaida Had Dirty Radioactive Bomb," *Pocono Record,* January 31, 2003, p. A5.

22. Jonathan Medalia, "Terrorist Nuclear Attacks on Seaports: Threat and Response," CRS Report for Congress. Washington, DC: Congressional Research Service—The Library of Congress, August 13, 2003, p. 4.

23. Associated Press, "Laboratories Set to Undergo Major Overhaul of Security," New York Times Online, www.nytimes.com, June 25, 2003.

24. Associated Press, "Security Probe Opens at Los Alamos Lab," New York Times. www.nytimes.com. July 19, 2004.

25. Matthew L. Wald, "Senator Questions Security at Nuclear Arms Laboratories," New York Times Online, www.nytimes.com, June 23, 2003.

26. Ibid.

27. Nuclear Regulatory Commission, *Protecting Our Nation Since 9-11-01.* Washington, DC: U.S. Nuclear Regulatory Commission, NUREG/BR-0314, September 2004, p. iii.

28. Ibid., p. 5.

29. Ibid., p. 18.

30. Matthew L. Wald, "Experts Say Nuclear Plants Can Survive Jetliner Crash," New York Times Online, www.nytimes.com, September 20, 2002.

31. Ibid.

32. *The National Strategy for the Physical Protection of Critical Infrastructures and Key Assets.* Washington, DC: The White House, February 2003, pp. 74–75.

33. Nuclear Regulatory Commission, *Protecting Our Nation Since 9-11-01.* Washington, DC: U.S. Nuclear Regulatory Commission, NUREG/BR-0314, September 2004, p. iii.

34. Mathew L. Wald, "Battle Swirls on Security at A-Plants," New York Times Online, www.nytimes.com, August 6, 2004.

35. Nuclear Regulatory Commission, *Protecting Our*

Nation Since 9-11-01. Washington, DC: U.S. Nuclear Regulatory Commission, NUREG/BR-0314, September 2004, p. 13.

36. Mathew L. Wald, "Battle Swirls on Security at A-Plants," New York Times Online, www.nytimes.com, August 6, 2004.

37. Nuclear Regulatory Commission, *Protecting Our Nation Since 9-11-01.* Washington, DC: U.S. Nuclear Regulatory Commission, NUREG/BR-0314, September 2004, p. 22.

38. Ibid., p. 24.

39. Nicholas J. Beeching, David A. B. Dance, Alastair R. O. Miller, and Robert C. Spencer," Biological Warfare and Bioterrorism," *Clinical Review,* Vol. 324, No. 9, February 2002, p. 336.

40. *Weapons of Mass Destruction Reference Guide—Protecting America: Nuclear, Biological, and Chemical Threat Reduction.* Washington, DC: Nuclear Threat Reduction Campaign, nd.

41. Office of Homeland Security, *National Strategy for Homeland Security.* Washington, DC: Office of Homeland Security, 2002, p. xii.

42. Office of Technology Assessment, "Technologies Underlying Weapons of Mass Destruction," OTA-BP-ISC-115, December 1993, p. 73.

43. John A. Jernigan et al., "Bioterrorism-Related Inhalation Anthrax: The First 10 Cases Reported in the United Sates," *Emerging Infectious Diseases,* Vol. 7, No. 6, November–December 2001, p. 933.

44. Associated Press, "Tabloid Headquarters to be Fumigated," New York Times Online, www.nytimes.com, July 10, 2004.

45. Allan Lengel, "Anthrax Probers Sill Seek Md. Leads," *Washington Post,* www.washingtonpost.com, July 18, 2004, p. C01.

46. Judith Miller, "Scientist Files Suit Over Anthrax Inquiry," New York Times Online, www.nytimes.com, August 27, 2003; Robert D. McFadden, "Doctor's Homes Are Searched in the Anthrax Investigation," New York Times Online, www.nytimes.com, August 6, 2004.

47. Judith Miller, "Scientist Files Suit Over Anthrax Inquiry," New York Times Online, www.nytimes.com, August 27, 2003.

48. Donald A. Henderson et al., "Smallpox as a Biological Weapon: Medical and Public Health Management," *Journal of American Medical Association,* Vol. 281, No. 22, June 9, 1999, p. 2136.

49. Donald G. McNeil, Jr., "National Programs to Vaccinate for Smallpox Come to a Halt." New York Times Online, www.nytimes.com, June 19, 2003.

50. Thomas V. Inglesby et al., "Plague as a Biological Weapon: Medical and Public Health Management," *Journal of American Medical Association,* Vol. 283, No. 17, p. 2281.

51. Ibid., p. 2282.

52. Ibid.

53. Ibid.

54. Stephen S. Arnon et al., "Botulinum Toxin as a Biological Weapon: Medical and Public Health Management," *Journal of American Medical Association,* Vol. 285, No. 8, February 28, 2001, p. 1060.

55. Ibid.

56. Ibid.

57. Nuclear Threat Reduction Campaign, *Weapons of Mass Destruction Reference Guide—Protecting America: Nuclear, Biological, and Chemical Weapon Threat Reduction.* Washington, DC: Nuclear Vietnam Veterans of America Foundation and the Justice Project, nd.

58. Donald G. McNeil, Jr., "Ricin, Made from Common Castor Beans, Can Be Lethal but Has Drawbacks as a Weapon," New York Times Online, www.nytimes.com, February 4, 2004.

59. Associated Press, "Feds Probe Cyanide in Texas Terror Case," New York Times Online, www.nytimes.com, January 20, 2004.

60. Ibid.

61. Philip Shenon, "Terrorism Drills Showed Lack of Preparedness, Report Says," New York Times Online, www.nytimes.com, December 19, 2003.

62. David Johnston, "Report Calls U.S. Agencies Understaffed for Bioterror," New York Time Online, www.nytimes.com, July 6, 2003.

63. Philip Shenon, "Terrorism Drills Showed Lack of Preparedness, Report Says," New York Times Online, www.nytimes.com, December 19, 2003.

64. Ibid.

65. Judith Miller, "Censored Study on Bioterror Doubts U.S. Preparedness," New York Times Online, www.nytimes.com, March 29, 2004.

66. Marc Santora, "New York Hospitals See Lack of Preparedness for Disaster," New York Times Online, www.nytimes.com, August 24, 2004.

67. Ibid.

68. Judith Miller, "Bush Issues Directive to Bolster Defense against Bioterrorism," New York Times Online, www.nytimes.com, April 28, 2004.

69. Patrick Healy, "After Many Flaws Are Detailed, Plum Island Security Is Stressed," New York Times Online, www.nytimes.com, October 21, 2003.

70. Daniel J. Wakin, "Report Cites Security Flaws at Plum Island," New York Times Online, www.nytimes.com, October 19, 2003.

71. Dee Ann Divis and Nicholas M. Horrock, "Living Terror Part 1: Deadly Laboratories," United Press International, www.upi.com/print.cfm?StoryID=20030630-122726-5144r, July 2, 2003.

72. William J. Broad, "Bioterror Researchers Build a More Lethal Mousepox," New York Times Online, www.nytimes.com, November 1, 2003.

73. Jeffrey Selingo, "New Advisory Board to Help

Safeguard Biological Research from Use by Terrorists," *The Chronicle of Higher Education,* http://chronicle.com/daily/2004/03/20004030505n.htm, March 5, 2004.

74. William J. Broad, "U.S. Selling Papers Showing How to Make Germ Weapons," New York Times Online, www.nytimes.com, January 13, 2002.

75. Tom Regan, "Politics of 'Fear Over Vision' Explored on British Television," *Christian Science Monitor,* www.csmonitor.com, October 18, 2004.

76. Ibid.

77. Ibid.

78. Associated Press, "School Weather Stations Could Track Attack," *Pocono Record,* April 5, 2003, p. A8.

79. Elizabeth Weise, "Pets May Be First Bioterrorism Alert," *USA Today,* March 31, 2003, p. 6D.

80. Andrew Pollack and William J. Broad, "Anti-Terror Drugs Get Test Shortcut," New York Times Online, www.nytimes.com, May 31, 2002.

81. Matthew L. Wald, "U.S. Plans to Offer Guidance for a Dirty-Bomb Aftermath," New York Times Online, www.nytimes.com, September 27, 2004.

82. Associated Press, "Government Provides Details of Bioterror Sensors in Cities," New York Times Online, www.nytimes.com, November 16, 2003.

83. Marc Santora, "City Opens a Secure Lab to Counter Bioterrorism," New York Times Online, www.nytimes.com, July 14, 2004.

8

The Day After

Rebuilding Main Street, USA

Gary Helfand, University of Hawaii–West Oahu
Ross Prizzia, University of Hawaii–West Oahu

Preventing needless damage after a terrorist attack poses as much or more of a challenge than actually preventing a terrorist attack.

The attacks of September 11, 2001, transformed the specter of a terrorist strike on U.S. soil into reality. The anthrax mailings of October 2001 provided sobering evidence of the vulnerability of this country to covert biological attack. Terrorists are actively working to obtain nuclear, radiological, chemical, and biological weapons for the stated purpose of killing large numbers of Americans. . . . And as September 11 demonstrated, terrorists are constantly seeking new tactics or unexpected means to cause mass casualties and inflict maximum damage.

—Homeland Security Organization, Lawrence Livermore National Laboratory, October 11, 2004

All Americans should begin a process of learning about potential threats so we are better prepared to react during an attack.

—READYAmerica, U.S. Department of Homeland Security, October 11, 2004

Chapter Outline

Learning Objectives

- The reader will appreciate how the United States government is striving to minimize damage and speed recovery in the event of a terrorist attack.
- The reader will understand the role of FEMA as a key agency for disaster response and planning.
- The reader will appreciate the importance of planning, partnerships, and preparation in disaster response.
- The reader will know the role emergency operations plans in disaster response.
- The reader will understand why mitigation is an important goal of disaster response.
- The reader will understand the guiding principles for the role of federal agencies in responding to a terrorist attack as outlined in the United States Government Interagency Domestic Terrorism Concept of Operations Plan (CONPLAN).
- The reader will know the primary federal agencies responsible for responding to a terrorist attack.
- The reader will appreciate the importance of identifying lead federal agencies and the role of the lead federal agency.
- The reader will realize how planning for emergency responses to weapons of mass destruction is different from planning for other disasters.
- The reader will appreciate the role of FEMA in providing assistance to state and local governments for planning for a terrorist attack.
- The reader will understand the role of mutual aid agreements and why they are a key strategy in responding to a terrorist attack.
- The reader will understand the importance of Continuity of Operations (COOP) and Continuity of Government (COG) in the event of a terrorist attack.

Introduction: The Day After

The numerous federal, state, and local agencies working to prevent another terrorist attack on U.S. soil have made tremendous progress in intelligence and prevention. However, the federal government and the Department of Homeland Security have acknowledged that despite all the efforts of these agencies, it may not be possible to prevent another 9/11-type attack.

The report of the *National Strategy for Homeland Security* identified the three goals of homeland security as (1) preventing terrorist attacks within the United States, (2) reducing America's vulnerability to terrorism, and (3) minimizing the damage and recovering from attacks that do occur. One of the key lessons of September 11, 2001, was that the ability to respond to terrorist attacks is a very important factor in minimizing loss of life and collateral damage. Some of the most severe criticisms of the *9/11 Commission Report* were its assessment of federal, state, and local capacity for emergency response and actions to minimize damage after the attacks. Emergency response efforts were hampered by lack of coordination among agencies, incompatible emergency communication equipment, lack of resource capacity by the healthcare providers, and lack of organization and command to coordinate the efforts of the numerous multilevel agencies responding to the attack and responsible for follow-up actions.

The previous chapters have addressed the efforts focused on achieving the first two goals of homeland defense: prevention and reducing vulnerability. This chapter examines the strategies and programs developed after September 11, 2001, to minimize damage and speed recovery in the event of a terrorist attack, especially an attack using weapons of mass destruction. In the event of another terrorist attack on U.S. soil, especially an attack involving weapons of mass destruction, the response of the government the day after will be an important factor in minimizing loss of life and injuries. Given the complexity of the task, many government agencies are involved in achieving this goal. However, the Federal Emergency Management Agency (FEMA) is a key agency in responding to this goal. This chapter will discuss FEMA's role in minimizing the damage and recovering from attacks that do occur and the plans that have been developed for responding to a terrorist attack in the United States.

The Federal Emergency Management Agency

The federal government and every state and local jurisdiction face the difficult challenge of ensuring that citizens, emergency responders, essential government services, and private property are protected from the consequences of a terrorist attack. The infrastructure that defines the ability to respond to terrorist attacks is the emergency disaster response strategies, agencies, and resources of the various governments and to some degree the disaster assistance provided by private and nonprofit agencies.

Historically, disaster response by states and the federal government has been fragmented. Each government agency often developed its own response plans without consideration of shared resources, coordination, and communication. Today, the primary federal government agency tasked with disaster response and planning is the Federal Emergency Management Agency (FEMA). The agency can trace its beginnings to the Congressional Act of 1803 when Congress provided federal disaster assistance to a New Hampshire town following an extensive fire. During the next 200 years the federal government provided disaster assistance in response to hurricanes, earthquakes, floods, and other natural disasters. The federal government approached disaster assistance with a piecemeal strategy and disaster assistance was provided by several different agencies, such as the Reconstruction Finance Corporation, the Bureau of Public Roads, the U.S. Army Corps of Engineers, and the Federal Disaster Assistance Administration.

In 1974, the Disaster Relief Act gave the president the power to declare an event a national disaster, thereby making federal assistance available to the victims of the disaster. However, there were more than 100 federal agencies involved in some aspect of disasters, hazards, and emergencies. Many of the federal programs were not coordinated with state programs.

In 1979, President Carter created the Federal Emergency Management Agency. Disaster assistance responsibilities that had been dispersed among many different agencies were transferred to FEMA. The agency was charged with providing assistance in a wide range of disasters, hazards, and emergencies, including civil defense, nuclear accidents, natural disasters, toxic contamination, and even the Cuban refugee crisis. Consequently, FEMA adopted an "all-hazards" approach to disaster assistance that included "direction, control and warning systems which are common to the full range of emergencies from small isolated events to the ultimate emergency—war."[1]

After September 11, 2001, FEMA focused on issues of national preparedness and homeland security. At first, FEMA coordinated its activities with the newly formed Department of Homeland Security (DHS) with the mission of helping to ensure that the nation's first responders were trained and equipped to deal with weapons of mass destruction. In March 2003, FEMA was merged under the Department of Homeland Security and tasked with responding to, planning for, recovering from, and mitigating against disasters. FEMA is one of the four major branches of DHS. It has about 2,500 full-time employees and more than 5,000 stand-by disaster reservists. Under the authority of the DHS, FEMA is responsible for acting as the federal portal for disaster assistance, especially in the event of a terrorist attack.

3 Ps: Planning, Partnerships, and Preparation

The Federal Emergency Management Agency is the key federal agency in promoting the 3Ps—planning, partnerships, and preparation (PPP)—to minimize the damage that would occur from a terrorist attack and to maximize the ability for the society and economy to recovery from a terrorist attack. Planning focuses on assessment of response capacity and developing specific and detailed plans of action, including what to do, when to do it, who will do it, and where it will be done in advance of a terrorist attack. Partnership focuses on interagency agreements and communication. Partnerships can be between local agencies, such as fire and police departments; between local and federal agencies; and between local/state and federal agencies. Also, there can be partnerships among state agencies and among federal agencies. Partnerships provide for the ability to fill resource gaps, to establish command and control structures in advance so that when multiple agencies respond to an incident there is effective leadership at the site, and to help make the costs of emergency response more affordable. Partnerships make emergency response more affordable in that if agencies can depend on equipment, personnel, and resources of other agencies, no single agency has to budget so much that it could respond alone.

One of the underlying principles of the concept of a federal lead agency such as FEMA for emergency response is the assumption that the complexity of the emergency response to a terrorist attack, especially one using weapons of mass destruction, would be so involved and of such a magnitude that no single agency—not even the federal government—has the equipment, personnel, and resources to respond alone. Preparation focuses on developing the ability to respond to a terrorist attack in a manner that would minimize loss of life and property and minimize public disorder and panic. Preparation focuses on the advance actions of local and state government agencies, federal government agencies, and individual citizens. The foundation on which PPP rests is the development of emergency operations

BOX 8.1 • *Up Close and Personal: The Optimism Bias*

Evaluations of the preparedness of the homeland for a terrorist attack have consistently indicated that the United States is unprepared. A 2004 poll by the *New York Times* indicated that the overwhelming majority of the people polled have done nothing to prepare for such an attack themselves.[2] The poll reported that most people are not worried that they or a family member will become a victim of terrorism. Also, the majority of the respondents reported that they do nothing different when the government raises the terror-alert level.[3]

Not only are individuals not prepared for a terrorism attack but government agencies are also not prepared for another terrorist attack. Despite the fact that biological and nuclear attacks rank as government officials' most feared types of terrorist attacks, a 2004 survey reported that "bio-terrorism preparedness planning still lacks strategic direction, well-defined priorities and appropriate levels of resources to match the needs,"[4] While one might expect New York and New Jersey to be better prepared because of their reported focus on preparation for another attack, they ranked near the bottom of the list of cities in the survey.[5]

Specific areas where the United States is rated as unprepared for a terrorist attacking using WMD include[6]:

- Hospitals and state and local public health agencies are not prepared to respond to a biological attack.
- Despite federal efforts to coordinate emergency response, experts report that there is confusion about who is in charge of preparations for, and response to, bio-attacks.
- Simulations indicate that communication to the public about the nature of the incident and what to do is still a major problem.
- There are insufficient vaccines and treatments available in the event of a bio-terrorism attack.
- There still is no technology to detect a biological attack as it occurs.

Studies suggest at the international level the world community is even less prepared to respond to a bio-terrorism attack.[7]

Critics point to several examples to demonstrate the actual lack of preparation for a terrorist attack despite the enormous amounts of time and money that have been invested in preparations. For example, over 100 chemical plants have been identified as having the potential to endanger one million or more people *each* in the event of a terrorist attack on one of these chemical plants.[8] Although the government has moved to secure airports, seaports are considered soft targets. Some experts speculate that the next terrorist attack may not occur on United States soil but in or near a harbor or the coastline. A supertanker filled with oil would not actually have to be in port to do catastrophic damage to the U.S. ecology and economy. A supertanker destroyed by a "dirty bomb" near the U.S. coastline would be an ecological nightmare. The clean-up costs would be in the billions of dollars.

Experts point to the accidents that do occur to indicate the unpreparedness of the United States for a terrorist attack. For example, trains carrying chlorine have crashed accidentally. If terrorists were to cause a crash of a train carrying chlorine near a major metropolitan area, 100,000 people could die within 30 minutes.[9] A simple fire in the New York subway system recently destroyed vital control equipment that will cripple the transportation system for six to nine months.[10] Despite increased security, strict regulations to discourage terrorists from gathering information about the operation of the subway system, and millions of dollars in security upgrades, the control room was not fireproof. Should it have been? Damage from similar fires was reported as far back as 1999. Despite this fact, the control room remained vulnerable to fire.[11]

David Ropeik of the Harvard School of Public Health finds no surprise in this state of affairs. He attributes the lack of initiative and response by individuals to the threat of terrorism to the "optimism bias." The theory of optimism bias says that individuals disproportionately believe that they will not be victims of a peril even though they widely acknowledge that it will occur.[12]

BOX 8.1 • Continued

Questions

1. Do you believe that many people suffer from optimism bias? That is to say, they believe that a terror attack is likely to occur but they do not believe that they will be a victim of or affected by the attack as demonstrated by their actions and lack of preparation. Why?

2. Do you suffer from optimism bias? Do you believe that the changes of another major terrorism attack is very likely but you have not taken any steps to prepare for such an attack and you do not change your behavior when the terror alert is raised? Why?

3. Another explanation as to why people do not take more steps to prepare for a terror attack, especially an attack using WMD, is that peo-

ple do not feel that there is anything they can do to prevent such an attack and the steps the government is urging them to take would make little impact in the event of an actual attack. For example, when the Department of Homeland Security urged people to stock up on duct tape and plastic sheeting for use in the event of a biological or chemical attack, many made fun of the advice and it was used as a source of jokes by many comedians. Which of these explanations—optimism bias or feelings of helplessness—do you feel best explains why so many Americans have not taken steps to prepare for a WMD attack? Explain your answer.

plans that are based on a realistic assessment of emergency response capacity and that provide detailed and specific action steps to be taken in the event of a terrorist attack.

Emergency Operations Plans

To enhance state and local coordination and planning, one of the key missions of FEMA is to provide funding and training for state and local governments to develop or update existing Emergency Operations Plans (EOP). These plans are considered the basic guidelines that provide for effective response to emergencies and disasters.

The Federal Emergency Management Agency not only provides EOP guidance for a terrorist incident but it also provides training and planning considerations that should be taken into account based on federal reports from the September 11 terrorist attacks at the World Trade Center and the Pentagon. Lessons learned from the terrorist attacks of 9/11 highlighted the importance that state and local governments need to ensure that response efforts are fully integrated and understood by all responders. Other lessons learned from the 9/11 attacks were that emergency response agencies need to adopt common command and control standards, to ensure equipment interoperability, and to implement mutual aid agreements. Moreover, the 9/11 attacks emphasized the importance of what is known as *continuity of operations* (COOP) and *continuity of state and local government/services* (COG) to ensure that operations and governmental authority are not disrupted. Although all of these program elements do not need to be included in the EOP itself, state and local jurisdictions need to address these issues as part of their comprehensive, strategic planning process.

The 9/11 attacks demonstrated that many EOPs were not current. Updated EOPs are important because they aid local jurisdictions and states in collecting information on their current response capability and adequacy of their strategic plans. FEMA is tasked with the responsibility to work with agencies at all levels of government to enhance their EOP and to coordinate with FEMA as the single point of federal coordination for local governments and states.[13] The collaboration between the state and local jurisdictions in developing or updating EOPs should be reflected in the state's strategic plan for addressing capability and resource needs. Each jurisdiction knows what its basic capabilities are, and accordingly, it should be intimately involved in the process to identify what capabilities it needs to enhance. Local jurisdiction involvement in determining the most prudent way to fill resource gaps is vital. The jurisdiction's input will provide the information needed to help states determine the resources needed to satisfy statewide requirements and the most appropriate source (mutual aid, other state and federal program funds) to provide the needed resources. Information derived from updating local EOPs will provide a means to help determine resource gaps. Effective disaster response requires that states should ensure that their EOPs and their strategic plans are coordinated and reflect a comprehensive, integrated approach to planning for and responding to terrorism, WMD incidents, and all other hazards, disasters, and emergencies.[14]

Many state and local jurisdictions have already completed Emergency Operations Plans. In light of the lessons learned from the September 11 terrorist attacks, federal funding is being provided to state and local governments to update these all-hazard plans, with a focus on WMD incidents. Each jurisdiction that receives federal funds to update its EOP should use the funds to ensure that the plan addresses all-hazards operations, with special emphasis on WMD terrorist incidents. In addition, states and local governments may use planning funds to implement the following activities in support of their EOP and state strategic plan.

- Identification and protection of critical infrastructure
- Inventory of critical response equipment and teams
- Interstate and intrastate mutual aid agreements
- Resource typing
- Resource standards to include interoperability protocols and a common incident command system
- State and local continuity of operations (COOP) and continuity of government (COG)
- Citizen and family preparedness, including Citizen Corps and other volunteer initiatives in responding to an incident

The purpose of this guidance is to help state and local governments fine-tune their all-hazards EOPs and address the critical planning considerations that have been discussed here. States should also encourage regional planning initiatives among its jurisdictions. Updating EOPs will not only aid jurisdictions in assessing current capability but it will also provide the basis for the preparation and refinement of state strategic plans and a foundation for mutual aid support.

BOX 8.2 • *Case Study: FEMA Strategic Plan (Fiscal Years 2003–2008)*

Vision: A Nation Prepared

Mission: Lead America to prepare for, prevent, respond to, and recover from disasters.

Core Values:
- Integrity
- Innovation
- Accountability
- Respect
- Trust
- Customer Focus
- Public Stewardship
- Partnership
- Diversity
- Compassion

Goals:
1. Reduce loss of life and property.
2. Minimize suffering and disruption caused by disasters.
3. Prepare the Nation to address the consequences of terrorism.
4. Serve as the Nation's portal for emergency management information and expertise.
5. Create a motivating and challenging work environment for employees.
6. Make FEMA a world-class enterprise.

GOAL 1: REDUCE LOSS OF LIFE AND PROPERTY.

Objective 1.1
Provide hazard and risk information using the best-suited technologies.

Objective 1.2
Ensure that the Nation's most vulnerable areas are covered by emergency management plans that can be implemented.

Objective 1.3
Ensure the capabilities of Federal, State, Territorial, Tribal, local, and other partners are in place to plan and prepare for disasters.

Objective 1.4
Help individuals, local governments, States, Territories, Tribal Nations, and Federal agencies make good risk management decisions.

Objective 1.5
Develop and implement a comprehensive training and education plan for emergency management planners and responders.

Goal 1: Performance Measures

Performance Measure 1.1
By Fiscal Year 2008, the average annual loss of life from fire-related events is reduced by 15% over the 1998 annual baseline of 4,500.

Performance Measure 1.2
By Fiscal Year 2008, $10 billion in potential property losses, disaster, and other costs have been avoided.

Performance Measure 1.3
By Fiscal Year 2008, 100% of States, Territories, and Tribal Nations report meeting collaboratively established, all-hazard, emergency management readiness capability standards.

GOAL 2: MINIMIZE SUFFERING AND DISRUPTION CAUSED BY DISASTERS.

Objective 2.1
Respond quickly and effectively when States, Territories, Tribal Nations, and local governments are overwhelmed.

Objective 2.2
Use the full range of State, Territorial, Tribal, and Federal capabilities in determining the most effective delivery mechanisms for disaster recovery and mitigation programs.

Objective 2.3
Provide timely and appropriate disaster assistance and payment of flood insurance claims.

Objective 2.4
Mitigate against potential future losses as part of every disaster recover effort.

Goal 2: Performance Measures

Performance Measure 2.1
By Fiscal Year 2008, FEMA has coordinated and established the capability to respond concurrently to four catastrophic and twelve non-catastrophic disasters.

(continued)

BOX 8.2 • Continued

Performance Measure 2.2
By Fiscal Year 2008, 100% of assessed public safety and service organizations meet established standards for interoperability of wireless communication systems.

Performance Measure 2.3
By Fiscal Year 2008, all disaster assistance and flood claim payments are provided within established performance standards.

GOAL 3: PREPARE THE NATION TO ADDRESS THE CONSEQUENCES OF TERRORISM.

Objective 3.1
Develop and implement a Federal program to support State, Territorial, Tribal, and local government incident management capability building.

Objective 3.2
Build a comprehensive State, Territorial, Tribal, and local capability for responding to the consequences of terrorism.

Objective 3.3
Ensure the means used to exchange information among Federal partners, State, Territorial, Tribal, and local responders, program officials, and the general public is coordinated with and delivered through a single National portal.

Goal 3: Performance Measures

Performance Measure 3.1
By Fiscal Year 2008, 100% of State and Territorial systems of first responders and other appropriate emergency personnel meet mutually-agreed upon baseline performance standards for responding to and recovering from terrorist incidents, including the unique threats posed by weapons of mass destruction.

GOAL 4: SERVE AS THE NATION'S PORTAL FOR EMERGENCY MANAGEMENT INFORMATION AND EXPERTISE.

Objective 4.1
Create and manage a single, convenient portal for emergency management information.

Objective 4.2
Serve as the Nation's knowledge manager and coordinator of emergency management information.

Objective 4.3
Establish a National warning capability.

Goal 4: Performance Measures

Performance Measure 4.1
By Fiscal Year 2008, 95% of those surveyed who accessed emergency management information through FEMA report that they found the information to be useful.

Performance Measure 4.2
By Fiscal Year 2008, a National network of warning systems is established with sufficient redundancy for 100% reliability in providing timely and accurate dissemination of alerts and crisis information to the general public throughout the Nation and to the emergency management community at all levels of government.

GOAL 5: CREATE A MOTIVATING AND CHALLENGING WORK ENVIRONMENT FOR EMPLOYEES.

Objective 5.1
Retain and recruit a capable, motivated, and diverse workforce.

Objective 5.2
Provide professional development training and opportunities for the betterment and advancement of employees.

Objective 5.3
Ensure employees understand their performance objectives and are recognized and rewarded appropriately.

Objective 5.4
Provide managers with the skills and authority they need to be successful and hold them accountable for their operational performance.

Objective 5.5
Provide a safe and healthy work environment to ensure FEMA employees feel valued and respected.

BOX 8.2 • Continued

GOAL 5: PERFORMANCE MEASURES.

Performance Measure 5.1
Maintain a positive Office of Management and Budget scorecard assessment (green light) in the area of Human Capital.

Performance Measure 5.2
By Fiscal Year 2008, the FEMA employee satisfaction rate in the area of Human Capital will be 5% over the Office of Personnel Management's government-wide survey average.

GOAL 6: MAKE FEMA A WORLD-CLASS ENTERPRISE.

Objective 6.1
Make FEMA a performance-based organization.

Objective 6.2
Plan and integrate FEMA's support functions to efficiently and effectively serve the Agency's strategic priorities, and both internal and external customers.

Objective 6.3
Ensure sound financial performance.

Objective 6.4
Communicate effectively with internal and external customers.

Objective 6.5
Provide customer-driven services.

Goal 6: Performance Measures

Performance Measure 6.1
External Partner Survey respondents report an annual incremental increase in satisfaction, over the 2003 baseline, with the efficient and effective delivery of FEMA's services.

Questions

1. FEMA's goal is to have 100 percent of state and territorial systems of first responders and other emergency personnel meet mutually agreed upon baseline performance standards for responding to and recovering from terrorist incidents, including the unique threats posed by weapons of mass destruction by fiscal year 2008. Do you think it will be possible to achieve this goal? Why?

2. FEMA is charged with and has adopted as their goal that FEMA would become the single source for emergency management information and expertise in the United States. Do you think having a single federal portal for emergency management information and expertise is the best strategy for emergency response? Would it be better if each state were to develop its own plan and resources? Why?

Emergency Response to Terrorism

When terrorism strikes, communities may receive assistance from state and federal agencies operating within the existing Integrated Emergency Management System. FEMA is the lead federal agency for supporting state and local response to the consequences of terrorist attacks.

Terrorism is often categorized as *domestic* or *international*. This distinction refers not to where the terrorist act takes place but rather to the origin of the individuals or groups responsible for it. For example, the 1995 bombing of the Murrah Federal Building in Oklahoma City was an act of domestic terrorism, but the attacks of September 2001 were international terrorism. For the purposes of consequence management, the origin of the perpetrator(s) is of less importance than the impacts of the attack on life and property; thus, the distinction between domestic and international terrorism is less relevant for the purposes of mitigation, preparedness, response, and recovery than understanding the capabilities of terrorist groups and how to respond to the impacts they can generate.

Hazard Mitigation

Mitigation is defined as any sustained action taken to reduce or eliminate long-term risk to human life and property from a hazardous event. Mitigation, also known as *prevention* (when done before a disaster), encourages long-term reduction of hazard vulnerability. The goal of mitigation is to decrease the need for response, as opposed to simply increasing the response capability. Mitigation can save lives and reduce property damage, and is cost effective and environmentally sound. This, in turn, can reduce the enormous cost of disasters to property owners and all levels of government. In addition, mitigation can protect critical community facilities, reduce exposure to liability, and minimize community disruption.

Mitigation planning grew out of a focus on planning for natural hazards. However, recent events demand that an all-hazard mitigation plan should also address hazards generated by human activities such as terrorism and hazardous material accidents. Although the term *mitigation* refers generally to activities that reduce loss of life and property by eliminating or reducing the effects of disasters, in the terrorism context it is often interpreted to include a wide variety of preparedness and response measures. For the purposes of FEMA's mitigation programs, the traditional meaning is assumed; that is, *mitigation* refers to specific measures that can be taken to reduce loss of life and property from human-caused hazards by modifying the environment to reduce the risk and potential consequences of hazards.

The role of FEMA in managing terrorism includes both anti-terrorism and counterterrorism activities. *Anti-terrorism* refers to defensive measures used to reduce the vulnerability of people and property to terrorist acts, whereas *counterterrorism* includes offensive measures taken to prevent, deter, and respond to terrorism. Thus, anti-terrorism is an element of hazard mitigation, while counterterrorism falls within the scope of preparedness, response, and recovery.

Although governments may not be able to prevent an attack, it is well within their ability to lessen the likelihood and/or the potential effects of an attack by implementing anti-terrorism measures. This is particularly so when government works cooperatively with community groups and the private sector to plan and implement anti-terrorism programs and strategies.

The process of mitigating hazards before they become disasters is similar for both natural and human-caused hazards; whether we are dealing with natural disasters or terrorism, we can use a process of (1) identifying and organizing resources, (2) conducting a risk or threat assessment and estimating losses, (3) identifying mitigation measures that will reduce the effects of the hazards and creating a strategy to deal with the mitigation measures in priority order, and (4) implementing the measures, evaluating the results, and keeping the plan up to date. This four-phase process is known as *mitigation planning*.

Capability Assessment for Readiness

The newly developed Terrorism Preparedness Supplement to the Local and Tribal Capability Assessment for Readiness (CAR) is designed to help local and tribal emergency managers to assess response capabilities and operational readiness for terrorism-related emergencies and disasters. This new terrorism supplement is based on information from the latest terrorism preparedness guidelines, including FEMA's "Managing the Consequences of Terrorist Incidents: Interim Planning Guide for State and Local Governments," the terrorism annex of the Federal Response Plan, the State Homeland Security Assessment and Strategy Program, and other relevant sources.

The terrorism supplement maintains the overall structure of the CAR, a survey-type system that is based on 13 functional areas of an emergency management program called Emergency Management Functions (EMF). Each EMF is subdivided into attributes or criteria by which performance in a particular area can be assessed. The attributes are further divided into characteristics—more detailed criteria that further clarify the area being assessed.

The CAR system is available in both electronic and manual formats. The automated version can generate tabulated results and reports and display results graphically. A FEMA web-based version of the Local and Tribal CAR was released in 2004.

FEMA and Federal Multiagency Coordination

In promoting effective planning, partnerships, and preparation, FEMA has to work with both federal agencies and state and local agencies. Each level of government requires a different strategy. Through the use of legislation, Presidential Decision Directives, and directives from the executive branch of government, to some degree federal interagency planning, partnership, and preparation can be facilitated. However, in dealing with sovereign states, FEMA must often rely on voluntary cooperation and mutual aid agreements to promote planning, partnerships, and preparation.

The United States Government Interagency Domestic Terrorism Concept of Operations Plan (CONPLAN) represents a concerted effort by a number of federal departments and agencies to work together to achieve a common goal.[15] The CONPLAN was developed through the efforts of six primary departments and agencies with responsibilities as identified in Presidential Decision Directive/NSC-39 (PDD-39).[16] This plan has been developed consistent with relevant PDDs, federal law, the Attorney General's Critical Incident Response Plan, the PDD-39 Domestic Guidelines, and the Federal Response Plan and its Terrorism Incident Annex. The FBI has worked with these departments and agencies to provide a forum to participate in planning and executing activities in order to develop, maintain, and enhance the federal response capability.

To ensure the policy is implemented in a coordinated manner, the CONPLAN is designed to provide overall guidance to federal, state, and local agencies concerning how the federal government would respond to a potential or actual terrorist threat or incident that occurs in the United States, particularly one involving weapons of mass destruction (WMD). The CONPLAN outlines an organized and unified capability for a timely, coordinated response by federal agencies to a terrorist threat or act. It establishes conceptual guidance for assessing and monitoring a developing threat; notifying appropriate federal, state, and local agencies of the nature of the threat; and deploying the requisite advisory and technical resources to assist the lead federal agency (LFA) in facilitating interdepartmental coordination of crisis and consequence management activities.

The actions each agency or department must perform during each phase of the response include crisis management and consequence management actions that are necessary to control and contain chemical, biological, nuclear/radiological, and conventional materials or devices. Prescribed actions will continue to be refined to better identify the mission, capabilities, and resources of supporting departments and agencies.

The CONPLAN establishes lead agencies and defines their responsibilities. Various departments and agencies agreed to support the overall concept of operations of the CONPLAN in order to carry out their assigned responsibilities under PDD-39 and PDD-62. The departments and agencies also agreed to implement national and regional planning efforts and to exercise activities in order to maintain the overall federal response capability.

Primary Federal Agencies

The response to a terrorist threat or incident within the United States will entail a highly coordinated, multiagency local, state, and federal response. In support of this mission, the following primary federal agencies will provide the core federal response:

- Department of Justice (DOJ) / Federal Bureau of Investigation (FBI)
- Federal Emergency Management Agency (FEMA)
- Department of Defense (DOD)
- Department of Energy (DOE)
- Environmental Protection Agency (EPA)
- Department of Health and Human Services (DHHS)

The Department of Justice and the Federal Bureau of Investigation will be the lead agencies for crisis management. The Federal Emergency Management Agency will be the lead agency for consequence management.

Although not formally designated under the CONPLAN, other federal departments and agencies may have authorities, resources, capabilities, or expertise required to support response operations. Agencies may be requested to participate in federal planning and response operations, and may be asked to designate staff to function as liaison officers and provide other support to the LFA.

The CONPLAN defines the responsibilities of the various federal agencies in the event of a terrorist attack.

Department of Justice (DOJ) / Federal Bureau of Investigation (FBI).   The Attorney General is responsible for ensuring the development and implementation of policies directed at preventing terrorist attacks domestically, and will undertake the criminal prosecution of these acts of terrorism that violate U.S. law. The Department of Justice has charged the FBI with execution of its LFA responsibilities for the management of a federal response to terrorist threats or incidents that take place within U.S. territory or those occurring in international waters that do not involve the flag vessel of a foreign country. As the lead federal agency for crisis management, the FBI will implement a federal crisis management response. The FBI will also designate a federal on-scene commander to ensure appropriate coordination of the overall government response with federal, state, and local authorities until such time as the Attorney General transfers the overall LFA role to FEMA. The FBI, with appropriate approval, will form and coordinate the deployment of a Domestic Emergency Support Team (DEST) with other agencies, when appropriate, and seek appropriate federal support based on the nature of the situation.

Federal Emergency Management Agency (FEMA).   As the lead agency for consequence management, FEMA will manage and coordinate any federal consequence management response in support of state and local governments in accordance with its statutory authorities. Additionally, FEMA will designate appropriate liaison and advisory personnel for the FBI's Strategic Information and Operations Center (SIOC) and deployment with the DEST, the Joint Operations Center (JOC), and the Joint Information Center (JIC).

Department of Defense (DOD).   The Department of Defense serves as a support agency to the FBI for crisis management functions, including technical operations, and a support agency to FEMA for consequence management. In accordance with DOD Directives 3025.15 and 2000.12 and the Chairman Joint Chiefs of Staff CONPLAN 0300-97, and upon approval by the Secretary of Defense, DOD will provide assistance to the LFA and/or the CONPLAN primary agencies, as appropriate, during all aspects of a terrorist incident, including both crisis and consequence management. Department of Defense assistance includes threat assessment; DEST participation and transportation; technical advice; operational support; tactical support; support for civil disturbances; custody, transportation, and disposal of a WMD device; and other capabilities, including mitigation of the consequences of a release.

The Department of Defense has many unique capabilities for dealing with a WMD and combating terrorism, such as the U.S. Army Medical Research Institute for Infectious Diseases, Technical Escort Unit, and U.S. Marine Corps Chemical Biological Incident Response Force. These and other DOD assets may be used in responding to a terrorist incident if requested by the LFA and approved by the Secretary of Defense.

Department of Energy (DOE).   The Department of Energy serves as a support agency to the FBI for technical operations and a support agency to FEMA for consequence management. The department provides scientific-technical personnel and equipment in support of the LFA during all aspects of a nuclear/radiological WMD terrorist incident. Assistance from the DOE can support both crisis and consequence management activities with capabilities such as threat assessment, DEST deployment, LFA advisory requirements, technical advice, forecasted modeling predictions, and operational support to include direct support of tactical operations. Deployable DOE scientific-technical assistance and support includes capabilities such as search operations; access operations; diagnostic and device assessment; radiological assessment and monitoring; identification of material; development of federal protective action recommendations; provision of information on the radiological response; rendering of safe operations; hazards assessment; containment, relocation, and storage of special nuclear material evidence; postincident clean-up; and on-site management and radiological assessment to the public, the White House, and members of Congress and foreign governments. All DOE support to a federal response will be coordinated through a senior energy official.

Environmental Protection Agency (EPA). The Environmental Protection Agency serves as a support agency to the FBI for technical operations and a support agency to FEMA for consequence management. The agency provides technical personnel and supporting equipment to the LFA during all aspects of a WMD terrorist incident. Assistance from the EPA may include threat assessment, DEST and regional emergency response team deployment, LFA advisory requirements, technical advice, and operational support for chemical, biological, and radiological releases. Assistance and advice from the EPA include threat assessment, consultation, agent identification, hazard detection and reduction, environmental monitoring, sample and forensic evidence collection/analysis, identification of contaminants, feasibility assessment and clean-up, and on-site safety, protection, prevention, decontamination, and restoration activities. The EPA and the United States Coast Guard (USCG) share responsibilities for response to oil discharges into navigable waters and releases of hazardous substances, pollutants, and contaminants into the environment under the National Oil and Hazardous Substances Pollution Contingency Plan (NCP). The Environmental Protection Agency provides the predestinated federal On-Scene Coordinator for inland areas and the USCG for coastal areas to coordinate containment, removal, and disposal efforts and resources during an oil, hazardous substance, or WMD incident.

Department of Health and Human Services (HHS). The Department of Health and Human Services serves as a support agency to the FBI for technical operations and a support agency to FEMA for consequence management. The department provides technical personnel and supporting equipment to the LFA during all aspects of a terrorist incident. The department can also provide regulatory follow-up when an incident involves a product regulated by the Food and Drug Administration. Assistance from the HHS supports threat assessment, DEST deployment, epidemiological investigation, LFA advisory requirements, and technical advice. Technical assistance to the FBI may include identification of agents, sample collection and analysis, on-site safety and protection activities, and medical management planning. Operational support to FEMA may include mass immunization, mass prophylaxis, mass fatality management, pharmaceutical support operations (National Pharmaceutical Stockpile), contingency medical records, patient tracking, and patient evacuation and definitive medical care provided through the National Disaster Medical System.

Policies and Federal Agency Authorities

The CONPLAN does not supersede existing plans or authorities that were developed for response to incidents under department and agency statutory authorities. Rather, it is intended to be a coordinating plan between crisis and consequence management to provide an effective federal response to terrorism. The CONPLAN is a federal signatory plan among the six principal departments and agencies named in PDD-39. It may be updated and amended, as necessary, by consensus among these agencies.

Federal Emergency Response Assistance

The federal response to a terrorist threat or incident provides a tailored, time-phased deployment of specialized federal assets. The response is executed under two broad responsibilities: crisis management and consequence management.

Crisis management is predominantly a law enforcement function and includes measures to identify, acquire, and plan the use of resources needed to anticipate, prevent, and/or resolve a threat or act of terrorism. In a terrorist incident, a crisis management response may include traditional law enforcement missions, such as intelligence, surveillance, tactical operations, negotiations, forensics, and investigations, as well as technical support missions, such as agent identification, search, rendering of safe procedures, transfer and disposal, and limited decontamination. In addition to the traditional law enforcement missions, crisis management also includes assurance of public health and safety.

The laws of the United States assign primary authority to the federal government to prevent and respond to acts of terrorism or potential acts of terrorism. Based on the situation, a federal crisis management response may be supported by technical operations and by consequence management activities, which should operate concurrently.

Consequence management is predominantly an emergency management function and includes measures to protect public health and safety, restore essential government services, and provide emergency relief to governments, businesses, and individuals affected by the consequences of terrorism. In an actual or potential terrorist incident, a consequence management response will be managed by FEMA using structures and resources of the Federal Response Plan (FRP). These efforts will include support missions as described in other federal operations plans, such as predictive modeling, protective action recommendations, and mass decontamination.

The laws of the United States assign primary authority to the state and local governments to respond to the consequences of terrorism; the federal government provides assistance, as required.

Lead Federal Agency Designation

The operational response to a terrorist threat will employ a coordinated, interagency process organized through a LFA concept. PDD-39 reaffirms and elaborates on the federal government's policy on counterterrorism and expands the roles, responsibilities, and management structure for combating terrorism. The lead federal agency responsibility is assigned to the Department of Justice, and is delegated to the FBI, for threats or acts of terrorism that take place in the United States or in international waters that do not involve the flag vessel of a foreign country. Within this role, the FBI Federal on-scene commander (OSC) will function as the on-scene manager for the U.S. government. All federal agencies and departments, as needed, will support the federal OSC. Threats or acts of terrorism that take place outside of the United States or its trust territories, or in international waters and involve the flag vessel of a foreign country are outside the scope of the CONPLAN.

In addition, these authorities reaffirm that FEMA is the lead agency for consequence management within U.S. territory. The Federal Emergency Management Agency retains authority and responsibility to act as the lead agency for consequence management through-out the federal response. The agency will use the Federal Response Plan structure to coor-dinate all federal assistance to state and local governments for consequence management. To ensure that there is one overall LFA, PDD-39 directs FEMA to support the Department of Justice (as delegated to the FBI) until the Attorney General transfers the LFA role to FEMA.[17] At such time, the responsibility to function as the on-scene manager for the U.S. government transfers from the FBI Federal OSC to the Federal Coordinating Officer (FCO).

Requests for Federal Assistance

Requests for federal assistance by state and local governments, as well as those from own-ers and operators of critical infrastructure facilities, are coordinated with the lead agency (crisis or consequence) responsible under U.S. law for that function. In response to a terror-ist threat or incident, multiple or competing requests will be managed based on priorities and objectives established by the JOC Command Group.

State and local governments will submit requests for federal crisis management assis-tance through the FBI. State and local governments will submit requests for federal conse-quence management assistance through standard channels under the Federal Response Plan. FEMA liaisons assigned to the DEST or JOC coordinate requests with the LFA to ensure consequence management plans and actions are consistent with overall priorities. All other requests for consequence management assistance submitted outside normal channels to the DEST or JOC will be forwarded to the Regional Operations Center (ROC) Director or the Federal Coordinating Officer for action.

Funding

As mandated by PDD-39, federal agencies directed to participate in counterterrorist opera-tions or the resolution of terrorist incidents bear the costs of their own participation, unless otherwise directed by the president.[18] This responsibility is subject to specific statutory au-thorization to provide support without reimbursement. In the absence of such specific authority, the Economy Act applies, and reimbursement cannot be waived.

Deployment/Employment Priorities

The multiagency JOC Command Group, managed by the Federal OSC, ensures that con-flicts are resolved, overall incident objectives are established, and strategies are selected for the use of critical resources. These strategies will be based on the following priorities:

1. Preserving life or minimizing risk to health (this constitutes the first priority of oper-ations)
2. Preventing a threatened act from being carried out or an existing terrorist act from being expanded or aggravated
3. Locating, accessing, rendering safe, controlling, containing, recovering, and disposing of a WMD that has not yet functioned
4. Rescuing, decontaminating, transporting, and treating victims (preventing secondary casualties as a result of contamination or collateral threats)

5. Releasing emergency public information that ensures adequate and accurate communications with the public from all involved response agencies
6. Restoring essential services and mitigating suffering
7. Apprehending and successfully prosecuting perpetrators
8. Conducting site restoration

Planning Assumptions and Considerations

The CONPLAN assumes that no single private or government agency at the local, state, or federal level possesses the authority and the expertise to act unilaterally on the difficult issues that may arise in response to threats or acts of terrorism, particularly if nuclear, radiological, biological, or chemical materials are involved.

The CONPLAN is based on the premise that a terrorist incident may occur at any time of day with little or no warning, may involve single or multiple geographic areas, and may result in mass casualties. The CONPLAN also assumes an act of terrorism—particularly an act directed against a large population center within the United States involving nuclear, radiological, biological, or chemical materials—will have major consequences that can overwhelm the capabilities of many local and state governments to respond and may seriously challenge existing federal response capabilities, as well.

Federal participating agencies may need to respond on short notice to provide effective and timely assistance to state and local governments. Federal departments and agencies would be expected to provide an initial response when warranted under their own authorities and funding. Decisions to mobilize federal assets will be coordinated with the FBI and FEMA.

In the case of a biological WMD attack, the effect may be temporally and geographically dispersed, with no determined or defined "incident site." Response operations may be conducted over a multijurisdictional, multistate region. A biological WMD attack employing a contagious agent may require quarantine by state and local health officials to contain the disease outbreak. Local, state, and federal responders will define working perimeters that overlap. Perimeters may be used by responders to control access to an affected area, to assign operational sectors among responding organizations, and to assess potential effects on the population and the environment. Control of these perimeters and response actions may be managed by different authorities, which will impede the effectiveness of the overall response if adequate coordination is not established.

If appropriate personal protective equipment and capabilities are not available and the area is contaminated with WMD materials, it is possible that response actions into a contaminated area may be delayed until the material has dissipated to a level that is safe for emergency response personnel to operate.

Training and Exercises

Federal agencies, in conjunction with state and local governments, will periodically exercise their roles and responsibilities designated under the CONPLAN. Federal agencies are charged with coordinating their exercises with the Exercise Subgroup of the Interagency Working Group on Counterterrorism and other response agencies to avoid duplication, and, more importantly, to provide a forum to exercise coordination mechanisms among responding agencies.

Federal agencies are charged with assisting state and local governments with the design and improvement of their response capabilities to a terrorist threat or incident. Each agency should coordinate its training programs with other response agencies to avoid duplication and to make its training available to other agencies.

Emergency Response to a Terrorist Attack Involving Weapons of Mass Destruction

The complexity, scope, and potential consequences of a terrorist threat or incident may require that there be a rapid and decisive capability to resolve the situation. The resolution to an act of terrorism demands an extraordinary level of coordination of crisis and consequence management functions and technical expertise across all levels of government. No single federal, state, or local governmental agency has the capability or requisite authority to respond independently and mitigate the consequences of such a threat to national security. The incident may affect a single location or multiple locations, each of which may be a disaster scene, a hazardous scene, and/or a crime scene simultaneously. There are three important factors that must be considered as FEMA interacts with federal agencies in planning, partnerships, and preparation for a possible terrorist attack. These three factors are (1) the difference that will be involved in PPP when responding to weapons of mass destruction as opposed to other types of terrorist attacks, (2) the threat level posed by the attack, and (3) the responsibilities of the lead federal agency.

Differences between WMD Incidents and Other Incidents

As in all incidents, those involving weapons of mass destruction may involve mass casualties and damage to buildings or other types of property. However, there are several factors surrounding WMD incidents that are unlike any other type of incidents that must be taken into consideration when planning a response. The first responders' ability to identify aspects of the incident (e.g., signs and symptoms exhibited by victims) and report them accurately will be key to maximizing the use of critical local resources and for triggering a federal response. Unfortunately, the situation and type of attack may not be recognizable until there are multiple casualties. Although it is important to distinguish between a chemical attack and a biological attack, most chemical and biological agents are not easily detectable by conventional methods. Lack of coordination and communication among local healthcare facilities may delay identifying common symptoms manifested by victims, thereby delaying early identification of the source and nature of the attack.

In an attack involving WMD there may be multiple events (e.g., one event in an attempt to influence another event's outcome). It is important that first responders are able to coordinate and communicate emergency response so that the "larger picture" emerges.

Responders to an attack involving WMD are placed at a higher risk of becoming casualties. Because biological and chemical agents are not readily identifiable, responders may become contaminated during emergency response and rescue before recognizing the agent involved. First responders may, in addition, be targets for secondary releases or explosions.

The location of the incident will be treated as a crime scene. As such, preservation and collection of evidence is critical. Therefore, it is important to ensure that actions on the scene are coordinated between emergency response organizations to minimize any conflicts between law enforcement authorities, who view the incident as a crime scene, and other emergency responders, who view it as a hazardous materials or disaster scene. Often, law enforcement and responders providing emergency response and rescue have conflicting objectives at the scene. Law enforcement officials need to preserve the crime scene, to gather evidence, and to be able to document the exact nature of the scene. Emergency responders and rescue personnel focus on saving lives, providing medical services to the injured, and minimizing the danger to others. (Preservation of property may also be a goal of emergency responders but it is usually secondary to saving lives, treating the injured, and locating and removing the dead.)

In an attack using weapons of mass destruction, contamination of critical facilities and large geographic areas may result. Victims can unknowingly carry an agent to public transportation facilities, businesses, residences, doctors' offices, walk-in medical clinics, and emergency rooms because they do not realize that they are contaminated. First responders also may be the source that contaminates others. They may carry the agent to fire or precinct houses, to hospitals, or to the locations of subsequent calls.

The scope of an incident involving WMD may expand geometrically and may affect mutual aid jurisdictions. Airborne agents flow with the air current and may disseminate via ventilation systems, carrying the agents far from the initial source.

In the event of a terrorist attack using weapons of mass destruction there will likely be a stronger reaction from the public than with other types of incidents. The thought of exposure to a chemical or biological agent or radiation evokes terror in most people. The fear of the unknown also makes the public's response more severe. Widespread panic is a distinct possibility in an attack using WMDs as compared to a fire or other natural disaster.

Time is working against responding elements in a WMD attack. Not only can the incident expand geometrically and very quickly, but the effects of some chemicals and biological agents worsen over time. Emergency response may be hindered by the fact that support facilities, such as utility stations and 911 centers along with critical infrastructures, are at risk as targets. Terrorists may deliberately target such facilities in order to promote maximum damage. For example, if at the same time of the 9/11 attacks on the Twin Towers in New York City, terrorists had attacked the city's emergency communication system and brought it down, it would have been much more difficult to coordinate emergency services.

Finally, one of the differences between a terrorist attack using weapons of mass destruction and other types of disasters is that in the event of a nuclear, biological, or chemical attack, specialized state and local response capabilities may be overwhelmed. Because of the high expense and limited demand for such specialized personnel, equipment, and resources, a large-scale attack could quickly overwhelm local, even regional, capacity to respond. The ability of FEMA to provide personnel, equipment, and resources from a broader geographical area and from many different agencies would be an essential element in responding to a terrorist attack using WMD.

Threat Levels

The CONPLAN establishes a range of threat levels determined by the FBI that serves to frame the nature and scope of the federal response. Each threat level provides for an escalating range of actions that will be implemented concurrently for crisis and consequence management. The federal government will take specific actions that are synchronized to each threat level, ensuring that all federal agencies are operating with jointly and consistently executed plans. The federal government will notify and coordinate with state and local governments, as necessary. The threat levels are:

- Level 4—Minimal threat
- Level 3—Potential threat
- Level 2—Credible threat
- Level 1—WMD incident

Level 4: Minimum threats do not warrant actions beyond normal liaison notifications or placing assets or resources on a heightened alert (agencies are operating under normal day-to-day conditions).

Level 3: A potential threat is characterized by intelligence or an articulated threat that indicates a potential for a terrorist incident. However, this threat has not yet been assessed as credible. Specific actions by federal agencies may not be possible to respond to the threat.

Level 2: A credible threat is when a threat assessment indicates that the potential threat is credible, and confirms the involvement of WMD in the developing terrorist incident. Intelligence will vary with each threat and will impact the level of the federal response. At a level 2 threat, the situation requires the tailoring of response actions to use federal resources needed to anticipate, prevent, and/or resolve the crisis. The federal crisis management response will focus on law enforcement actions taken in the interest of public safety and welfare, and is predominantly concerned with preventing and resolving the threat. The federal consequence management response will focus on contingency planning and pre-positioning of tailored resources, as required. The threat increases in significance when the presence of an explosive device or WMD capable of causing a significant destructive event, prior to actual injury or loss, is confirmed or when intelligence and circumstances indicate a high probability that a device exists. In this case, the threat has developed into a WMD terrorist situation requiring an immediate process to identify, acquire, and plan the use of federal resources to augment state and local authorities in lessening or averting the potential consequence of a terrorist use or employment of WMD.

Level 1: A level 1 WMD incident threat is when a WMD terrorism incident has occurred that requires an immediate process to identify, acquire, and plan the use of federal resources to augment state and local authorities in response to limited or major consequences of a terrorist use or employment of WMD. This incident results in mass casualties. The federal response is primarily directed toward public safety and welfare and the preservation of human life.

Lead Federal Agency Responsibilities

In the event of a terrorist attack the lead federal agency, in coordination with the appropriate federal, state and local agencies, is responsible for formulating the federal strategy and a coordinated federal response. To accomplish that goal, the LFA must establish multiagency coordination structures, as appropriate, at the incident scene, area, and national level. These structures are needed to perform oversight responsibilities in operations involving multiple agencies with direct statutory authority to respond to aspects of a single major incident or multiple incidents. Oversight responsibilities include coordinating the operation, assessing the situation, and providing public information. First, the LFA is responsible for coordinating the determination of operational objectives, strategies, and priorities for the use of critical resources that have been allocated to the situation, and communicating multiagency decisions back to individual agencies and incidents. Second, the LFA is responsible for assessing the situation to evaluate emerging threats, to prioritize incidents, and to project future needs.

Finally, a very important responsibility of the LFA is to provide public information. As the spokesperson for the federal response, the LFA is responsible for coordinating information dissemination to the White House, Congress, and other federal, state, and local government officials. In fulfilling this responsibility, the LFA ensures that the release of public information is coordinated between crisis and consequence management response entities.

The LFA is responsible for establishing a Joint Information Center under the operational control of the LFA's Public Information Officer, as a focal point for the coordination and provision of information to the public and media concerning the federal response to the emergency. The JIC may be established in the same location as the FBI Joint Operations Center or may be located at an on-scene location in coordination with state and local agencies. The following elements should be represented at the JIC: (1) FBI Public Information Officer and staff, (2) FEMA Public Information Officer and staff, (3) other federal agency Public Information Officers, as needed, and (4) state and local Public Information Officers.

FEMA and State and Local Multiagency Coordination

State and local governments face a difficult challenge in preparing for the consequences of a terrorist attack. They must ensure that their emergency operations plans are updated to address the unique planning requirements associated with terrorism and weapons of mass destruction. These planning requirements include special response procedures, preidentified risk areas and evacuation routes, provisions and protocols for warning the public and disseminating emergency public information, requirements and instructions on the types of protective equipment and detection devices responders must wear, the operational and safety protocols that must be followed when working in or near a "hot zone," among other tasks. These planning requirements may be included as part of the emergency response plan through the use of appendices, tabs, and attachments, and may include such things as maps, charts, tables, checklists, resource inventories, and summaries of critical information. The detail of these plans is very specific and massive but the data must be readily available, accurate, and up to date.

Thus, state and local governments must consider the changing nature of emergency operating plans. Changes in threat, organizational capabilities, and the jurisdiction's emergency services resource base may diminish the emergency response capacity of the agency. The state and local agency must be alert to the need to fix deficiencies identified in disaster response after action reports, exercises, program reviews, and changes in mutual aid arrangements. State and local government emergency operating plans must also ensure that time-sensitive information is updated. Some data important for emergency response remains relatively constant. For example, maps showing the location of natural gas pipelines may remain accurate much longer than data on ships in a dock and the nature of their cargo. Thus, jurisdictions should review, test, and evaluate their emergency operating plans on a regular basis. This requirement may present a challenge to state and local agencies that are often limited by budget and personnel constraints.

One of the key missions of FEMA is to provide information to state and local agencies on planning, partnerships, and preparation. To fulfill this mission, FEMA strives to provide guidance documents to address essential preincident, initial response, and follow-up operational actions that should be accomplished to ensure that the unique requirements associated with responding to a WMD terrorist attack are understood and implemented by federal, state, and local governments. Thus, one of the roles of FEMA is to provide state and local agencies with the information they need to formulate emergency operating plans, to establish partnerships, and to assist in preparation.

To help jurisdictions with the overall terrorism planning process, FEMA prepares various publications with specific and detailed information on planning, partnerships, and preparation. The agency strongly encourages state and local jurisdictions to use this information as a starting point when they update their emergency operating plans and in their broader strategic planning efforts.

Key documents regarding emergency response to a terrorist attack involving weapons of mass destruction are *Managing the Emergency Consequences of Terrorist Incidents, Interim Planning Guide for State and Local Governments,* and *Tool Kit for Managing the Emergency Consequences of Terrorist Incidents.* These documents provide information about the unique terrorism response planning considerations that should be included in each jurisdiction's all-hazard emergency operating plans. These guidance documents are intended to help the state and local agencies to examine the jurisdiction's emergency operating plans for attacks involving WMD. They will help in determining if the special and unique response procedures, notifications, protective actions, emergency public information, and other needs generated by this hazard are adequately addressed in the emergency response plan. The documents provide state and local emergency planners with a framework for developing emergency operations plans that address the consequences of terrorist acts involving weapons of mass destruction. The use of such documents by state and local agencies is encouraged by FEMA because it is believed that if state and local agencies use a common guide and standard for emergency planning, a consistent planning approach will foster efficient integration of state, local, and federal terrorism consequence management activities.

One of the documents that FEMA recommends as the guideline for state and local emergency planning is the *Tool Kit.* This document was adopted from FEMA's Emergency Management Institute's new Terrorism Planning Course and is a companion document to the *Interim Planning Guide for State and Local Governments.* It provides emergency planners with additional information on the special planning and response requirements for terrorism incidents, including the following:

- Actions associated with assessing terrorist threats.
- Information on emergency response planning and other preparedness actions associated with direction and control, communications, disseminating warnings, emergency public information, protective actions, mass health and medical needs, managing resources, and responder roles and responsibilities

- Information on nuclear, biological, chemical, radiological, and agri-terrorism agents, and cyber-terrorism[19]
- Planning checklists for WMD incidents
- Functional checklists for WMD incidents
- Basic job aids for emergency responders
- ICS forms for emergency responders

Other Planning Considerations

State and local governments have other planning considerations that play an important role in minimizing damage from a terrorist attack or in helping to speed recovery after a terrorist attack. Often these other considerations are specific to each state or local government; thus, general guidelines are helpful but have limited value. Some of these other planning considerations are

- Identification and protection of critical infrastructure
- Inventory of response assets
- Mutual aid agreements
- Resource typing
- Resource standards
- Continuity of Operations (COOP) and continuity of state and local government and services (COG)
- The role of citizen and family preparedness, including Citizen Corps

Identification and Protection of Critical Infrastructure

Our society is dependent on a number of critical infrastructures that are oftentimes not apparent until a disaster occurs. Many of these critical infrastructures are under the direct or indirect control of state and local agencies. According to the President's Commission on Critical Infrastructure, critical infrastructures are systems whose "incapacity or destruction would have a debilitating impact on the defense or economic security of the nation." For state and local governments, these services can include:

- Telecommunications
- Electrical power systems
- Gas and oil
- Banking and finance
- Transportation
- Water supply systems
- Government services
- Emergency services such as police, fire, and medical services

States and localities may have different definitions of what constitutes a critical infrastructure, and each entity is presented with different challenges in identifying and conducting a threat vulnerability of critical infrastructure in their area. State and local governments are responsible for ensuring the continuation of critical infrastructure service operations to communities impacted by natural, technological, and WMD terrorist disasters. Protection of critical infrastructures helps reduce negative impacts on rescue operations, communications, health and medical services, and the economy, among others.

Because the protection of critical infrastructure affects emergency preparedness and operations, FEMA encourages state and local governments to prepare and maintain current emergency operating plans with information on what steps they are taking to identify and protect critical infrastructures. Planners must assess the vulnerability of, and provide critical infrastructure protection measures for, the systems and assets they identify as critical infrastructure. Many states and localities have already accomplished this task for FEMA's Capability Assessment for Readiness (CAR) or for other federal agency assessments. Although many major cities have reassessed their emergency response plans following the 9/11 attacks, some jurisdictions have not updated their plans. To encourage agencies to update their plans and to promote a single standard for judging the adequacy of emergency operating plans for responding to a terrorist attack, FEMA provides publications, guidance, websites, and training to help state and local governments update planning, partnerships, and preparation. FEMA publishes a series of *State and Local Mitigation Planning How-To Guides,* including *Understanding Your Risks: Identifying Hazards and Estimating Losses* and *Integrating Human Caused Hazards into Mitigation Planning.*[20]

Inventory of Critical Response Assets

Given the increase in availability of federal funds and domestic preparedness assistance provided since the 9/11 attacks, many state and local governments have developed or acquired additional emergency response assets through federal subsidies and grants. However, some agencies have added these new assets but have not updated their emergency operating plans to reflect these changes. The Federal Emergency Management Agency encourages jurisdictions to maintain current and accurate inventories of their emergency response resources and to include new assets in their emergency operating plans. Emergency response equipment that is not reflected in the current inventory of emergency response plans can cause just as many problems as lack of equipment. If the equipment is not reflected in the inventory, there is a good chance that the emergency operating plan does not provide information to first responders regarding this equipment.

Not only will this information help determine a jurisdiction's current capability but it will also help jurisdictions identify the resource shortfalls they must fill through mutual aid or other resources to successfully execute an operation. States should ensure that this information is integrated into their strategic plan for addressing capability and resource needs statewide.

Interstate and Intrastate Mutual Aid Agreements

The severity of disasters may at times overwhelm state and local response resources. All scenarios regarding what would happen in the event of a terrorist attack using a weapon of mass destruction predict that no city, not even the largest cities, will be able to respond to the attack without assistance from numerous local, state, and federal agencies. Mutual aid

BOX 8.3 • *Consider This: Who's Liable for Injuries the Day After*

Most World Trade Center (WTC) ground-zero workers still suffer health problems after the September 11 attacks. Many do not have health insurance to obtain the treatment they need and there are insufficient federal funds to provide for the healthcare needs of these victims.[21] Those affected include police officers, firefighters, emergency response personnel, and construction workers. Congressional inquiries reveal that the health problems of many of these afflicted workers occurred after the attack during clean up, not during the attack. For example, construction workers who worked to help clean up the debris have developed chronic breathing problems and many are at risk for developing cancer in the next decade.[22]

In addition to ground-zero workers, many tens of thousands of people who live and work in Lower Manhattan and Brooklyn claim to have been endangered by the way federal officials mishandled the environment hazards caused by the collapse of the World Trade Center.[23] In March 2004, some of these victims filed a lawsuit accusing the Environmental Protection Agency of "shockingly deliberate indifference to human health," failure to test thousands of homes and business for potential toxic contamination and providing misleading information about air quality.[24]

Families of firefighters who died in the WTC have filed a lawsuit claiming that the firefighters died unnecessarily because the city had issued them radios that did not work in high-rise buildings.[25] They claim the city broke the law in providing equipment that they knew or should have known was inadequate to perform in high-rise buildings and as a result firefighters in the WTC did not hear the call to evacuate the WTC's north tower.[26]

New York City received over $54 million in Department of Homeland Security grants for improving radio interoperability but budget cuts will result in the inability for firefighters to obtain new radios and establish protocols to link to the police at a large-scale emergency.[27]

Questions

1. FEMA and other federal agencies have placed great emphasis on the importance of planning, partnerships, and preparation. The lessons learned from the 9/11 attacks seem to suggest that state and local governments were not prepared for the 9/11 attacks and are not close to achieving this goal in the near future. What could be done to improve state and local disaster planning?

2. As a result of inadequate planning and resources, thousands are claiming that they suffered needless injury from the 9/11 attacks. If as many who claim they are injured actually are, the injuries from the aftermath of the 9/11 attacks may exceed the injuries directly caused by the attacks. However, those suffering from injury after the attack find that they do not have access to government healthcare or compensation. Should free government healthcare be available to those injured in a terrorist attack or do you believe healthcare is the responsibility of the individual? Explain your answer.

3. If first responders and clean-up workers die, are seriously injured, or are disabled as a result of inadequate planning, equipment, or environmental projection, what should be the liability of the city, state, and/or federal government?

---

agreements provide an opportunity for neighboring jurisdictions to assist in providing personnel and resources to their impacted counterparts, thus ensuring the continued safety of both responders and citizens.

There are three types of mutual aid agreements. The first is mutual aid agreements with adjacent jurisdictions. These are called *intrastate mutual aid agreements*. The advantage of intrastate mutual aid agreements is that the agencies operate under a common state law and have a single executive—the governor—who has emergency authority and power over all agencies in the state and share similar financial structures. That is to say, the tax structure and state funding provides for the common good of the agencies within the state. Mutual aid agreements between states or between agencies of different states are called *interstate mutual aid agreements*. The final type of mutual aid agreement is between *local and/or state government and the federal government*. Often these mutual aid agreements are for "serious" emergencies in that it takes a greater disaster to invoke their operation as compared to intrastate or interstate agreements.

All three types of mutual aid agreements are an effective means for states and local governments to leverage existing and new assets to the maximum extent possible. Creating and updating mutual aid agreements require participating organizations to have an awareness and understanding of each other's personnel, equipment, and technological resources.

Team compositions and structures, equipment and communications interoperability, and training and accreditation standards are frequently addressed in mutual aid agreements. Ultimately, mutual aid agreements demonstrate a formal commitment of effort by participating jurisdictions to provide a unified and coordinated response structure.

Mutual aid agreements may require that agencies change behaviors, participate in joint-training exercises, and have common standards regarding communication equipment or other actions and responsibilities that must be worked out in advance. For these reasons it is necessary that state and local governments should develop and refine interstate, intrastate, and federal mutual aid assistance agreements well in advance of their need. For example, if a mutual aid agreement requires all of the agencies involved to have radios that are able to communicate with the various agencies, it is highly unlikely that all of the agencies will have such capacity prior to the agreement. It will take time and money for the agencies to update their communication equipment. Also, if agencies are to work together as a team in responding to an emergency, it will be necessary for them to train together or at least train using a common standard and procedure. Such training may take months or even years to fully implement.

Mutual aid agreements should specifically address the unique response requirements and resource needs associated with responding to a WMD terrorist event and this planning should be reflected in the emergency operating plans of all the agencies that are partners to the agreement. A greater burden falls on local agencies in forming mutual aid agreements for responding to a terrorist event. Local agencies are most likely the least equipped, trained, and capable of responding to a terrorist incident involving a weapon of mass destruction. Large cities such as New York, Los Angles, Chicago, Dallas, and Philadelphia may be much better equipped but there are numerous small cities and suburbs surrounding large metropolitan areas that do not have adequate resources to respond to a terrorist attack. Because of the independence of local governments, each small city has its own tax base, police department, fire department, political leaders, and city planners. Seldom are the resources of small cities adequate to respond to a terrorist incident. Even if the attack was on a larger city, neighboring small suburban cities would be involved and impacted by the attack. Thus, small and medium-sized cities often find that mutual aid agreements are much more necessary for them if they are to be able to respond to a terrorist attack.

Therefore, it is important for local governments and states to examine their mutual aid agreements such as the Emergency Management Assistance Compacts (EMAC) and related regional agreements and consortiums. This will help determine the types of support local governments and states are prepared and able to provide to help each other and the shortfalls that exist to meet critical resource needs. The FEMA publication *Managing the Emergency Consequences of Terrorism Incidents, Interim Planning Guide for State and Local Governments* has examples of mutual aid agreements.

Some of the specifics that an effective mutual aid agreement will address are issues such as (1) liability; (2) reimbursement; (3) the identification, availability, and location of needed resources; and (4) the ability to accurately track the resources from request to return.

Resource Typing

To make mutual aid more effective, resources must be clearly described by function and capability in common and universal terms and classified by levels of capability or capacity. In order to efficiently request and offer resources under mutual aid, it is essential for state and local governments to address resource typing in their emergency operating plans.[28]

In the event of a terrorist attack using a weapon of mass destruction it is possible to predict the need for specific types of resources that will be needed by the targeted city. These common needs are referred to by FEMA as "teams" or "task forces." The following teams are resources that cities will need in the event of a terrorist attack:

• *Weapons of Mass Destruction-Civil Support Team (WMD-CST):* A Weapons of Mass Destruction-Civil Support Team is a team that supports civil authorities at a domestic chemical, biological, radiological, nuclear, or high-yield explosive (CBRNE) incident site by identifying CBRNE agents/substances, assessing current and projected consequences, advising on response measures, and assisting with appropriate requests for state support. The National Guard Bureau fosters the development of WMD-CSTs.

• *Disaster Medical Assistance Team (DMAT):* A Disaster Medical Assistance Team is a group of professional and paraprofessional medical personnel (supported by a cadre of logistical and administrative staff) designed to provide emergency medical care during a disaster or other event. The National Disaster Medical System (NDMS), through the U.S. Public Health Service (PHS), fosters the development of DMATs.

• *Disaster Mortuary Operational Response Team (DMORT):* A Disaster Mortuary Operational Response Team works under the guidance of local authorities by providing technical assistance and personnel to recover, identify, and process deceased victims. These teams are composed of private citizens, each with a particular field of expertise, who are activated in the event of a disaster. The National Disaster Medical System, through the U.S. Public Health Service, and the National Association for Search and Rescue (NASAR), fosters the development of DMORTs.

• *National Medical Response Team-Weapons of Mass Destruction (NMRT-WMD):* The National Medical Response Teams-Weapons of Mass Destruction is a specialized response force designed to provide medical care following nuclear, biological, and/or chemical incident. This unit is capable of providing mass casualty decontamination, medical triage, and primary and secondary medical care to stabilize victims for transportation to tertiary care facilities in a hazardous material environment. There are four NMRTs-WMD geographically dispersed throughout the United States. The National Disaster Medical System, through the U.S. Public Health Service, fosters the development of NMRTs.

• *Urban Search and Rescue Task Force (US&R):* An Urban Search and Rescue Task Force is a highly trained team for search-and-rescue operations in damaged or collapsed structures, hazardous materials evaluations, and stabilization of damaged structures and can provide emergency medical care to the injured. The US&R team consists of a partnership between local fire departments, law enforcement agencies, federal and local governmental agencies, and private companies. FEMA fosters the development of US&R Task Forces.

• *Incident Management Team (IMT):* An Incident Management Team is a team of highly trained, experienced individuals who are organized to manage large and/or complex incidents. They provide full logistical support for receiving and distribution centers. Each IMT is hosted and managed by one of the United States Forest Service's Geographic Area Coordination Centers.

Resource Standards

Resource standards are an integral piece of preparedness planning efforts and should be incorporated into every jurisdiction's emergency operating plan. Standards provide state and local emergency management and first responder organizations with a baseline capability that should be achieved to respond to natural and human-made emergencies. They also allow for consistency among response elements within a given jurisdiction and across jurisdictions as well. Numerous commissions, the Bush Administration, Congress, and state and local associations have reinforced the crucial requirement for these standards and their respective complementary guidelines. National standards for emergency management will allow for the successful integration of federal, state, and local resources in the emergency response process, promoting the seamless interface of existing critical incident management systems.

The federal government and FEMA have developed and disseminated a number of standards that are considered essential to effective emergency response planning. Examples of some of these resource standards include the following:

• *Incident Command System (ICS):* The Incident Command System, a national tool for command, control, and coordination of emergency response, provides a means to coordinate the efforts of federal, state, and local agencies in stabilizing an incident while protecting life and property. Currently the standard emergency response system for numerous states, ICS has been adopted and endorsed by numerous federal agencies and organizations.
• *OSHA 1910.120 Q:* The Occupational Safety and Health Administration specifies procedures for handling emergency response in OSHA 1910.120, Hazardous Waste Operations and Emergency Response, paragraph Q. It includes the minimum requirements for inclusion in an emergency response plan, the use of ICS, and training.
• *The National Fire Protection Association (NFPA):* The National Fire Protection Association has developed over 300 consensus codes and standards that address plan-

ning, exercises, training, and equipment acquisition. The National Fire Protection Association 1600 was used as the foundation for development of the EMAP standard.

Continuity of Operations (COOP) and
Continuity of Government (COG)

One of the most important aspects to address in disaster planning and one of the most frightening scenarios resulting from a terrorist attack is the loss of government services or government officials. The need to preserve ongoing government services is called *continuity of operations (COOP)* and the need to preserve the functioning of government is called *continuity of government (COG)*.

It is important for state and local governments to consider developing or updating contingency plans for the continuity of operations of vital government functions. Jurisdictions must be prepared to continue their minimum essential functions throughout the spectrum of possible threats from natural disasters through acts of terrorism. Planning for COOP facilitates the performance of state and local government and services during an emergency that may disrupt normal operations.[29] The lack of essential government services or leadership in a crisis would contribute to public panic, loss of public safety, and the disruption of the broadcast of essential emergency response information, and would result in loss of decision-making ability in the direction of first responders and deployment of emergency resources. Again, COOP and COG take on special importance for small and medium-sized cities because government leadership for these may rest in the hands of just a few people. A city of 25,000 probably has less than a dozen key leaders (e.g., the mayor, city manager, city planner, chief of police, chief of the fire department, city council members, and health officials). Unless there are plans to "carry on" in the absence of some or all of these key government leaders, a terrorist attack may result in many more causalities and much more damage than necessary.

Goals for COOP planning should include an all-hazards approach, the identification of alternate facilities, and the ability to operate within 12 hours of activation, as well as sustain operations for up to 30 days. Elements of a viable COOP capability should include plans for such contingencies as:

- Line of succession
- Delegation of authorities
- Alternate facilities
- Safekeeping vital records
- Administration and logistics
- Operating procedures
- Personnel issues
- Security
- Communications
- Exercises and training

Also, it is important for state and local governments to develop or update contingency plans for the continuity of state and local government/services (COG). In the case that elected, appointed, or professional government leaders are not available to provide critical command and leadership, there should be an alternative plan to ensure continued line of governmental authority and responsibility.[30]

The Role of Citizen and Family Preparedness, Including Citizen Corps

Volunteers are valuable resources for expanding response capability, and states and local jurisdictions should plan how to manage the additional numbers of volunteers provided during an emergency or disaster. State and local jurisdictions can use Citizen Corps councils to partner with the volunteer community.[31] The president's new Citizen Corps initiative is designed to bring together leaders from first responder groups, emergency management, volunteer organizations, local elected officials, and the private sector to form Citizen Corps councils. The councils serve as a focal point for engaging citizens in homeland security and in promoting community and family safety practices in three principle ways: through public education and outreach, through training opportunities, and through volunteer programs drawing on special skills and interests.

State and local jurisdictions should include Citizen Corps councils and State Voluntary Organizations Active in Disaster (VOAD) in developing a plan on how to coordinate volunteers and include this information in their emergency operating plans.[32] And, finally, states should consider donations coordination when updating their emergency operating plans. As seen in response to the September 11 attacks, donations flooded Washington, D.C., and New York, requiring warehouse space and inventorying of donated services. Blood donations far exceeded the need. The Red Cross had to call for a cessation of donations. Yet, at the same time as this excess, there were victim needs that "fell through the cracks" and were not met. Furthermore, it takes resources and personnel to organize, distribute, and administer the influx of donations in a crisis.

Conclusion: Alphabet Soup—Confusion or Cure?

It is a daunting effort to completely comprehend the enormity of the intergovernmental coordination effort that currently exists to combat terrorism and protect the homeland. However, complexity is inevitable in a country as large as the United States that has a federal or multilevel system of government, with separate federal, state, and local government bureaucracies. It is to this country's credit that our nation has responded so quickly in developing an overall coordination plan that will no doubt continue to evolve as terrorist-related events continue to unfold.

The desired end state for this planning effort is for local, state, and federal governments to develop current detailed and accurate emergency operating plans to enhance the capability for responding to a terrorist attack, especially an attack involving weapons of mass destruction. Local, state, and federal governments can best prepare to minimize the damage of a terrorist attack and speed recovery by developing emergency operating plans and partnerships and taking steps to prepare for recovery from an attack. These strategies should provide for the protection of critical infrastructure and the continuity of operations and government to ensure that essential services can continue without interruption, the needs of victims can be met, and the government can respond. Finally, mutual aid agreements are key strategies in responding to a terrorist attack, as no single agency has the resources to respond alone.

At one time the focus of emergency planning was on natural disasters and civil defense against a Soviet nuclear attack. Natural disasters will always be a constant threat but fears of a Soviet nuclear attack have diminished. These have been replaced with a focus on homeland defense against terrorism. No one wants to think that another 9/11-type attack will happen, but government officials continue to warn the public that such an attack is a real possibility. Despite the resources funneled into preventing another attack, the United States cannot rely on these efforts to prevent terrorists from striking the homeland again. A plan to minimize the damage of an attack and to recover as quickly as possible is absolutely necessary. Because there are tens of thousands of government agencies at all levels, the coordination and direction of these agencies is a massive task. The federal government has designated FEMA as the key agency to prepare the homeland for responding to a terrorist attack. The strategic plans developed to defend the homeland read like alphabet soup. There are thousands of acronyms describing the various agencies, strategies, and plans. However, in the event of a terrorist attack it will be necessary for these agencies, strategies, and plans to work effectively and efficiently in harmony and precision to minimize the damage from the attack and to speed recovery.

Chapter Summary

- One of the goals of homeland defense is to minimize damage and speed recovery in the event of a terrorist attack.
- FEMA is the key agency for disaster response and planning.
- The essential elements of disaster response planning are planning, partnerships, and preparation.
- The foundation of disaster response is emergency operations plans.
- In the event of a terrorist attack the goal is mitigation or actions to reduce or eliminate long-term risk to human life and property from the hazard event.
- The guiding principles for the role of federal agencies in responding to a terrorist attack are outlined in the United States Government Interagency Domestic Terrorism Concept of Operations Plan (CONPLAN).
- The primary federal agencies responsible for responding to a terrorist attack are DOJ, FBI, FEMA, DOD, DOE, EPA, and HHS.
- One of the key planning strategies is the identification of which federal agency will be the lead federal agency in the event of a terrorist attack and the responsibilities of the lead federal agency and other agencies.
- Planning for emergency response to a WMD is different from planning for other disasters.
- FEMA plans an important role in state and local planning for a terrorist attack and publishes resources to assist state and local governments in planning, partnerships, and preparation.

- Mutual aid agreements are a key strategy in responding to a terrorist attack, as no one agency has the resources to respond to a terrorist attack using weapons of mass destruction.
- Continuity of operations (COOP) and continuity of government (COG) are important goals of emergency planning to respond to a terrorist attack.

Terrorism and You

Understanding This Chapter

1. What federal agency has the primary responsibility for minimizing the damage and speeding recovery from a terrorist attack?

2. Why are emergency operating plans important in responding to a weapons of mass destruction terrorism incident?

3. What is mitigating planning and why is it important in planning for recovery from a terrorism attack?

4. What is CONPLAN and what role does it play in responding to a terrorism attack?

5. Why is it important in responding to a terrorism attack to identify a lead federal agency? Why are there different lead federal agencies for different events?

6. Why is continuity of operations and continuity of government important in minimizing the damage from a terrorism attack?

7. What is the role of mutual aid agreements in responding to a terrorism attack?

Thinking about How Terrorism Touches You

1. Are you aware of any plans by your local or state government for responding to a terrorism attack? If so, how did you learn about them? If not, does it concern you that you are not aware of any emergency response plans?

2. Do you think the city you live in is prepared to respond to a terrorism attack using weapons of mass destruction? Why?

3. To a large degree emergency response to a terrorism attack depends on an enormous amount of cooperation among local, state, and federal governments. Do you think it would be more effective if there were legislation requiring local, state, and federal cooperation? Why or why not?

4. One of the keystones of emergency response to a terrorism attack is dependence on mutual aid agreements based on the assumption that no one agency has the necessary resources to respond to such an attack. Do you think this is the best strategy or should the federal government create a terrorism emergency response agency with enough funds, equipment, and personnel to respond to a WMD attack without the need to rely on voluntary mutual aid agreements? Support your answer.

5. In the event of a WMD attack do you think local, state, and federal governments will cooperate? Why or why not? Do you think lack of cooperation among agencies was a problem during the 9/11 recovery effort? Explain your answer.

6. Have you prepared personal emergency plans and do you have the personal supplies and equipment recommended by FEMA in the event of a emergency? If not, why? What would you do in the event of a terrorism attack using weapons of mass destruction?

Important Terms and Concepts

Capability Assessment for Readiness (CAR)
Consequence Management
Continuity of Operations (COOP)
Continuity of State and Local Government/Services
   (COG)
Crisis Management
Critical Infrastructure
Domestic Emergency Support Team (DEST)
Emergency Operations Plans (EOP)
Federal Emergency Management Agency (FEMA)
Hazard Mitigation

Joint Information Center (JIC)
Joint Operations Center (JOC)
Lead Federal Agency (LFA)
Mutual Aid Agreements
On-Scene Commander (OSC)
Regional Operations Center (ROC)
United States Government Interagency Domestic
   Terrorism Concept of Operations Plan
   (CONPLAN)
Weapons of Mass Destruction (WMD)

Endnotes

1. "FEMA History," www.fema.com, February 15, 2005.

2. Calvin Sims, "Poll Finds Most Americans Have Not Prepared for a Terror Attack." New York Times Online, www.nytimes.com, October 28, 2004.

3. Ibid.

4. Marc Santora, "Region Unable to Counter Biological Hit, Study Says," New York Times Online, www.nytimes.com. December 18, 2004.

5. Ibid.

6. John Miztz and Jody Warrick, "U.S. Unprepared Despite Progress, Experts Say," *Washington Post,* November 8, 2004, p. 1A.

7. John Mintz, "Bioterrorism War Game Shows Lack of Readiness," *Washington Post,* January 15, 2005, p. 12A.

8. "Our Unnecessary Insecurity," New York Times Online, www.nytimes.com, February 20, 2004.

9. Ibid.

10. Joyce Purnick, "Underground, Both Security and Logic Fail," New York Times Online, www.nytimes.com, January 27, 2005.

11. Ibid.

12. Calvin Sims, "Poll Finds Most Americans Have Not Prepared for a Terror Attack," New York Times Online, www.nytimes.com, October 28, 2004.

13. A. D. Beresford, "Homeland Security as an American Ideology: Implications for U.S. Policy and Action," *Journal of Homeland Security and Emergency Management,* Vol. 1, No. 3, Article 301, 2004.

14. R. Prizzia and G. Helfand, "Emergency Preparedness and Disaster Management in Hawaii," *Disaster Prevention and Management: An International Journal,* Vol. 10, No. 3, 2001.

15. CONPLAN: United States Government Interagency Domestic Terrorism Concept of Operations Plan, www.fbi.gov/publications/conplan/conplan.pdf. Updated: "The United States Government Interagency Domestic Terrorism Concepts of Operations Plan," Department of Homeland Security (DHS), September 2003. http://www.fema.gov/rrr/conplan/conpln2p.shtm.

16. William J. Clinton, *U.S. Policy on Counterterrorism.* Presidential Decision Directive 39, June 21, Washington, DC: White House, 1995.

17. Ibid.

18. Ibid.

19. T. W. Graham and A. G. Sabeinikov, "How Much Is Enough: Real-Time Detection and Identification of Biological Weapon Agents," *Journal of Homeland Security and Emergency Management,* Vol. 1, No. 3, Article 303, http://www.bepress.com/jhsem/vol1/iss3/303, 2004.

20. The guides are available on FEMA's website at www.fema.gov/fima/planresource.shtm or the U.S. Critical Infrastructure Assurance Office website at www.ciao.gov/resource/index.html.

21. Associated Press, "Doctors: Most 9-11 Workers Still Ailing," New York Times Online, www.nytimes.com, October 29, 2003.

22. Ibid.

23. Anthony DePalma, "Group Is Suing Federal

Agency Over Post-9/11 Health Hazards," New York Times Online, www.nytimes.com, March 11, 2004.

24. Ibid.; Anthony DePalma, "A Sampling of Apartments to Be Retested for 9/11 Ills," *New York Times,* March 2, 2004, p. B3.

25. Sabrina Tavernise, "Suit by Firefighters' Families Cites 9/11 Radio Failures," New York Times Online, www. nytimes.com, December 23, 2003.

26. Ibid.

27. Corey Kilgannon, "Emergency Workers Imperiled by Loss of Funds, Schumer Says," New York Times Online, www.nytimes.com, February 15, 2004.

28. Detailed information on resource typing is available at the National Emergency Management Association, www.nemaweb.org/index.cfm.

29. Specific information on COOP plans are available from the following documents: Recent Presidential Decision Directives on COOP, such as PDD-39, Counter-Terrorism; PDD-62, Unconventional Threats; PDD-63, Critical Infrastructure Protection; and PDD-67, Enduring Constitutional Government and Continuity of Government Operations. Recent Federal Preparedness Circulars such as FPC-65, Federal Executive Branch Continuity of Operations (COOP); FPC-66, Test, Training and Exercise Program for Continuity of Operations (COOP)—72 KB; and FPC-67, Acquisition of Alternate Facilities for Continuity of Operations (COOP)—74 KB.

30. Information on COG is provided in PDD-67, Enduring Constitutional Government and Continuity of Government Operations.

31. For more information on Citizen Corps, visit www. citizencorps.gov.

32. For more information on National and State Voluntary Organizations Active in Disaster, visit www.nvoad. org.

9

Defending Liberty

Today and Tomorrow

Enhancing national security to prevent a terrorist attack often requires the solving of other problems, such as cyber-security and immigration control. Terrorists can use the Internet to cause more destruction than a bomb. If illegal immigrants can easily enter the United States by the thousands daily, then terrorists can just as easily enter the country.

> *America's immigration system is also outdated, unsuited to the needs of our economy and to the values of our county. We should not be content with laws that punish hardworking people who want only to provide for their families, and deny businesses willing workers, and invite chaos at our border. It is time for an immigration policy that permits temporary guest workers to fill jobs Americans will not take, that rejects amnesty, that tells us who is entering and leaving our country, and that closes the border to drug dealers and terrorists.*
>
> —President George Bush, State of the Union Address, February 2, 2005

Chapter Outline

Learning Objectives

- The reader will understand why additional efforts are necessary to defend the homeland against terror attacks.
- The reader will understand how cyber-terrorism could be a greater threat than bombs.
- The reader will understand how terrorists use the Internet and will know the advantages of the Internet to the terrorists.
- The reader will realize why terror-proofing the Internet is a very difficult task.
- The reader will know of the government's response to cyber-security threats.
- The reader will appreciate the difficulty of the task of border security and immigration control.
- The reader will know the various programs initiated to enhance border security and immigration control.
- The reader will understand the role of deportation in immigration control.
- The reader will appreciate the impact of border security and immigration control initiatives on the U.S. relationship with Canada and Mexico.

Introduction: A Threat with No End in Sight

Following the September 11, 2001, attacks the United States took immediate actions to address what were considered the most threatening vulnerabilities to attacks by terrorists: airline security and prevention of nuclear, biological, and chemical terrorist attacks. However, the prevention of terrorism is not limited to these threats. As the United States strives to prevent terrorists from striking homeland targets, it has become evident that in addition to the first steps that were taken to defend the homeland, additional actions are necessary. For example, in his 2005 State of the Union Address, President Bush pointed out the problem with securing the U.S. borders against terrorism while at the same time permitting the flow of legitimate persons and commerce. Defending the homeland against terrorism requires a two-prong strategy: (1) defending against immediate threats and (2) defending the homeland by identifying problems and future threats that must be addressed.

One of the most significant problems in fighting terrorism is maintaining the high level of vigilance necessary for identifying and responding to possible future threats for an indefinite period of time.[1] For example, as election day approached for the 2004 presidential elections, federal and local government agencies maintained a high level of alert in anticipation of a possible terrorist attack. Police officers in major cities were required to work 12-hour shifts with few or no days off. New York City and Washington, D.C., spent millions of dollars in overtime pay. Many cities spent money they did not have to respond to the heightened security alert preceding the presidential elections.[2] After the election, the Department of Homeland Security (DHS) lowered the terror alert for the financial sector in New York, Washington, and northern New Jersey and many were relieved to "have gotten by without any major terrorist attacks." However, after the elections in November it was necessary to again gear up for possible terrorist attacks for the presidential inauguration ceremonies. It is a never-ending cycle of continuous preparation against possible terrorist attacks.

The process of staying prepared for a terrorist attack is an ongoing challenge and a challenge that can change from day to day. Staying prepared requires accurate information, equipment, training, funding, and, most important, the ability to anticipate what the threats of terrorism could be tomorrow. The federal government and the DHS have focused their major efforts on responding to the threat of terrorist attacks on aviation and using nuclear, chemical, and biological weapons of mass destruction. This chapter discusses two other concerns that may require more serious counterterrorism attention in the immediate future: (1) cyber-terrorism and (2) immigration control and border security.

Continuous Vigilance

The Department of Homeland Security warned that the relaxing of vigilance against terrorism is a "very dangerous train of thought"[3] and that there is every indication that attacks on the homeland by foreign-sponsored terrorists continues to be a significant concern.[4] The DHS has also warned that there are signs that terrorist groups have long-term plans for attacking the United States. In support of this assertion, DHS points out that the Osama bin Laden video released just before the 2004 presidential elections came with English subtitles. Also, a 75-minute video in English from "Azzam the American" released to ABC news on

October 22, 2004, was obviously intended for an American audience. Al-Qaida is targeting Americans with their warnings of violent jihad. There is evidence that al-Qaida's anti-American diatribe is having an affect on some in the United States, as there are more and more reports of persons arrested for rendering support to foreign terrorist groups.

In fact, intelligence officials are beginning to examine why the United States has not experienced another terrorist attack.[5] Did the vigilance of the DHS and other federal and local agencies detour planned attacks? Has the operational capacities of such terrorist groups such as al-Qaida been reduced by overseas military actions and stepped up anti-terrorism actions by foreign nations? Whatever the explanation, counterterrorism experts warn that continuous vigilance is "a relatively new phenomenon" in the United States and that local and federal governments need to develop permanent, long-term plans for vigilance against terrorism. Shortsighted plans that assume vigilance will be maintained by working overtime and deficit spending will result in burnout and decreased response capacity. Already some large-city police departments are experiencing this burnout among their officers, evidenced by high absenteeism rates as officers are calling in sick from working 12-hour shifts for an extended period of time.[6]

Experts are warning that local governments are going to have to be more innovative in building a response capacity and may have to effect change in policies and permanent increases in staffing levels to maintain the vigilance necessary to meet the threat. The Police Executive Research Forum, a Washington-based think tank that helps large police departments, has warned that defense of the homeland against terrorist attacks "is a threat with no end in sight."[7] Counterterrorism experts remind the public and government agencies that Israel has endured over three decades of terrorist attacks with no end in sight.

There are two major vulnerabilities the United States has identified as needing immediate attention: cyber-terrorism and immigration control and border security. To enhance anti-terrorism security and to defend the homeland against terror attacks it will be necessary make major changes to improve anti-terrorism security.

Cyber-Terrorism

The *National Strategy to Secure Cyberspace* report said that in the 1950s and 1960s the federal government created a national system to protect against the new threat of attack from aircraft and missiles.[8] In the twenty-first century the *National Strategy to Secure Cyberspace* calls for similar actions by the federal government to protect against a new and different kind of national threat—attacks through cyber-space. Defending cyber-space is a new challenge that emerged with the invention of the Internet. Defending cyber-space from attack by terrorists is a new threat that has become a prominent concern since the 9/11 attacks.

The Federal Bureau of Investigation has defined *cyber-terrorism* as "the premeditated, politically motivated attack against information, computer systems, computer programs, and data which result in violence against noncombatant targets by sub national groups or clandestine agents."[9] This definition includes actions by both domestic terrorists and international terrorists operating either in the United States or in a foreign country. There have been no documented cases of a "pure cyber-attack" by international terrorists but the National Research Council has warned that "tomorrow's terrorist may be able to do more damage with a keyboard than with a bomb." Former cyber-security czar Richard Clarke warned Congress in 2003 that there is a "dangerous tendency to dismiss the consequences of an attack on the nation's computer networks because no one has died in a cyber-attack and there has never been a smoking ruin for cameras to see."[10]

Even before the 9/11 attacks experts have warned that cyber-terrorism presents a great potential threat to the United States. Since the 9/11 attacks experts have warned of the specter of a "digital Pearl Harbor."[11] Former Central Intelligence Agency Director Robert Gates warned, "Cyberterrorism could be the most devastating weapon of mass destruction yet and could cripple the U.S. economy."[12]

Terrorists could use the strategy of cyber-terrorism in the following four ways: (1) use of the Internet to promote terrorism; (2) use of the Internet to gather information for attacks (cyber-attacks) and as a tool to attack businesses and websites to disrupt the economy and cause financial loss (cyber-intelligence); (3) attacks on critical infrastructures using the Internet to effect physical damage, and (4) cyber-warfare.

Use of the Internet to Promote Terrorism

Military action by the United States has disrupted the terrorist training camps in Afghanistan and Iraq. Also, the United States has increasingly pressured other Middle Eastern nations to take actions against terrorist training camps within their borders. The result is that terrorist groups are turning to the Internet as their new sanctuary.[13] The Internet has become a key tool for both domestic and international terrorist organizations. For international terrorist groups such as al-Qaida the Internet is their new "base." Anonymous Arabic-language Internet websites provide cyber-sanctuaries for terrorists that are often more difficult to detect and eliminate than physical training camps. Deputy Defense Secretary Paul D. Wolfowitz, in testimony before the House Armed Services Committee, said that terrorists use the Internet as a tool "to conceal their identities, to move money, to encrypt messages, even to plan and conduct operations remotely."[14] It is known that al-Qaida and its affiliates have always used email and the Internet as communication tools. The Internet allows al-Qaida to use a legitimate technology to assist in planning terrorism, recruiting new members, and gathering information that will assist them in their attacks. The Internet has become one of the prime tools of the terrorists.[15]

In addition to using the Internet to communicate with each other, terrorist groups use the Internet to distribute their violent messages and call for jihad worldwide. Al-Qaida can use the Internet to develop a global supply chain of angry people to fill their ranks.[16] There are several hundreds of jihadist sites on the Internet.[17] Often the Internet company hosting the Arabic-language jihadist websites is not aware of the nature and purpose of the website.[18] Al-Qaida even has a "virtual university" on the Internet that teaches "electronic jihad."[19] Besides urging attacks against American and Israeli targets, these websites provide information resources for terrorists. Website visitors can read instructions on using a cell phone to remotely detonate a bomb, instructions for manufacturing small missiles, advice on the art of kidnapping, and instructions on military tactics.[20]

Federal agencies, including the National Security Agency, the FBI, and the Department of Homeland Security, monitor suspected terror sites on the Internet and sometimes track users. However, the sheer number and anonymity of these jihadist websites makes it virtually impossible to stem the flow of radical Islamic propaganda.[21] Another problem in stopping violent jihadist groups from using the Internet is that censoring Internet websites often raises the constitutional challenge of First Amendment rights. For example, many of the jihadist websites distribute videos of kidnapped hostages pleading for their lives or graphic uncensored videos of beheadings. Terrorists have been quick to understand the power of graphic images and the powerful tool that atrocity footage can be. For example, websites showing beheadings usually get 200,000 visitors a day.[22] However, censoring these violent images "opens the floodgates to really marginalizing a lot of the free speech that has been a hallmark of the American legal and political system."[23] Thus, these websites are able to distribute videos of retributive humiliation and vengeful, purifying executions that encourage terrorism and spread its propaganda of fear and humiliation. The videos proclaim that there are no innocent foreigners and that the United States, with all its power and might, is unable to ensure the protections of civilian immunity. Also, terrorists hope the images on these websites will be a crucial fist step toward cracking the will to continue the fight.[24] This strategy has been particularly evident in Iraq. There, some of the citizens of coalition forces have been so influenced by the emotional videos showing kidnapped civilians pleading for their lives and their subsequent execution that they have pressured their government to withdraw their troops or support from the war in Iraq.

Cyber-Intelligence and Cyber-Attacks

Cyber-Intelligence.   In addition to being an effective method for the distribution of propaganda, the Internet is a strategic tool for terrorists to gather intelligence to assist in planning attacks and a tool to attack businesses and websites to disrupt the economy and cause financial loss.

The Internet has proven to be one of the most valuable sources of intelligence for planning attacks for terrorists. Prior to the 9/11 attacks the amount of information that could be of strategic importance to terrorists that could be accessed by the Internet was overwhelming. Routinely, data about electrical power, gas and oil storage, transportation, banking and finance, water supply, emergency services, and the continuity of government operations were available from the Internet. Even information that would clearly be of value in the planning of an attack—such as the operational status information of nuclear plants, toxic-release inventory, a listing of all factories and other sources that emit poisonous pollution, information about dangerous pesticides and detailed maps of power lines, gas lines, and locations of critical emergency supplies used by state Emergency Management Offices—was easily accessible as public documents on the Internet. Even after the 9/11 attacks many sites did not remove information that could equip potential terrorists to carry out an attack, such as the location of fuel storage tanks, maps of electrical grids, information on dams and reservoirs, and building floor plans of state and federal buildings.

Removal of information from the Internet has prompted some cries of censorship and infringement of freedom of speech and information. For example, environmental protection groups used to use information that was available on the Internet to monitor nuclear power plants, hazardous waste sites, and other toxic waste information. States have removed most of this information from the Internet and now the environmental groups must use the Freedom of Information Law to obtain such information. However, some states are even refusing to release information under the Freedom of Information Law, claiming that the information "serves no other purpose than to equip potential terrorists."[25]

The search to find the correct balance between the right of the public to know and the duty of local, state, and federal governments to secure information that could be used by terrorists to inflict damage is ongoing. Activist groups accuse the government of making information secret to protect administrative mismanagement, to cover up failure to comply with clean air and toxic guidelines, and to make it more difficult to monitor compliance. These groups often charge that the removal of the information from the Internet does not protect against terrorist attacks but does protect government and businesses from lawsuits and fines. Government officials deny such charges and claim their actions do not deny the public access to legitimate information. For example, following the 9/11 attacks, New York State Energy Department erased a detailed map of power lines and substations from its site. Requests for the information under the Freedom of Information Act can be censored if it is determined that release of the information would endanger people's lives or compromise criminal investigations. Citing these exemptions, officials are refusing to release information such as the diameter and location of a suspension bridge's cables and fasteners, fencing and gates around nuclear plants, and access roads leading to water reservoirs.[26]

Cyber-Attacks.   Security experts have warned for several years that cyber-terrorism presents a great potential threat to the United States.[27] Even before the 9/11 attacks, the information technology revolution was quietly and quickly changing the way business and government operate. The Internet has become the world's communications network linking banking, businesses, manufacturing, and utilities. In the past, waterways, surface transportation, and air transportation were the vital communication and transportation systems considered to be the engine of commerce. Today, networked computers and the Internet is the lifeline of businesses and government. Unfortunately, however, the Internet was developed without a great deal of thought about security.[28] This great dependence on information transferred by the Internet and networked computers has created a new vulnerability for society with the potential to bring commerce to a halt and to impact the lives of millions of people worldwide. Intelligence gathered from confiscated computers from al-Qaida members, interrogations of captured terrorists, and past actions clearly indicate that terrorist groups are planning attacks to disrupt or disable the Internet and other global communications networks.[29]

Cyber-attacks did not originate with terrorists. In fact, terrorists account for only a small fraction of such attacks. It is estimated that about 90 percent of the cyber-attacks are perpetrated by amateurs. Of the remaining 10 percent, 9.9 percent are perpetrated by professional hackers or corporate spies. That leaves only 0.1 percent of cyber-attacks that can be attributed to terrorists and enemy nations. Some experts dismiss the threat of cyber-terrorism. According to one panel of security experts, "The nation's computer networks face greater threats from non-terrorist hackers, viruses and poorly designed software than from a major cyberterrroism attack."[30] Although the threat of cyber-terrorism is minimum according to some, many fear that the *fear* of cyber-terrorism is greater than the actual threat that can be documented. In addition, although there have been no catastrophic cyber-attacks by terrorists, the same could be said of attacks using airplanes as flying missiles prior to September 11, 2001. Thus, cyber-terrorism is a great concern by both governments and businesses.

Computer systems and networks are vulnerable for two major reasons: (1) inadequate security to prevent unauthorized users from obtaining access and (2) software and network flaws that allow unauthorized users to exploit a flaw in the software or network to gain unauthorized access to the computer system or network. Such flaws are called *bugs*. The term originated in 1945 when Rear Admiral Grace Murray Hopper discovered that the cause of a computer malfunction was a moth trapped between relays in a Navy computer. She called it a "bug" and the term has been used since to refer to problems with computers and networks. *Debugging* is the term used to describe efforts to fix computer and network problems.

One of the most common causes of bugs is a flaw in the software. Companies such as Microsoft are constantly issuing "patches" to fix flaws or bugs in their software. However, sometime hackers and terrorists learn of this flaw before a patch is distributed or use this flaw to gain access to computers that have not installed the software update. Unfortunately, rather than experiencing a decrease in vulnerabilities due to software and hardware flaws, there has been a significant increase in such vulnerabilities. From 2000 to 2002 the number of known vulnerabilities in software and hardware that could permit unauthorized access or allow an attack to cause damage increased from 1,090 to 4,129—a four-fold increase. Microsoft, the leading software company, reported 128 publicly disclosed security flaws in Windows during the 12-month period from June 1, 2002, to May 31, 2003. From the time a security flaw is disclosed to the time a patch is issued and applied, companies are at risk of a cyber-attack. Microsoft reported an average of 25 days between disclosure and release of a fix, and this performance is one of the best in the software business, as other operating system software companies report up to 82 days between the disclosure and release of a patch.

Companies and governments use software and network security programs and devices to defend against unauthorized entry whether due to a software vulnerability or to the efforts of a hacker. These software programs are called *anti-virus programs.* Another defense against unauthorized entry into a computer system or network is a *firewall,* which is an intrusion-detection system designed to detect unauthorized users and not allow them entry into the system. Surveys of computer networks report that about 90 percent of network systems use anti-virus programs, firewalls, and intrusion-detection systems. Nevertheless, 90 percent reported that security breaches had taken place, with 85 percent reporting their systems had been damaged by computer viruses.

Reports by the General Accounting Office have repeatedly warned that federal systems are not being adequately protected from computer-based threats, even though these systems process, store, and transmit enormous amounts of sensitive data and are indispensable to many federal agency operations.[31] Tests of government computer systems in 2001, 2002, and 2003 indicated that nearly all of the 24 agencies tested have "significant information security weaknesses that place a broad array of federal operations and assets at risk of fraud, misuse, and disruption." Among these agencies were the Department of Defense, the Department of State, the Department of Energy, and the Federal Emergency Management Agency. All four of these agencies have primary roles in the war on terrorism.[32]

Viruses and Worms. Computers and networks can be attacked using Trojan horses, worms, and viruses. All three of these are called *malicious code* and all three are similar in that they are software programs or instructions that when executed cause the computer to perform a task. However, they have unique characteristics. A *Trojan horse* is a software program that claims to be one thing while in fact it has a "hidden" software program that performs another task—often unknown to the user. A Trojan horse software program usually promises the user to perform some useful function to cause the user to install the program. Once installed, another program is launched that operates in the background, unknown to the user. A common Trojan horse program is a program that promises to place local weather information on the user's computer. The program performs this function but it also sends information about the user's visits to websites to a predetermined Internet address so that this information can be used to target the user to receive advertisements related to the sites he or she visits. This type of Trojan horse is commonly called *spyware*. Terrorists could use a Trojan horse program to have government or private company computers send confidential information to them.

Worms usually exploit software vulnerabilities and propagate without user intervention. Engineers at Xerox Palo Alto Research Center first discovered the computer worm. The worm was a short program that scours a network of idle processors in order to provide more efficient computer use. Modern worms are a form of a computer virus that does destructive damage to data on computers. Some well-known cyber-attacks using worms—none of them initiated by terrorists—are the Code Red worm in 2001, the Klex worm in 2002, the Slammer worm in 2003, and the MyDoom worm in 2004.

Viruses are a type of malicious code that requires the user to execute the program. Opening an email attachment or going to a particular webpage could trigger this action. One of the first PC viruses ever created was "The Brain" released in 1986 by programmers in Pakistan. Some well-known viruses—none of them initiated by terrorists—are the Melissa and the Chernobyl virus released in 1999, the I Love You virus released in 2000, the Anna Kournikova virus released in 2001, and the SoBig.F virus released in 2003. It is estimated that nearly 63,000 viruses have rolled through the Internet, causing an estimated $65 billion in damages.[33] Despite the fact that none of these viruses has been linked to terrorism, half of those surveyed by the Pew Internet and American Life Project said they worried about terrorists damaging the Internet.[34]

Types of Cyber-Attacks.   There are five main types of cyber-attacks: (1) incursion, (2) destruction, (3) disinformation, (4) denial of service, and (5) defacement of websites. *Incursion attacks* are carried out with the purpose of gaining unauthorized access to a computer system or network. Such attacks are most commonly carried out to obtain data or to manipulate information. The motive for incursion attacks among nonterrorists is for financial gain, such as embezzlement, or for sabotage. For example, disgruntled employees or former employees may want to cause economic damage to the database. Young males, sometimes preteen boys, seeking thrills and notoriety, commit a good number of incursion attacks. Successful incursion attacks are usually carried out by taking advantage of loopholes in computer systems and networks, insider information (e.g., knowledge of passwords), or flaws in the software that allow unauthorized "backdoor" entries.

Destruction involves entry into a computer system or network for the purpose of inflicting severe damage or destroying them. Such destruction usually causes significant financial loss to the target. The damage can be erasing databases, corrupting data, releasing sensitive data to the public or competitors, and causing the system to crash. This type of attack is usually carried out by disgruntled employees or former employees seeking revenge or criminal hackers as a kind of vandalism. For terrorists, the motivation would be to cause economic damage to private business or to disrupt government operations.

Disinformation attacks are used to spread rumors or information that can have severe impact to a particular target. Such cyber-attacks can be carried out using legitimate bulletin boards or by creating websites, some claiming to be "news" websites, to disseminate the disinformation. A common criminal use of this type of cyber-attack is to influence the price of a company's stock. This type of cyber-attack is commonly used by radical jihadist websites. Many of the websites purport to be "news" sites but they disseminate false information about U.S. actions and policies. During war this is commonly referred to as *propaganda.*

Denial of service (DOS) is one of the most common forms of cyber-attack. The main objective in a DOS attack is to disable or disrupt the online operations of a website by flooding the targeted servers with a huge number of packets or requests for service. A DOS attack usually involves a worm that takes control of remote computers without the knowledge of the computer user. The worm is programmed to initiate requests for service on a predetermined time or event. A successful DOS attack will cause the target server to shut down due to its inability to handle the incoming messages. A denial of service attack in 2002 generated such a volume of messages that it nearly overwhelmed the entire Internet.[35]

The final type of cyber-attack is *defacement of websites.* This type of attack is a form of digital vandalism. The targeted website can be changed totally to include messages and images from the cyber-attacker. The attack can cause the website to be taken down to avoid embarrassment caused by the defacement and can cause financial losses and loss of services as legitimate users are denied access to the website while the vulnerability is detected and patched and the website restored. The motivation for this type of attack is primarily propaganda or publicity. Defacement of website attacks have been successfully executed against the White House website, the Department of Defense website, and George Bush's reelection campaign website.

Attacks on Critical Infrastructures Using the Internet

Cyber-terrorist attacks can be grouped into three main categories: (1) simple–unstructured, (2) advanced–structured, and (3) complex–coordinated.[36] *Simple–unstructured* attacks are directed against individual systems using software created by other people. This is the most common form of hacking by amateurs. *Advanced–structured* attacks are directed toward multiple systems or networks and the hacker may use hacking software he or she created. *Complex–coordinated* attacks are capable of causing mass disruptions against integrated and heterogeneous defenses. Using complex–coordinated attacks, terrorists have the ability to use the Internet as a direct instrument of bloodshed. These complex–coordinated cyber-attacks do more than cause damage to computer databases and networks. They have the ability to give terrorists control of the physical structures controlled by computers.[37]

What gives terrorists the ability to use computers to cause damage in the real world are the use of digital control systems (DCS) and supervisory control and data acquisition systems (SCADA). These specialized digital devices are used by the millions as the brains of critical infrastructure in the United States.[38] The report of *The National Strategy to Secure*

Cyberspace states that over the last 20 years DCS and SCADA control systems have transformed the way many industries in the United States control and monitor equipment. These two systems do tasks such as collect measurements, throw railway switches, close circuit breakers, and adjust values in the pipes that carry water, oil, and gas. They can also be designed to control a single device or to monitor and control multiple devices. They can be programmed to make decisions as to what to do and when to do it. The use of DCS and SCADA systems has allowed industry to replace many tasks that were previously performed manually with digital controls. They are used in almost every sector of the economy, including water, transportation, chemicals, energy, and manufacturing.[39] Using the Internet to take control of DCS and SCADA systems, terrorists could use virtual tools to destroy real-world lives and property. Terrorists could combine physical attacks, using explosives with cyber-attacks to escalate the damage caused by a physical attack. For example, terrorists could detonate a truck bomb and simultaneously disable the 911 communications systems to prevent officials from responding to the situation.

When DCS and SCADA systems were designed it was not anticipated that there would be public access to these digital control systems, as they were controlled by local computers without access to the Internet. During the last 20 years many of these systems have been connected to the Internet because this allows companies to reduce personnel and costs. However, connecting these digital control systems to the Internet has created new vulnerabilities. A statement by the Commerce Department's Critical Infrastructure Assurance Office warns that the prevalence of these digital control systems connected by the Internet to run physical assets places the nation at risk. "Digital controls are so pervasive that terrorists might use them to cause damage on a scale that otherwise would not be available except through a very systematic and comprehensive physical attack."[40]

There have been no documented cases of al-Qaida conducting such cyber-attacks. However, there have been cases where cyber-attacks on DCS and SCADA systems by persons who are not international terrorists have been successful in causing physical damage or could have caused damage. In 1998, a 12-year-old hacker broke into the computer system that runs Arizona's Roosevelt Dam. He had complete command of the SCADA system controlling the dam's floodgates. Had he been more malicious or a terrorist, he could have opened the floodgates and caused extensive damage.[41] In 2000, computer hacker Vitek Boden, age 48, was able to gain access to the digital control system of the Maroocky Shire wastewater system in Queensland, Australia. He was able to take control of the digital control system and dump hundreds of thousands of gallons of putrid sludge into parks, rivers, and the manicured grounds of a Hyatt Regency hotel. The release of wastewater killed marine life, polluted creek water, and made it impossible for people to use the beaches. What is astonishing is that he was able to make 46 successful incursions without being detected. The utility's managers could not determine why the wastewater system's controls were malfunctioning until Boden was captured.[42]

In the United States there have been a number of successful cyber-attacks on the 911 system and the telephone system. Successful cyber-attacks on the Internet have brought down police and fire departments emergency communication systems and disrupted telephone services to thousands of customers.[43] In January 2003, a cyber-attack shut down the monitoring system of a nuclear power plant. Fortunately the plant was off-line or the cyber-attack would have resulted in a major disaster.[44]

A major concern of government officials is the vulnerability of the North American power grid. Equipment failures not due to cyber-attacks by terrorists have demonstrated that it is possible for the grid to go down and that disruption of the power grid causes enormous financial damage, causes fear and disruption of everyday life, and exposes cities to vulnerabilities due to disruption of communications and emergency services such as fire and police. The Commerce Department has conducted mock cyber SCADA attacks against the power grid. These mock attacks have always succeeded in bringing down the power grid.[45]

Cyber-Warfare

Cyber-attacks by terrorists are a concern, but some government officials, including Richard A. Clarke, former head of the Office of Cyberspace Security under President Bush, consider cyber-attacks by nation-states "the most dangerous threat to this country's computer security."[46] Clarke has indicated that he suspects that about five or six nation-states have attempted cyber-attacks on national security computers.[47] The report of *The National Strategy to Secure Cyberspace* stated that in 1998, attackers carried out a sophisticated, tightly orchestrated series of cyber-intrusions into the computers of the Department of Defense, the National Aeronautical and Space Administration (NASA), and government research labs. The intrusions were targeted against those organizations that conduct advanced technical research on national security, including atmospheric and oceanographic topics as well as aircraft and cockpit design.[48] In 1999 and 2000, unidentified hackers downloaded scores of "sensitive but unclassified" internal documents from the Los Alamos and Livermore national laboratories. Defense Department investigators traced the electronic trail back to an unnamed foreign country.[49] Officials in the United States believe it is possible that a foreign government helped create the Code Red virus that took control of 314,000 servers in 2001 and directed them to attack White House computers.[50]

Tests of the security of national military and security computers have indicated that the government's computers and security networks are vulnerable.[51] Continued testing of the Department of Defense computer and network security by the Government Accounting Office continues to reveal security flaws that make unauthorized intrusion possible. The concern with lax cyber-security is two-fold: (1) agents of nation-states may take information that would prove harmful to United States security and (2) agents of nation-states may place malicious software such as a virus, worm, or Trojan horse program on network computers with the goal that the malicious software would be transferred to more sensitive networks.[52]

It is easy for the perpetrators of a cyber-attack to conceal their identity; thus, cyber-attacks have proven attractive strategies for attacking the United States, especially by poorer nations. Nations that would never consider a military assault against the Untied States may be tempted to launch a cyber-attack. Cyber-warfare could be carried out at a fraction of the cost of a conventional war, expose the attacker to much less risk of retaliation, and be initiated anywhere in the world. It is not necessary to physically enter the United States to launch a cyber-attack. Mock attacks by the Central Intelligence Agency and the National Security Agency have concluded that cyber-terrorism could be the most devastating weapon of mass destruction and could cripple the U.S. economy.[53]

The Internet is a prime target of terrorists because the high-tech economy of the United States is dependent on it. Furthermore, the economy of countries from which most terrorists originate is usually not as dependent on the Internet. Therefore, a disruption of the Internet would have a far greater impact on the United States.[54] Former Central Intelligence Director Robert Gates has warned that as terrorists become more motivated by radical religion, the less the terrorists are concerned about the scale of their violence and the number of innocent lives they are prepared to take.[55] Thus, concerns about both cyber-attacks from terrorists and cyber-attacks from nations have caused the federal government and military to take actions to develop robust defense capacities against cyber-attacks.

Whereas the United States worries about cyber-attacks by foreign nations, the nation has also given consideration to the use of cyber-weapons against nations. For example, in the 1999 U.S. military action in Kosovo, the U.S. military jammed Serbian computer networks.[56] However, the United States has never conducted a large-scale, strategic cyber-attack.[57] The extent of the U.S. arsenal of cyber-weapons, offensive capacity, and defense capacity is "among the most tightly held national security secrets, even more guarded than nuclear capabilities."[58] It is known that National Security Presidential Directive 16, a classified document issued in July 2002, directed government and military officials to develop a national-level policy for determining when and how the United States would launch cyber-attacks against enemy computer networks.[59]

In considering the rules of engagement for cyber-weapons, the United States needs to consider such factors as expected outcomes and military advantages of cyber-attacks and collateral damage. For example, a computer attack on an enemy nation's electric power grid intended to disable military facilities may also cut off power to civilian users, such as hospitals.[60] Also, the United States has to consider that U.S. businesses and governmental entities depend on technology to a far greater degree than do relatively underdeveloped countries, rogue nations, and terrorist groups. If the United States initiates offensive cyber-attacks against such countries, it could trigger counter–cyber-attacks that would be much more harmful to the United States than to the nation the United States attacked.[61]

Defending Cyber-Space

Defense against cyber-attacks is somewhat different from defense against physical attacks by terrorists. In defending against physical attacks, the primary goal is to prevent such attacks through intelligence, preparation, and target hardening. The primary goal in cyber-attacks "is not to prevent cyber-attacks but to withstand them."[62] Cyber-networks are constantly exposed to anonymous cyber-attacks in the United States. There is no way to prevent such attacks, so the primary defense is to develop firewalls, hardware, and software that can detect a cyber-attack and prevent the malicious program from gaining access to the network or damaging data. In developing a defense strategy against cyber-terrorism, the federal government has had to contend with three unique obstacles that make cyber-terrorism different from traditional terrorism: (1) hackers versus terrorists, (2) private initiatives, and (3) the role of the federal government.

Hackers versus Terrorists.   First, most cyber-based attacks are crimes, not attacks, by cyber-terrorists.[63] Furthermore, most of cases of major cyber-attacks have been initiated by amateurs or hackers, not terrorists. Some of the cyber-attacks have been initiated by teenagers as young as 14 years old. It is difficult for the federal government to develop a national policy and national agency to respond to a problem that should be the responsibility of law enforcement officials. The problem is that law enforcement and the courts are not effective agents in preventing cyber-terrorism. Laws against cyber-terrorism do not keep pace with the technology of the crime. For example, it was not possible to prosecute the person who was responsible for the "I Love You" virus that did 7 billion dollars worth of damage, because his native country did not have laws against releasing the malicious code and there was no U.S. law that allowed him to be extradited for prosecution in the United States.

Even when there are laws against cyber-attacks, such laws are very difficult to enforce and often carry only minimum punishments. David Smith, the person responsible for the Melissa virus, which was responsible for millions of dollars of damage, received only a 20-month sentence for sending the virus. Also, many of those responsible for cyber-attacks are teenagers who are often protected from harsh punishment by the juvenile courts. The federal government has taken some steps to remedy this problem, however. In November 2003, legislation was passed making certain computer crimes federal crimes punishable by harsher sentences. For example, under the new legislation a person who is responsible for a cyber-attack that intends to cause deaths, such as tying up 911 emergency telephone lines or shutting down the power grid, could face a life sentence. However, for the most part, local and state law enforcement authorities are not well equipped to detect and prosecute those responsible for cyber-crime.

Private Initiatives Necessary.   The second problem in defending against cyber-attacks is that most critical infrastructures, and the cyber-space on which they rely, are privately owned and operated.[64] Not only is there no single government oversight agency responsible for cyber-security but also the federal government often has no authority or responsibility at all. Thus, cyber-security to a great deal depends on private initiatives. Often the most the federal government can do is to encourage individuals and private businesses to take steps to increase cyber-security.[65] The report of the *National Strategy to Secure Cyberspace* indicated that the majority of security vulnerabilities could be mitigated through good security practices.[66] However, many individuals and businesses may not be willing to pay the additional costs necessary to promote cyber-security.[67] For example, one of the most deadly cyber-attacks by terrorists would be an attack where terrorists took control of digital control systems and supervisory control and data acquisition systems with the purpose of overriding critical controls of nuclear power plants, dams, wastewater treatment, traffic signal controls, or other devices that could cause real damage and death. One of the simple ways to prevent such a disaster is to provide human control in all vital systems so as to prevent misuse by such terrorists. However, the very reason that such digital control systems were initiated was to save the cost of human supervision.

Efforts by both the government and consumers to encourage private software developers to eliminate vulnerabilities in their software has not eliminated one of the most common causes of cyber-insecurity—software with vulnerabilities that allow intrusions and malicious code attacks by exploiting vulnerabilities in the software. Some have argued for software companies to be held legally responsible for damages due to software vulnerabilities. They suggest that software developers should be held accountable for what they produce, sell, and distribute to the public.[68] Critics have argued that leaving it to software companies to improve their software security has not worked and that regulation and legislation is necessary. If adopted, such regulations and legislation would mandate the use of firewalls, anti-virus software, and increased security practices.

A 2003 survey by the Pew Internet and American Life Project indicated that nearly 60 percent of Internet users say they favor the government requiring U.S. corporations to disclose more information about their vulnerabilities. Most do not believe that voluntary efforts to secure the Internet are sufficient.[69] Many business, however, fear that regulation would place financial burdens on them that would destroy their ability to be competitive in the marketplace. For example, broadband Internet providers argue that if they modify their services, as suggested in several legislative proposals to make it easier for police to perform wiretaps, such costs would be prohibitive.[70] Colleges say that to modify their campus-based networks to make it easier for law enforcement to monitor Internet-based voice conversations could cause colleges to incur significant costs without compensation.[71] Other advocates argue that if the government is allowed to require security enhancements to the Internet, such regulations would "dumb down the genius of the Net to match the limited visions of the regulator."[72]

The Federal Government's Role.   The report of the *National Strategy to Secure Cyberspace* concluded that "public-private engagement is a key component of our strategy to secure cyberspace."[73] However, although the report concluded that the federal government alone cannot sufficiently defend America's cyber-space, the report also concluded that the federal government plays a key role in securing cyber-space.[74] Worms and viruses can infect millions of computers in a very brief time and can cause millions or billions of dollars in damage. The speed and anonymity of cyber-attacks makes the distinction among the actions of terrorists, criminals, and nation-states difficult. Often this distinction is only possible after the attack occurs.[75] Thus, the task is to define the role of the federal government in cyber-security.

In October 2001, President Bush issued Executive Order 13231, authorizing a federal cyber-protection program that consists of continuous efforts to secure information systems for critical infrastructure, including emergency preparedness communications and the physical assets that support such systems.[76] Unlike the federal role in aviation security, the federal government has chosen to take a limited role in cyber-protection that depends to a great extent on partnerships with private businesses and individuals. The report of the *National Strategy to Secure Cyberspace* concluded that private-sector organizations and all individuals must make their own decisions as to what security measures they will adopt based on cost effectiveness analysis and risk-management and mitigation strategies.[77] The federal government has taken the role of encouraging rather than legislating that the public and private institutions and cyber-centers perform analysis, conduct watch and warning activities, enable information exchange, and facilitate restoration efforts.[78] Basically, the federal government's position is that "each American who depends on cyberspace, the network of information networks, must secure the part that they own or for which they are responsible."[79]

The federal government under President Bush's Executive Order 13231 and President Clinton's Presidential Directive Decision 63 (May 22, 1998) has outlined its responsibility for cyber-security and the partnerships it envisions with the public and private sector. Operating under these directives, the federal government established lead agencies responsible for various infrastructure sections. The overall critical infrastructure protection responsibilities of the federal government are summarized in Table 9.1. Each lead agency is responsible for developing its own plan (1) to protect those computers and networks for which it is responsible and (2) to partner with the various public and private infrastructure sectors for which it is the lead agency to encourage policies and actions that will enhance cyber security.

With the creation of the Department of Homeland Security, the DHS assumed a key role in cyber-security. One of the directorates of the DHS is the National Cyber Security Division (NCSD). This division is the federal government's cornerstone for cyber-security coordination and preparedness, including implementation of the *National Strategy to Secure Cyberspace*. The operational arm of the NCSD is the United States Computer Emergency Readiness Team (US-CERT), established in September 2003. The DHS defines the *US-CERT* as "a public-private partnership charged with improving computer security preparedness and response to cyber attacks in the United States." The specific mission of US-CERT is to (1) analyze and reduce cyber-threats and vulnerabilities, (2) disseminate cyber-threat warning information, and (3) coordinate incident response activities.

In January 2004, the National Cyber Security division of DHS initiated the National Cyber Alert System. This system is similar to the DHS color-coded threat alert advisories in that it delivers "timely and actionable information" to pubic and private sectors concerning computer security vulnerabilities and cyber-attacks. Unlike the National Threat Advisory

TABLE 9.1   *Critical Infrastructure Lead Agencies*

Lead Agency	Sectors
Department of Homeland Security	• Information and telecommunications • Transportation (aviation, rail, mass transit, waterborne commerce, pipelines, and highways, including trucking and intelligent transportation systems • Postal and shipping • Emergency services • Continuity of government
Department of the Treasury	• Banking and finance
Department of Health and Human Services	• Public health (including prevention, surveillance, laboratory services, and personal health services) • Food (all except for meat and poultry)
Department of Energy	• Energy (electric power, oil and gas production, and storage)
Environmental Protection Agency	• Water • Chemical industry and hazardous materials
Department of Agriculture	• Agriculture • Food (meat and poultry)
Department of Defense	• Defense industrial base

Source: The National Strategy to Secure Cyberspace, Washington DC: GPO, February 2003, p. 16.

System, those concerned with computer security have to sign up with the National Cyber Alert System (www.US-CERT.gov/cas) to receive information by email concerning vulnerabilities and threats. There is no charge for this service; even individuals can sign up for cyber-security tips, bulletins, and alerts. Private businesses have offered a similar service for a fee. For example, both Symantec, an independent security services and software publisher, and IBM offer a similar cyber-threat warning network. Similar to the US-CERT National Cyber Alert System, the services of Symantec and IBM provide "a first-line defense" against cyber-attack

Immigration Control and Border Security

The 9/11 Commission criticized the former office of Immigration and Naturalization Services (INS), claiming that INS failed to prevent terrorists involved in the 9/11 attacks from entering the United States even though some of them were listed on the State Department's watch list. The commission also claimed that INS failed to monitor and take steps to remove potential terrorists who entered the United States illegally or who remained in the United States after their visas had expired. The public and the Bush Administration apparently shared this concern, as a crackdown on immigration control and border security was quickly initiated.

Concern over ineffective immigration control and porous border security led to the dismantling of INS and the transfer of responsibility for immigration control and border security to the newly created Department of Homeland Security. The Immigration and Naturalization Service (INS) was abolished March 1, 2003, and its functions and units incorporated into the new DHS.[80] Immigration enforcement functions were placed within the directorate of Border and Transportation Security (BTS), either directly, or under Customs and Border Protection (CBP), which includes the Border Patrol and INS Inspectors or Immigration and Customs Enforcement (ICE). ICE assumed responsibility for the enforcement and investigation components previously performed by INS, such as investigations, intelligence, detention and removals.[81]

The challenge of securing the borders against terrorists is staggering in its scope. There are more than 300 legal ports of entry but the 8,000 miles of Canadian and Mexican borders, plus the Atlantic and Pacific coastlines, provide virtually an unlimited number of possible illegal points of entry. Congress limits the number of legal immigrations into the United States but even with the number of immigrants capped, a tremendous number of people must be screened and processed. In 2002, there were 1,063,732 legal immigrations into the United States, and in 2003, there were 705,827 legal immigrations.[82] On top of this number of legal immigrations, DHS must also detect and remove illegal immigrants. The number of illegal immigrants who enter the United States is as many or more than the number of legal immigrants. For example, there were 1 million deportable aliens located by DHS during 2003, 186,000 deportations, and more than 79,000 criminal alien deportations.[83]

To enhance border security and protect against terrorists entering the United States, the Department of Homeland Security and the newly created departments of Bureau of Customs and Border Protection and the Bureau of Immigration and Customs Enforcement undertook a number of aggressive programs to change existing policies and to enact new policies to defend the homeland against terrorism. The purpose of these programs was to

BOX 9.1 • *Up Close and Personal: May I See Your ID?*

Official identification documents are a major concern in the war on terrorism. The DHS wants to stop terrorists from being able to obtain government identification cards. This concern was sparked by the fact that two of the 9/11 hijackers illegally obtained Virginia identification cards. Following the 9/11 attacks many states tightened rules on issuing identification cards and driver's licenses. Many states refuse to issue drivers license to illegal immigrants; whereas other states argue that it is better to have illegal immigrants licensed rather than driving without testing that a license would require. Without a license or state identification card, immigrants find that they are unable to open bank accounts and to utilize services that require the user to provide official identification. The problem extends not only to illegal immigrants but also to legal immigrants who find that their paperwork is not in order or does not meet the new more stringent DHS standards. Often these immigrants find that although they were able to obtain identification cards and driver's licenses prior to 9/11, they are now unable to renew their ID cards and driver's licenses.[84]

To enhance national security, the government has focused on the merits of a national identification card and a standardized driver's license. Each state issues a driver's license of its own design with whatever information on the license deemed appropriate by the state. The Department of Homeland Security has argued for a single standard "look" with certain information being required on all state driver's licenses. The agency maintains that this would help law enforcement officials, airline security officials, and immigration and customs officials to be able to spot fraudulent identification documents.

Since each state can issue a driver's license of its own design, disputes can arise as to what can be required to obtain a driver's license. Lultaana Freeman, formerly Sandra Keller, was denied a Florida driver's license because she refused to have her photograph taken without her veil. She previously had been issued a driver's licenses from the state of Illinois and the state of Florida in which she was photographed in her veil. However, following the 9/11 attacks, Florida changed its policy and issued her a letter advising that she would have to have a new photograph taken without her veil or her driver's license would be canceled. Citing objections based on religious practices of the Muslim faith, she refused to be photographed without her veil.

The American Civil Liberties Union filed suit to force the state of Florida to issue a driver's license with a photograph of her veiled. The ACLU claimed that the requirement to be photographed without a veil was arbitrary, as a driver's license can be obtained without a photograph in 14 states. The court ruled against Lultaana Freeman, accepting the lawyers' for state argument that a driver's license showing only a covered face would hinder law enforcement officials. Florida Circuit Judge Janet C. Thorpe said the state of Florida was justified in required persons to be photographed without a veil. Judge Thorpe stated in her ruling, "Although the court acknowledges the plaintiff herself most likely poses no threat to national security, there likely are people who would be willing to use a ruling permitting the wearing of full-face cloaks in driver's license photos by pretending to ascribe to religious beliefs in order to carry out activities that would threaten lives."

Questions

1. Freeman was photographed without a veil after she was arrested in 1998 on a domestic battery charge. Also, Muslim women in the Middle East are required to be photographed without their veil for passports. Do you agree with the State Court's ruling that people should not be able to obtain a driver's license without a photograph in which the person can be identified? Why or why not?

2. The ACLU argued the state of Florida does not have compelling state interest in having a face photograph of Freeman on her driver's license without her veil and if required to do so the state would be forcing Freeman to violate her religious beliefs. When there is a conflict between religious beliefs and concern for national security, what should be the criteria in balancing the two conflicting rights?

stop terrorists from entering the United States and to ensure that aliens who entered the United States illegally and those who entered legally but lost their legal status were detected and deported. These new border security strategies and programs have focused on (1) controlling and identifying who enters and exits the United States, (2) more scrutiny of foreign students entering the United States for the alleged purpose of attending school, and (3) enhancing security by the adoption of "smart" passports.

Immigration Control

The Department of Homeland Security initiated several programs with the goal of enhancing border security by identifying and deporting people with criminal backgrounds or indirect ties to terrorism. Among these new programs, the most controversial was one that sought to identify "special-interest" immigrants who allegedly had direct or indirect connections to terrorist groups. This program resulted in the arrest of more than 700 people, most from Middle Eastern countries, who were charged with violating immigration laws.[85] Additional security screening for visa applications was required for applicants from 26 predominately Muslim countries. Also, DHS initiated the Absconder Apprehension Initiative. The purpose of the program was to identify and expedite the expulsion of immigrants who were facing deportation from countries with an al-Qaida presence.

US-VISIT. The DHS has initiated new requirements for travelers to the United States. Two of the most sweeping policies are the fingerprinting and photographing of foreign visitors and passenger screening. The new policy, known as United States Visitor and Immigrant Status Indicator Technology, or US-VISIT, requires foreign visitors to be fingerprinted and photographed when they enter the United States at first applied only to those visitors from countries for which entry visas were required. However, fearing that terrorists may take advantage of the exemption of foreign visitors from European countries and other nations—such as Brunei, Singapore, Japan, Australia, and New Zealand—the policy was changed in April 2004 to require fingerprints and photographs of *all* visitors. The program started with air travelers but will eventually extend to most if not all airports, seaports, and land border crossings. Foreign visitors' reactions to the new fingerprint and photo requirement have been mixed, with some visitors praising the efficiency of the system and others saying the new requirement "makes them feel like a criminal."[86]

The policy requires that foreign visitors be photographed and provide a digital fingerprint of their left and right index finger. The procedure usually takes less than a minute. One of the shortcomings of the policy is that fingerprints are not checked against the Federal Bureau of Investigation databank of fingerprints. The FBI fingerprint database, one of the most comprehensive in the world, contains more than 47 million prints. The digital fingerprints of travelers are checked only against the limited database of the DHS. The reason for this practice is that the FBI fingerprint database uses fingerprints from all 10 fingers, whereas the DHS database uses only fingerprints from the index fingers. The DHS and the FBI have not developed a common database that will share the fingerprint data collected from foreign travelers. A small percentage of the fingerprints from foreign travelers is cross-checked with the FBI database, but 99 percent of foreign visitors to the United States do not have their fingerprints checked against the FBI database.[87] The Department of Homeland Security has defended the incompatibility of the two fingerprint databases, saying that to take all 10 prints of the millions of visitors would be "expensive, time-consuming and unnecessary" and that the DHS fingerprint database was "not designed for booking criminals."[88]

Airline Passenger Screening.   The second strategy initiated by DHS to enhance border security is passenger screening. In 2004, DHS formalized plans to screen airline passengers against a list of potential terror suspects. This screening was previously performed by the airlines. Passenger name screening requires that the names of passengers provided by the airlines are checked against government watch lists to ensure that suspected terrorists do not board airplanes and that law enforcement officials are promptly notified of potential security risks.[89]

The DHS administration of passenger screening was suppose to result in greater efficiency and was to be less intrusive. However, bugs in the passenger screening system have resulted in passenger lists being screened after the airplane has departed for the United States. Some of these flights have been turned back and the offending passenger made to deplane. Some flights have actually landed in the United States only to discover a passenger on the no-fly list.

One of the more prominent errors of this sort was when Yusuf Islam, better known to Americans as Cat Stevens, the musician popular in the 1960s and 1970s, was flagged in a flight from London to New York in September 2004. The musician's name was not discovered until it was too late to turn the plane back. The airplane was diverted to Bangor, Maine, where Yusuf Islam, or Cat Stevens, was removed, taken into custody, and deported back to London. The deportation of Cat Stevens resulted in a questioning of the effectiveness of the passenger screening program and furthermore a questioning of the criteria used to place names on the list. Many argued that Cat Stevens is known for his peace activities, including opposition to the U.S. war effort, and that he is a moderate Muslim and has taken a public stance against terrorism.[90] Such critics argue that the watch lists "demonstrate the failure of American domestic and security policy, both tactically and strategically, to discern who the bad guys really are."[91] This potential flaw in the passenger screening system was again emphasized when Senator Edward M. Kennedy (D-MA) found he was on the no-fly list from March 1 to April 6, 2004, as a suspected terrorist.[92] While on the no-fly list, Senator Kennedy found that he could not purchase an airline ticket and that the airlines would not explain to him why they refused to allow him to board. Even after the mistake was allegedly corrected by DHS, Senator Kennedy reported that he continued to be stopped from boarding flights.[93]

The Challenges Facing DHS.   The Department of Homeland Security's efforts to secure the borders were evaluated by the 9/11 Commission. The commission concluded that immigration policies initiated by DHS have been "ineffective, producing little, if any, information leading to the identification or apprehension of terrorists."[94] These programs have neither prevented potential terrorists from entering the country nor clearly distinguished potential terrorists who should be removed from the country. For example, after assuming control over visas, the new DHS supervised departments issued visas to 105 foreign men who should have been prevented from entering the United States because their names appeared on government lists of suspected terrorists.[95]

Furthermore, DHS has struggled to keep foreign tourists informed of the new requirements. A significant number of foreign travelers who were not previously required to have visas have found themselves afoul of the new immigration policies. The treatment of these travelers has generated international criticism of U.S. policies. In late 2004, a significant number of British travelers found themselves arrested, handcuffed, and confined without access to a lawyer or the ability to inform others of their situation.[96] The treatment of foreign travelers from countries previously exempt from visa requirements received significant media attention in 2004 when approximately 15 journalists and actress Olivia Newton-John were handcuffed, arrested, fingerprinted, held in detention, and finally deported because they had failed to obtain the newly required special visa, known as an *I-visa,* when visiting the United States for professional reasons.

The I-visa requirement has its roots in the 1952 McCarthy era as a strategy to screen subversives from entering the United States. Foreign journalists and professional news media organizations have criticized the policy of greater scrutiny for journalists as discriminatory practices.[97] When applying for I-visas, journalists are required to declare who they are going to interview, the nature of the article they plan to write, and the fee they will be paid. Foreign journalists can be rejected for visas. If rejected, they have no right to appeal. Foreign journalists object to having to reveal this information, especially since U.S. journalists entering Britain and other European countries covered by this requirement are not required to disclose similar information about their visits.[98] Following the negative press over the

BOX 9.2 • *Case Study: Security or Discrimination?*

People who look like they are of Middle Eastern descent are claiming they are being discriminated against because others assume they are terrorists. In December 2001, an Arab American member of President Bush's Secret Service security detail was denied passage on an American Airlines flight after the flight's pilot questioned the validity of the agent's credentials.[99]

In 2002, an Indian doctor who was a naturalized citizen and former U.S. Army major was detained by air marshals but later released without charge allegedly because they "didn't like the way [he] looked."[100] On September 13, 2003, two Canadian Islamic leaders were denied entry into the United States and detained for 16 hours and jailed because security officials found a business card that contained the name of an organization allegedly tied to terrorism. The Canadian Islamic leaders alleged, "One of the agents told them, 'You guys have picked the wrong time to fly.'"[101] In July 2003, the Federal Bureau of Investigation's highest-ranking Arab American agent filed a racial discrimination lawsuit against the bureau, charging that he was kept out of the investigation of the

September 11, 2001, hijackings because of his ancestry.[102] On December 29, 2004, U.S. border agents detained, searched, fingerprinted, and photographed approximately 30 persons returning from a religious conference in Toronto. A spokesperson for the Department of Homeland Security's Customs and Border Protection Bureau said that agents had orders to detain anyone who said they attended the three-day convention, entitled "Reviving the Islam Spirit," on the belief that such gatherings could promote terrorism.[103] The order to stop all persons attending the conference was justified by the statement that "the threat of terrorism provided no room for error."[104]

Questions

1. Do you believe that heightened security to detect terrorists who may attempt to enter the United States has resulted in unintended discrimination against innocent persons of Middle East ancestry?
2. What would you suggest as guidelines for airlines and customs and immigration for screening for possible terrorists?

policy, the DHS issued new guidelines allowing for more flexibility in admitting first-time offenders.

International Students: Separating Friend from Foe

Several of the hijackers in the 9/11 attacks entered the United States claiming they were entering to study. The screening used by INS prior to 9/11 was a manual system that made it very difficult to determine the legitimacy of immigrants' claims that they were students. To enter as a student, the government issues what are known as *I-20 visa permits*. However, under the system in place prior to the 9/11 attacks, it was very difficult for custom officials to know if a student enrolled and attended the college or program indicated on his or her application.

To close this vulnerability a new tracking system for international students was implemented. The new system converted what was a manual procedure into an automated process and provided stricter monitoring of the activities of international students. The new system, called the Student and Exchange Visitor Information System (SEVIS), is a web-based system for maintaining information on international students and exchange visitors in the United States. It is administered by U.S. Immigration and Customs Enforcement (ICE) and U.S. Customs and Border Protection (CBP). Immigration and Customs Enforcement asserts that "SEVIS is designed to keep our nation safe while facilitating the entry and exit process for foreign students in the United States and for students seeking to study in the United States."[105] The cost of the SEVIS program is paid for by fees collected from those applying for the student, exchange visitor, or scholar visa.

In 2004, more than 770,000 students and exchange visitors and more than 100,000 dependents of students registered with SEVIS. Unlike the previous I-20 visa system, SEVIS provides tracking of students from entry to exit. If an international student enters the United States but does not register and attend classes at the university or school on record, ICE is alerted to this fact. In 2004, 36,600 potential student violators were reported to ICE Compliance Enforcement Unit (CEU). More than 2,900 of these reported violators were "no shows," or students who entered the country but failed to register and attend classes. As a result of investigations triggered by reported violations, CEU made 155 arrests in 2004.

In addition to registering and tracking all student and scholar visitors, SEVIS has the added advantage of being an effective tool to detect corrupt school officials who sell fraudulent Forms I-20 and transcripts. U.S. Immigration and Customs Enforcement has proclaimed, "SEVIS is one of the pillars of ICE's mission of restoring integrity to the immigration system."[106]

Although ICE has praised SEVIS, many U.S. universities have expressed the opinion that the new immigration policies concerning students and scholars has made it difficult for legitimate international students to come to the United States. These universities have also complained that international students have been subjected to misunderstandings and misinterpretations of the regulations, often resulting in their deportation for minor violations or differences of opinions as to the requirements of the law.[107] The number of international students entering the United States has dropped significantly and many credit the drop to the difficulties students are having in getting approval of their visas due to the new screening requirements.[108]

In addition to entry screening, the DHS and the FBI have engaged in active programs to investigate students, especially those from predominately Muslim countries.[109] These investigations often involve on-campus interviews with university administrators and students. Under these new regulations, university officials are "data monitors for the government" and fulfill a "law enforcement" role in tracking the compliance of students.[110] In addition to casting a new relationship between the student and the university, there are charges that although providing new scrutiny against terrorists entering as students, these new policies have adversely impacted important research being performed by international scholars and scientists in the United States.[111] For example, one review of the impact of these policies reported that due to delays and barriers in obtaining visas or permission to reenter the United States, research projects have been delayed, including research programs to create new HIV drugs, work on a vaccine for West Nile virus, research on leukemia, and work on sensors that could detect bio-warfare agents.[112]

High-Tech Passports: The Promise for More Secure Borders?

The passport is one of the primary means of establishing the identity of international visitors to the United States. The fraudulent use of passports has been a concern, as one estimate is that there are as many as 400,000 stolen blank passports.[113] To enhance passport security, the Department of State has initiated a program to move toward "smart" passports. Smart passports would contain microchips with approximately 64 kilobytes of data. The electronic passports would contain data about the traveler, such as name, birth date, and issuing office, as well as biometric identifier data, such as a photograph of the holder's face, digital fingerprints, and iris scans. The technology would permit computers to query the chip on selected data, including the use of facial recognition technology that would match the image on the passport with the traveler. Furthermore, the electronic passports are designed to be able to be read by wireless technology. This would allow travelers to pass through a checkpoint with their passports and have their data confirmed electronically. This feature would greatly speed up the processing of international travelers through customs. The biometric system would cut down the subjectivity in photo identification. The current technology of biometric systems can discriminate the difference between identical twins.[114]

The use of smart passports was initiated in 2004. Initially, the United States had proposed that citizens from most of the countries in Western Europe would be required to have smart passports with machine-readable biometric data by the end of 2004. However, this deadline proved unworkable, as many countries failed to convert their old passports over to the new smart passports. The State Department has endorsed proposals calling for the implement of smart passports within one to three years of the original deadline.[115]

The adoption of biometric technologies has been held back for years by concerns about privacy, reliability, and the lack of international uniform standards.[116] The 9/11 attacks were the tipping point, resulting in the decision to go with enhanced security rather than worry about privacy concerns. Using the new smart passports, a traveler entering the United States puts his or her index fingers on scanners and stands in front of facial recognition cameras. The traveler's fingerprints and photograph are compared to that on his or her passport. This system provides fast, positive identification of the traveler.

However, the system also provides the potential for abuse. Concern is expressed that electronic passports may be vulnerable to electronic snooping. The wireless technology of the machine-readable passport could enable someone to capture identification data by merely being in close proximity to the traveler's passport with appropriate equipment to read the data illegally. This practice, called *skimming,* is a common technology used by identity thefts.[117] One of the reasons electronic passports would be so vulnerable to snooping is the lack of encryption of the data in the current design. The reason cited for the lack of data encryption is that all countries will need to be able to read the passports and encryption could be a barrier. Thus, the data are not encrypted and anyone skimming the data would have no problem capturing enough information about the traveler to engage in identity theft. One low-tech solution to this problem may be simply to incorporate a layer of metal foil into the cover of the passport so that it can be read only when opened.[118]

The American Civil Liberties Union has raised the concern that the new smart passports could contribute to the continuing loss of privacy.[119] Such passports would make it possible to monitor the movement of individuals globally. Smart passports could be used to track not only the entry and exit of international travelers but also track their movement within the United States. It should be noted that U.S. citizens will also be required to have smart passports. This change is spurred by both DHS initiates and initiates by foreign governments. As the United States requires international travelers to have smart passports, foreign countries in turn are requiring U.S. citizens to have similar passports.

Deportation: A Simple Solution or Misguided Bureaucracy?

As stricter immigration controls have been adopted, the need for enforcement action and sanctions has become more important. Strict immigration controls without enforcement would be useless. The Department of State and the Department of Homeland Security have aggressively pursued deportation as one of the primary strategies to respond to violations of immigration polices. This new aggressive use of deportation has been championed as an effective strategy to defend the United States against terrorist.

Prior to September 11, 2001, the Immigration and Naturalization Service was responsible for enforcing immigration law and INS was criticized for its lax enforcement of immigration laws and removal of aliens who no longer were entitled to remain in the United States. Following the 9/11 attacks this function was transferred to the Department of Homeland Security (DHS) and immigration laws were enforced with a new vigor. Old laws that had not been enforced by INS were strictly enforced by DHS. The Department of Homeland Security placed a never before seen emphasis on strict enforcement of immigration status and deportation of those found to be in violation of their immigration status. For example, in the months following the 9/11 attacks 762 people were arrested for immigration violations.[120] In 2003, DHS removals of illegal aliens increased to more than 186,000. The investigative actions of DHS resulted in the identification of 1 million deportable aliens in 2003. New policies, most of them evoked with the purported purpose of fighting terrorism, have subjected many more aliens to deportation.

Removal from the United States.   Aliens can be removed from the United States primarily by three means: voluntary departure, withdrawal of application for admission, and

BOX 9.3 • *Consider This: Getting under Your Skin*

The Department of Homeland Security has recommended a national identification card and a standardized format for a driver's license. The federal government is moving toward the adoption of a single governmentwide ID card for federal employees and contractors, known as Personal Identity Verification Project, to prevent terrorists, criminals, and other unauthorized people from getting into government buildings and computer systems. New identification cards are containing more and more information, as new high-tech identification cards can be encoded with a fairly large amount of digital information.

However, these forms of identification fall far short of the under-the-skin identity badge developed by Applied Digital Solutions based in Delray Beach, Florida. Applied Digital Solutions has developed an under-the-skin identification badge, known as VeriChip, that has been approved for implantation by the Food and Drug Administration. Implanted ID tags have been commonly used with livestock and pets for years. Applied Digital Solutions has developed a radio frequency identification tag that is 12mm by 2.1mm, or about the size of a large grain of rice, that can be inserted under the skin with nothing more than a syringe—the same technology used to insert identification tags in animals. The radio frequency identification tag uses passive technology and cannot be used to track a person by satellite or other surveillance technology. The information on the chip can be read only by a scanner that cannot be more than a few feet away. The chips used by Applied Digital Solutions are not encoded with personal data. The chips are encoded with a unique 16-digit identification number. The technology is relatively low cost, with each chip costing about $200.

Applied Digital Solutions is emphasizing the uses of the chips primarily for medical purposes whereby a patient's medical records would be tied to the chip's identification number. However, there is nothing to prevent the chip's technology from being used in other ways. In fact, Applied Digital Solutions is marketing its use for other purposes, including homeland security. Applied Digital Solutions reports that government officials in Mexico are using the implanted identification chips to identify people to control access to secure rooms and documents, and some businesses offer the chip as an alternative to traditional identification cards for identifying customers.[121] Applied Digital Solutions has promoted the chip as a means to provide positive identification of children in the event they are kidnapped or abducted. The implanted ID chip could also supplement existing identification systems or it could replace traditional identification cards and could be used to control access to nuclear power plants and government buildings. The techonlogy could also replace dog tags as military identification. In addition, the government could adopt such technology to identify and track criminals and parolees. The government could also use such a chip to track visitors to the United States.

It is not unreasonable to assume that the chip's technology will evolve and it is not unrealistic to expect that a chip could be developed that could track a person's movement or at least could be read from a greater distance. With further development of the chip's technology, it is not science fiction to imagine that frequent flyers who had such chips implanted could be quickly and positively screened through expedited check-in lines or passengers could be matched to their baggage by such technology.

Questions

1. Applied Digital Solutions is emphasizing the implanted identification chip's use to identify medical records of a patient. Do you believe the use of such technology could quickly expand to other nonmedical uses such as security control? How widely do you think this technology will be accepted? Is this going to be the new identification card of the future or will this technology be rejected? Why?
2. What are your feelings about such technology? If you worked in a secure facility—such as a nuclear power plant, a government

(continued)

BOX 9.3 • Continued

building, a bio-chemical laboratory, or a weapons research facility—and your employer offered employees the option of an implanted identification chip in lieu of a traditional identification card, which would you choose? Why?

3. What, if any, are the possible abuses or problems that you can see if such identification technology were to become commonly used in the United States?

formal removal of an alien. Of the approximately 1.5 million removals of aliens in 2003, the largest number of removals was by voluntary departure. More than 99 percent of the 887,115 aliens deported through voluntary departure involved aliens who were apprehended by the Border Patrol and removed quickly. *Voluntary departure* is the most common procedure with noncriminal aliens who are apprehended by the Border Patrol during an attempted illegal entry. In voluntary departure, aliens agree that their entry was illegal, waive their rights to a hearing, remain in custody, and are removed under supervision.[122] Most of the aliens removed through voluntary departure were apprehended crossing the United States–Mexican border.

The next largest numbers of aliens are removed by *withdrawal of application for admission.* In 2003, 431,807 aliens withdrew their application for admission. Somewhat similar to voluntary departure, in withdrawal of application for admission, aliens who customs inspectors determine are inadmissible during the custom processing phase are allowed to withdraw their application for admission.

Of the 1.5 million aliens removed from the United States in 2003, only 186,151 were formally removed. Actions to initiate the *formal removal of an alien* from the United States are commenced when the presence of that alien is deemed inconsistent with public welfare.[123] Under new policies adopted after 9/11 an immigration officer may determine that an arriving alien is inadmissible because the alien engaged in fraud or misrepresentation or lacks proper documents. Under these circumstances the officer can order the alien removed without further hearing or review, unless the alien states a fear of persecution or an intention to apply for asylum.[124] Furthermore, aliens who are formally removed are subject to fines or imprisonment. In 2003, 79,395 of the 186,073 formal removals were for criminal activity by the alien. Nine countries accounted for almost 92 percent of all formal removals. None of these countries were Middle East countries. (See Table 9.2.)

One controversial aspect of formal removal or deportation of aliens has been the secrecy with which formal removals can be executed. After the 9/11 attacks the court has upheld the right of immigration authorities to hold hearings in secret on possible immigration violations. If immigration officials cite possible terrorists ties as the reason for the formal removal, the Court has upheld that national security justifies the withholding of the names of persons arrested on immigration charges. The courts have ruled that disclosing the names of people arrested on immigration charges could help al-Qaida discover how law enforcement officials were conducting the nation's antiterrorist campaign.[125]

TABLE 9.2   *Nine Top Countries Accounting for Formal Removals in 2003*

Country	Number Removed	Number of Criminals
Mexico	137,819	62,518
Honduras	7,700	1,862
Guatemala	6,674	1,483
El Salvador	4,933	1,982
Brazil	3,797	210
Dominican Republic	3,284	2,139
Colombia	2,081	1,319
Jamaica	1,999	1,480
Haiti	1,032	516

Source: Department of Homeland Security, *2003 Yearbook of Immigration Statistics,* Washington, DC: GPO, September 2004, p. 150.

The Department of Homeland Security has aggressively sought to identify and remove aliens from the United States. After the 9/11 attacks INS and DHS began a policy of strict enforcement of immigration laws, particularly focused against immigrants from predominantly Muslim countries.[126] One of the first programs to focus on enforcing immigration policies was the Alien Absconder Apprehension Initiative. Prior to the 9/11 attacks INS had a poor record for deporting aliens who were no longer legally qualified to remain in the United States.[127]

In the post-9/11 environment, many aliens have been deported for offenses that prior to 9/11 most likely would not have come to the attention of immigration officials. For example, aliens who have legal permanent status can be and are deported for committing misdemeanors crimes. Officials at the Department of Homeland Security regularly scrutinize the records of jails and prisons in search of aliens eligible for deportation. In New York City's Rikers Island jail, an average of 226 inmates per month for the later part of 2004 were identified as deportable aliens.[128] Immigration proceedings are civil, thus, unlike those accused of criminal offenses, aliens identified for deportation hearings have no right to a public defender if they cannot afford counsel. Some foreign visitors have found themselves deported for suspected terror-related activities when law enforcement authorities have become suspicious of what they were photographing. Visitors have been formally deported for photographing bridges, overpasses, nuclear power plants, water-treatment plants, and other similar structures that could be possible terrorist targets.[129]

Children and Citizenship.   Immigration authorities do not differentiate between children and adults in their enforcement. As a result, about 5,000 unaccompanied minors were apprehended in 2004 and processed for deportation.[130] In some cases children are processed for deportation but in other cases parents have been deported while minor children have remained in the United States. For example, children born in the United States of immigrants who have been found to be no longer qualified to remain in the United States can stay even though their parents are deported. It is estimated that tens of thousands of children every year lose a parent to deportation.[131]

In the post-9/11 environment even citizenship has proven no guarantee against deportation. For example, In January 2005, U.S. Immigration and Customs Enforcement sought to remove a Haitian American who obtained citizenship six months prior to being convicted of a felony.

Our Neighbors: Canada and Mexico

The crackdown on border security and immigration control has had the largest impact not on Middle Eastern countries but on our neighbors to the north and south, Canada and Mexico. Although neither country is associated with terrorist groups, fear that Middle East terrorists could enter the United States through Canada or Mexico has resulted in enhanced border security between the United States and these countries.

Canada.   Historically, the United States–Canadian border has been a "good-neighbor" border with large stretches of the border unguarded and fairly easy for one to cross illegally. For example, prior to the 9/11 attacks only 35 agents guarded more than 450 miles of border between Erie, Pennsylvania, and Watertown, New York. Also, despite the large expanse of the border, much of the border lacked air surveillance.[132] Increased concern that terrorists could descend on the United States from Canada has resulted in increased surveillance, border-crossing checkpoints, and the adoption of high-tech border monitoring equipment.

The Canadian border poses difficult challenges to close to terrorists because it is possible to cross the border by air, water, and land, and much of the border is relatively deserted wilderness. A compounding factor is the fact that new immigration controls can cause strain on the "good-neighbor" policy between the United States and Canada whereby U.S. citizens and Canadian citizens cross the border freely and frequently for business and tourism. For example, when the United States set up border-crossing checkpoints on Interstate 87 north of Albany, several major crashes resulting in traffic fatalities occurred that were attributed to unsafe conditions near or at the checkpoints.[133] Also, as aliens desire to cross the Canadian–United States border illegally, some Canadian citizens may be tempted to provide illegal border-crossing services for the lucrative profit that can be realized from guiding people across the border. Few aliens seeking to cross from Canada into the United States attempt the crossing without a guide. Smuggling people across the border is lucrative business; depending on the nationality of the alien, one can make as much as $40,000 for each adult they help cross the border.[134]

Mexico.   The closing of the United States–Mexican border to terrorists is complicated by a long-standing history of a great number of illegal crossings by Mexicans seeking employment in the United States. Furthermore, the amount of commercial traffic resulting from North American Free Trade Agreement (NAFTA) and tourist traffic crossing the United States–Mexico border is so great that any delay in border inspections would cause a tremendous back-up of traffic at border crossings. For example, Laredo, Texas, each year has 4.6 million pedestrians, 1.4 million trucks, 6.8 million private vehicles, and more than 40,000 buses cross its four international bridges, according to U.S. Customs and Border Protection.[135] Thus, while border inspections are necessary, timely inspections are essential, thereby creating conflict between efficiency and border security.

Unlike the Canadian–United States border, relations between the United States and Mexico over illegal immigration has always been strained. Illegal immigration, inspired primarily by the desire for better economic well-being, has resulted in a porous border with thousands of illegal crossings per week, despite fences, guards, checkpoints, high-tech night surveillance, and aerial surveillance of the border. It is difficult to separate discussion of preventing terrorists from crossing the border from stemming illegal immigration by Mexican citizens seeking jobs in the United States. Plus, border security is compounded by the desire to stop the flow of illegal drugs into the United States, as the United States–Mexico border is a major route for illegal drug traffic. Thus, border security is a triple challenge as DHS strives to keep out illegal immigrants, drug smugglers, and terrorists. Due to the large number of illegal crossings, DHS has declared that the U.S.–Mexican border "is not a secure border."[136]

For example, prior to the 9/11 attacks there were many "unofficial" but illegal border-crossing points where people crossed back and forth without difficulty or oversight of the border patrol. One example of such an unofficial crossing was near the small town of Lajitas, Texas, where prior to 9/11 residents of both countries could freely cross from one to the other by a short boat ride. People had been using this unofficial crossing for decades and its frequent use was reflected by the fact that the illegal boat ride across the border cost only $1 from Mexico to the United States and $2 from the United States to Mexico. After the 9/11 attacks the unofficial, illegal crossing was closed and anyone caught crossing the river now faces a $5,000 fine and possible jail time.[137]

The Department of Homeland Security continues to invest millions of dollars to enhance border security with Mexico. The fear is that if it so easy for illegal immigrants to cross, terrorists could cross with the same ease. However, U.S. officials have expressed concern that the Mexican government has not viewed border security with the same perspective. One of the examples cited by U.S. officials of the Mexican government's apparently lax attitude toward illegal border crossings was the Mexican government's publication of 1.5 million copies of a 32-page "comic book" format guide for migrants. These pamphlets instructed migrants on how to illegally cross into the United States and how to minimize the possibility of getting caught by American law enforcement officials once in the United States. Mexico's ambassador to the United States denied that the intent of the book was to promote illegal immigration. He claimed the purpose of the book was to promote safety by instructing those engaging in illegal border crossings about the hazards of drowning or dehydration.[138] However, U.S. officials claimed the guide book is "tantamount to the Mexican government printing a 'how-to' guide to illegally entering the United States."[139] U.S. lawmakers point out that although the book discusses the hazards of crossing the border illegally, it also provides advice on how to avoid arrest and detection by U.S. law enforcement officials after crossing into the United States.[140]

Conclusion: Can the United States Be Terror-Proofed?

Is it possible to turn off the Internet? No. Is it possible to stop illegal immigration into the United States? No. The threats of terrorism stemming from possible cyber-attacks and illegal immigration are threats that have no end in sight. The United States will always be at risk from cyber-attacks. The changing nature of the Internet make it impossible to design software and hardware that would provide 100 percent protection against cyber-attacks and still allow the Internet to be used as it was intended.

Also, there is no solution in sight for the problem of illegal immigration, especially at the southern border of the United States. Following the 9/11 attacks one Customs Service official declared, "Short of building a wall from the Pacific Ocean to the Gulf of Mexico, the task of actually securing the border, most agree, is impossible. It would take a million people, I suppose—maybe more."[141] Three years after the 9/11 attacks and all the effort, money, and resources that that have gone into securing the border of the United States, a survey of border agents and immigration inspectors reported that 60 percent of border patrol agents and immigration officers surveyed said the DHS could do more to stop potential terrorists from entering the country.[142] Responding to data reported by the survey, the President of the National Border Patrol Council said, "Prior to September 22, 2001, it was extremely easy to enter the United States illegally. Incredibly, this has not changed in any meaningful way."[143]

The war on terrorism has had tremendous influence on government policies, actions, and strategies to enhance domestic security to prevent another 9/11-type attack by terrorists. In trying to defend the homeland it is important to understand the larger picture. Often the problem is to shift the focus from the terrorist to the root cause of the problem or the primary reason for the vulnerability. For example, terrorists may be able to use the Internet to execute a crippling cyber-attack on the United States not because terrorists are "super computer programmers" but because the Internet and the computer software and hardware used to access the Internet are full of bugs, flaws, defects, and vulnerabilities. It has been demonstrated that small children with only limited computer skills can hack into databases and control systems. To provide an effective deterrent against cyber-attacks by terrorists it will be necessary to focus attention on the practices of computer users and the quality of software and hardware used by private citizens, commercial companies, and the government.

Likewise, additional border patrol agents, immigration officers, high-tech passports, fences, and surveillance cannot solve border security, especially the United States–Mexican border. Given the incredible number of persons entering the United States, it is impossible for DHS to identify terrorists from among the hundreds of millions of persons who enter the United States each year.[144] However, so long as every person entering the United States is scrutinized as a possible terrorist, DHS will have to continue to demand more and more resources. Some critics argue that the DHS and the U.S. government have taken the wrong approach to securing the United States–Mexican border. They maintain that the waves of illegal immigrants who cross into the United States from Mexico is primarily a labor-market regulation issue rather than a border-security issue.[145] Millions of Mexican citizens will continue to enter the United States illegally so long as there is poverty in Mexico and jobs in the United States. If DHS devotes its time and resources to screening the millions of nonterrorists, it will make it more and more difficult for border agents to focus on identifying potential terrorists. Many argue that the solution to terror-proofing the borders is not more border agents and surveillance but better intelligence so that emphasis can be placed on identifying terrorists attempting to enter the United States.[146]

Finally, the race to secure the borders against terrorists must face the reality that in 2004, 34 million U.S. residents were born outside the United States. Nearly one-third of the total U.S. foreign-born population is from Mexico.[147] Census data project that Hispanics will become the largest single group of minority persons in the United States and that in the southwestern states, including California, Hispanics may eventually be the majority rather than a minority population. Given this demographic shift, it will be necessary to give serious consideration to what the immigration policy of the United States should be.

Cyber-terrorism, border security, and immigration control are not the only long-term challenges the United States will face in the war on terrorism. There are many other threats that need to be addressed to defend the homeland against terrorists. The war on terrorism is going to be one of the most protracted conflicts the United States has seen. Just as the Cold War following World War II in which the United States feared attack from communist countries lasted decades, there is every indication that the war on terrorism will last decades. Given this possibility, it will be necessary to take the time and effort necessary to address the root causes of potential threats rather than throw money at temporary fixes to the symptoms of the problem.

Chapter Summary

- In addition to the anti-terrorism efforts immediately following the 9/11 attacks there are other security issues that need to be addressed, and the need for constant vigilance will continue indefinitely.
- Two threats important to homeland security are cyber-terrorism and immigration control and border security.
- Some fear that tomorrow's terrorist may be able to do more damage with a keyboard than with a bomb.
- The primary tool of the cyber-terrorist is the Internet. Terrorists can use the Internet for intelligence gathering, education, communication, and to launch cyber-attacks.
- Terrorists do not initiate most cyber-attacks but the terrorists use the same tools: viruses, Trojan horses, worms, denial of service, and defacement of websites.
- Internet attacks on digital control systems (DCS) and supervisory control and data acquisition systems could enable a terrorist to do damage to physical infrastructure resulting in economic damage or loss of life.
- Nation-states could use cyber-attacks as a form of cyber-warfare.
- Defending against cyber-attacks is difficult because the Internet is under private control.
- Department of Homeland Security has assumed a key role in cyber-security through the National Cyber Security Division and the United States Computer Emergency Reading Team (US-CERT). Similar to the color-coded terror alerts issued to the public by DHS, US-CERT issues national cyber-alerts.
- Following the 9/11 attacks immigration control and border security were considered so lacking that a major overhaul resulted in these responsibilities being transferred to the Department of Homeland Security.
- Those departments under DHS responsible for immigration control and border security have undertaken aggressive programs to stop illegal immigration, apprehend and deport aliens residing illegally in the United States, and identify terrorists attempting to enter the United States.

- Major initiatives by DHS include the Absconder Apprehension Initiative, the registration of certain male aliens from predominantly Muslim countries, SEVIS, smart passports, and US-VISIT.
- Efforts to enhance border security have had a major impact on the U.S. relations with Canada and Mexico.
- The war on terrorism is going to be one of the most protracted conflicts the United States has seen, and it will be necessary to constantly examine vulnerabilities and adopt new strategies to enhance security.

Terrorism and You

Understanding This Chapter

1. Why is it necessary to look beyond the threats of hijacking and nuclear, biological, and chemical attacks at other potential terror attacks?

2. How is it possible for terrorists to use the Internet to launch a terrorist attack on the United States? Could terrorists do physical harm or cause the loss of life by the use of an Internet attack? Explain your answer.

3. What makes the Internet and computer systems vulnerable to terror attacks?

4. Why is there a concern over attacks on DCS and SCADA systems?

5. What has been the response of the United States in answering the threat of cyber-attacks? What are the primary agencies responsible for cyber-security?

6. Why were responsibilities for immigration control and border security transferred to the Department of Homeland Security?

7. What programs did DHS initiate to enhance immigration control and border security? What have been the criticisms of these programs?

8. How has immigration control and border security affected relationships with Mexico and Canada?

Thinking about How Terrorism Touches You

1. Efforts to enhance Internet security have resulted in the removal of certain information from the Internet. Have you been affected by the removal of any information from the Internet? Do you think removal of sensitive information that could be used by terrorists is a prudent decision or an infringement on freedom of speech? Why?

2. Have you suffered an attack by a virus, worm, or Trojan horse? If so, how did this affect you?

3. Should the private software and hardware industry be made liable for damage due to cyber-attacks if the software or hardware contained bugs that make the attack possible? If this would increase the cost of software and hardware, how much more would you be willing to pay?

4. Do you know of any international student who has been adversely impacted by the new DHS immigration policies? If yes, what were the circumstances?

5. If your name was accidentally placed on the "no-fly" list, how do you think this would affect you? What would you do to correct the error? How long do you think it would take to correct the error?

6. Does it concern you that your passport may contain personal data and biometric data that could be scanned by identify thieves? Why or why not?

Important Terms and Concepts

Absconder Apprehension Initiative
Anti-Virus Programs
Bugs
Customs and Border Protection (CBP)
Cyber-Terrorism
Digital Control Systems (DCS)
Directorate of Border and Transportation Security (BTS)
Executive Order 13231
Firewall
Formal Removal
Hacker
Immigration and Customs Enforcement (ICE)
Internet
National Cyber Alert System
National Cyber Security Division (NCSD)

National Security Agency
Patches
Smart Passports
Student and Exchange Visitor Information System (SEVIS)
Supervisory Control and Data Acquisition Systems (SCADA)
Trojan Horses
United States Computer Emergency Readiness Team (US-CERT)
US-VISIT
Viruses
Voluntary Departure
Withdrawal of Application
Worms

Endnotes

1. Sari Horwitz, "Police Show Strain from Endless Alerts," *Washington Post,* October 18, 2004, p. A1.

2. Ibid.

3. Associated Press, "Gov't: Al-Qaida Threat Still Significant," New York Time Online, www.nytimes.com, November 13, 2004.

4. Ibid.

5. Ibid.

6. Sari Horwitz, "Police Show Strain from Endless Alerts," *Washington Post,* October 18, 2004, p. A1.

7. Ibid.

8. *The National Strategy to Secure Cyberspace.* Washington DC: GPO, February 2003, p. 19.

9. Ronald L. Dick, "Cyber Terrorism and Critical Infrastructure Protection," www.fbi.gov/congress/congress02/nipc072402.htm, July 24, 2002.

10. Brian Krebs, "Feds Falling Short on Cybersecurity," *Washington Post,* www.washingtonpost.com, April 8, 2003.

11. John Schwartz, "Decoding Computer Intruders,"
New York Times Online, www.nytimes.com, April 24, 2003.

12. Associated Press, "Ex-CIA Chief Gates Warns on Cyberterror," New York Times Online, www.nytimes.com, December 5, 2004.

13. Tom Regan, "Terrorism and the 'Net," *Christian Science Monitor,* www.csmonitor.com, October 7, 2004.

14. Eric Lipton and Eric Lichtblau, "Even Near Home, a New Front Is Opening in the Terror Battle," New York Times Online, www.nytimes.com, September 23, 2004.

15. Tom Regan, "Terrorism and the 'Net," *Christian Science Monitor,* www.csmonitor.com, October 7, 2004.

16. Thomas L. Friedman, "Origin of Species," New York Times Online, www.nytimes.com, March 14, 2004.

17. Eric Lipton and Eric Lichtblau, "Even Near Home, a New Front Is Opening in the Terror Battle," New York Times Online, www.nytimes.com, September 23, 2004.

18. Ibid.

19. Tom Regan, "Terrorism and the 'Net," *Christian Science Monitor,* www.csmonitor.com, October 7, 2004.

20. Eric Lipton and Eric Lichtblau, "Even Near Home, a New Front Is Opening in the Terror Battle," New York Times Online, www.nytimes.com, September 23, 2004.

21. Ibid.

22. Michael Ignatieff, "The Terrorist as Auteur," New York Times Online, www.nytimes.com, November 14, 2004.

23. Eric Lipton and Eric Lichtblau, "Even Near Home, a New Front Is Opening in the Terror Battle," New York Times Online, www.nytimes.com, September 23, 2004.

24. Michael Ignatieff, "The Terrorist as Auteur," New York Times Online, www.nytimes.com, November 14, 2004.

25. James C. McKinley, Jr, "State Pulls Data from Internet in Attempt to Thwart Terrorists," New York Times Online, www.nytimes.com, February 26, 2002.

26. Ibid.

27. John Schwartz, "Decoding Computer Intruders," New York Times Online, www.nytimes.com, April 24, 2003.

28. *The National Strategy to Secure Cyberspace.* Washington, DC: GPO, February 2003, p. 5.

29. Brian Krebs, "U.S. Government Flunks Computer Security Tests," *Washington Post,* www.washingtonpost.com, November 19, 2002.

30. Patrick Marshall, "Cyberterrorism: A Clear and Present Danger?" *Federal Computer Week,* November 22, 2004.

31. United States General Accounting Office, *Critical Infrastructure Protection: Significant Challenges in Safeguarding Government and Privately Controlled Systems from Computer-Based Attacks.* Washington, DC: GAO, September 2001, p. 5.

32. Brian Krebs, "U.S. Government Flunks Computer Security Tests," *Washington Post,* www.washingtonpost.com, November 19, 2002; Brian Krebs, "Ex-Officials Urge U.S. to Boost Cybersecurity," *Washington Post,* April 9, 2003, p. E5.

33. Martha Mendoza, "Computer Virus Writers Rarely Go to Jail," *Pocono Record,* August 31, 2003, p. 5A.

34. Amy Harmon, "Digital Vandalism Spurs a Call for Oversight," New York Times Online, www.nytimes.com, September 1, 2003.

35. David McGuire and Brian Krebs, "Attack on Internet Called Largest Ever," *Washington Post,* www.washingtonpost.com, October 22, 2002.

36. Shamsuddin Abdul Jalil, "Countering Cyber Terrorism Effectively: Are We Ready to Rumble? www. giac. org/practical/GSEC/Shamsuddin_Abdul_Jalil_GSEC.pdf, 2003.

37. Barton Gellman, "Cyber-Attacks by Al Qaeda Feared," *Washington Post,* June 27, 2002, p. 1A.

38. Ibid.

39. *The National Strategy to Secure Cyberspace.* Washington, DC: GPO, February 2003, p. 32.

40. Barton Gellman, "Cyber-Attacks by Al Qaeda Feared," *Washington Post,* June 27, 2002, p. 1A.

41. Ibid.

42. Ibid.

43. Associated Press, "'Net Attack Did Extensive Damage," *Pocono Record,* January 28, 2003, p. A5.

44. Jim Bencivenga, "Software: Weak Link in Cyber-security?" *Christian Science Monitor,* www.csmonitor.com, April 2, 2004.

45. Barton Gellman, "Cyber-Attacks by Al Qaeda Feared," W*ashington Post,* June 27, 2002, p. 1A.

46. Ariana Eunjung Cha and Jonathan Krim, "White House Officials Debating Rules for Cyberwarfare," *Washington Post,* August 22, 2002, p. A2.

47. Ibid.

48. *The National Strategy to Secure Cyberspace.* Washington, DC: GPO, February 2003, p. 50.

49. Ariana Eunjung Cha and Jonathan Krim, "White House Officials Debating Rules for Cyberwarfare," *Washington Post,* August 22, 2002, p. A2.

50. Ibid.

51. Robert O'Harrow, Jr. "Sleuths Invade Military PCs with Ease," *Washington Post,* August 16, 2002, p. A1.

52. Ibid.

53. Associated Press, "Ex-CIA Chief Gates Warns on Cyberterror," New York Times Online, www.nytimes.com, December 5, 2004.

54. Ibid.

55. Ibid.

56. Ariana Eunjung Cha and Jonathan Krim, "White House Officials Debating Rules for Cyberwarfare," *Washington Post,* August 22, 2002, p. A2.

57. Bradley Graham, "Bush Orders Guidelines for Cyber-Warfare," *Washington Post,* February 2003, p. A1.

58. Ibid.

59. Ibid.

60. Bradley Graham, "Bush Orders Guidelines for Cyber-Warfare," *Washington Post,* February 2003, p. A1.

61. Ariana Eunjung Cha and Jonathan Krim, "White House Officials Debating Rules for Cyberwarfare," *Washington Post,* August 22, 2002, p. A2.

62. Ibid.

63. *The National Strategy to Secure Cyberspace.* Washington, DC: Government Printing Office, 2003, p. 28.

64. Ibid.

65. Jonathan Krim, "Cyber-Security Strategy Depends on Power of Suggestion," *Washington Post,* February 15, 2003, p. E1.

66. *The National Strategy to Secure Cyberspace.* Washington, DC: Government Printing Office, 2003, p. 9.

67. Jim Benclvenga, "Software: Weak Link in Cyber-security?" *Christian Science Monitor,* www.csmonitor.com, April 2, 2004.

68. Ibid.

69. Amy Harmon, "Digital Vandalism Spurs a Call for

Oversight," New York Times Online, www.nytimes.com, September 1, 2003.

70. Jim Benclvenga, "Software: Weak Link in Cybersecurity?" *Christian Science Monitor,* www.csmonitor.com, April 2, 2004.

71. Andrea L. Foster, "Colleges Fear that Agencies' Surveillance Request will Require Expensive Network Changes," *Chronicle of Higher Education,* http://chronicle.com/daily/2004/042004041402n.htm, April 14, 2004.

72. Stephen Labatron, "Easing the Internet Regulations Challenges Surveillance Efforts," New York Times Online, www.nytimes.com, January 22, 2004.

73. *The National Strategy to Secure Cyberspace.* Washington, DC: Government Printing Office, 2003, p. ix.

74. Ibid., p. xiii.

75. Ibid., p. viii.

76. Ibid., p. 14.

77. Ibid., p. 3.

78. Ibid.

79. Ibid., p. 11.

80. U.S. Citizenship and Immigration Services. "INS into DHS," http://uscis.gov/graphics/othergov/roadmap.htm, January 20, 2005.

81. Ibid.

82. Department of Homeland Security, *2003 Yearbook of Immigration Statistics.* Washington, DC: Government Printing Office, September 2004, p. 3.

83. Ibid.

84. Rachel L. Swarns, "Immigrants Feel the Pinch of Post-9/11 Laws," New York Times Online, www.nytimes.com, June 25, 2003.

85. Michael Janoesky, "9/11 Panel Calls Policies on Immigration Ineffective," New York Times Online, www.nytimes.com, April 17, 2004.

86. Rachel L. Swarns, "Foreign Travelers Face Fingerprints and Jet Lag," New York Times Online, www.nytimes.com, October 1, 2004.

87. Elisabeth Bumiller, "Report Finds Infighting Over Prints," New York Times Online, www.nytimes.com, December 30, 2004.

88. Ibid.

89. "Government to Begin Passenger Screening," New York Times Online, www.nytimes.com, August 27, 2004.

90. Mansoor Ijaz, "One Way to Alienate Moderate Muslims: Depart Cat," *Christian Science Monitor,* www.csmonitor.com, September 24, 2004.

91. Ibid.

92. Rachel L. Swarns, "Senator? Terrorist? A Watch List Stops Kennedy at Airport," New York Times Online, www.nytimes.com, August 20, 2004.

93. Ibid.

94. Michael Janoesky, "9/11 Panel Calls Policies on Immigration Ineffective," New York Times Online, www.nytimes.com, April 17, 2004.

95. Associated Press, "U.S. Issued Visas to 105 Men on Anti-Terror List, *Pocono Record,* November 27, 2002, p. A5.

96. Rachel L. Swarns, "Detention of British Travelers Brings New Policy," New York Times Online, www.nytimes.com, August 16, 2004.

97. Tom Regan, "Foreign Reporters Cry Foul," *Christian Science Monitor,* www.csmonitor.com, June 8, 2004.

98. Elena Lappin, "Your Country Is Safe from Me," New York Times Online, www.nytimes.com, July 4, 2004.

99. "Guard for Bush Isn't Allowed Aboard Flight," New York Times Online, www.nytimes.com, December 27, 2001.

100. Associated Press, "Air Passenger Cries Racism," New York Times Online, www.nytimes.com, September 19, 2002.

101. Associated Press, "Canadian Imams Detained, Told They 'Picked Wrong Time to Fly,'" *Pocono Record,* September 13, 2003, p. A5.

102. David Johnston, "F.B.I. Is Accused of Bias by Arab-American Agent," New York Times Online, www.nytimes.com, July 2003. Washington DC: GPO, February 2003.

103. Associated Press, "Islamic Group Protests Detention at Border," New York Times Online, www.nytimes.com, December 20, 2004.

104. Ibid.

105. U.S. Immigration and Customs Enforcement, "Fact Sheet SEVIS: One Year of Success," www.ice.gov/graphics/news/factsheets/sevis_1year_success.htm, August 3, 2004.

106. Ibid.

107. "Closing the Gates," *Chronicle of Higher Education,* April 11, 2003, pp. A12+.

108. Burton Bollag, "Enrollment of Foreign Students Drops in U.S." *Chronicle of Higher Education,* November 19, 2004, pp. 1+.

109. Michael Arnone, "Watchful Eyes: The FBI Steps Up Its Work on Campuses, Spurring Fear and Anger Among Many Academics," *Chronicle of Higher Education,* April 11, 2003, pp. A14+.

110. "Closing the Gates," *Chronicle of Higher Education,* April 11, 2003, pp. A13.

111. Lila Guterman, "Stalled at the Border," *Chronicle of Higher Education,* April 11, 2003, pp. 20–21.

112. Ibid.

113. Associated Press, "Interpol Says Hundreds of Thousands of Stolen Blank Passports Aid Terrorists," *Pocono Record,* February 28, 2004, p. A5.

114. Jennifer Lee, "Passports and Visas to Add High-Tech Identity Features," New York Times Online, www.nytimes.com, August 24, 2003.

115. Philip Shenon, "New Passport Rules are Put Off by U.S." New York Times Online, www.nytimes.com, September 9, 2003.

116. Jennifer Lee, "Passports and Visas to Add High-Tech Identity Features," New York Times Online, www.nytimes.com, August 24, 2003.

117. Matthew L. Wald, "New High-Tech Passports Raise Snooping Concerns," New York Times Online, www.nytimes.com, November 26, 2004.

118. Ibid.

119. Ibid.

120. Eric Lichtblau, "Treatment of Detained Immigrants Is Under Investigation," New York Times Online, www.nytimes.com, June 26, 2003.

121. Barnaby J. Feder and Tom Zeller, Jr., "Identity Badge Worn Under Skin Approved for Use in Health Care," New York Times Online, www.nytimes.com, October 14, 2004.

122. Department of Homeland Security, *2003 Yearbook of Immigration Statistics.* Washington, DC: Government Printing Office, September 2004, p. 146.

123. Ibid.

124. Ibid.

125. Neil A. Lewis, "Secrecy Is Backed on 9/11 Detainees," New York Times Online, www.nytimes.com, June 18, 2003.

126. Nina Bernstein, "Old Deportation Orders Put Many Out Unjustly, Critics Say," New York Times Online, www.nytimes.com, February 19, 2004.

127. Ibid.

128. Nina Bernstein, "When a MetroCard Led Far Out of Town," New York Times Online, www.nytimes.com, October 11, 2004.

129. Kirk Semple, "Man Arrested Over Photos After 9/11 Is Deported," New York Times Online, www.nytimes.com, August 14, 2004.

130. Nina Bernstein, "Children Alone and Scared, Fighting Deportation," New York Times Online, www.nytimes.com, March 26, 2004.

131. Nina Bernstein, "A Mother Deported, and a Child Left Behind," New York Times Online, www.nytimes.com, November 24, 2004.

132. David Staba, "A Canadian Gate Where Illegal Immigrants Knock," New York Times Online, www.nytimes.com, June 15, 2004.

133. Al Baker, "Checkpoint Near Canada Called Unsafe," New York Times Online, www.nytimes.com, October 23, 2004.

134. David Staba, "A Canadian Gate Where Illegal Immigrants Knock," New York Times Online, www.nytimes.com, June 15, 2004.

135. Associated Press, "New Border Security Technology Faces Test," New York Times Online, www.nytimes.com, November 15, 2004.

136. Eric Lichtblau, "U.S. Takes Steps to Tighten Mexican Border," New York Times Online, www.nytimes.com, March 16, 2004.

137. Jim Yardley, "Because of 9/11, a Uniting River Now Divides," New York Times Online, www.nytimes.com, August 1, 2002.

138. Mary Jordan, "Guide for Mexican Migrants Draws Ire," New York Times Online, www.nytimes.com, January 6, 2005.

139. Ibid.

140. Ibid.

141. Tim Weiner, "Border Customs Agents Are Pushed to the Limit," New York Times Online, www.nytimes.com, July 25, 2002.

142. Rachel L. Swarns, "Study Finds Most Border Officers Feel Security Ought to Be Better," New York Times Online, www.nytimes.com, August 24, 2004.

143. Ibid.

144. Kris Axtman and Peter Grier, "What It Will Take to Terror-Proof Border," *Christian Science Monitor,* www.csmonitor.com, December 10, 2004.

145. Ibid.

146. Ibid.

147. Associated Press, "Summary: Foreign-Born Population Tops 34M," New York Times Online, www.nytimes.com, November 23, 2004.

10

The Cost of Freedom

Terrorism is cheap. Anti-terrorism is very expensive and requires extensive efforts by all levels of government and all citizens. Protecting against a terrorist attack involves more than a one-time response and expense. The United States has become a terror-focused government. Defending the homeland has become its key mission and, to a great extent, the measure of success.

*America's prosperity requires restraining the spending appetite of the federal govern-
ment. I welcome the bipartisan enthusiasm for spending discipline. . . . In the three and
a half years since September the 11, 2001, we've taken unprecedented actions to protect
Americans. We've created a new department of government to defend our homeland,
focused the F.B.I. on preventing terrorism, begun to reform our intelligence agencies,
broken up terror cells across the country, expanded research on defenses against
biological and chemical attack, improved border security and trained more than a half
million first responders. Police and firefighters, air marshals, researchers, and so many
others are working every day to make our homeland safer, and we thank them all.*

—President George W. Bush, State of the Union Address, February 2, 2005

Chapter Outline

Learning Objectives

- The reader will understand how terrorism is financed.
- The reader will understand what the United States is doing to cut off funding for terrorism.
- The reader will appreciate how much is spent on the war on terrorism and the problems that arise in determining how much and how to spend this money.
- The reader will understand that in addition to economic costs there are noneconomic costs in the war on terrorism that can be just as important or more important than the economic costs.
- The reader will appreciate the worldview of the United States as it becomes a terror-focused country and to appreciate how other countries have addressed their terror problems.

Introduction: Counting the Costs

The United States has entered an era of terror-focused government. There is a price tag—a hefty price tag—for this new focus. In his 2005 State of the Union Address, President Bush promised economic discipline and spending restraints. He also promised international and domestic security against terror. This chapter will examine the cost of the war on terrorism. It will look at both economic and noneconomic costs. Noneconomic costs such as psychological well-being, trust in government, and loss of privacy are difficult or impossible to quantify but they have a great impact on quality of life. Often these are the measures that define the standards of a democratic society. This chapter will also discuss the very important topic of foreign relations. This book has focused on domestic issues in the war on terrorism but there are important lessons to be learned from looking at the worldview.

How Terrorists Get Their Money

The cost of terrorism is relatively inexpensive, and terrorists seem to have the money they need to engage in a protracted conflict. The September 11 attacks cost al-Qaida an estimated $500,000. However, the al-Qaida network spent less than $50,000 on each of its major attacks.[1] For example, the Madrid (Spain) train bomb attack is estimated to have cost about $10,000 to carry out. The attack on the U.S. destroyer *Cole* in October 2000 is estimated to have cost about $5,000 to $10,000. These cost estimates cover materials as well as gifts to family members of the suicide bombers.

The ability to finance worldwide terrorist attacks is one of the most valuable assets of the al-Qaida network. The wellspring of cash that finances terrorism is a network of illegal enterprises, including unscrupulous charities, drug trafficking, robbery, extortion, kidnapping, credit card fraud, cigarette smuggling, blackmailing, and arms smuggling. American government officials recognize that cutting off terrorists' funding is an important means of disrupting their operations and to that end have engaged in significant efforts to do so.[2] These efforts have affected the financial health of al-Qaida, as it is estimated its annual budget has been reduced from $35 million prior to September 11, 2001, to $5 million to $10 million in 2003, and more than $200 million in terrorists' assets has been frozen worldwide since the 9/11 attacks. Despite significant efforts to cut off funding for terrorism, a United Nations report on the effect of U.N. sanctions against al-Qaida and the Taliban has indicated that terrorists' networks have shown great flexibility and adaptability in keeping the pipeline of money flowing to fund their activities.[3]

Fund-Raising for Terrorism

The United States Treasury Department reports that unwitting or unscrupulous charities are among the biggest financiers of global terrorism. One of the factors that enables unscrupulous charities to raise large amounts of money and to divert the cash to fund terrorism is that observant Muslims consider giving to charity a religious obligation. Generally, Muslims are expected to give 2.5 percent of their annual income to charity. Taking advantage of this religious tenet, terrorist groups have established a network of charities to funnel money to fund terrorism. This network is worldwide and operates extensively in the United States. Since 9/11 the Bush Administration has designated more than 390 groups and individuals as "global terrorists" and has frozen the assets of these groups and individuals and banned charitable giving to these groups and individuals.[4] Of this number, 27 have been Islamic charities that have been designated as financiers or supporters of terrorism. Most are international relief agencies that for years canvassed the mosques and raised millions.[5] Persons donating to these banned "charities" can be investigated and may be arrested for supporting terrorism.

Charities are important in funding terrorism in two ways. First, charities serve as a direct source of income. One of the biggest Islamic charity funneling money to support terrorism in the United States was the Holy Land Foundation. In July 2004, five former leaders of the Holy Land Foundation were arrested on charges that they funneled $13 million to Palestinian terrorists to support suicide bombers and their families.[6] Former Attorney General John Ashcroft claimed the Holy Land Foundation was the "North American front for Hamas."[7] Many who contribute to these charities that support terrorism do so unwittingly, as the charities claim that they support needy Islamic families and children and hide their support of terrorism from the public. For example, Global Relief Foundation, an Illinois-based charity, sent 90 percent of its donations abroad in 2003 for the support of the al-Qaida, Osama bin Laden, and other known terrorist groups, but most people who contributed to Global Relief Foundation were probably not aware of this fact.[8]

Second, charities are important because they provide a conduit to move money worldwide that has been raised through various illegal enterprises. For example, money that has been raised by various enterprises, including criminal activities, can be "donated" to these charities that support terrorists. Then the charities, under the cover of transferring the money from the United States to overseas, can legally move the money overseas where it will be siphoned off by various terrorist front organizations.

Funding Terrorism through Criminal Enterprises

Of the various criminal enterprises to fund terrorism, drug trafficking is at the top of the list of illegal money-raising activities. The 1992 United Nations International Narcotics Control board report warned of the link between illegal drugs and terrorism. President George W. Bush declared, "It's important for Americans to know that the traffic in drugs finances the work of terror, sustaining terrorists, that terrorists use drug profits to fund their cells to commit acts of murder." The Drug Enforcement Agency (DEA) warns the public that there is a link between drug trafficking and global terrorism, as terrorists use the drug trade to fund attacks.[9] The Islamic terrorists responsible for the Madrid train bombings financed their plot with sales of hashish and Ecstasy.

In the United States there have been a number of specific incidences that demonstrate the link between the funding of terrorism and the illegal drug trade in the United States. For example, a series of DEA drug raids in January 2002 uncovered a methamphetamine drug operation in the Midwest involving men of Middle Eastern descent who were shipping money made from drug sales back to Middle East terrorist groups such as Hezbollah. In January 2004, two Michigan men were charged in connection with a drug ring that authorities alleged provided financial support for Hezbollah.[10] In March 2004, two men pleaded guilty in federal court in San Diego in a scheme to trade hashish and heroin for anti-aircraft missiles that in turn were to be supplied to the Taliban and al-Qaida.[11]

One of the largest sources of income for terrorism from the drug trade is opium from Afghanistan. Despite the U.S. invasion of Afghanistan and the displacing of the Taliban from power, in 2004, opium from Afghanistan accounted for 87 percent of the world supply, according to data from the United Nations. The opium drug trade accounted for about 60 percent of Afghanistan's 2003 gross domestic product. The opium trade is so ubiquitous in Afghanistan and the link to terror so direct that Antonio Maria Costa, executive director of the Vienna-based United Nations Office on Drugs and Crime, commenting on the illegal drug trade in Afghanistan, said, "The terrorists and traffickers are the same people."[12] The Afghanistan opium drug trade was estimated at about $2.8 billion dollars in 2004. However, little of the profits from the illegal drug trade goes to those who grow the poppies used to produce opium. Most of the profits from the drug trade go to the drug traffickers, warlords, and militia leaders, according to the United Nations.

Cutting Off the Flow of Cash

Overseas the United States is attempting to cut off the cash terrorists realize from drug trafficking by a two-prong strategy. First, the United States has various in-country programs to reduce drug production. For example, the United States and the United Nations have various programs in Afghanistan to discourage farmers from growing poppies and to encourage cultivation of other crops. One of the difficulties in discouraging farmers from growing poppies is the large difference in price between poppies and legal crops. An Afghanistan farmer may realize about $390 (U.S. dollars) per hex acre income from wheat but the same hex acre of poppies will net $4,600 (U.S. dollars). Thus, it is little surprise that a 2004 United Nations survey of opium production in Afghanistan indicated opium production up 64 percent from 2003. The survey indicated that there were about 2.3 million people, or about 10 percent of the total population, cultivating opium, up 35 percent from 2003.

Second, to cut off the flow of cash to terrorism from drug trafficking overseas, the United States Navy and Coast Guard patrol the high seas to detect and apprehend drug traffickers. Using intelligence and photo imaging data of ship movements, the United States Navy and Coast Guard intercept and inspect ships suspected of transporting illegal drugs. For example, in December 2003, the United States Navy seized two tons of hashish in the Persian Gulf, worth about $8 million to $10 million.[13] In September 2004, the Coast Guard seized about 27 tons of cocaine in the Eastern Pacific. For 2004, the Coast Guard seized in excess of $7.3 billion in illegal drugs.[14]

A new tactic being used in the United States to cut off the flow of illegal cash to terrorists has been the scanning of financial records of persons and organizations suspected to have ties with terrorism to detect "high-risk" financial transactions. In December 2004, the Department of Homeland Security began using various computer databases to allow investigators to match financial transactions against a list of some 250,000 people and firms with suspected ties to terrorist financing, drug trafficking, money laundering, and other financial crimes. Using a network of various private databases, the Department of Homeland Security tries to match financial transactions with people and organizations on the department's terrorist watch list.[15]

Numerous federal agencies are involved in the effort to cut off the funds of terrorists. Table 10.1 lists the various key U.S. government entities responsible for deterring terrorist financing. The list includes the Central Intelligence Agency, the Department of Homeland Security, the Department of Justice, the National Security Council, the Department of State, and the Department of Treasury.

The Cost of the War on Terrorism

The cost of terrorism may be cheap but the cost of the war on terrorism is terribly expensive. In 2004, the Department of Homeland Security spent $5 million to buy an entire 640-acre town and 1,200 surrounding acres in New Mexico for the purposes of training first responders in simulated terrorist attacks and other disasters.[16] The cost of airline security continues to rise, which means passengers and airlines have to pay more and more. In 2004, the report of the National Commission on Terrorist Attacks Upon the United States said it would cost at least $1 billion annually for the next five years in order to close the remaining gaps in airline security.[17] The security surcharge enacted to have passengers pay for additional security screening is providing insufficient funds to cover all of the new security procedures, which is resulting in proposals to double the surcharge. Both the airline industry and passengers are becoming concerned about the rising cost of security.[18] In addition to security costs are the costs of research. For example, the Department of Homeland Security awarded the University of Maryland $12 million to develop a new research center on the behavioral and social underpinnings of terrorism. The goal of the research is to help the government predict when and where attacks will occur, to better prepare the public for attacks, and to recover more quickly.[19] The cost of the war on terrorism impacts not only federal agencies but also state and municipal agencies. For example, in 2004, Washington D.C., police spent $10.6 million on overtime and equipment for security checkpoints.[20] During the Orange terror alert of 2004, the Delaware River Joint Toll Bridge Commission spent $2 million for state police in New Jersey and Pennsylvania to patrol five of its most critical bridges.[21]

It is impossible to calculate the total spending of all government and private agencies in the war on terrorism. However, the 2004 budget for only the key federal agencies involved in the war on terrorism was $52.8 million. Figure 10.1 shows that the majority of this ($23.9 million) went to the Department of Homeland Defense and the Department of Defense received the second highest amount ($15.2 million). This amount to fight the war on terrorism does not include the $200 billion for the U.S. military troops and equipment in Afghanistan and Iraq. There is no end sight to the cost of the war on terrorism. The Bush Administration has asked for an increase in the 2005 Department of Homeland Security budget and all indications are that the cost of the war on terrorism to other agencies will continue to rise.

Kinks in the System

Not only is the war on terrorism costly but there is also considerable debate as to how the money is spent. The nation's counterterrorism budget has been described by New York City Mayor Michael Bloomberg as "pork barrel politics at its worst."[22] The reason for Bloomberg's criticism is that the formula for distributing federal grants and subsidies to

TABLE 10.1 *Key U.S. Government Entities Responsible for Deterring Terrorist Financing*

Department	Bureau/Division/Office	Role
Central Intelligence Agency		Leads gathering, analyzing, and disseminating intelligence on foreign terrorist organizations and their financing mechanisms; charged with promoting coordination and information-sharing between all intelligence community agencies.
Homeland Security	Bureau of Customs and Border Protection	Detects movement of bulk cash across U.S. borders and maintains data about movement of commodities into and out of the United States.
	Bureau of Immigration and Customs Enforcement (ICE—formerly part of the Treasury's U.S. Customs Service)	Participates in investigations of terrorist financing cases involving U.S. border activities and the movement of trade, currency, or commodities.
	U.S. Secret Service	Participates in investigations of terrorist financing cases, including those involving counterfeiting.
Justice	Bureau of Alcohol, Tobacco, Firearms, and Explosives (ATF)	Participates in investigations of terrorist financing cases, including alcohol, tobacco, firearms, and explosives.
	Civil Division	Defends challenges to terrorist designations.
	Criminal Division	Develops, coordinates, and prosecutes terrorist financing cases; participates in financial analysis and develops relevant financial tools; promotes international efforts and delivers training to other nations.
	Drug Enforcement Administration (DEA)	Participates in investigations of terrorist financing cases involving narcotics and other illicit drugs.
	Federal Bureau of Investigation (FBI)	Leads all terrorist financing investigations and operations; primary responsibility for collecting foreign intelligence and counterintelligence information within the United States.
National Security Council		Manages the overall interagency framework for combating terrorism.
State	Bureau of Economic and Business Affairs	Chairs coalition subgroup of a National Security Council Policy Coordinating Committee, which leads U.S. government efforts to develop strategies and activities to obtain international cooperation.
	Bureau of International Narcotics and Law Enforcement Affairs	Implements U.S. technical assistance and training to foreign governments on terrorist financing.
	Office of the Coordinator for Counterterrorism	Coordinates U.S. counterterrorism policy and efforts with foreign governments to deter terrorist financing.
Treasury	Executive Office for Terrorist Financing and Financial Crime	Develops U.S. strategies and policies to deter terrorist financing, domestically and internationally; develops and implements the National Money Laundering Strategy as well as other policies and programs to prevent financial crimes.
	Financial Crimes Enforcement Network (FinCEN)	Supports law enforcement investigations to prevent and detect money laundering, terrorist financing, and other financial crime through use of analytical tools and information-sharing mechanisms; administers the Bank Secrecy Act.
	Internal Revenue Service (IRS) Criminal Investigation	Participates in investigations of terrorist financing cases with an emphasis on charitable organizations.

(continued)

TABLE 10.1   Continued

Department	Bureau/Division/Office	Role
Treasury *(continued)*	IRS Tax Exempt and Government Entities	Administers the eligibility requirements and other IRS tax law that apply to charitable and other organizations that claim exemption from federal income tax.
	Office of Foreign Assets Control	Develops and implements U.S. strategies and policies to deter terrorist financing; imposes controls on transactions; and freezes foreign assets under U.S. jurisdiction.
	Office of the General Counsel	Chairs Policy Coordination Committee for Terrorist Financing, which coordinates U.S. government efforts to identify and deter terrorist financing; coordinates U.S. government actions regarding implementation of, and imposition of, economic sanctions under Executive Order 13224 with respect to the freezing of terrorist-related assets.
	Office of International Affairs	Provides advice, training, and technical assistance to nations on issues including terrorist financing deterrence.

Source: Terrorist Financing (Washington, D.C.: GAO, November 2003), pp. 8–9.

states and cities uses a state-by-state allocation system rather than a threat-based formula. Starting with the assumption that any city could be a terrorist target, Congress allocated federal grants and subsidies with the goal to provide something to everyone, rather than focus on high-risk cities. Using this system, states that have had no or little threat of attack by terrorists have received substantial federal counterterrorism funding. This funding formula re-

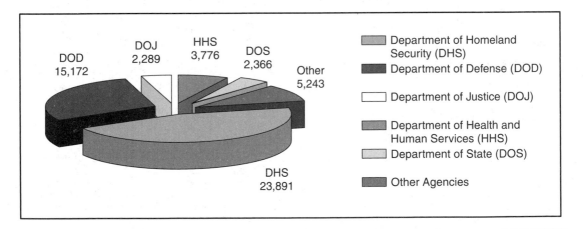

FIGURE 10.1   *Budget Authority for Combating Terrorism by Agency for Fiscal Year 2004 (Total Budget Authority Is $52,732 Million)*

Source: GAO Subcommittee on National Security, Emerging Threats, and International Relations, Committee on Government Reform, House of Representatives, *Combating Terrorism: Evaluation of Selected Characteristics in National Strategies Related to Terrorism.* GAO-04-408T (Washington, D.C.: GAO, February 3, 2004).

Note: "Other Agencies" includes the Departments of Energy ($1,588 million), Agriculture ($368 million), Transportation ($283 million), Commerce ($153 million), Veterans Affairs ($145 million), Interior ($115 million), Treasury ($90 million), Labor ($67 million), Housing and Urban Development ($2 million), and 18 other independent agencies (totaling $2,432 million).

BOX 10.1 • *Consider This: 88009*

The Department of Homeland Defense owns Playas, New Mexico, 88009. The 640-acre township includes a 25-unit apartment complex, community center, grocery store, medical clinic, fitness centers, a bank, a gas station, a post office, a bowling alley, and an airstrip. The DHS also purchased 1,200 acres surrounding the town. The town is located in a remote area of southwestern New Mexico. Playas was built in the early 1970s to house the employees and infrastructure of the Phelps Dodge copper smelter. Once a town of about 1,000, the company shut down in 1999, leaving a virtual ghost town of about 40 families. When the copper-smelting operation shut down in 1999, the Phelps Dodge Corporation put the town up for sale.

The DHS wanted Playas so it could transform the town into a terrorist response training center. When approached by DHS to help facilitate the $5 million purchase of Playas, Senator Pete Domenici responded, "Are you crazy?" The residents living in Playas will be allowed to continue to live in one end of the town.

The DHS partnered with New Mexico Tech and New Mexico State University to open the Play-as Research and Training Center. The agency will use Playas for national homeland security training and research programs. New Mexico State University will focus on agricultural and food supply security. The Department of Homeland Security will use Playas as a real-world training center for training first responders, including medical personnel, and for emergency operations and training in prevention and response to suicide bombings and other related programs.

New Mexico Tech, a state-supported research university, has signed a five-year contract with DHS to operate the Playas Research and Training Center. It is probably the only university in the United States to own an entire town.

Question

1. The purchase price for Playas was $5 million but annual operating costs and training costs will also cost millions. Do you think it is a worthwhile investment for the DHS to buy an entire town for training purposes? Why or why not?

sults in Alaska, which has 649,000 residents, receiving nearly $92 per resident in security funds in 2003 and 2004, compared with states such as New York, which received $32 per resident, California, which received $22, and Texas and Florida, which received $21 each.[23] As a result, high-risk cities are unable to fund needed security improvements, whereas rural states are trying to find ways to spend the money.

A proposal to provide extra security aid to high-risk cities was vetoed by the House in June 2004. However, in December 2004, the Department of Homeland Security shifted a larger share of its annual $3.5 billion in anti-terrorism grants to the nation's largest cities.[24] Recognizing the importance of getting adequate counterterrorism funding to high-risk cities, the DHS will funnel 42 percent of its aid to New York, Washington, and Los Angeles.[25] Another change is that DHS funding will be shifted to directly funding cities rather than using state programs as conduits for federal counterterrorism funding. State programs tend to diffuse the federal subsidies to both urban and rural areas in response to political pressure. According to DHS officials the new policy reflects the high-risk threat to these cities due to the large number of possible targets such as bridges, signature buildings, government facilities, and symbolic targets.[26]

In addition to criticisms regarding the distribution of federal funds, states and cities are complaining that the funds authorized by Congress are not reaching the local authorities.[27] A Congressional analysis found that in 2004, more than 80 percent ($5 billion) of the counterterrorism money approved by Congress to help cities, counties, and states remains stuck in the administrative pipeline.[28] For various reasons the money is not getting to the agencies that need it to buy equipment, train personnel, pay overtime, and provide for security enhancements. Much of the blame for the delay is due to delays at the state level. State agencies have been unable to develop criteria, guidelines, and administrative procedures to distribute the federal money they receive to counties and cities.[29]

Of greater concern to some is not that money is stuck in the pipeline but the fear that federal counterterrorism grants and subsidies will stop flowing through the pipeline. Many states and cities have exhausted their reserve funds in building up their capacity to respond to terror threats and must rely on federal funding to continue to be able to protect tunnels, ports, airports, building, financial districts, schools, transportation arteries, and other possible terror targets. States and cities are relying more on federal funding, but the federal government is having difficulty providing the funds that states expect and need. The federal government is engaged in deficit spending and the cost of the war in Iraq continues to escalate. As a result, the federal government is finding it necessary to cut back both on its own counterterrorism spending and on its grants and subsidies to states and cities. For example, in October 2004, a budget shortfall of about $500 million at the department of Immigration and Customs Enforcement restricted ICE's ability to conduct terror investigations and forced ICE to release on bond 25,000 illegal immigrants because it lacked space to incarcerate them.[30] Federal cutbacks in the funding given to states in turn have forced states and cities to cut back spending on counterterrorism programs.[31]

Terror-Related Fraud

The nation's financial crisis has caused some to question the $40 million second inauguration of President Bush as they wondered if the money could not be better spent.[32] Although some may consider the inauguration excessive, of greater concern has been terror-related fraud. Millions of dollars have been siphoned off by terror-related fraud, committed by individuals, by businesses, and by the government.

Immediately following the 9/11 attacks many unscrupulous individuals engaged in criminal schemes to claim compensation or to establish fraudulent charities to bilk the public for money. For example, an Arkansas woman tried to defraud a fund for victims of the September 11, 2001, attacks, claiming that her dead brother was a firefighter who was killed in the attacks. The scope of the fraud can be appreciated when you consider that the average settlement paid to families of firefighters averaged more than $4 million.[33] In another case, a Michigan man claimed that his brother died in the collapse of the Twin Towers. The man received more than $268,000 before it was discovered that the claim was fraudulent. Insurance companies allege that numerous businesses have filed fraudulent 9/11-related claims.[34] Even state governments have been accused of using anti-terrorism funds improperly. The governor of Alaska proposed to buy a personal jet with anti-terrorism funds, claiming it was necessary for responding quickly to possible terror attacks. An audit of the state of Texas spending of anti-terror funds indicated that nearly $600 million in federal anti-terrorism funds was spent improperly.[35] Despite the potential seriousness of such misappropriation, some of the alleged abuses appear mind-boggling. For example, it is alleged that one jurisdiction purchased a trailer that was used to haul lawn mowers to "lawn mower drag races," claiming the trailer was "emergency equipment."[36]

The Other Costs of the War on Terrorism: Extremism in the Defense of Liberty

The human rights group Amnesty International released a statement in 2003, saying, "The world has become more dangerous, and governments more repressive, since the effort to fight terrorism began after the September 11, 2001, attacks on the United States. What would have been unacceptable on September 10, 2001, is now becoming almost the norm."[37] One of the difficult costs to calculate in the war on terrorism is the cost of extremism in the defense of liberty. Extremism in the name of protecting the homeland deprives citizens of liberty, creates conflict, diminishes the stature of the United States as perceived by foreign countries, and can be counterproductive in fighting true threats of terrorism.

Extremism in the defense of liberty can manifest itself in numerous ways—often in unexpected situations. For example, consider the debate between community residents of Little Egg Harbor, New Jersey, when a National Guard F-16 fighter jet's accidental release of gunfire resulted in the strafing of Little Egg Harbor Intermediate School with 27 rounds of 20mm cannon fire in November 2004. While some residents expressed concern and fear for their safety and that of their children, others argued that it was "profoundly unpatriotic to question the military during a time of war."[38] In another example where national defense was offered as the defense, three laboratory workers at Boston University were exposed to harmful bacteria at a bio-defense laboratory in January 2005. When some community residents expressed concerns over community safety, the risk was justified with the defense, "The nation needs this lab."[39]

Government agencies have used and continue to use the war on terrorism as the overriding reason in responding to criticisms of community safety and actions that otherwise would not be justified or permitted. At times the government agencies use the claim of national security to circumvent exiting laws. For example, the Defense Department has claimed that to sustain the national defense mission, it needs waivers from environmental laws, such as the Clean Air Act, toxic waste disposal requirements, and the endangered species laws.[40] The Defense Department requested and received exemptions from Congress to these laws and regulations, claiming that compliance would impede the Defense Department's ability to conduct combat exercises and weapons testing necessary for national security.[41] Environmental groups decry the circumvention of environmental controls in the name of national security and have filed lawsuits to force the Department of Defense to comply with Clean Air laws and toxic waste disposal regulations.

Two concerns that constantly emerge in the discussion of excessive actions by the government that are justified by arguments of national security are (1) infringement on privacy rights and government secrecy and (2) the government's alleged use of torture in interrogating terrorists. The war on terrorism has resulted in government actions in these two areas that alarm many critics.

The War on Terrorism and Privacy

As a result of the search for terrorists in the United States and abroad, U.S. citizens are losing more and more of their privacy while government is keeping more and more

BOX 10.2 • *Case Study: Freedom of Speech*

From the time of the Revolutionary War freedom of speech has always been restricted during war. If not by legislation, freedom of speech has been chilled by public opposition against anti-war speech. The war on terrorism is no exception. Professor Ward Churchill of the University of Colorado at Boulder is the lightning rod of the free speech controversy in the war on terrorism. Churchill, who teaches ethic studies, called those who died in the 2001 attacks "little Eichmanns." In an essay he wrote he said that the victims of the 9/11 attack "were not innocent civilians but a technocratic corps at the very heart of America's global financial empire."[42] Churchill has written other essays and books critical of the United States and Israel and their policies toward the Palestinians, including charges of genocide against the Palestinians. He has been denounced by families of victims of the 9/11 attack, the governor of Colorado, Bill O'Reilly of Fox TV, and others. Churchill's public speaking engagements have been canceled and one college has refused to pay him his speaker's fee, which he claims is owed to him.

Professor Churchill issued a defense of his remarks, saying,

I am not a defender of the September 11 attacks, but simply pointing out that if U.S. foreign policy results in massive death and destruction abroad, we cannot feign innocence when some of that destruction is returned. . . . I have never characterized all the September 11 victims as "Nazis." What I said was that the "technocrats of empire" working in the World Trade Center were the equivalent of "little Eichmanns." It should be emphasized that I applied the "little Eichmanns" characterization only to those described as "technicians." Thus, it was obviously not directed to the children, janitors, food service workers, firemen and random passers-by killed in the 9/11 attack.

Fox TV commentator Bill O'Reilly has called for the firing of Professor Churchill as has the governor of Colorado and numerous other public officials and citizens.[43] The University of Colorado Boulder Faculty Assembly called his remarks "controversial, offensive, and odious" but expressed support for his right to express them.[44] The American Civil Liberties Union renounced the calls for his termination. The ACLU said,

Freedom of faculty members to express views, however unpopular or distasteful, is an essential condition of an institution of higher learning that is truly free. We deplore threats of violence heaped upon Professor Churchill, and we reject the notion that some viewpoints are so offensive or disturbing that the academic community should not allow them to be heard and debated. Also reprehensible are inflammatory statements by public officials that interfere in the decisions of the academic community.

Questions

1. Professor Churchill has received hundreds of death threats, his public speeches have been disrupted by violent demonstrators, and his vehicle has been vandalized. The Colorado Senate and House have passed resolutions denouncing Churchill's comments as "evil and inflammatory." Does the right to freedom of speech protect Churchill's remarks or is there a line at which point "freedom of speech" becomes treason? If so, do Churchill's remarks cross that line?

2. What are the standards for the acceptable limits on freedom of speech? Who gets veto power over controversial speakers and when should retaliation occur for those who voice unpopular dissent?

3. Some have compared the reaction to Professor Churchill's remarks to McCarthyism and have argued that "well-meaning college administrators who sought to defuse controversy by treating the principle of free speech as one that was expendable in a time of international crisis and domestic anxiety" have done the greatest damage to academic freedom. Does freedom of speech guarantee a professor the right to express any opinion, even if there are strong beliefs that his opinions are not based on fact or truth?

4. Many figures in history have expressed controversial opinions during their lifetimes.

BOX 10.2 • Continued

Some of these persons have been recognized by history as great leaders who expressed what were unpopular opinions at the time, but these opinions would later become guiding principles for society. For example, during his lifetime many of the speeches of Martin Luther King, Jr. were denounced as Communist-inspired and detrimental to the welfare of the nation. Nelson Mandela was imprisoned for his rhetoric against apartheid in South Africa. How can society distinguish between free speech that denounces popular beliefs that are later to be recognized as social evils and treason or other harmful speech that should be banned?

information from the public. One of the most intrusive and influential factors in the loss of privacy is the USA Patriot Act of 2001. The Patriot Act has had far-reaching impact on privacy. Its provisions for secret searches, less restrictions on wiretaps, and a general lowering of the standard of proof for certain law enforcement actions are well known and have been previously discussed. However, there are provisions of the Patriot Act and other laws and regulations that are less well known but just as intrusive. The anti–money-laundering compliance laws, for example, require that persons purchasing real estate submit to a name check to determine if their name is on the government's list of people blocked from participating in "any transaction or dealing . . . in property or interests" within the United States. People on this list have been identified by White House Executive Order 132224 "to have committed, or to pose a significant risk of committing, acts of terrorism."[45] If a person's name matches a name on the list, the transaction must be immediately halted and a report filed with the Treasury Department.[46] The buyer pays the fee for the name search.

Following the 9/11 attacks stricter employment documentation and screening laws were passed based on the rationale that it would make it more difficult for "sleeper" terrorists to remain in the United States or to obtain jobs where they could use their employment to carry out a terror attack. As a result of this legislation, thousands of airline workers lost their jobs. Especially controversial was the provision that required U.S. citizenship for certain airline workers when U.S. citizenship is not even a requirement for military service. Also, new restrictions prohibit persons with felon convictions from obtaining employment on federal contract jobs or military bases. Because there is no time limit on when one was convicted, some workers with long-past felony convictions found themselves unemployed due to the Patriot Act.[47]

News reporters have also experienced the impact of post-9/11 legislation and policies regarding privacy. They have expressed concern over the government's attempts to gather information against suspected terror suspects by issuing subpoenas for reporters' notes and confidential sources.[48] The news media argue that without the protection of the First Amendment to protect confidential sources and interview and investigation records of the reporter, it is not possible to have a free press.[49]

While government agencies have reduced the privacy rights of citizens, they have increased government secrecy. Some members of Congress accuse the Bush Administration of excessive secrecy in the war on terrorism.[50] Senator Charles E. Grassley (R-IA) cited the retroactively classifying of information the Justice Department gave to Congress as an example of government secrecy that appears to do "harm to transparency in government, and it looks like an attempt to cover up the F.B.I.'s problems in translating intelligence."[51] In 2002, Congress heard testimony from a Federal Bureau of Investigation translator who accused the FBI of incompetence and a lack of urgency in translating intelligence documents. In 2004, two years after the testimony, the Justice Department retroactively classified the information and warned congressional members and staffers not to disseminate the information contained in the briefings. Also, the FBI refused to allow the translator to testify in lawsuits filed by families of the September 11 attack victims, claiming her testimony would violate "the state secret privilege."[52] Congressional members expressed surprise at the Justice Department's actions and suggested that the purpose of the action was to "quash Congressional oversight."[53]

Many have become fearful that the government's encroachment on privacy rights has or will become excessive. Not only do critics of government's encroachment on privacy claim violation of constitutional rights by current practices but they also point to possible future violations as the government positions itself to collect even more data on individuals. One example cited of data gathered by the government that could be subject to misuse is the Department of Education's proposal to create a comprehensive database of enrollment records of all college and university students in the United States.[54] The record-keeping proposal is justified by the argument that Congress needs the data to provide accountability in elementary and high schools by having the ability to see which students go on to postsecondary education and to track their progress. The Department of Education issued assurances that the data would not be used for other purposes or given to other federal agencies such as the Department of Homeland Security. Critics counter by arguing, "Since the September 11 attacks, the balance between privacy and the public interest [has] been shifting. We're in a different time now, a very different climate. There's the huge possibility that the database could be misused."[55]

The skepticism of the critics that such a database would not be available to DHS or other government agencies is based on the fact that over the years many databases that initially appeared to have no connection to homeland security have been appropriated by the DHS. In fact, DHS has come to rely on databases gathered by private companies as a primary source of intelligence about individuals. One of the largest private companies that provides personal data about individuals to the DHS, which it in turn uses for actionable intelligence, is ChoicePoint Inc.[56] ChoicePoint gathers comprehensive personal data about individuals, including financial data, data about relatives, DNA identification data, criminal records, testing for illegal drug use, criminal background, personal data, and credit record. ChoicePoint even has access to private databases, such as lists of employees who have admitted to shoplifting whether they were charged and convicted or just admitted the offense to their employer.[57] ChoicePoint claims to have "billions of details" about individuals in their databases and "the ability to access all relevant information with a single query."[58] Thus, it is little surprise that the Department of Homeland Security has contracted with ChoicePoint for intelligence data to assist in investigating terrorist activity and to track down people who pose a threat.

The War on Terrorism and Torture

The pictures of what appears to be the torture of the prisoners of Abu Ghraib prison in Iraq shocked the citizens of the United States and resulted in the investigation and prosecution of those who allegedly were responsible for the torture and mistreatment of Iraqi prisoners. Since the revelation of alleged torture at Abu Ghraib, numerous other allegations of torture of alleged terrorist suspects have emerged. Investigations by the International Committee of the Red Cross have charged that "the American military has intentionally used psychological and sometimes physical coercion tantamount to torture on prisoners at Guantanamo Bay, Cuba."[59] Allegations of torture closer to home come from aliens of Middle East descent who were detained in New York following the 9/11 attacks who claim they were mistreated and physically abused by correctional officials.[60]

The U.S. government has claimed that "a few bad apples" were responsible for the abuse of prisoners at Abu Ghraib, but there is evidence to suggest that the United States has chosen to systematically engage in or permit the torture of terror suspects. Critics of the government's alleged torture of terror suspects accuse the U.S. government of being so shocked by the September 11 attacks that "the United States government was willing to consider doing almost anything—including actions previously thought morally suspect—to prevent another such catastrophe."[61] The emergence of "torture memos" exchanged between the Justice Department and the president seem to suggest that the Bush Administration operated on the premise that in a time of necessity, the president and the military could disregard torture conventions, international treaties, and the law of the land.[62] In legal memorandums by the Justice Department and the Defense Department, President Bush was advised that the Geneva Convention and other anti-torture covenants do not apply to suspected terrorist detainees.[63] President Bush has publicly declared that the United States rejects the use of torture, but allegations by accused terror suspects and various investigations seem to suggest that the United States has used what many would call torture in interrogating suspected terrorists.

Another charge against the Bush Administration is that the Central Intelligence Agency and the government has engaged in a practice called *rendition*. Rendition is when the U.S. government arranges for the transfer of a suspected terrorist from the United States or another country to a country such as Pakistan or Egypt, where the suspect can be interrogated by the use of torture by local authorities. The CIA and the Bush Administration deny any involvement in such alleged clandestine transfer of terror suspects, but various investigations and charges by persons who have allegedly been the victims of such torture appear to provide evidence that such charges are credible.[64]

The Bush Administration has retreated from an August 2002 legal memorandum that defined torture extremely narrowly. The 2002 memorandum asserted that "mistreatment rose to the level of torture only if it produced severe pain equivalent to that associated with organ failure or death."[65] The 2002 memorandum advised the President that "the Geneva Conventions did not bind the United States in its treatment of detainees captured in the fighting in Afghanistan."[66] In December 2004, the Bush Administration redefined its definition of torture while still denying that the administration sanctioned or had sanctioned the use of torture. However, to some it appears that from 2002 to 2004, the 2002 memorandum reflected the policy and practice of the Bush Administration. This charge is reinforced by the assertion of the International Committee of the Red Cross that U.S. personnel have engaged in torture of detainees, both in Iraq and at Guantanamo.[67] The sanctioned use of torture by government officials and the failure to condemn such use when evidence suggests charges are credible is a high price to pay for the war on terrorism. It is a challenge to the Constitution and the rights that citizens believe are held sacred.

Correcting Extremism

Although there are charges that the United States has engaged in extremism in the defense of the homeland, one must also consider the "self-correction" that occurs as extreme practices are made public and criticized, and the government retreats from the abusive practice or policy. There are several examples that can be cited to illustrate this self-correcting process, including (1) the Treasury Department's restrictions on U.S. publications by authors in embargoed countries, (2) DHS's rules against disclosure of nonclassified information by its employees, (3) the Department of Defense's policy on mandatory anthrax shots, (4) the CIA's proposal for domestic spying, and (5) the Transportation Security Administration's policy on search of females.

As discussed in previous chapters, the United States can direct foreign policy by prohibiting individuals and businesses from engaging in economic trade with countries under sanctions. The U.S. Treasury Department Office of Foreign Assets Control (OFAC) applied sanctions against U.S. citizens who were alleged to have engaged in trade with Iraq prior to the U.S. invasion of Iraq. In 2003, OFAC issued advisories that essentially made it impossible for authors from sanctioned nations to have scholarly writings published in the United States. Critics quickly pointed out that the ban in effect discouraged the publication of dissident speech from within these oppressive regimes. Publishers joined in a successful lawsuit to effect a change in the policy. In December 2004, OFAC issued new guidelines that eased the restrictions on authors from sanctioned countries to allow U.S. publishers to work with them as long as they are not government representatives.[68]

In another example of a reversal of a policy criticized as overly repressive was the DHS's policy that "prohibits department employees from giving the public sensitive but unclassified information" and authorized the government to "conduct inspections at any time or place to ensure that the agreement is obeyed."[69] The two unions that represent the DHS employees, the National Treasury Employees Union, and the American Federation of Government Employees, argued that the policy was overly broad in what information it restricted employees from disclosing and that it gave "government unprecedented leeway to search employee homes and personal belongings in violation of the Fourth Amendment."[70] In January 2005, responding to threats of lawsuits, DHS dropped its requirement for new employees to sign the oppressive nondisclosure agreement and instituted a program to provide training on the proper education and training for handling sensitive information.[71] The two unions and civil liberties groups approved of the change in policy but still expressed concern of the "broad and vaguely defined" definition of information that was prohibited from disclosure.[72]

The Department of Defense feared that front-line troops may be exposed to deadly bio-warfare agents and wanted to inoculate troops against such agents if possible. An experimental vaccine against anthrax was developed and the Department of Defense adopted a mandatory vaccination program. Soldiers who refused vaccination were subject to disciplinary action and/or dismissal from the service. Numerous soldiers objected to the mandatory vaccinations and some health experts called into question the safety of the experimental vaccine. Soldiers opposed to the mandatory vaccination filed suit against the Department of Defense. The courts sided with the soldiers and ruled that the mandatory vaccination program was illegal. The court ruled, "Congress has prohibited the administration of investigational drugs to service members without their consent. This court will not permit the government to circumvent this requirement."[73] Lawyers for the soldiers said they would initiate an effort to ensure the government reverses all punishments that were imposed for refusing an order to take the vaccine and will seek compensation for service members who contended they were harmed.[74]

The previous examples illustrate how the court can be a significant force in correcting extremism in the defense of liberty. However, not all self-corrections have required court intervention or the threat of court intervention. Two examples of how public opinion and debate can cause a change in government polices are the discontinuation of the Total Information Awareness (TIA) program by the CIA and the change of policy of the TSA on search of females.

The CIA wanted to develop a program called Total Information Awareness, a secret program that would allow the CIA to develop the ability to spy on American citizens in the United States and to develop a database that could track a person's entire existence.[75] The program would have authorized spy agencies to gather intelligence inside the United States and would have allowed them to recruit citizens as informants on other citizens.[76] The agency would not have to disclose to citizens that intelligence data had been gathered nor would the agency have to have probable cause of terror-related activities or to have approval of the courts to gather intelligence on citizens. When the program concept became known to the public, both public opposition and congressional opposition forced the CIA to abandon the program. Congress refused to fund the program and the firestorm of public criticism discouraged the government from developing the program.[77]

When two women blew up Soviet airliners by smuggled bombs on board the aircraft by secreting them in their bras, the Transportation Security Administration instituted new search procedures for female travelers in the United States. The new search procedures required TSA personnel to search between the breasts of female passengers when performing pat-down security searches. Furthermore, the new policy did not require TSA screeners to have reasonable suspicions to justify the search of females passengers. The policy allowed men to perform the search and the search was conducted at the security checkpoint without any privacy. If the woman was wearing heavy outer clothing, such as a jacket, she was required to remove it. Many women complained that the underclothing they were wearing under their jacket was not appropriate to expose in public. There were numerous complaints from women about the new policy. Women complained that they were being "groped," randomly selected for searches, treated rudely during the search, and sometimes asked personal and inappropriate questions by the TSA personnel. The policy required TSA screeners to use the "back of their hand" to perform the search but many women complained this procedure was not followed. After many complaints and much negative media coverage of the policy, in December 2004, TSA changed the policy and TSA screeners stopped searching between female passengers' breasts during the pat-down search.

These examples indicate that extremism can be tempered. Policies that allegedly violate constitutional rights can be changed. Practices that are intrusive and offensive but do little to enhance security can be stopped. Thus, while there are indeed numerous criticisms of the overzealousness of the government in defending the homeland against terrorism, there is reason to believe that bad policy and practices can be changed.

The Growing Conflict with Foreigners

Hidden costs associated with the war on terrorism can be so enormous that the costs can be unbearable. One of these costs is the changing attitude of Americans toward foreigners—particularly those from Mexico and Middle Eastern countries. Suspicion and distrust of Hispanic immigrants was prevalent prior to the 9/11 attacks but it seems the new focus on national security has highlighted these feelings. Although there is little to connect Hispanic immigrants to terrorism, it appears that many persons conceal their prejudice toward Hispanic immigrants using the guise of national security. In many communities, and not just limited to southwestern-border states, Hispanics find local residents bitter or even violently opposed to the presence of Hispanics in their city.[78]

Hispanic immigrants, and even Hispanic American citizens, often are fearful and mistrusting of law enforcement officials. Some communities report that Latinos are reluctant to contact the police if they are victims of a crime or a witness to a crime.[79] Even when law enforcement attempts to build bridges with the Latino community, residents are suspicious of their motives. For example, when the Fairfax County police held a Spanish-language child safety seat demonstration in Herndon, Virginia, despite a large Latino population, no one showed up. Police officials said they believe the lack of attendance was because the "Hispanic community thought it was a ploy to snare the undocumented."[80] Law enforcement officials report that fear of the police is so widespread that some immigrants hoard food and stay indoors because "they are afraid of venturing outside their homes, believing they will get stopped by police and asked to produce documents that prove their immigration status."[81]

Some argue that Hispanic immigration threatens to "disrupt the political and cultural integrity of the Untied States."[82] Dr. Samuel Huntington, chair of Harvard University's Academy for International and Area Studies, warns that Hispanic immigration threatens the United States with the loss of its "core Anglo-Protestant culture and may soon be divided into two peoples with two cultures (Anglo and Hispanic) and two languages (English and Spanish)."[83]

The greatest conflict, however, is developing between Americans and Muslims. A national poll reported that one in four Americans holds a negative stereotype of Muslims, and almost one-third respond with a negative image when they hear the word *Muslim.*[84] A 2003 poll by the Pew Research Center reported that 46 percent of Americans believe that Islam is more likely than other religions to encourage violence among its believers and 42 percent of Americans believe all Muslims are anti-American.

Muslims are aware of the prejudice of Americans toward them. A poll by the University of Michigan in 2004 of Arab Americans and Muslim Americans in the Detroit area (the largest concentration of Arab Americans in the United States) reported that 60 percent say they are worried about the future of their families. Fifteen percent say they have suffered some form of harassment or intimidation. People who appear to be of Middle Eastern descent, even if they are from India or some other country not identified with the war on terrorism, say they have a feeling of persecution. They feel especially singled out during high terror alerts and at airport security checkpoints. In New York and New Jersey, Muslim residents of communities say they feel there is conflict and tension between the Muslim community and their neighbors.[85] The Federal Bureau of Investigation has issued warnings that tend to confirm this bias toward the Muslim community. The FBI has cautioned that terrorist attacks or the Iraq war could prompt a wave of hate crimes against Arab Americans, Muslims, and other minorities in the United States. Other indicators of bias against people who appear to be from Middle Eastern countries are reports of discrimination by private businesses and reported dismissals from jobs with little or no explanation other than vague reasons citing national security. Many Muslim parents report that they fear that their children may become targets of bigotry.[86]

Racial Profiling

Prior to September 11, 2001, racial profiling was not considered an acceptable practice by law enforcement officers. A 1999 Gallup Poll reported that 81 percent of the public disapproved of racial profiling. Prior to the 9/11 attacks racial profiling referred primarily to selective enforcement against Latinos and blacks. Although the public still disapproves of racial profiling against Latinos and blacks in routine law enforcement investigations, there is support for racial profiling of young Middle Eastern men at airports and national security checkpoints. There is also support for racial profiling in identifying illegal immigrants from Mexico.

The DHS and the Justice Department have been careful to deny that their policies related to immigration enforcement and investigation screening are based on racial profiling. Actions by the DHS and the Justice Department, however, seem to suggest that race often is a primary, perhaps the only, factor in selecting a person for an interview, further screening, or additional security.

Some have argued that "Middle Eastern males should be targeted for search because, 'based on historical experience, [they] seem more likely than others to include suicide bombers or just bombers.'"[87] Thus, although there is still a general disapproval for racial profiling when applied to Latinos and blacks, the public approves of profiling young, Middle Eastern or Islamic men at airports or other high-risk security venues.[88]

Studies have indicated that since the 9/11 attacks in some cities the number of Middle Easterners cited for offenses by law enforcement has been significantly higher than all others charged with offenses.[89] This statistic raises the question: Is there racial profiling of Middle Easterners? Local law enforcement officials deny targeting Middle Eastern males. They claim that any increase in citations to Middle Eastern males is due to changes in patrol or police procedures, not racial profiling. The Justice Department denies that there is racial profiling by federal law enforcement agencies. The department said it conducted a survey of federal operations and concluded that racial profiling by federal law enforcement agents does not appear to be a systemic problem.[90]

In 2003, the Bush Administration issued a policy statement from the Justice Department regarding guidelines on racial profiling. The guidelines govern the conduct of 70 federal law enforcement agencies. The guidelines do not ban racial profiling. They do bar federal agents from using race or ethnicity in their routine investigations but the guidelines allow for clear exemptions for investigations involving terrorism and national security matters.

International Relations

The focus of this book has been on defending the homeland against terrorism, but it is also necessary to examine how U.S. domestic policy aimed at fighting terrorism has influenced foreign relations that in turn has influenced the effectiveness of the United States to fight terrorism. In his 2005 Inaugural Address, President Bush told Americans that spreading liberty around the world was "the calling of our time." In spreading liberty around the world, he said that America "will not impose our own style of government on the unwilling. Our goal instead is to help others find their own voice, attain their own freedom and make their own way." There is a high cost to be paid for this calling.

The Bush Administration has at times has compared the war on terrorism to the Cold War with the Soviet Union. The rhetoric has painted an image of the United States and "freedom-loving" nations in a united fight against terrorism. In this "international" war on terrorism American politicians claim they are leading a popular war against an unpopular enemy. President Bush declared in his 2005 State of the Union Address that in leading the war on terrorism the United States will behave as a benevolent superpower. He said, "The United States has no right, no desire, and no intention to impose our form of government on anyone else. This is one of the main differences between us and our enemies. They seek to impose and expand an empire of oppression, in which a tiny group of brutal, self-appointed rulers control every aspect of every life." Most Americans accept this premise and believe that "while the U.S. necessarily shapes foreign polices to support our national interests, those same interests are not necessarily in opposition to the interests of other nations and cultures. . . . To the contrary, Americans are convinced that the U.S. . . . elevates values emphasizing freedom."[91] The rest of the world does not share this viewpoint.

Terrorism is not a common enemy of the nations of the world. It is a philosophy, a policy, a tactic. The use of terrorism by one group does not unite them and identify them with a worldwide network of terrorists with common goals. The terrorist attacks on the United States are perpetuated by a specific group of enemies, not by a single worldwide group of terrorists. Unlike the Cold War, where sides were divided into those who supported the Soviet Union and communism and those who supported the United States and democracy, the war on terrorism has multifactional fronts, groups, and players. There is no overarching theme that unites the United States and its allies against a common enemy.[92]

There are two key reasons many nations do not attach the same significance to the U.S. war on terrorism as Americans do. First, many nations have endured their own war on terrorism for years or decades. Simply stated, the war on terrorism is old news to them. In 2003, there were 175 worldwide significant terrorism events according to the U.S. State Department Patterns of Global Terrorism report. Only 1.5 percent of terrorism's casualties in 2003 were U.S. citizens. Many countries are fighting and have been fighting their own war on terrorism. Groups around the world have used terror tactics to attack their government. Terrorism is and has been a significant problem in Israel, the Philippines, Russia, Peru, Spain, numerous countries in Africa, and many other nations. Many nations have been engaged in a war on terrorism much longer and with greater ferocity than the United States. For example, since 2000, Israel has had more than 120 suicide bombings. African nations have experienced terrorism on a scale described by some as genocide and Iraq experiences nearly daily suicide bombings or assassinations by terrorists. Russia has been battling the Chechens for decades and Spain has suffered attacks by the Basque terrorists for decades.

Indonesia has had nearly constant conflicts with terrorists, as has Peru in battling the Shinning Path. Terror is a global struggle but each nation battles enemies unique to it, whereas the Bush Administration has described the war on terrorism as a global battle against a common enemy. Thus, many nations find that the U.S. war on terrorism is not the universal pivotal global struggle of the age.[93]

Some nations are critical of the tactics that the United States has adopted in its war on terrorism and the impact of these tactics on their nation. For example, President Luiz Inácio Lula da Silva of Brazil criticized the U.S. strategy, saying, "The exploitation of fear is a highly developed and refined science, but Brazil is not convinced by this culture that triumphed in the American election. What concerns us in Latin America is that, in the name of defending its security, the United States will escalate the wars it has begun."[94]

The second reason that many nations are less concerned than the United States with the war on terrorism is because many of them have more pressing priorities, such as poverty, clean water, economic revival, trade, and other internal economic issues that pose grave dangers to their country. The United States enjoys a level of economic prosperity and well-being that far exceeds that of most nations of the world. In many countries the issues of adequate health care, clean water, transportation infrastructure, education, and other services that are taken for granted in the United States are major concerns of the government.

President Bush has said that the lack of support for the war on terrorism from certain Middle Eastern countries is because they "hate our freedom." This analysis as to the cause of the unpopularity of the United States fails to take into account the impact of U.S. policy on those countries. The Report of the Defense Science Board Task Force on Strategic Communication concluded that Middle Eastern countries do not hate America's freedom, but rather they hate America's policies. In particular, they object to "what they see as one-sided support in favor of Israel and against Palestinian rights, and the long-standing, even increasing, support for what Muslims collectively see as tyrannies, most notably Egypt, Saudi Arabia, Jordan, Pakistan and the Gulf states." French terror expert Xavier Raufer asserts that the Bush Administration is "20 years behind the curve" in understanding international terrorism and the opposition to the United States.

Polls of international opinion toward the United States show that approval of the United States has significantly dropped since the 9/11 attacks. Among Arab countries the favorable attitudes toward the United States are extremely low and are dropping. Table 10.2 reports the results of public opinion polls conducted in 2004 on how Arabs view the United States. This poll indicates that even among so-called Arab "allies," such as Egypt, which receives over $2 billion annually in foreign aid from the United States, public disapproval of the United States is at record lows. In June 2004, 98 percent of Egyptians polled stated they had an unfavorable view of the United States. In Saudi Arabia, another "ally" in the war on terrorism, only 4 percent of those polled had a favorable attitude toward the United States. A large majority in Saudi Arabia believe that the United States "seeks to weaken and dominate Islam itself."[95] The highest approval rating among the Arab countries polled was 20 percent (Lebanon).

Even among European "friends," the percent of people polled who report they view the United States favorably is dropping. Table 10.2 indicates that in England, France, and Germany approval rate of the United States has dropped 17 to 26 percent. Only in Britain did more respondents report a favorable attitude (58 percent) toward the United States than an unfavorable attitude. These polls tend to support the assumption that the United States has become more alienated from other nations because of its strategy on the war on terrorism.

TABLE 10.2   *Arab Opinion of the United States*

Country	June 2004		April 2002	
	Favorable	*Unfavorable*	*Favorable*	*Unfavorable*
Morocco	11	88	38	61
Saudi Arabia	4	94	12	87
Jordan	15	78	34	61
Lebanon	20	69	26	70
UAE	14	73	11	87
Egypt	2	98	15	76

Source: "Impressions of America 2004: How Arabs View America, How Arabs Learn about America," A Six Nation Survey Conducted by Zogby International, July 2004.

Lessons from Others

As mentioned, many other countries have had to deal with the problem of terrorism. Like the United States, many of these countries face the problem of how to defend their homeland against terror without "trampling on individual rights or risking charges of discrimination."[96] Many of these countries face the same problems as the United States in striking this balance and, thus, there are lessons to be learned by studying their response to terrorism.

A common struggle among "democratic" countries has been what to do with "suspected" terrorists, especially foreign terror suspects. Often the country does not have sufficient evidence to arrest, try, and convict the suspected terrorist but fears that if left at liberty the person may commit terrorist acts. Like the United States, many allow suspected terrorists to be held without charges or trial. However, some countries, unlike the practices of the Bush Administration, place a limit on how long terrorist suspects can be held without charges. For example, in Spain, terrorism suspects can be held for up to 13 days without charge and as long as four years without trial.[97]

Some countries have laws that provide for punishments very different from those in the United States. For example, in France, it is against the law to associate with terrorists.[98] In the United States, such a law most likely would be considered a violation of the First Amendment. Israel imposes "collective punishment" on all who provide "aid and comfort" to terrorists, even if they had no part in the terror act. The United States has no such similar punishment, and "collective punishment" for those not responsible for a terrorist crime most likely would be unconstitutional in the United States. However, in Israel, to deter suicide

TABLE 10.3   *Percentage of People Who View the U.S. Favorably*

Country	Summer 2002	March 2003	May 2003	March 2004
Britain	75%	48%	70%	58%
France	63%	31%	43%	37%
Germany	61%	25%	45%	38%

Source: Pew Research Center for the People and the Press, 2004.

bombings the military has the authority to destroy the home of the suicide bomber—even if the bomber was not the owner of the home and even if others without knowledge of the actions of the bomber lived in or owned the house. Nearly always this punishment causes "innocent" parties to suffer homelessness. For example, when a relative living in a home with others commits a suicide bombing, the house where they lived is destroyed, even if the other family members can demonstrate they had no knowledge of the bomber's intention. The government says such harsh retaliation is necessary to motivate family members to encourage people living in the same house from deterring other household members from becoming involved in terrorism. Since 2001, Israel has demolished more than 612 homes of Palestinian militants involved in attacks on Israelis, resulting in approximately 4,000 people being left homeless.[99] Without doubt, collective punishment would be unconstitutional in the United States.

Often foreign countries face the same ethical dilemmas as the United States in responding to terrorism. For example, following the 9/11 attacks Germany passed a law, the Air Safety Act, that, like the United States, allows the defense minister to order hijacked aircraft shot down. In January 2005, President Hörst Kohler voiced concern that the law may be unconstitutional. The German debate as to the legal and ethical authority to take innocent lives as a measure to stop a greater harm by terrorists is not that different from the debate in the United States. In the 9/11 attacks the order to shoot down the third hijacked aircraft came too late to execute. However, the debate as to the ethical and legal consequences of "what if" the order had been executed and the military shot down the aircraft is still of great concern to many. Is it ethical to take the lives of hundreds of innocent people for the greater good of protecting the homeland?

Britain has had a similar problem as the United States with foreigners suspected of terrorism. Like the United States, Britain practiced indefinite detention of foreigners suspected of terrorism without charging or trying them. However, in December 2004, the British Court ruled that indefinite detention without trial or charges violated European human rights laws. In ruling on the practice of indefinite detention, Judge Lord Leonard Hoffman said in his criticism of the practice, "It calls into question the very existence of an ancient liberty of which this country has until now been very proud: freedom from arbitrary arrest and detention. The real threat to the life of the nation, in the sense of a people living in accordance with its traditional laws and political values, comes not from terrorism but from laws such as these."[100]

Unable to hold suspected foreign terrorists without charge or trial, Britain had to come up with alternative policies that would protect the public but preserve civil liberties. In January 2005, the British government unveiled its new policies. Instead of imprisoning suspected foreign terrorists, the Home Secretary will have the power to give suspects curfews, tag them with electronic bracelets, limit their access to telephones and the Internet, restrict their communications with "named individuals," and, if necessary, place them under house arrest.[101] As the U.S. courts consider the constitutionality of "enemy combatants" being held without charge or trial, it may be necessary for the government to examine the new British policies in case the courts rule against the government.

The United States is spending millions of dollars to explore the causes of terrorism. Many European countries, especially France and Spain, offer insight into this question, as they are finding that their prisons are becoming breeding grounds for new recruits for radical Islamic terror groups. The problem is most severe in France, where Muslims make up only 10 percent of the country's population but account for approximately 60 percent of the prison population.[102] In Europe, Islam is becoming the religion of the repressed. The United States may want to examine the effect of repression and economic distress as a cause of terrorism. If repression and economic distress are identified as key factors in promoting terrorism, this finding may influence policies and practices governing illegal immigration from Mexico. Many claim that the key motivation for illegal immigrants is economic distress.

Conclusion: A Terror-Focused Government

The U.S. government has become a terror-focused government. Defending the homeland has become its key mission and, to a great extent, the measure of success. Many have joined ranks with the government in defending the homeland against terrorism and are working to root out potential threats. For example, Member of Freedom House, a conservative-learning rights organization based in New York, searched Mosques in the United States to see if they could find evidence of any threat to America. They reported that books and publications containing the hate-filled, vitriolic writings of the minority Muslim Wahhabi sect were found in mosques throughout America.[103] Some examples of the anti-American and anti-Jewish writings include such statements as "It is a religious obligation to hate Christians and Jews" and "It is forbidden for a Muslim to become a citizen of a county (such as the United States) governed by infidels."

Officials throughout the United States have embraced the fight against terrorism, sometimes too enthusiastically. For example, in October 2003, Lt. General William G. Boykin, in a speech before an evangelical Christian audience, likened the war against Islamic militants to a battle against "Satan," resulting in criticism by Muslims that his rhetoric encouraged prejudice against all Muslims.[104] Sometimes government officials have invoked the analogy of the war on terrorism in inappropriate circumstances, as when in February 2004, Education Secretary Rod Paige called the nation's largest teachers' union a "terrorist organization."

Financing the war on terrorism has become a key component of the government's budget at all levels: local, state, and federal. Also, there are many hidden costs in conducting the war on terrorism, including financial costs and intangible costs, such as psychological well-being, trust in government, and erosion of privacy. Who pays for the various counterterrorism actions often is at the heart of the debate in determining how to better defend the homeland. For example, the federal government wants states to adopt a "standard" driver's license and to verify that applicants are U.S. citizens or legal immigrants before issuing an applicant a license. State officials do not dispute the wisdom and intent of the measure but argue that such federal mandates would be a massive unfunded mandate on the states and would require state officials to take on the role of immigration officers.[105]

Counterterrorism actions are not only expensive, they sometimes ensnarl innocent citizens in a maze of red tape causing them to suffer emotional and economic loss or cause some to question the legitimacy of the government's action. For example, citizens who have discovered their names placed on government watch lists find that there is no explanation as to how their names were placed on the list or how to remove the names from the list if they believe the names are listed without cause. In November 2004, 680 people had filed complaints with the DHS that their names have been mistakenly placed on the watch list. Some citizens have had to resort to suing the government, as they have been unable to have their names removed from the watch list.

Floo Floo Bird Syndrome

In examining the response of the United States to the war on terrorism, columnist William Safire said, "The architect Frank Lloyd Wright warned of the floo floo bird, 'the peculiar and especial bird who always flew backward . . . because it didn't give a darn where it was going, but just had to see where it had been.'"[106] Safire accused that in responding to the war on terrorism, the United States was similar to the floo floo bird. He said, "With our eyes fixed on our rearview mirror, we obsessively review catastrophes past when we should be looking thorough our windshield at dangers ahead." The United States has spent millions of dollars examining the 9/11 attacks. Millions more have been spent on aviation security to make sure that there is not a repeat of the 9/11 attacks. At the slightest hint of a possible security weak point, new policies and practices have been adopted to further ensure that there is not a repeat of a 9/11-type attack. Many are critical that such focus on preventing future attacks like the past attacks will lead to the same situation that made the 9/11 attacks possible in the first place: a lack of anticipation of new threats. At the time of the 9/11 attacks airline security focused on threats that were identified in the 1960s and 1970s. Despite warnings from various sources of the danger of terrorists using aircraft in a way that had never before been experienced in the United States, government officials and airline security officials did not anticipate this new strategy.[107]

Another danger of the floo floo bird syndrome is that sometimes blame is assessed against people based on present information but information that was not known to them or others at the time of the incident. One example is the tendency to accuse or suspect those who donated to Muslim "charities" that are now on the government's list of supporters of terrorism as supporting terrorism when they did not know of the charity's support of terrorism at the time of their donation. For example, an investigation of a mosque accused of ties with terrorism revealed that the mosque was established and financed by the former Houston Rockets star Hakeem Olajuwon. Olajuwon issued a statement that said, "he had not known of any links to terrorism when the donations were made, before the government's crackdown on the groups, and would not have given the money if he had known."[108]

The war on terrorism is an expensive war. It will take a great toll on the United States, both economically and noneconomically. It will be a long war. It is a difficult mission to defend the homeland against all possible attacks. The consequences of a nuclear, biological, or chemical attack could be so devastating that all costs in preventing such attacks would pale if such an attack were successful. A successful cyber-attack by terrorists could cause billions of dollars in damage and could result in causalities exceeding that of the 9/11 attacks. If a cyber-attack caused such damage, there would be much regret that more was not spent on cyber-counterterrorism. However, there is not an endless pot of money for counterterrorism. Although terrorism may be cheap, the war on terrorism is expensive. Deciding what is the right amount to spend on counterterrorism will be one of the major decisions by local, state, and federal government for years, perhaps decades, to come in this new age of terror-focused government.

BOX 10.3 • *Up Close and Personal: Should Those Wrongly Accused Be Compensated?*

On a tip, Tarek Albasti, and eight other Evansville, Indiana, Muslim men, were rounded up by Federal Bureau of Investigation agents, shackled, paraded in front of a newspaper photographer, and jailed for a week. Forty agents investigated them for a week and in the end, the tip turned out to be false and the men were released. But four of the men were then listed in the national crime registry as having been accused of terrorism, even though they were never charged. The branding prevented them from flying, renting apartments, and landing jobs.[109] (They were later removed from the watch list.)

The source of tips accusing persons of terrorism can often come from unreliable sources. Vindictive family members provide some tips as a means to get back at the accused due to a family feud. Some tips are provided by people who hope that by providing federal agents with information it will help them with their own immigration problems. Some tips are provided by ex-wives as a way of striking back at their former husbands. If the same tips were received accusing a person of criminal activity, few courts would authorize a search warrant, much less an arrest warrant.

However, the policy of the Department of Homeland Security and the Department of Justice is that in the event of charges of terrorism, suspects are to be immediately imprisoned and held without bail, if possible, until it can be determined if the suspects have terrorist ties. Often suspects are arrested and detained without interviewing or assessing the validity of the information provided by the tipster. As a result, numerous people have been detained on suspicion of terrorism based on false allegations. For example, Mohamed Alajji, a Michigan trucker born in Yemen, was jailed for seven days before agents interviewed his accuser, who turned out to be making false claims against him to press a family feud.[110] Alajji was set free but the or-

deal destroyed his business and he was forced to return to Yemen. In another case, Esshassah Fouad was accused by his former wife of plotting terrorism. He was jailed until it was determined the charges against him were false. However, Fouad was charged with violating his immigration status by not attending school, despite his defense that he had missed school because he was in jail.[111]

Questions

1. The Justice Department defends the immediate jailing of those accused of terrorism before the facts of the case can be verified, claiming, "With terrorism you do not have the luxury of sometimes waiting to figure out if the guy is truly a terrorist." Do you believe the risk of failing to apprehend a terrorist outweighs the risk of imprisoning an innocent person? Why or why not?

2. Is jailing those accused of terrorism without first confirming or investigating the evidence a "double-standard" in that in the criminal justice system normally the assumption of innocence requires that the prosecutor provide evidence to justify the jailing of a suspect? Explain your answer.

3. Should people who are falsely imprisoned while the government investigates the tips against them be financially compensated by the government? Why or why not?

4. Should there be a punishment against federal agents for falsely imprisoning suspects? Why or why not?

5. Other than false imprisonment of innocent persons, what are the potential harms that can result from a policy in which accused suspects are imprisoned first and the tip verified after they have been imprisoned?

Chapter Summary

- The United States has entered an era of terror-focused government.

- The cost of terrorism is relatively inexpensive. The average terrorist attack costs about $50,000.
- Terror is financed by criminal enterprises. The major source of funding from criminal enterprises comes from drug trafficking.
- Terror is financed by unwitting or unscrupulous charities.
- Many government agencies are working to cut off the flow of cash to terror groups.
- The cost of counterterrorism is very expensive to local, state, and federal governments.
- Local and state governments have relied on the federal government for funding but the federal government is having difficulty providing them the funds they need.
- Some counterterrorism funding is misspent.
- In addition to economic costs, the war on terrorism has noneconomic costs. Chief among these are extremism in the defense of liberty, loss of privacy, and loss of trust in government.
- Some extreme policies and practices are self-correcting in that the government takes actions to reverse these policies and practices. Sometimes this action is spurred by the courts.
- Prejudice against foreigners, particularly Hispanics and those of Middle Eastern descent, is a concern.
- Many foreign nations do not approve of U.S. actions and policies in the war on terrorism.
- Foreign countries have similar problems with terror as the United States, and there are lessons that the United States could learn from observing how these countries respond.
- The United States must anticipate new strategies that terrorists may use and not become focused on defending the homeland against the same terror tactics that have been used in the past.

Terrorism and You

Understanding This Chapter

1. How is terror financed?

2. What is the federal government doing to cut off the flow of cash to terrorists?

3. Why is the war on terrorism so expensive?

4. What are some of the noneconomic costs of the war on terrorism?

5. What are some examples of extremism in the defense of liberty?

6. What are some examples of self-correcting actions taken by the government in the correction of extremism in the defense of liberty?

7. How has the war on terrorism affected relations with and attitudes toward Hispanics and persons of Middle Eastern descent in the United States?

8. What is the worldview of the U.S. actions in the war on terrorism?

Thinking about How Terrorism Touches You

1. What impact, if any, do you think that the government's crackdown on charities that support terrorism has on "legitimate" charities that help needy people in the Middle East?

2. Do you think that people in the United States who use illegal drugs believe that they are supporting terror? Explain.

3. Have you felt any loss of privacy or personal freedom due to the war on terrorism? Explain.

4. Do you think the use of extreme interrogation tactics to obtain information from terror suspects is justified? Why?

5. Do you think TSA agents at airline checkpoints should pay more attention to Arab-looking people than other passengers? Why?

6. What do you think of the fact that many countries view the United States as an aggressive superpower and disapprove of the nation's in the war on terrorism?

7. In the 2004 presidential election, did the candidates' stand on terrorism influence your vote? Explain.

Important Terms and Concepts

Collective Punishment
Extremism in the Defense of Liberty
Floo Floo Bird Syndrome
Global Relief Foundation
Holy Land Foundation
Playas Research and Training Center
Pork Barrel Politics
Racial Profiling

Rendition
Terror-Focused Government
Torture
Total Information Awareness
U.S. Treasury Department Office of Foreign Assets
    Control (OFAC)
Ward Churchill

Endnotes

1. Associated Press, "U.N.: Most Terror Attacks Cost Under $50G," *New York Times* Online, www.nytimes.com, August 27, 2004.

2. "Terrorist Financing." Washington, DC: GAO-01-163, November 2003, p. 1.

3. Associated Press, "U.N.: Most Terror Attacks Cost Under $50G," *New York Times* Online, www.nytimes.com, August 27, 2004.

4. David B. Ottaway, "Islamic Group Banned by Many Is Not on U.S. Terrorist List," *Washington Post,* Washingtonpost.com, December 27, 2004.

5. Laurie Goodstein, "Since 9/11, Muslims Look Closer to Home," *New York Times* Online, www.nytimes.com, November 15, 2004.

6. Eric Lichtblau, "Arrests Tie Charity Group to Palestinian Terrorists," *New York Times* Online, www.nytimes.com, July 28, 2004.

7. "Terrorist Financing." Washington, DC: GAO-01-163, November 2003, p. 14.

8. Ibid., p. 15

9. Donna Leinwand, "Exhibit Links Terror, Drug Traffic," *USA Today,* September 13, 2004, p. 6D.

10. Associated Press, "Hezbollah Allegedly Linked to Drug Ring," *New York Times* Online, www.nytimes.com, January 21, 2004.

11. "National Briefing: West," *New York Times* Online, www.nytimes.com, March 4, 2004.

12. Associated Press, "Drug Profits in U.S. Linked to Middle East Terrorists," *Pocono Record,* September 2, 2002, p. A5.

13. Thom Shanker, "Navy Seizes Hashish; Sees Ties to Al Qaeda," *New York Times* Online, www.nytimes.com, December 20, 2003.

14. Department of Homeland Security, "27 Tons of Co-

caine Seized from Two Vessels in Pacific," www.DHS.gov/dhspublic/display?content=4046, September 27, 2004.

15. Eric Lichtblau, "Homeland Security Department Experiments with New Tool to Track Financial Crime," New York Times Online, www.nytimes.com, December 12, 2004.

16. Associated Press, "N.M. Town Is Anti-Terror Training Center," New York Times Online, www.nytimes.com, December 2, 2004.

17. Sara Kehaulani Goo, "Deadlines Urged for Terror Fixes," *Washington Post,* August 17, 2004, p. A13.

18. Eric Lichtblau, "Color Crazed: Terror Policy: Between Fear and Freedom," New York Times Online, www.nytimes.com, January 11, 2004.

19. Kelly Field, "U. of Maryland Wins Federal Grant for Research Center on What Makes a Terrorist," *Chronicle of Higher Education,* http://chronicle.com/daily/2005/01/2005011103n.htm, January 11, 2005.

20. Spencer S. Hsu and Sari Horwitz, "Spending on Capital Checkpoints at Issue," *Washington Post,* November 21, 2004, p. C7.

21. Kedvin Amerman, "$2 Million Police Presence for Toll Bridges," *Pocono Record,* February 24, 2004, p. A3.

22. Philip Shenon and Kevin Flynn, "Mayor Tells Panel 'Pork Barrel Politics' Is Increasing Risk of Terrorism for City," New York Times Online, www.nytimes.com, May 20, 2004.

23. Dean E. Murphy, "Security Grants Still Steaming to Rural States," New York Times Online, www.nytimes.com, October 12, 2004.

24. Eric Lipton, "Big Cities Will Get More in Antiterrorism Grants," New York Times Online, www.nytimes.com, December 22, 2004.

25. Ibid.

26. Ibid.

27. Eric Lichtblau and Joel Brinkley, "$5 Billion in Antiterror Aid Is Reported Stuck in Pipeline," New York Times Online, www.nytimes.com, April 28, 2004.

28. Ibid.

29. Ibid.

30. John Mintz, "Cutbacks Threaten Work of Homeland Security Unit," *Washington Post,* October 31, 2004, p. A6.

31. Josh Benson, "Codey Fears Cutbacks in Security," New York Times Online, www.nytimes.com, December 9, 2004.

32. Anne E. Kornblut, "Laura Bush Defends Gala in Time of War and Disaster," New York Times Online, www.nytimes.com, January 15, 2005.

33. Associated Press, "$38.1B Said Paid to Those Affected by 9/11," New York Times Online, www.nytimes.com, November 9, 2004.

34. Michael Slackman, "2 Insurers Say Bank's Suit Tries to Capitalize on 9/11," New York Times Online, www.nytimes.com, August 26, 2003.

35. Associated Press, "Audit Finds Texas Improperly Spent Terror Funds," New York Times Online, www.nytimes.com, January 8, 2005.

36. Ibid.

37. Sarah Lyall, "Amnesty Calls World Less Safe," New York Times Online, www.nytimes.com, May 29, 2003.

38. Associated Press, "Strafing of School Divides N.J. Region," New York Times Online, www.nytimes.com, November 28, 2004.

39. Scott Shane, "Exposure at Germ Lab Reignites a Public Health Debate," New York Times Online, www.nytimes.com, January 24, 2005.

40. Felicity Barringer, "Pentagon Is Pressing to Bypass Environmental Laws for War Games and Arms Testing," New York Times Online, www.nytimes.com, December 28, 2004.

41. Ibid.

42. Brian Braiker, "The Patriot Search," *Newsweek,* June 9, 2004.

43. Ibid.

44. Scott Smallwood, "Colorado Regents Will Investigate Professor Who Compared September 11 Victims to Nazis," *Chronicle of Higher Education,* http://chronicle.com/daily/2005/022005020405n.htm, February 4, 2005.

45. Scott Smallwood, "Anatomy of a Free-Speech Firestorm: How a Professor's 3-Year-Old Essay Sparked a National Controversy," *Chronicle of Higher Education,* http://chronicle.com/daily/2005/0220005021003n.htm, February 10, 2005.

46. Associated Press, "UC Faculty Backs Professor on Free Speech," New York Times Online, www.nytimes.com, February 2, 2005.

47. Associated Press, "Patriot Act Affects Ex-Con from Nebraska," *Seattle Post-Intelligencer,* June 4, 2004.

48. Julia Preston, "Reporters' Subpoenas Are Being Fought in the Case of Lawyer Accused of Aiding Terrorism," New York Times Online, www.nytimes.com, June 15, 2004.

49. Ibid.

50. Eric Lichtblau, "Material Given to Congress in 2002 is Now Classified," New York Times Online, www.nytimes.com, May 20, 2004.

51. Ibid.

52. Ibid.

53. Ibid.

54. Diana Jean Schemo, "Federal Plan to Keep Data on Students Worries Some," New York Times Online, www.nytimes.com, November 29, 2004.

55. Ibid.

56. Robert O'Harrow, Jr., "In Age of Security, Firm Mines Wealth of Personal Data," *Washington Post,* January 20, 2005, p. A1.

57. Ibid.

58. Ibid.

59. Neil A. Lewis, "Red Cross Finds Detainee Abuse in

Guantanamo," New York Times Online, www.nytimes.com, November 30, 2004.

60. Nina Bernstein, "Lawyers Sue Over Tapes with Detainees," New York Times Online, www.nytimes.com, July 2, 2004.

61. Peter Grier, "Bush Team and the Limits on Torture," *Christian Science Monitor,* June 10, 2004, p .1.

62. Ibid.

63. Ibid.

64. Dana Priest, "Jet Is an Open Secret in Terror War," *Washington Post,* December 27, 2004, p. A1.

65. Neil A. Lewis, "Justice Dept. Broadens Definition of Torture," New York Times Online, www.nytimes.com, December 31, 2004.

66. Ibid.

67. Neil A. Lewis, "Justice Dept. Toughens Rule on Torture," New York Times Online, www.nytimes.com, January 1, 2005.

68. Lila Guterman, "Treasury Department Removes Restrictions on U.S. Publications by Authors in Embargoed Countries, *Chronicle of Higher Education,* http://chronicle.com/daily/2004/12/2004121602n.htm, December 16, 2004.

69. Brian Wingfield, "Unions for Border Workers Criticize Rules on Disclosure," New York Times Online, www.nytimes.com, November 30, 2004.

70. Ibid.

71. John Files, "Security Dept. Eases Its Nondisclosure Rule," New York Times Online, www.nytimes.com, January 18, 2005.

72. Ibid.

73. Marc Kaufman, "U.S. Barred from Forcing Troops to Get Anthrax Shots," *Washington Post,* October 28, 2004, p. A1.

74. Ibid.

75. Tom Regan, "Terrorism & Security," *Christian Science Monitor,* www.csmonitor.com/2004/0223/dailyUpdate.html, February 23, 2004.

76. Tom Regan, "Pentagon Seeks OK to Spy on Americans," Christian Science Monitor, www.csmonitor.com/2004/0617/dailyUpdate.html, June 17, 2004.

77. Tom Regan, "Terrorism & Security," *Christian Science Monitor,* www.csmonitor.com/2004/0223/dailyUpdate.html, February 23, 2004.

78. Patrick Healy, "L.I. Clash on Immigrants Is Graining Political Force," New York Times Online, www.nytimes.com, November 29, 2004.

79. David Cho and Tom Jackman, "Law Raises Immigrants' Suspicions," *Washington Post,* July 11, 2004, p. C1.

80. Ibid.

81. Ibid.

82. David Glenn, "Critics Assail Scholar's Article Ar-

guing that Hispanic Immigration Threatens U.S.," *Chronicle of Higher Education,* http://chronicle.com/daily/2004/02/200402401.htm, February 24, 2004.

83. Ibid.

84. Caryle Murphy, "Distrust of Muslims Common in U.S., Poll Finds," *Washington Post,* October 5, 2004, p. A2.

85. Associated Press, "N.J. Killings Spark New Anti-Muslim Bias," New York Times Online, www.nytimes.com, January 22, 2005.

86. Anemona Hartocollis and Charlie LeDuff, "Parents Fear Their Children Will Be the Targets of Bigotry," New York Times Online, www.nytimes.com, September 15, 2001.

87. Tracey Maclin, "'Voluntary' Interviews and Airport Searches of Middle Eastern Men: The Fourth Amendment in a Time of Terror," *Mississippi Law Journal,* January 21, 2005, p. 521.

88. Ibid.

89. Associated Press, "Dearborn, Mich., Arabs Cited More Often," New York Times Online, www.nytimes.com, November 20, 2003.

90. Eric Lichtblau, "Bush Issues Federal Ban on Racial Profiling," New York Times Online, www.nytimes.com, June 17, 2003.

91. *Report of the Defense Science Board Task Force on Strategic Communication.* Washington, DC: Defense Science Board, 2004. p. 44.

92. Bruce Nussbaum, John Rossant, and Stan Crock, "Fighting A New Cold War," *Business Week,* www.keepmedia.com/pubs/BusinessWeek/2004/03/29/397908, March 29, 2004.

93. Roger Cohen, "An Obsession the World Doesn't Share," New York Times Online, www.nytimes.com, December 5, 2004.

94. Ibid.

95. *Report of the Defense Science Board Task Force on Strategic Communication.* Washington, DC: Defense Science Board, 2004, p. 46.

96. Craig S. Smith, "Dutch Try to Thwart Terror Without Being Overzealous," New York Times Online, www.nytimes.com, November 25, 2004.

97. Ibid.

98. Ibid.

99. Associated Press, "Israel Destroys Teen Suicide Bomber's Home," *Pocono Record,* November 3, 2004, p. A7.

100. Lizette Alvarez, "Britain's Highest Court Overturns Anti-Terrorism Law," New York Times Online, www.nytimes.com, December 16, 2004.

101. Lizette Alvarez, "Britain Offers Plan to Restrain, Not Jail, Foreign Terror Suspects," New York Times Online, www.nytimes.com, January 27, 2004.

102.   Craig S. Smith, "In Europe's Jails, Neglect of Islam Breeds Trouble," New York Times Online, www.nytimes.com, December 8, 2004.

103.   John Mintz, "Report Cites 'Hate' Writings in U.S. Mosques," *Washington Post,* February 6, 2005, p. A18.

104.   Douglas Jehl, "U.S. General Apologizes for Remarks about Islam," New York Times Online, www.nytimes.com, October 18, 2003.

105.   Associated Press, "House Agrees to Citizenship Check for Licenses," New York Times Online, www.nytimes.com, February 10, 2005.

106.   William Safire, "The Floo Floo Bird," New York Times Online, www.nytimes.com, April 5, 2004.

107.   Eric Lichtblau, "9/11 Report Cites Many Warnings about Hijackings," New York Times Online, www.nytimes.com, February 10, 2005.

108.   Associated Press, "Terror Fronts Got Money from Olajuwon's Mosque," New York Times Onine, www.nytimes.com, February 10, 2005.

109.   Michael Moss, "False Terrorism Tips to F.B.I. Uproot Lives of Suspects," New York Times Online, www.nytimes.com, June 19, 2003.

110.   Ibid.

111.   Ibid.

Index